Yearbook of the Maimonides Centre for Advanced Studies 2017

Yearbook of the Maimonides Centre for Advanced Studies

Edited by
Giuseppe Veltri

Yearbook of the Maimonides Centre for Advanced Studies 2017

―

Volume Editor
Bill Rebiger

The Yearbook is published on behalf of
the Maimonides Centre for Advanced Studies.

ISBN 978-3-11-052796-4
e-ISBN (PDF) 978-3-11-052797-1
e-ISBN (EPUB) 978-3-11-052809-1

This work is licensed under the Creative Commons Attribution-Non Commercial-No Derivatives 4.0 Licence. For details go to http://creativecommons.org/licenses/by-nc-nd/4.0/.

Library of Congress Cataloging-in-Publication Data
A CIP catalog record for this book has been applied for at the Library of Congress.

Bibliographic information published by the Deutsche Nationalbibliothek
The Deutsche Nationalbibliothek lists this publication in the Deutsche Nationalbibliografie; detailed bibliographic data are available in the Internet at http://dnb.dnb.de.

© 2017 Walter de Gruyter GmbH, Berlin/Boston
Cover image: Staats- und Universitätsbibliothek Hamburg, Ms Cod. Levy 115, fol. 158r: Maimonides, More Nevukhim, Beginn von Teil III.
Printing and binding: CPI books GmbH, Leck
♾ Printed on acid-free paper
Printed in Germany

www.degruyter.com

Contents

Editorial —— VII

Part I: **Articles**

Rachel Aumiller
Epoché as the Erotic Conversion of One into Two —— 3

Emidio Spinelli
Some Blunt Instruments of Dogmatic Logic: Sextus Empiricus' Sceptical Attack —— 15

Teresa Caligiure
In antiquam litem relabimur. Sceptical Hints in Petrarch's *Secretum* —— 29

Bill Rebiger
Sceptical Strategies in Simone Luzzatto's Presentation of the Kabbalists in his *Discorso* —— 51

Michela Torbidoni
The Italian Academies and Rabbi Simone Luzzatto's *Socrate*: the Freedom of the *Ingenium* and the Soul —— 71

Guido Bartolucci
Jewish Thought vs. Lutheran Aristotelism: Johann Frischmuth (1619–1687) and Jewish Scepticism —— 95

Giuseppe Veltri
Negotiating the Principle of (Non)-Contradiction: Johann Frischmuth on the Rabbinic Dialectic Discussion —— 107

Libera Pisano
Silence, Translation, and Grammatical Therapy: Some Features of Linguistic Scepticism in the Thought of Rosenzweig and Wittgenstein —— 121

Harald Bluhm
Was Leo Strauss a Zetetic Political Philosopher? —— 145

Roi Benbassat
Jewish Faith and Scepticism—The Example of Yeshayahu Leibowitz —— 161

Part II: Lectures

Josef Stern
What is Jewish Philosophy? A View from the Middle Ages —— 185

WORKSHOP: Jewish-Christian Polemics in the Middle Ages and in the Early Modern Period —— 205

1. Daniel J. Lasker

2. Lawrence Kaplan

3. Racheli Haliva

4. Michael Engel

5. Paolo L. Bernardini

Jonathan Garb
Doubt and Certainty in Early Modern Kabbalah —— 239

Wilhelm Schmidt-Biggemann
Lingua Adamica and Philology: The Rise and Destruction of a Concept —— 247

Part III: Reports

Activities and Events —— 269

Stephan Schmid and Yitzhak Melamed
Report on the Sceptical Atelier on Maimon's *Lebensgeschichte* (6–9 February, 2017) —— 293

Michela Torbidoni
Report on the Sceptical Atelier on Simone Luzzatto's *Socrates*: Reading the Forthcoming First English Translation (22–24 May, 2017) —— 299

Silke Schaeper
Report on the Library of Jewish Scepticism —— 303

Editorial

This Yearbook presents some results of the research done at the Maimonides Centre for Advanced Studies – Jewish Scepticism in its second academic year 2016-17. The contributions collected in this volume show the broad scope of the Centre's main topic, that is, scepticism. First and foremost, scepticism is a philosophical tradition beginning in antiquity and persisting into the present. Sceptical elements, concepts, methodologies and strategies are present also in philology, political thought, religion, and, generally, in culture and language. This variety and abundance of sceptical topics and methods are mirrored in the present Yearbook.

The aim of the Yearbook is to document the research, activities, and events that were accomplished at the Maimonides Centre. It is divided into three parts: articles, lectures, and reports.

The section of articles, subject to a double-blind peer review, offers a broad range of topics and approaches and follows a chronological order. They reflect the interests of the fellows, which range from classical sceptic topics such as the suspension of judgment, Sextus Empiricus' logic, the principle of non-contradiction, and critiques of dogmatism to new insights in specialized areas of the history of philosophy and religion such as sceptical strategies in anti-Kabbalistic tendencies, sceptical references in Petrarch, the Italian academies, and Luzzatto's *Socrates*.

One of the main features of the Maimonides Centre is the many lectures given not only by the fellows but also by other distinguished scholars from all over the world. The second part of our Yearbook displays a few of these inspiring moments. We are very happy to publish the opening lecture held by Josef Stern in October 2015. We also highlight the papers presented at the workshop 'Jewish-Christian Polemics in the Middle Ages and in the Early Modern Period' and two lectures given by Jonathan Garb and Wilhelm Schmidt-Biggemann as part of our ongoing lecture series on scepticism.

The last part of the Yearbook consists of reports including an annotated listing of the Centre's activities and events, a summary of two Sceptical Ateliers, and, finally, a bibliographical report of the Centre's librarian. The Centre's new event series, introduced for the first time in 2017, takes the form of the Sceptical Atelier. The Sceptical Atelier is designed as a discussion forum, in which specialists from diverse fields contribute to the understanding of a certain topic or historical phenomenon. Thus, the participants will not have prepared a particular talk or paper, but will rather have studied the object of common enquiry in advance so as to share their notes and thoughts about it in the joint discussion. Detailed reports on the ateliers on Salomon Maimon's *Lebensgeschichte* and on Simone Luzzatto's *Socrates* are presented in the third section.

We owe many thanks for the excellent language editing by Katharine Handel. In addition, we are thankful to Rachel Aumiller who also revised parts of this volume. We would also like to acknowledge the *Deutsche Forschungsgemeinschaft* for the generous financial support that made the creation of the Centre possible, to the Board of Trustees for their supervisory role, the advisory board for their help and assistance in selecting the fellows, and the President of the Universität Hamburg, Dieter Lenzen, the Chancellor, Martin Hecht, the Dean of the faculty, Oliver Huck, and the head of the Philosophy department, Benjamin Schnieder for their active presence in maintaining an international centre to its high standard.

Hamburg, August 2017

Giuseppe Veltri (Chief Editor)
Bill Rebiger (Volume Editor)

Part I: **Articles**

Rachel Aumiller
Epoché as the Erotic Conversion of One into Two

This philosophical essay interprets the *epoché* of ancient scepticism as the perpetual conversion of the love of one into the love of two. The process of one becoming two is represented in Plato's *Symposium* by Diotima's description of the second rung of 'the ladder,' by which one ascends to the highest form of philosophical devotion (Pl. *Sym.* 209e-210e). Diotima's ladder offers a vision of philosophy as a total conversion of both the lover and the object of love (or philosopher and object of knowledge). I suggest that scepticism, however, is found in the frustration of Platonic ascension, which results in a partial conversion. Because the process of conversion (from the love of one to the love of One) remains suspended midway, the sceptic's transformation is erotic—this is to say, driven by a desire that is characterised by a split (which may be identified between subject and object, between incompatible objects of desire or knowledge, or within the subject herself).

In contrast to the understanding of conversion as the transition from one (spiritual/intellectual/political/sexual) orientation to another, I consider how conversion operates as an *epoché* by splitting the timeline of an individual or community into two irresolvable, conflicting orientations. In an effort to achieve peace and unity, we may try to completely abandon the old for the new. However, remnants of our 'former' life tend to resurface disrupting our vision of a life that is unified by our professed beliefs. I suggest that the sceptic is one who embraces the failure of conversion to achieve unity. What would the life and philosophy of one who openly embraces such contradiction look like? I consider how both the content and form of Diogenes Laertius' specific depiction of Pyrrho offers us a picture of both a life and a text of a sceptic as a enactment of *epoché* as the erotic space of the in-between.

To further explore the paradox as *epoché* as a kind of transformation that occurs through suspension, I identify two kinds of Platonic conversion narratives: one dogmatic and one sceptical. The first model, represented by Augustine's *Confessions*, is the familiar portrayal of conversion as a transformative event in which one abandons a former way of being-in-the-world for a worthier pursuit. The exchange of objects of love/knowledge at first seems to result in a new ontological stance: the apparent death of the old gives birth to the new. However, Augustine's own struggles to adhere to his 'new being' call this dogmatic model of conversion into question. The second model of conversion, as depicted in Apuleius' *Metamorphoses*, is a tale of partial conversion, which leaves one suspended between two incompatible ways of being in the world. Both experiences introduce a crisis that conversion fails to overcome. And yet the sceptic's acceptance of her repeated failure to ascend results in the transformation of the crisis itself into something that is experienced with pleasure.

Overturning Diotima's Ladder

Conversion begins with a moment of crisis when my unquestioned devotion to one (philosophical/theological/political/ethical framework) is threatened by my unanticipated attraction to a second. My fundamental understanding of my relationship to the world is disrupted by a competitor in the form of an equally appealing framework that throws my relationship with my current beliefs into conflict. Crisis is overcome when my split attraction for two is mastered by a return to my devotion to one. Two becomes one either when I reject the temptation of the second or when I abandon my first (intellectual, spiritual, carnal) love, giving myself over to a second *beauty so old and so new*.

In the first movement of conversion one becomes two in the crisis of being-in-between. The moment of crisis splices an autobiographical narrative, introducing an alternative timeline. The splice between the first and second timeline becomes the crack that both holds together and separates two incompatible ways of grasping the world. I could once identify myself positively in my belief, but in the ec-static moment of the crisis I am nothing more than the crack between two. I become the negative space of indeterminacy.

In the last instance, the exhaustion of indecision or the exhaustion of resisting the seduction of the new drives me to make a decision. Two returns to one in the resolution of choosing one over the other. I destroy one side of conflict in the name of truth. The final decision, an arbitrary act for which I later provide myself many reasonable accounts, dissolves the tension of contradiction. I am of one mind again, standing firmly in my conviction.

Each rung of Diotima's ladder—leading from one love to another, from the love of many bodies to the love of many activities and customs, from the articulation of many ideas to One ineffable form—itself represents a kind of conversion. With each shift both the lover/philosopher and beloved/object of knowledge undergo transformation. Platonic ascent transforms one's childish and stubborn devotion to *this* particular one into the philosophical love of the One.

While other seekers of beauty or truth scramble to the top of the ladder, sceptics are content to dwell in the middle with a far-reaching view of many bodies, activities, customs and ideas. A peculiar trait of Pyrrho's sceptics, however, is their place at the second rung of Diotima's ladder. At the second rung, the sceptic is still in touch with the myth of an original one and thus the fantasy of an ultimate One. Other varieties of sceptics—such as the academics and their contemporary postmodern counterparts—no longer themselves experience the devastating dissolution of one or the tension between two, each of which claim to be *the* one. At the second rung, however, where one is still a possibility that is constantly overturned, the sceptic is touched by the perpetual conversion of conviction into crisis.

From the humble vantage point of the second rung, the sceptic has the impression that those who claim to gaze upon the One have perhaps never progressed past their love for their first one. It is possible that the dogmatist appears to confuse the first rung for the top rung, declaring this particular one to be his One (and only). Perhaps he has never properly allowed himself to be seduced by another. Observing the comic effort of the dogmatist, who repeatedly seems to confuse his first one for the One, the sceptic contemplates how One is *no more* top than bottom, *no more* up than down. She considers the possibility of throwing away the ladder altogether (Sext. Emp. *M.* 8.481).

Epoché—the sceptic's mode of suspension at the second rung—may be grasped as the perpetual conversion of one into two. With the introduction of 'the second'—be it in the form of a tempting new companion or a tempting counter-proposal—desire itself is split into two. Desire is divided by the multiplication of its object. When desire is split into two its drive becomes erotic. The experience of the erotic space of the in-between disrupts the relatively good thing I had going on with 'my first.' The crisis of one becoming two is far from what most would identify as the good life. The second introduces complications.

There are various philosophical modes of resistance that shut down the second before it can cause any serious disturbance to my commitments to my first. The stoic, for example, may say 'no' to the second, dismissing it as a potential waste of his time. The epicurean might say 'no' based on his speculation that the complications of the second are likely to bring more headache than pleasure. The cynic says 'no' dismissing the strangeness of the new as pretentious or absurd. Ironically, the sceptic, who is marked by her refusal to assent to anything absolutely, is the most likely to say 'yes' to this other (at least for the sake of experimentation). Her refusal to commit to anything in particular allows her to be open to the equal consideration of everything that happens to come her way.

In her pedagogical role of the lover, the sceptic may be identified as the one who initiates crises in the lives of her interlocutors through her questions, refutations, and counter-proposals. Her dialectics introduces a seductive alternative both to her companion's deepest commitments and to his seemingly simple observations. One becomes two either when the sceptic presents an equally compelling but competing account to what seems certain to her interlocutor or by guiding her interlocutor to the contradiction within his own accounts, showing that one was already two (continuity is constituted by paradox). In the active position of the lover, the sceptic may be seen either as the one who causes crisis or as the one who brings visibility to a crisis that certainty concealed.

In her involuntary role of the beloved, however, the sceptic undergoes her own conversion. She experiences herself as the site of crisis. But conversion for the sceptic is very different from the conversion of the dogmatist who abandons one path to happiness, virtue, or truth for an alternate timeline, which promises the same if the traveler abandons his original path. A dogmatic account of conversion is a relationship of simple negation in which one must renounce the gods of one's childhood to serve a new god (in whatever form these gods may take). The sceptic however neither renounces nor declares devotion to any god in particular. She instead becomes the *daimonic* space in-between what some call sacred or profane (Pl. *Sym.* 202b-203a).

While traditional conversion involves the rejection of the old in the affirmation of the new, conversion as *epoché* is *no more* a 'yes' than a 'no.' Conversion is traditionally understood as the story of a moment of decision. Crisis is overcome when one is chosen over another and two returns to one. In taking up a new position, transformation occurs as one way of being-in-the-world is forsaken for a new ontological orientation. While traditional conversion narratives are about a transformation that occurs through a decisive turning point by which crisis is overcome, the sceptic's transformation occurs through the sustained tension between two. Crisis itself is not overcome but transformed in the refusal to allow two to resolve back into one. *Epoché* is a mode of yea-saying: a saying yes to the new, for the sake of experimentation. However, *epoché* is also a mode of resistance: the resistance of giving oneself over to any one absolutely.

Diotima offers a picture of philosophy as the transformative movement of ascension: by fully assenting to a new object of desire, which appears more worthy than my former pursuits, I myself am transformed into a higher being. Scepticism, in contrast, pictures philosophy as the transformative practice of 'stuckness.' Transformation occurs through the suspension of movement in the paralysis of choice.

Being In-Between Two Ways of Being

Ancient scepticism is often described as a way of being in the world rather than a philosophical doctrine or theory. But perhaps we could further suggest that scepticism is not a way of being but instead the experience of being-stuck-in-between (at least) two ways of being in the world. To live a life in-between ways of being might be to live a life committing to nothing in particular but partaking in a bit of everything as it comes. This entails not only observing the appearance of contradiction in others' experiences and accounts of the world, but also living a life that actively enacts such contradiction. Perhaps it is appropriate that *nothing more* remains of Pyrrho himself other than inconsistent second hand accounts. While Sextus' effort to present a comprehensive philosophical account of Pyrrhonean scepticism is often treated as definitive, it is worth considering how 'less coherent' or 'philosophical' presentations of scepticism perhaps better lend themselves to depicting the life and philosophy of a sceptic as an enactment of contradiction. For example, Diogenes Laertius' genre of historical fragments offers a depiction of scepticism through a playful collection of hearsay. Diogenes suggests that although everyone had something to say about Pyrrho, none of these things were consistent. To name a few of these inconsistencies:

According to Ascanius of Abdera, Pyrrho led a life consistent with his philosophical doctrine, while Aenesidemus insists that Pyrrho applied his sceptical method only to his philosophy without extending his theory to his own life (Diog. Laert. 62).

Antigonus of Carystus tells us that Pyrrho went out of his way for nothing, taking no precautions, but walked directly into any danger that came his way. His friends had to constantly rescue him from trouble (62). Still others say that the sceptic does not fail to take precautions when it comes to his everyday life. A sceptic avoids trouble (106). This is evident from the fact that Pyrrho lived nearly to the age of ninety (62).

As Antigonus also tell us, Pyrrho withdrew from the world, committing himself to a life of solitude, showing himself only on rare occasion to a family member. He delivered his speeches in front empty audiences and was often caught talking to himself. But the same account presents a very different picture. The gregarious philosopher spent his time in the city and would find a walking companion in whomever he met by chance. He would engage his interlocutors in tireless debate and lecture at great length, attracting prestigious admirers such as the young Nausiphanes and Epicurus. He was a hero of the people who declared him not only a citizen of Athens and but also a high priest. (63)

Anaxarchus praises Pyrrho for his indifference toward society and the everyday life of others, even if this made him a rather odd fellow. He walked around talking to himself oblivious of everything. He neglected even his friends when they were in obvious need of help (for example, when Anaxarchus himself fell into a ditch) (63). And yet we often are told that the sceptic behaves according to what is customary (105).

Posidonius claims that Pyrrho was a man of great composure. He tells the tale of traveling with Pyrrho on a ship during a great storm. While the other travelers worried for their safety, Pyrrho modeled himself after the pig, who unperturbed by the storm, continued to calmly eat his slop. The wise person should mimic the unperturbed state of the little pig (69). And yet it is said that Pyrrho admitted that no person is above human weakness. Other accounts suggest that Pyrrho was easily raddled, as seen in his terrified response to a dog that chased after him (66). Likewise, his closest students miserably failed to keep their composure. His student Eurylochus, for example, when asked a tricky question in response to his lecture, allegedly panicked, stripped naked, and jumped into a river to swim away (68).

All of the small discrepancies in the fragmented accounts of Pyrrho's life add up to the underlying paradox of scepticism. Since Pyrrho did not put forth a doctrine one cannot be called a Pyrrhonean sceptic according to one's philosophical positions. As Theodosius puts it, 'If the movement of the mind in either direction is unattainable by us, we shall never know for certain what Pyrrho really intended, and without knowing that, we cannot be called Pyrrhoneans.' Thus, since Pyrrho did not hold any positive tenets, a 'Pyrrhonian' can only be said to be the one whose manners and life resembled Pyrrho (70). And yet Diogenes' account, which is packed full of opposing anecdotes of Pyrrho's manners and life, indicates that modeling oneself after Pyrrho would be quite the impossible task, since his 'way of life' is as unattainable as his mindset.

On one level, Diogenes' text depicts Pyrrho's life as the enactment of contradiction. On another level, the text itself seems to self-consciously perform contradiction in every statement. Diogenes offers some explanation about this method. Many say that a sceptic refrains altogether from saying anything positive about the world; and yet others point to the impossibility of staying silence, suggesting that the sceptic's philosophical speech must enact the failure of philosophical speech to grasp the world. As Diogenes explains in a passage that captures the playfulness at the core of scepticism:

> The sceptics, then, were constantly engaged in overthrowing the dogma of all schools, but enunciated none themselves; and though they would go so far as to bring forward and expound the dogmas of the others, they themselves laid down nothing, not even the laying down of nothing. So much so they even refuted their laying down of nothing. (74)

In saying, 'we determine nothing,' the sceptic openly confesses to self-contradiction, since in professing to refrain from determining anything, one makes a positive statement about determining nothing. Scepticism testifies to the impossibility of remaining neutral, since even claims to neutrality fall into contradiction. The agnostic who claims allegiance to nothing, commits herself to nothing, and therefore exposes her positive allegiance to the nothing itself.

> Even this statement (implying the negative of all determinations) contains its own antithesis, so that after destroying others it turns round and destroys itself, like a purge which drives the substance out and then in its turn is itself eliminated and destroyed. (76)

Sometimes the sceptic speaks to the impossibility of self-consistency by remaining silent. Other times she speaks in such a way that her words openly turn on themselves, demonstrating the way each concept already seems to contain its contrary. One is always already two. *Epoché* as the suspension of judgment does not pretend to remain impartial or neutral, offering a pure description of the phenomenal world. It instead is an act of constant self-defeat, a repeated grasp upon the world that slips through one's fingers. To borrow Sextus' famous imagery, the fire after consuming the wood turns around to consume itself. Silence can disguise itself as neutrality, but a sceptic's philosophy is a text that openly exposes its own inconsistencies— throwing itself and the reader into crisis. As Aenesidemus describes it in his introduction to *Pyrrhonics*, the sceptic's account 'is but a report on phenomena or on any kind of judgment, a report in which all things are brought to bear on one another and in the comparison are found to present much anomaly and confusion' (Diog. Laert. 78).

There seems to be a metaphysical stirring within the sceptic's professed attempt to avoid metaphysics. We find this metaphysical tickle within the suggestion that the content of all things—whether in the form of our experience or theory, the world or the self—is *no more* one thing than the other—*no more* than contradiction itself. The sceptic witnesses the way the crack (of subjectivity? of existence?) continually rises to the surface of every appearance, while the dogmatist frantically tries to mend the crack, restoring the illusion of oneness. Many experience anguish at the experience of the reappearance of the crack (within themselves or within their accounts of the world). What allows the sceptic to experience the repeated crisis of one becoming two with a spirit of tranquility?

Conversion as Tragedy and Comedy

I turn to two conversion narratives of (late) antiquity, both products of the development of Platonism in Roman Africa: Apuleius' second-century *Metamorphoses* or *The Golden Ass* and Augustine's fourth-century *Confessions*. Although the former presents itself as a fictional account of conversion, many readers have noted suspicious similarities between the author and his protagonist; and although the latter presents itself as autobiographical, many readers have noted the suspicious similarities between the author's account of his real life with the epic tales of fictitious characters (such as Aeneas). The sceptical reader might concede that neither conversion tale can be declared more fictional or autobiographical than the other. Both narratives begin with a protagonist who recklessly partakes in the messy delights of a little bit of everything the world has to offer. At the climax of each narrative the protagonist discovers 'the light' and dramatically turns from his love of the many to his love of the One. In other words, both tales are explicitly about the conversion of the sceptic into the dogmatist. And yet, the overall structure of Apuleius' narrative may nevertheless be read sceptically.

Both narrators of the two conversion stories recall the 'misplaced' desire of their younger selves who partake in many varieties of carnal and spiritual pleasures. Both figures move from venture to venture until their journeys lead them to a point of crisis. Their crisis is resolved when they undergo a conversion, committing themselves to a life-long religious vocation (Augustine turns to Christianity and Apuleius' narrator, Lucius, to the cult of the goddess Isis). Yet, despite these similarities, the attitude of the narrator of Apuleius' conversion story and that of Augustine's narrative are dramatically different. Augustine's conversion narrative takes the form of a confession, whereas Apuleius' narrative takes the form of a comedy. Augustine weeps over lingering remnants of his past life that do not fully die in his conversion. Lucius laughs over his own experience of self-contradiction. What is experienced as a crisis for the dogmatist is the pleasure of the sceptic.

The dramatic structure of comedy shares a close connection with the sceptic's transformation (which occurs without movement), while the dogmatist' conversion follows the structure of ancient tragedy. Both tragedy and comedy are composed of two sides, which are equally right according to their own logic but equally wrong according to the logic of the other. Tragic resolution aims to overcome its conflict between two incompatible positions through a return oneness. The side that is identified as introducing conflict must be destroyed in order for two to return to one. The myth of an original unity is momentarily restored until the same conflict resurfaces in the next generation. In the case of a dogmatic conversion story, an old way of life must die in order for a new life to be born. And yet, despite the appearance of the victory of the new, remnants of the old inevitably resurface, reintroducing the struggle between two ways of being, which conversion had promised to overcome.

Structurally, tragedy and comedy may be said to be the same. However, while tragedy can only grasp itself from the perspective of one of the sides of its conflict, the comic perspective grasps itself from the (non)perspective of the crack itself. In the perpetual repetition of the same formal stage, an imperceptible shift in contents takes place. The anguish of tragedy is transformed into the laughter of comedy: the hiss between two positions that logically cannot coexist and yet nevertheless persist in contradiction. Likewise a conversion narrative—a story of two incompatible ways of being—is most often told from the perspective of one side of the transformative turning point (nearly always from the new self). The sceptic's story of conversion, however, is comic in the way it tells its narrative from the perspective of the splice between two ontological orientations that persist within the experience of a single subject.

The values that Augustine holds as a Christian bishop dominate the narration of the events that took place before his conversion. His post-conversion self hovers over his pre-conversion self as he laments what he wished he had known earlier. In this way, the narrator recalls his journey while self-consciously distancing himself from his former actions that are out of line with his current commitments. Augustine's post-conversion self attempts to suppress the sceptical appetite of his younger self, but is not always successful. This failure is most thematic in Augustine's early *Soliloquies*, an inner dialogue between Augustine's 'rational' and 'irrational' sides, which discuss the tension between his pre-conversion and post-conversion selves: the tragedy of the desire for unity told from the perspective of a fractured subject. Augustine repeatedly professes fidelity to his new object of devotion in an effort to convince himself, rather than his God, of his singular devotion to one: 'Now I love *only* you, I follow *only* you, I seek *only* you!' (Aug. *sol.* 1.5). While Augustine insists that he has entirely abandoned his former way of being, his lingering desire for his first loves (his longing for a wife, for example) puncture his current convictions. In the middle of trying to convince himself of his singular devotion to One, he drifts to sleep. His dreams about the companionship of a woman betray him (1.11.18). Augustine is split once again between his wakeful declarations and his unconscious fantasies. Augustine's rational voice is quick to catch him in his inconsistencies. He pushes himself on the issue of his split desire until the dogmatic side of himself—the side that desires fidelity, unity, truth—cracks: 'Silence, I beg you, silence! Why do you cause me so much trouble; why do you challenge me? Now I weep uncontrollably!' (1.14.25-26).

The final conclusion of the *Soliloquies* has a sceptical ring: reason exposes the quest for a unified way of being in the world—a unity that comes through a devotion to one true object of love/knowledge—as an irrational desire. The only thing reason has to offer is to point to the contradictions within itself. The text enacts a number of failures and contractions: the failure of reason to provide an adequate account of the self and the world, the failure to the dogmatist to honour that which he declares true, the failure of self to correspond to itself (both over a lifetime and within the same moment). On a performative level, the text fails in that Augustine abandoned the work, which was never finished, testifying to the genuine frustration of the author's inability to transcend contradiction. Augustine's former interest in scepticism clearly peeks through this early work, and yet the dialogue—between his two selves—lacks the ease of a sceptic who takes strange delight in his own failure.

The tragic-comedy of the dogmatist's ascension to truth is that the resolution of his conversion comes full circle leading him back to the partial conversion of being stuck in-between.

In contrast to Augustine, who painfully revisits the events of his youth through the lens of his current failed commitments, Apuleius' narrator, Lucius, delights in retelling old events as if he is experiencing the thrill of each old flame for the first time. Lucius seems to take genuine pleasure in recalling his life before his conversion and does not spare the reader a single seductive detail of his 'folly.' He admits that he is grateful for his curious nature that (literally) made an ass out of him (Apul. *Met.* 9.15). Augustine too expresses gratitude for the detours of his youth because he sees them as leading him to his current position in divine truth; Lucius, however, seems to find his youthful adventures valuable, or at least entertaining, for their own sake.

Apuleius himself was a devote follower of Plutarch, who might be attributed for making Eros thematic in his sceptical reading of the *Theaetetus*. Beyond his schooling in 'erotic scepticism,' Apuleius' own life resembles that of a sceptic in that he openly took up many opposing positions and participated in many opposing activities, devoting himself to the study of philosophy, poetry, geometry, and rhetoric. When accused of seducing his friend's widowed mother by means of dark magic, Apuleius does not exactly deny the charges. Instead, in the fashion of a true sceptic, he defends his commitment to nothing in particular by confessing his openness to everything: as he tells his accusers, if he had dabbled in things related to magic it was in relation to his many other pursuits: his interest in bodily hygiene (Apul. *Apol.* 7), his experiments with medical practice (27, 51), his investigation of natural science (27), his participation in religious rituals (26-27). (A defense, which evades guilt by confessing to more and more, running along the lines of: 'Well yes, it's true that I slept with your wife, but I also slept with your daughter and sister.')

Although Apuleius' diverse life and texts speak to his schooling in philosophical scepticism, he does not declare himself so. Likewise, his *Metamorphoses* makes no commitment to any one philosophical school, but instead takes the form of a comedy: an invitation for the reader to doubt what she believes to be certain and reconsider what strikes her as incredible. The protagonist espouses contrasting views and values at different points in the narrative. Up until his religious conversion in the final eleventh book of the novel, Lucius proudly declares himself to be one who is curious about everything (*curiousus alioquin*) (Apul. *Met.* 2.6). The narrator beckons the reader to follow him along a string of extraordinary tales ranging from romantic and silly to sexually graphic and grotesque to philosophical and religious. A reader who lacks a hearty appetite for curious matters has little motivation to commit herself to an ass' episodic tales about magical transformations, adulterous scandal, and sensational goddesses and witches. *The Metamorphoses* has a bit of something for every kind of reader but is ideal for someone who, like Lucius (not to mention Apuleius himself), takes interest in a little bit of everything.

One can read Apuleius' entire narrative from the pious perspective of Lucius at the end of the novel. In this case the rest of the novel's tantalizing adventures must be taken as a moralistic warning. Indeed many scholars of Apuleius choose this 'high road,' but a sceptic continues to question the indeterminacy between such moral highs and lows. A sceptical reading treats the prologue with equal weight as the conclusion, just as she treats the fantastic with equal weight as what appears realistic. While Apuleius' tale concludes dogmatically, it opens with an invitation to read the text sceptically, letting one's resistance to anything absolutely be an openness to a bit of everything.

The prologue opens with a direct debate of the merits of saying 'yes' or 'no' to the seduction of a second. The narrator on his way to Thessaly eavesdrops on two quibbling travelers. He recounts:

> I saw two men trudging along together a short distance ahead of me, deep in conversation. I walked a little faster, curious to know what they were talking about, and just as I drew abreast one of them burst into a loud laugh and said to the other: 'Stop, stop! Not another word! I can't bear to hear any more of your absurd and monstrous lies.' (Apul. *Met.* 1.2)

The cynical travelers' protest against what he takes to be his friend's outrageous story immediately spikes Lucius' interest. He interrupts the conversation, encouraging the first traveler to retell his story from the beginning. Lucius promises not only to enjoy the tale but also to give every word serious consideration no matter how ridiculous it may initially seem. The sceptic overturns the cynic's 'no' with his insistent 'yes.' The prologue can be read as Apuleius' way of encouraging the reader to embrace the forthcoming series of stories, which will surely strike the reader as fantastical and obscene. Lucius' eagerness to hear the storyteller's tale precisely because it has been forbidden lures the reader into indulging in Apuleius' novel even when the presented values are contrary to the traditional values of its age. Apuleius invites his readers to go precisely where his contemporaries advise their readers not to go.

Lucius as the protagonist of *Metamorphoses* is divided between the sceptical persona in the introduction and the dogmatic persona of the conclusion. However, Lucius as the narrator of events experienced by 'both selves' seems to find equal value in both sides of a life split by radical conversion. Although the dogmatic commitments of 'post-conversion' Lucius would deny any legitimate value in his former lifestyle, the narrator continues to take equal pleasure in recounting all of his experiences. Conversion narratives, like tragedy and comedy, attempt to grapple with conflicting objects of desire, ethical frameworks and metaphysical systems held by one individual or community over a lifetime or within the same moment. A sceptical conversion (of the experience of conversion) is in the insight that when one is unable to achieve unity, which perhaps no honest person can, one can wade in the pleasure of opposing attractions.

The content of scepticism appears empty both in terms of establishing any philosophical positions and in terms of offering us practical advice for our daily life. It turns out that scepticism is *no more* a way of life than it is a philosophical framework. Perhaps the only insight that we can take away from the contradictory lives and philosophical positions of figures like Socrates, Pyrrho, Apuleius, and even the young Augustine, is that the lives of sceptics are the very enactment of the contraction they identify in every philosophical statement. Both their texts and lives are *nothing more* than an enactment of the *nothing more*. The sceptic is not only one who identifies discrepancies in others' account of the world and therefore remains above such contradiction; by assenting to no position absolutely she instead commits herself to dwelling in the tension of contradiction. Scepticism is a resistance to a kind of dramatic resolution that comes too easily in the superficial reduction of two to One. The sceptic dwells in the space of crisis—in perpetual partial conversion—until the indecision that throws others into panic is transformed into something that she experiences as serene.

Emidio Spinelli
Some Blunt Instruments of Dogmatic Logic: Sextus Empiricus' Sceptical Attack

1 The Feeble Power of Dogmatic Logic

Even without delving into the abundant historiographical and doxographical details to be found in the treatment offered by Sextus Empiricus in the parallel passages of his *Against the Mathematicians* (*Adversus Mathematicos* = *M* VII and VIII), it must be acknowledged that the more succinct and introductory analysis he presents in the second book of his *Outlines of Pyrrhonism* (= *PH*) may already satisfy the reader wishing to investigate questions of truth and falsehood, in relation to both dogmatic philosophies and the objections raised by the sceptics.

The underlying argument of Sextus' book systematically addresses a series of topics familiar to anyone seeking to establish the truth of those key epistemological tools exploited by currents of thought purporting to state 'how things really stand': an easy target for Pyrrhonian criticism.

Following a few introductory sections (*PH* II 1–12) of crucial importance for understanding—and especially justifying, against all sterile dogmatist polemics—a genuine form of sceptical *zetein*,[1] Sextus examines (and attempts to demolish) some central concepts in dogmatic 'logic.' The semantic field covered by 'logic' here is far broader than the one usually attributed to it, insofar as it extends to questions that may be seen to fall under the labels of epistemology, semiotics, the philosophy of language, and so on.

From first to last, Sextus pays special attention to the following notions:

---

[1] See therefore: Jacques Brunschwig, "Sextus Empiricus on the κριτήριον," in idem, *Papers in Hellenistic Philosophy* (Cambridge: Cambridge University Press, 1994): 224–241; Emidio Spinelli, *Questioni scettiche. Letture introduttive al pirronismo antico* (Rome: Lithos, 2005): 114–117 (now also online: http://scholarlysource.daphnet.org/index.php/DDL/issue/view/18); Katja M. Vogt, "Skeptische Suche und das Verstehen von Begriffen," in *Wissen und Bildung in der antiken Philosophie*, eds. Christoph Rapp and Tim Wagner (Stuttgart: J.B. Metzler, 2006): 325–339; Filip Grgić, "Sextus Empiricus on the Possibility of Inquiry," *Pacific Philosophical Quarterly* 89 (2008): 436–459; Lorenzo Corti, *Scepticisme et langage* (Paris: Vrin, 2009): 185–206; Gail Fine, "Sceptical Inquiry," in *Definition in Ancient Philosophy*, ed. David Charles (Oxford: Oxford University Press, 2010): 493–525; eadem, "Concepts and Inquiry: Sextus and the Epicureans," in *Episteme, etc. Essays in Honour of Jonathan Barnes*, eds. Ben Morison and Katherina Ierodiakonou (Oxford: Oxford University Press, 2012): 90–114 [= now eadem, *The Possibility of Inquiry: Meno's Paradox from Socrates to Sextus* (Oxford: Oxford University Press, 2014): chs. 10 and 11]; and Anna Tigani, "A New Answer to an Old Puzzle: Νοεῖν ἁπλῶς (Sextus Empiricus, *PH* II 1.10)," *Logical Analysis & History of Philosophy/Philosophiegeschichte und Logische Analyse* 19 (2016): 188–211.

- criterion (*PH* II 14–79; cf. *M* VII 25–37 and 46–445);[2]
- the true and truth (*PH* II 80–96; cf. *M* VII 38–45; VIII 1–140);[3]
- sign (*PH* II 97–133; cf. *M* VIII 141–299);[4]
- demonstration (*PH* II 134–192; cf. *M* VIII 300–481);[5]
- syllogism (*PH* II 193–203);
- induction and definition (*PH* II 204 and 205–212);[6]
- division, whole/parts, genus/species, and accidents (*PH* II 213–228), examined in this contribution;
- sophisms (*PH* II 229–259).[7]

Within this conceptually homogeneous logical-epistemological arsenal that reflects a perspective marked by the dichotomy of true/false, I would like to focus on one of the 'logical' sections. These are unique in Sextus' work and hence find no parallels in the more meticulous analysis provided in *M* VII and VIII. This uniqueness does not merely concern the dogmatic theories pertaining to the notions of syllogism, induction/definition, and sophism, but extends to a range of points made with regard to logical-demonstrative argumentation, and which appear to play a leading role in the doctrines that Sextus seeks to refute.

---

[2] See, Anthony A. Long, "Sextus Empiricus on the Criterion of Truth," *Bulletin of the Institute of Classical Studies* 25 (1978): 35–49; Jacques Brunschwig, "Sextus Empiricus on the kriterion: the Sceptic as Conceptual Legatee," in *The Question of 'Eclecticism': Studies in Later Greek Philosophy*, eds. John M. Dillon and Anthony A. Long (Berkeley: University of California Press, 1988): 145–175; Tad Brennan, "Criterion and Appearance in Sextus Empiricus," in *Ancient Scepticism and the Sceptical Tradition*, ed. Juha Sihvola (Helsinki: Hakapaino O., 2000): 63–92; and Rosario La Sala, "Argumentative Strategien bei Sextus Empiricus. Das Beispiel des Kriteriums," *Acta Universitatis Carolinae, Philologica 1-Graecolatina Pragensia* 21 (2006): 63–75 [= idem, *Die Züge des Skeptikers. Der dialektische Charakter von Sextus Empiricus' Werk* (Göttingen: Vandenhoeck & Ruprecht, 2005): 96–107].
[3] See Emidio Spinelli, "Vero. verità, vita. Deficienze epistemologiche e soluzioni pragmatiche?," *Iride* 76 (2015): 625–639.
[4] See, Theodor Ebert, "The Origin of the Stoic Theory of Signs in Sextus Empiricus," *Oxford Studies in Ancient Philosophy* 5 (1987): 83–126; James Allen, *Inference from Signs: Ancient Debates about the Nature of Evidence* (Oxford: Clarendon Press, 2001): 87–146; Pierre Pellegrin, "Scepticisme et sémiologie médicale," in *De Zénon d'Élée à Poincaré. Recueil d'études en hommage à Roshdi Rashed*, eds. Régis Morelon and Ahmad Hasnawi (Louvain and Paris: Peeters, 2004): 645–664; and Richard Bett, "Le signe dans la tradition pyrrhonienne," in *Signe et prédiction dans l'antiquité*, ed. José Kany-Turpin (Saint-Étienne: Publications de l'Université de Saint-Etienne, 2005): 29–48.
[5] See Emidio Spinelli, "Non si dimostra il vero: la critica di Sesto Empirico ai procedimenti apodittici," *Elenchos* 36 (2015): 297–316.
[6] See Spinelli, *Questioni scettiche*, ch. 3.
[7] See Emidio Spinelli, "Dialectic and Sophisms: the Sceptical Dissolution of Dogmatic Logic" (forthcoming).

2 Logical Division and Its Four Aspects

Sextus' first target is the concept of division. Before discussing its more questionable aspects, in *PH* II 213 Sextus invokes the authority of 'some dogmatists' who considered dialectic 'the science of deduction, induction, definition and division,' apparently in an attempt to apply the same scheme to his own exposition. Sextus states that, in addition to his previous analysis of the notions of criterion, sign, and demonstrative *logoi*, he has already discussed syllogisms, inductions, and definitions. He now deems it appropriate to also examine, however briefly (*brachea*), the last section of dialectic: that pertaining to division (*PH* II 213–228), whose specific weight within the philosophical tradition embodied by Platonic and Peripatetic philosophers is undeniable.[8]

Presumably relying once again on the authority of the dogmatists mentioned at the beginning (*phasi*), Sextus presents—and sets out to criticise, what in his view seems to be easily (*rhadion isos*)—a distinction between four modes of *diairesis*, namely the division:

1. of the name into its relative meanings;
2. of the whole into its parts;
3. of the genus into its species;
4. of the species into individuals.[9]

If we start from the division of the name into its meanings, we will immediately notice an underlying feature of Sextus' argumentative strategy. The premise on which it rests in *PH* II 214 (= fr. 65 Hülser) is the acceptance—and perhaps not just *disserendi*

---

[8] On this aspect, see Benson Mates, *The Skeptic Way: Sextus Empiricus's* Outlines of Pyrrhonism (Oxford: Oxford University Press, 1996): 285. One should also note that Sextus' 'thematic index'—apart from the inversion of the topic examined: division, definition, induction, and syllogism—corresponds to the partition attested by Alcinous in his *Didaskalikos* (III, 153, 30–32 Hermann); cf. Sextus Empiricus, *Outlines of Scepticism*, trans. Julia Annas and Jonathan Barnes (Cambridge: Cambridge University Press, ²2000): 126, n. 313, where another passage of the *Didaskalikos* (156 Hermann), as well as Ammonius, *in Int.* 15, 16–18, are quoted. On some textual difficulties posed by these texts, see Whittaker's cautious observations in *Alcinoos. Enseignement des doctrines de Platon*, ed. John Whittaker (Paris: Les Belles Lettres, 1990): ad loc., and also Michelangelo Giusta, "Due capitoli sui dossografi di fisica," in *Storiografia e dossografia nella filosofia antica*, ed. Giuseppe Cambiano (Turin: Tirrenia, 1986): 177–178, especially n. 60.

[9] For a similar scheme of division, see also other sources: for example, Alcinous, Seneca, Galen, and Alexander of Aphrodisias, as well as Ps.-Gal. *Hist. phil.* ch. 14 and Clement of Alexandria (on his treatment of the topic, see Riccardo Chiaradonna, "Definitions, Species, Wholes, Parts. Clem. *Strom.* VIII.6.19.2–20.2," forthcoming). On their structure and mutual analogies or differences, apart from some useful references offered in *The So-Called Eighth* Stromateus *by Clement of Alexandria* (Leiden: Brill, 2016): ad loc. and also by Jonathan Barnes, *Porphyry: Introduction* (Oxford: Clarendon Press, 2003): 339–342, see especially Jaap Mansfeld, *Heresiography in Context: Hippolytus' Elenchos as a Source for Greek Philosophy* (Leiden: Brill, 1992): 80 ff. and 125 ff., who insists on the comparison between *PH* II 219–227 and Ps.-Hyppolitus, *ref.* VII 16–18.

causa, as the formula *kai eikotos* might be taken to suggest—of a widely accepted thesis in the dogmatist milieu (*phasin*): true knowledge, namely 'science' or *episteme*, is something firm and immutable. As such, it falls within the realm of *physei* entities and not of conventional products that are likely to undergo sudden changes and are subject to our judgement, which is to say—as Sextus points out—that it falls within the sphere of what is *eph'hemin*. May this thesis be traced back, first of all, to a Platonic Academic philosophical background, one also shared by Aristotle (see especially *An. post.* I 33)? The way in which it is presented, particularly the emphasis on the characteristic of immutability (*ametaptotos*, which like the following *eumetaptotos* is a *hapax* in Sextus), does not seem to suggest a Platonic echo and polemical target,[10] but perhaps allows a further speculation. One might suppose that Sextus here has a Stoic thesis in mind, a 'heterodox' thesis, possibly because it was still too Socratic in its distinctive traits (see in particular *SVF* I 413). It might be the radical thesis upheld by Herillus, who identified *telos* with a form of science intended as 'constant disposition.'[11]

Leaving aside the question of the origin of this doctrine, the mentioning of it allows Sextus to strategically highlight the unscientific nature, or, if we like, the incapacity, of operating on the firm and incontrovertible level of truth of diairetic activity, which some scholars have taken to amount to a merely lexicographical exercise in the clarification of homonyms.[12] The semantic function of names is presented as a merely conventional product by means of arguments that also occur, albeit in relation to different polemical aims, in other sections of Sextus' corpus: what we have is, on the one hand, the reciprocal linguistic incomprehension between Greeks and barbarians, and, on the other, the arbitrary and ever-changing connection between names and the things they signify.[13]

---

[10] One may however remember the continuous reference to the bebaios character of the so-called *epistemonikos logos*, again in Alcinous' *Didaskalikos* (see p. 154, 29, 30 Hermann = p. 5 Whittaker).
[11] See therefore *SVF* I 409; 411; 414–417 and Anna Maria Ioppolo, "Lo Stoicismo di Erillo," *Phronesis* 30 (1985): 58–78 [now in eadem, *Dibattiti filosofici ellenistici. Dottrina delle cause, Stoicismo, Accademia scettica*, eds. Bruno Centrone, Riccardo Chiaradonna, Diana Quarantotto, and Emidio Spinelli (Sankt Augustin: Academia, 2013): 119–135].
[12] See Mates, *The Skeptic Way*, 285.
[13] On the alleged Diodorean origin of this last *logos*, see Catherine Atherton, *The Stoics on Ambiguity* (Cambridge: Cambridge University Press, 1993): 430; more generally, on Diodorus Chronus' theory of language, see Francesco Verde, *Elachista: La dottrina dei minimi nell'Epicureismo* (Leuven: Leuven University Press, 2013): 210 ff. For other passages, in which Sextus insists on forms of linguistic conventionalism, see *PH* II 256; III 266–268; *M* XI 239–243; *M* I 36–38 e 144–147, as well as some useful observations in David K. Glidden, "Parrots, Pyrrhonists and Native Speakers," in *Language*, ed. Stephen Everson (Cambridge: Cambridge University Press, 1994): 129–148; Sextus Empiricus, *Contro gli etici*, ed. Emidio Spinelli (Naples: Bibliopolis, 1995): 393–394; Sextus Empiricus, *Against the Ethicists (Adversus Mathematicos XI)*, ed. Richard Bett (Oxford: Clarendon Press, 1997): 244–248; and Sextus Empiricus, *Against the Grammarians (Adversus Mathematicos I)*, ed. David L. Blank (Oxford: Clarendon Press, 1998): 105–107.

On the doxographical level too this passage from Sextus offers some interesting insights: the final demolition of the definition of dialectic as the science of signifiers and things signified—here recorded in an anonymous form (*hos oiontai tines*)—can, and indeed must, be seen to find its remote yet certain origin in Chrysippus (see *DL* VII 62).

3 Splitting the Whole into Its Parts

After having demolished the notion of division in a terse and schematic way, in *PH* II 215–218 Sextus turns his attention to the issue of the relation between the whole and its parts. In these sections, leaving open the question of the existence or non-existence of the whole and its parts, Sextus exclusively directs his criticism 'against the possibility of dividing a whole into its parts, a topic with which he does not deal at all in *M* 9.331–358.'[14] It is undeniable that this general question was very dear to the philosopher, since he repeatedly examines it, not merely occasionally in different sections of his works,[15] but also under more specific 'rubrics,' such as, for instance:

1. in the sections devoted to 'physics,' as he himself mentions at the beginning of *PH* II 215;[16]
2. in the technical context of the 'grammatical' partition of a *logos* into its parts (see *M* I 132–141; cf. also *M* I 162–168);[17]
3. in the context of a more specifically 'arithmetical' discussion (see *M* IV 23–33).

---

[14] Katherina Ierodiakonou, "Wholes and Parts: M 9.331–358," in *Sextus Empiricus and Ancient Physics*, eds. Keimpe Algra and Katherina Ierodiakonou (Cambridge: Cambridge University Press, 2015): 111.

[15] See, for example, *PH* III 45–46 and 85–96; *M* III 35–36; IX 258–264 and 308–319.

[16] The closest reference seems to be *PH* III 98–101. If this is true (and if therefore one should posit a coherent plan of composition behind Sextus' treatment of these topics), it is legitimate to refer not only to *PH* III 85–93 but also, on the one hand, to the 'parallel' section in *M* IX 297 ff. and, on the other, albeit the examples used are not always identical, to the above-mentioned relevant chapters in *M* IX 331–358. With regard to the latter, one can usefully read Ierodiakonou, "Wholes and parts," and especially the very stimulating analysis in Jonathan Barnes, "Bits and Pieces," in *Matter and Metaphysics*, eds. Jonathan Barnes and Mario Mignucci (Naples: Bibliopolis, 1988): 228, especially nn. 10–12. On some questions related to the doxographical (Stoic?) paternity of these Sextan passages, especially *M* IX 352, see also Dirk Baltzly, "Who are the mysterious dogmatists of Adversus Mathematicus ix 352?," *Ancient Philosophy* 18 (1998): 145–170 and the very cautious position adopted by Ierodiakonou, "Wholes and parts," 120–129.

[17] See the careful commentary by David Blank in Sextus Empiricus, *Against the Grammarians*, 170–175, who rightly affirms: 'the topic of part and whole [...] was of capital importance for the dogmatists, who promised to speak truly about the "all" or "whole," that is, the universe, and then for the sceptics, who needed it as an example of the dogmatists' rashness' (*ibidem*, 170–171).

In the passage under scrutiny, Sextus embarks on a general investigation of one of the possible aspects of *diairesis* without ever losing sight of his aim: to disprove the logical devices commonly employed by the dogmatists so as to undermine their truth claims. Sextus resorts to a numerical example, the number 10 and its parts,[18] in keeping with a mode of arguing that—as he himself consciously notes—is typical of the sceptics.[19]

The criticism unfolds along two distinct lines:
(a) the impossibility of dividing 10 *into* its parts;
(b) the impossibility of conceiving the parts *within* 10 in a non-contradictory way.

    a. Let us suppose that we divide 10 into the following parts—1+2+3+4—and, clearly stretching the argument to some extent, let us consider division to be almost a synonym of subtraction.[20] The first of the divided parts, 1, will then be subtracted from 10, which will become 9 and hence lose its peculiarity as a whole, and the same applies to the other elements in the division/subtraction.

    b. Given any division of the whole, moreover, its parts must necessarily be encompassed by the whole itself.[21] However, taking once again our chosen numerical example, if 10 is divided into 9+1 and then into 8+2, 7+3, and so on, it must be admitted that 10 encompasses, in addition to itself, the full sum of its parts (9+8+7+6+5+4+3+2+1=45). We must therefore grant that '10 encompasses 45.'

These absurd conclusions—which also apply on the 'geometric level,' which is to say in the case of magnitudes, to be intended however as continuous and not discrete quantities—[22] ought to show that it is impossible to divide a whole into parts. Faced with this unlikely claim, which seems to run against the most basic rules of common sense, one could raise some substantial doubts and objections, so as to highlight its 'sophistic' character, so to speak.[23] Sextus himself seems to be aware of this, since he introduces his polemical *logoi* with the kind of cautious language

---

18 Is this another implicit yet transparent allusion to the 'holy' Pythagorean decade? See Mansfeld, *Heresiography in Context*, 170.
19 *Hos ethos tois apo tes skepseos*, as we read in *M* IX 311; for a possible Platonic antecedent, see *Theaet.* 204b-c; see also Barnes, "Bits and Pieces," 237, n. 27, and Ierodiakonou, "Wholes and parts," 115–116.
20 See also *PH* III 85 and Eugen Pappenheim, *Erläuterungen zu des Sextus Empiricus pyrrhoneischen Grundzügen* (Leipzig: Meiner, 1881): 147.
21 On the meaning and textual distribution/diffusion of the verb *emperiechesthai* (or even of the simple *periechesthai*), see again Barnes, "Bits and Pieces," 234, n. 21.
22 Sextus would here appear to overlook the evident difference between the two thematic fields, a difference which he himself admits elsewhere; see, for example, *M* IV 1.
23 This 'sophistic' spirit has been stressed by many scholars; see, for example, Mates, *The Skeptic Way*, 285 and especially Barnes, "Bits and Pieces," 270 (with additional textual references to Locke and Leibniz).

that distinguishes Pyrrhonian formulations: he 'qualifies' them using semantically restrictive *phonai* (such as *tacha*, *PH* II 216, or *isos*, *PH* II 218) that are far removed from the dogmatist exposition of logical and linguistic statements as absolute, incontrovertible truths.

4 Genera and Species: Mental Concepts or Substantial Entities?

Sextus shifts the focus of his attack to a web of notions that carries even greater implications in terms of the claim of possessing the truth in the sections which he devotes to an examination of the dogmatist use of genera/species as a pair of terms (*PH* II 219–227).[24]

At the very beginning, in § 219, we find a sort of cross-reference, a crucial element for anyone wishing to further investigate and better understand Sextus' overall argument, as well as the connections which might be seen to lend coherence to his polemical exposition. Sextus writes that he will be returning to the question of the relationship between genera/species in greater detail elsewhere (*platyteron men en allois*). However, the philosopher does not keep this important promise, at any rate judging from his surviving writings.[25] We must make do, then, with the succinct analysis he offers in his *Outlines*, an analysis that from the very beginning is marked by the explicit identification of two polemical targets:

(a) A first group of dogmatists maintains that genera and species are merely conceptual products. Sextus regards the position of these thinkers—in all likelihood, Stoics—to have already been refuted through the aporias raised against the governing part (of the soul, the *hegemonikon*) and the notion of 'representation' (*phantasia*).[26]

---

[24] For a clear and accurate analysis of these paragraphs, see Mansfeld, *Heresiography in Context*, 125–131, whose conclusions I shall accept in what follows. For a very peculiar application of the genera/species pair to the notion of *genike gramme*, see *M* III 92 ff., and Wolfgang Freytag, *Mathematische Grundbegriffe bei Sextus Empiricus* (Hildesheim: Olms, 1995): 83–95.

[25] On this point, see *Sexti Empirici Opera*, recensuit Hermann Mutschmann, vol. I: Πυρρωνείων ὑποτυπώσεων *libros tres continens*, editionem stereotypam emendatam curavit, addenda et corrigenda adjecit Juergen Mau (Leipzig: Teubner, 1958): XXVII; one may however imagine that Sextus examined that question in one of the lost books antecedent to *M* VII-XI. For this hypothesis, see especially Karel Janáček, "Die Hauptschrift des Sextus Empiricus als Torso erhalten?," *Philologus* 107 (1963): 271–277 [now in idem, *Studien zu Sextus Empiricus, Diogenes Laertius und zur pyrrhonischen Skepsis*, eds. Jan Janda and Filip Karfík (Berlin and New York: De Gruyter, 2008): 124–131] and Jerker Blomqvist, "Die *Skeptika* des Sextus Empiricus," *Grazer Beiträge* 2 (1974): 12–24, as well as Mansfeld, *Heresiography in Context*, 130, who suggests that Ps-Hyppolitus too might depend on the same, more detailed Sextan passage.

[26] See *PH* II 70–71. The Stoic origin of the theses attacked here seems to be confirmed by the presence of some very technical terms belonging to their lexicon. This notwithstanding, *PH* II 219 is ab-

(b) A second group of philosophers instead grants genera and species self-subsistence (*idia hypostasis*). Based on cross-references with texts by Seneca, Alcinous, and Clement of Alexandria, it has been reasonably suggested that this 'second group consists of Middle Platonists (that is to say, inclusive of the Middle Platonist Plato and the *Aristoteles interpretatus*).'²⁷

The theses upheld by this second group of opponents may have struck Sextus as being more challenging or better argued, since he does not limit himself to providing a swift, terse refutation, but examines them in greater detail in *PH* II 220–222. Given the actual existence of genera (*disserendi causa*, of course), it thus seems as though those wishing to highlight their limits are faced with two possibilities:
(a) there are as many genera as species;
(b) there is only one genus, common to all the species that fall under it.

The first alternative forces us to deny the very possibility of a *diairesis* of the genus, i.e., of that process enabling us to acknowledge a multiplicity of species to be subsumed under the *single* and same *genos*. The second alternative, instead, entails a series of contradictions; in fact, it presupposes the creation of some real fictions (*eidolopoieseis*, *PH* II 222: a noun that constitutes a *hapax* in Sextus). In order to expose these contradictions, Sextus sets out to reveal certain dogmatic incongruities through a range of objections that carry considerable weight within the Pyrrhonian polemical arsenal and whose presence in this section of the corpus is certainly noteworthy.²⁸ At this point, one might also speculate: can Sextus' formulation find an authoritative precedent in Plato's *Parmenides* (see especially *Parm.* 131a ff.)? Or, at least, may it constitute a conscious counterpart to some sort of Middle Platonist reading of these Platonic pages?²⁹

The richness of the possible philosophical background of Sextus' objections and the objective strength they display in their attempt to demolish two cornerstones of the much-flaunted dogmatist ability to build cogent arguments, as far as the identification of the truth is concerned, suggest that we should examine the development of Sextus' polemic more closely. Sextus' criticism revolves around two key points:

---

sent from *SVF* and also from Hülser's collection; see Mansfeld, *Heresiography in Context*, 126, n. 50. The term *ennoema*, attested only here and in *M* IX 355–356, would also appear to be Stoic; see *DL* VII 60.

27 Mansfeld, *Heresiography in Context*, 126.
28 In *PH* II 222, these Pyrrhonian *logoi* are labelled as *skeptikai ephodoi*, a formula used also in *PH* II 258, on which, see Theodor Ebert, *Dialektiker und frühe Stoiker bei Sextus Empiricus. Untersuchungen zur Entstehung der Aussagenlogik* (Göttingen: Vandenhoeck & Ruprecht, 1991): 256–257, n. 22 and Fernanda Decleva Caizzi, "Sesto e gli scettici," *Elenchos* 13 (1992): 296, n. 41 (now also online: http://scholarlysource.daphnet.org/index.php/DDL/article/view/130). For similar objections, see also *PH* III 158 ff.
29 See, for example, Alcinous, *Didask.* VI 159, 35 H. and Mansfeld, *Heresiography in Context*, 126–127; Sextus Empiricus, *Outlines of Scepticism*, 128, n. 323, referring back to *PH* III 158–162.

1. Not every species can participate in the whole genus, because otherwise it would exhaust that genus in itself, so to speak, and hence it could not be 'participated' in by any other species.
2. Not every species can participate even in a part of the genus, for at least for two reasons:
    a. Because if it did, we would not find the whole genus in the species and would have to say, for example, that man is only substance, and not the other parts of the 'animal' genus (for example, animated or endowed with sensation);
    b. Because not every species participates in the same part of the genus (for this would give rise to the same difficulties encountered under point 1), nor do different species participate in different parts. In the latter case, 'they will either be generically different, which conflicts with the notion of a common genus, or each genus will become infinite, being divided not only into entirely different species but also into entirely different empirical individuals.'[30]

With no scruples about doxographical homogeneity, and with little concern about switching from one dogmatist family to another in his polemic, Sextus seems to shift from a remote Platonist or Middle Platonist terrain[31] to one of his favourite targets. From *PH* II 223 (= fr. 718 Hülser), his polemical focus is yet another doctrine typical of the Stoics. The latter identify (*phasin*) 'something' (*ti*) as the supreme genus (see *PH* II 86). Purely by way of hypothesis and for the sake of argumentative completeness (*logou eneken*), Sextus puts forward three alternatives. This supreme category, the *ti*, is:

(a) all things;
(b) only some things;
(c) no things.

Alternative (c) is immediately discarded, since it is tantamount to positing that the supreme genus is nothing at all. Hypothesis (a) also raises some glaring contradictions,[32] for if the supreme genus is both corporeal/incorporeal, true/false, white/black, and so on, then the species and individuals 'in which it is found' also

---

30 *Ibidem*, 126 and n. 53, where Sextus' correct form of argumentation is explicitly praised.
31 Although one should not forget the Platonic 'adoption,' in Severus, of the Stoic doctrine of the *ti*; see also David Sedley, *Stoic Metaphysics at Rome*, in *Metaphysics, Soul, and Ethics in Ancient Thought: Themes From the Work of Richard Sorabji*, ed. Ricardo Salles (Oxford: Oxford University Press, 2005): 117–142.
32 The example used here (§ 224: the animal as 'an animate sensitive substance') seems to be a standard, quasi-'scholastic' definition, possibly a 'common asset' of the Platonic, Peripatetic, and Stoic traditions at the time; see Sextus Empiricus, *Outlines of Scepticism*, 120.

ought to be such,³³ a conclusion obviously in contrast with reality. Finally, alternative (b) suggests that we can only identify the *ti* with, for example, the body or with rationality, which automatically implies the non-existence of 'something' incorporeal or non-rational (conclusions that openly conflict with established Stoic theses).

Faithful to his 'diabolically ecumenical' intention to spare no possible commentator who makes a dogmatic claim of possessing the truth, Sextus takes a sort of exegetical turn at the end of *PH* II 225 by focusing on the further dogmatist attempt to describe the genus as something that is all things *in potency* (*dynamei*) but not *in act*: an attempt that has a Peripatetic 'flavour' to it and carries markedly polemical implications.³⁴ Once again, this dogmatist suggestion, anchored in the dialectical relation between potency and act, proves fruitless in Sextus' eyes. He plays with basic concepts that are well established in the philosophies he attacks, since he 'jumps from the relative to the absolute sense of "not being."'³⁵ For Sextus, the dogmatist (or possibly Peripatetic) is first of all forced to define what the genus itself is in act; yet as soon as he does so, he finds himself caught in the aporias already examined with regard to the aforementioned alternative (a), and hence is forced to abandon his hypothetical yet fragile way out.

In this progressive accumulation of polemical targets, attacked in relation to the alleged explicative or heuristic strength of the *genos*, there is another dogmatist short-cut which does not escape Sextus' attention: the thesis that the genus coincides with some things in act and others only in potency. For example, if the *ti* is 'actually' (*energeia*) corporeal, it cannot be *dynamei* incorporeal. Sextus' argument here proves particularly effective, insofar as it denies that the genus encompasses, at least potentially, the different qualities, or even opposite or contradictory qualities (white/black, true/false, etc.), of its species. The argument can apparently be applied to any opponent seeking to uphold this thesis.³⁶

Sextus' last objection, put forward in *PH* II 227, concerns a well-known example that was no doubt widely used in dogmatist milieus. It revolves around the impossibility of regarding the word 'man' as being truly and unqualifiedly common to all the particular entities that ought to fall within it. Let us grant that statements such as 'Alexander is taking a walk' and 'Paris is taking a walk' are both either true or false, since the proper nouns used are absolutely homonymous. This is not the case when the subject of a statement is a common noun, as this would give a linguistic character to its genus. In his example, Sextus seems to be mocking the discussions and dialectical arguments typical of his opponents' schools. If we say 'a man is taking a walk,' we must grant that this proposition is not always true or al-

---

33 On this distinctive Sextan interpretation of the relationship between genera/species and individuals and for some parallels in Plotinus, see again *ibidem*, 127, n. 55.
34 See Long, "Sextus Empiricus on the Criterion of Truth," 48, n. 25.
35 Mansfeld, *Heresiography in Context*, 129.
36 As is later the case with Porphyry; see *Isag.* 10. 22–11–6.

ways false, but rather true in the case of Theon, who is indeed taking a walk, and false in the case of Dion, who is seated.

In this case too, then, Sextus' polemic combines notions more specifically related to the field of logic with what characterises the linguistic expressions exploited by the various dogmatist schools. The latter—judging at least from Sextus' cumulative and far from neutral reconstruction—all share an obstinate desire to assign our assertions an ontologically cogent value on the semantic level.

5 Common Accidents or Private Properties?

The set of criticisms advanced against the background of this complex logical, linguistic, and conceptual network culminates in *PH* II 228 with an attempt to disprove the notion of common accidents. Moving directly on from the objections examined in the previous sections, Sextus extends his criticism to those qualifications that seem to be transversally 'promiscuous,' which is to say common to several entities, when in fact in each case they turn out to apply only to one subject (the adjective used here, *idion*, may be an allusion to Stoic doctrine)—or, to be more precise, to a particular condition or situation in which the entity in question finds itself, as though these qualifications were an integral part of a sort of metaphysical *principium individuationis*.[37] The examples of *symbebekota* chosen by Sextus (sight and breathing) show that the apparently common predicability with respect to Dion or Theon, for instance, no longer applies the moment one of the two subjects radically changes his status. Sight and breathing 'perish,' so to speak, with the death of the subject in relation to whom they were enunciated; nor is it reasonable to suppose that they endure as self-subsistent entities.

6 Beyond Theory, but Towards Life ...

Retracing the steps of Sextus' attack on the various notions examined in certain sections of the second book of the *Outlines of Pyrrhonism*—often schematic or even inadequate steps, at times compelling or cogent ones—has proven to be a rather useful exercise in two respects. On the one hand, the analysis of Sextus carried out in these pages and the sharp *pars destruens* they deliver have enabled us—with obvious benefits on the doxographical level—to highlight some of the argumentative tools, or at any rate some of the main points of reference, in the reasoning developed by individ-

---

37 The way in which Sextus here examines and solves the problem seems to justify the conclusion that 'the present section is very Leibnizian,' see Mates, *The Skeptic Way*, 286. The difficult question of a reliable *principium individuationis* was at any rate also a crucial topic for ancient medicine; see therefore Riccardo Chiaradonna, "Universals in Ancient Medicine," in *Universals in Ancient Philosophy*, eds. Riccardo Chiaradonna and Gabriele Galluzzo (Pisa: Edizioni dela Normale, 2013): 381–423.

ual dogmatist currents. Each of these currents sought to consolidate its solid knowledge, its established *episteme*, as the unquestionable province of truth. On the other hand, behind Sextus' persistent arguments it has been possible to grasp a fully and distinctly Pyrrhonian *pars construens*: the progressive demolition of the cornerstones of the logical structure of dogmatism enables the true sceptic to fully exercise his most genuine *dynamis*. In *PH* I 8, this is praised as a crucial sceptical

> ability to set out oppositions among things which appear and are thought of in any way at all, an ability by which, because of the equipollence in the opposed objects and accounts, we come first to suspension of judgement and afterwards to tranquillity.[38]

This intellectual effort does away with all truth claims and, ultimately, probably rejects even the alleged primacy of the *bios theoretikos*.[39] In his critical enquiry, the Pyrrhonian philosopher does not investigate conflicting dogmatist theses on the level of the strict rules of Aristotelian logic, i.e., in the light of the alleged mutually exclusive contradictory status between what is absolutely true and what is absolutely false.[40] Rather, he bases the assessment of these theses on their credibility, which is psychologically experienced as being equipollent and hence capable of leading to a morally fruitful suspension of judgement.[41] With this comes something capable of providing guidance in the complexity of everyday life, namely the acceptance of a series of apparent values and phenomena that prove pragmatically effective insofar as they are governed by the non-dogmatic four-fold rule for directing one's mind. Sextus sums it up as follows (*PH* I 23):

> Thus, attending to what is apparent, we live in accordance with everyday observances, without holding opinions—for we are not able to be utterly inactive. These everyday observances seem to be fourfold, and to consist in guidance by nature, necessitation by feelings, handing down of laws and customs, and teaching of kinds of expertise.[42]

In other words, if it is true that we can do without the truth, it will be useful to gaze at reality with different eyes, with a less presumptuously definitive or absolute per-

---

38 Sextus Empiricus, *Outlines of Scepticism*, 4.
39 For more details, see Emidio Spinelli, "Beyond the Theoretikos Bios: Philosophy and Praxis in Sextus Empiricus," in *Theoria, Praxis, and the Contemplative Life after Plato and Aristotle*, eds. Thomas Bénatouïl and Mauro Bonazzi (Leiden: Brill, 2012): 101–117.
40 In this case too, let me refer back to Emidio Spinelli, "Sextus Empiricus et l'ombre longue d'Aristote," *Philosophie Antique* 12 (2012): 275–277.
41 I focus on some crucial aspects related to the sceptical notion of *epoche* in Emidio Spinelli, "Sesto Empirico: iceberg scettico della nozione di ἐποχή," *Archivio di Filosofia* 83 (2015): 193–207. On the notion of equipollence, see also Diego Machuca, "Argumentative Persuasiveness in Ancient Pyrrhonism," *Méthexis* 22 (2009): 101–126 and Svavar H. Svavarsson, "Sextus Empiricus on Persuasiveness and Equipollence," in *Strategies of Argument. Essays in Ancient Ethics, Epistemology, and Logic*, ed. Mi-Kyoung Lee (Oxford: Oxford University Press, 2014): 356–373.
42 Sextus Empiricus, *Outlines of Scepticism*, 9.

spective. We can then shape our being in the world in the light of different criteria, criteria that may be weaker and less appealing perhaps, but are no less fruitful: *primum vivere, deinde philosophari* [...].[43]

---

[43] In conclusion, let me warmly thank Riccardo Chiaradonna and Francesco Verde, who offered useful comments on a first draft of this paper.

Teresa Caligiure
In antiquam litem relabimur.
Sceptical Hints in Petrarch's *Secretum**

> Cum enim neque melius quaeri veritas possit,
> quam interrogando et respondendo.
> (Augustine, *Soliloquium*, II:7,14)

Introduction

Francesco Petrarch's *Secretum*[1] is a Latin dialogue in three books composed between 1347 and 1353.[2] The aim of this paper is to investigate certain sceptical hints emerging

---

* This contribution includes the first results of the research I have had the privilege to carry out at the Maimonides Centre for Advanced Studies. I would like to express my gratitude to Giuseppe Veltri and to all my other colleagues at the Maimonides Centre, particularly Harald Bluhm and Warren Zev Harvey, as I have had the pleasure of discussing some aspects of the subject of this research with them. Some of the issues put forward in this article were presented during a talk on Petrarch's *Secretum* at Masaryk University in Brno thanks to the hospitality of Paolo Divizia. I thank Bill Rebiger for the patience he has shown as the editor of this article.

1 The Latin text is as established by Enrico Carrara in Francesco Petrarca, *Secretum*, in idem, *Prose*, eds. Guido Martellotti, Pier Giorgio Ricci, Enrico Carrara, and Enrico Bianchi (Milan and Naples: Ricciardi, 1955): 22–215, amended with corrections from Bufano's edition in Francesco Petrarca, *Opere latine*, vol. 1, ed. Antonietta Bufano (Turin: UTET, 1975): 44–258. The English text follows Mann's excellent translation in Petrarch, *My Secret Book*, ed. and trans. Nicholas Mann (Cambridge, Mass.: Harvard University Press, 2016). Paragraph numbers refer to Fenzi's outstanding annotated edition, Francesco Petrarca, *Secretum. Il mio segreto*, ed. Enrico Fenzi (Milan: Mursia, 1992), which gives the pages from Carrara's edition.

2 On the dating of the composition, cf. Francisco Rico, *Vita u obra de Petrarca. I: Lectura del 'Secretum'* (Padua: Antenore, 1974). In his impressive analysis, Rico demonstrated that the action of the dialogue takes place between 1342 and 1343. According to him, the first redaction dates from 1347 and was followed by a second in 1349 and a final edition, thoroughly re-elaborated, completed in 1353. In 1358, Petrarch is supposed to have merely re-read the text, adding some marginal notes that confirm the proposed chronology of the three editions. We can read those marginal notes in the copy of the *Secretum* made by Tebaldo della Casa, reproduced in the current Codice Laurenziano XXVI sin. 9 of the Biblioteca Mediceo-Laurenziana in Florence, cc. 208–243. Hans Baron, *Petrarch's 'Secretum.' Its Making and its Meaning*, Medieval Academy of America (Cambridge: Mass., 1985) proposes a different reconstruction of the *Secretum*: his important analysis roots the interpretation and the proposed dates more solidly in the biographical data. Bortolo Martinelli, *Il Secretum conteso* (Naples: Loffredo, 1982) and Giovanni Ponte, "Nella selva del Petrarca: la discussa data del Secretum," *Giornale storico della Letteratura italiana* 167 (1990): 1–63, also discussed—with different hypotheses—the complex question of establishing the chronology of the *Secretum*'s composition. For a careful reconstruction of the many hypotheses concerning the editing and dating of the *Secretum*, see Fenzi, *Secretum*, 5–77 (introduction).

OpenAccess. © 2017 Teresa Caligiure, published by De Gruyter. This work is licensed under the Creative Commons Attribution-NonCommercial-NoDerivatives 4.0 License.
https://doi.org/10.1515/9783110527971-003

from the dialogue which underpinned the conception of Francesco's character and his relationship with the quest for Christian truth.

It would be proper to begin with the *Proem*, as it anticipates the ideological cores of the *Secretum* by delineating Francesco's moral character, that of a man prone to anxious brooding about the human condition: 'Not long ago, while I was yet again meditating with astonishment on how I had come into this life and how I would depart from it.'[3] Next, Truth[4] appears in the shape of a woman whose presence plays a specific role, as she herself explains:

> Taking pity on your errors I have come down from afar to help you in your hour of need. Until now you have often all to often gazed upon the earth with clouded eyes; if so far you have found mortal things delightful, how much more can you not hope for if you look up to things eternal? [...] So I gazed, eager to look at her, but my mortal eyes could not bear the celestial light, and I lowered them again. Seeing this, she was silent for a moment, and then, repeatedly breaking into speech, she forced me with brief and almost insignificant questions to respond and to discuss a multitude of things. I recognised that this was doubly to my advantage: I became a little wiser, and at the same time, feeling more confident as a result of our discussion, I began to be able to look more openly at the face.[5]

Francesco dwells in error because his interests aim solely at mundane goods. Truth, whom he described in his Latin poem *Africa*[6] and with whom he is therefore well acquainted, comes to his rescue. After a brief silent pause,[7] during which Francesco shivers in awe, unable to bear the gaze of such celestial splendour, Truth, through

---

3 'Attonito michi quidem et sepissime cogitanti qualiter in hanc vitam intrassem, qualiter ve forem egressurus.' Cf. Seneca, *Ad Lucil.*, XXII:14 ss; Boethius, *Cons. Phil.*, I:1, Augustine, *Sol.*, I:I,1. On the semantic richness of the *incipit* and the intricate web of classical and medieval references, see Rico, *Secretum*, 16–20.

4 On the character of Truth in the *Proem*, see the *ad locum* comments of Rico and Fenzi.

5 *Proem*, 22–24: 'Errores tuos miserata, de longinquo tempestivum tibi auxilium latura descendi. Satis superque satis hactenus terram caligantibus oculis aspexisti; quos si usqueadeo mortalia ista permulcent, quid futurum speras si eos ad eterna sustuleris? [...]. Rursus igitur in terram oculos deicio; quod illa cognoscens, brevis spatii interveniente silentio, iterumque et iterum in verba prorumpens, minutis interrogatiunculis me quoque ut secum multa colloquerer coegit. Duplex hinc michi bonum provenisse cognovi: nam, et aliquantulum doctior factus sum, aliquantoque ex ipsa conversatione securior spectare coram posse cepi vultum illum, qui nimio primum me splendore terruerat.'

6 In fact, the received text of the poem *Africa* contains no description of Truth or of her palace, contrarily to what Francesco writes in the *Proem*. The same question concerns Book III of the dialogue, in which Augustine repeatedly refers to the poem. On this issue, also connected to chronological aspects of the work, see Enrico Fenzi, "Dall'*Africa* al *Secretum*. Il sogno di Scipione e la composizione del poema," in idem, *Saggi petrarcheschi* (Florence: Cadmo, 2003): 305–365; idem, *Secretum*, 23–39 (introduction); 399–400, n. 327; 407, n. 376; 411–412, n. 402 (commentary).

7 On the topic of silence in Petrarch, understood as inner recollection, far from the distractions of the city, and for its different meanings relating to *otium* see, including the references to previous studies, Arnaud Tripet, "Pétrarque, la parole silencieuse," *Italique* 8 (2005): 9–25 and Ilaria Tufano, "I silenzi di Petrarca," in *Silenzio*. Atti del terzo colloquio internazionale di letteratura italiana, Napoli, 2–4 ottobre 2008, ed. Silvia Zoppi Garampi (Rome: Salerno Editrice, 2011): 105–120.

minutae interrogatiunculae,⁸ initiates a conversation intended to bring about the moral elevation of her interlocutor. Nonetheless, the task of reaching deep into the depths of Francesco's soul and diverting his desires from earthly vanities is entrusted to Augustine, because 'it is the human voice that penetrates the ear of mortal man.'⁹ Francesco recognises the saint at once because of his posture, his African outfit and Roman eloquence, and his eagerness to question him;¹⁰ however, Truth addresses Augustine first. Truth asks Augustine to come out of his silent brooding ('taciturna meditatio'), since Francesco is moribund because of his own sin and, furthermore, is dangerously far from understanding the nature of his own sickness: that is why he needs a physician who is an expert in mundane passions.¹¹ Augustine,¹² to whom Francesco is devoted as he views him as the intellectual closest to his own sensitivity, is an example to follow, since he also wandered in error before reaching a path of truth-seeking.¹³ In fact, Petrarch considered Augustine his own master. The saint accepts the task, initiating a three-day exchange with the disciple in the silent presence of Truth.¹⁴

'Sola virtus animum felicitat'

The structure of the work, as the *auctor* highlights, draws from the model of Platonic and Ciceronian dialogues.¹⁵ Its constant and crucial references are Boethius' *Conso-*

---

8 This is a Ciceronian syntagm opening the proem of the *Paradoxa stoicorum ad Marcum Brutum* I:2.
9 *Proem*, 24: 'Aurem mortalis hominis humana vox feriat.'
10 *Ibidem*: 'iam interrogationis verba dictaveram' ('I was already preparing to frame my question').
11 *Ibidem*: 'quod cum ita sit, passionum expertarum curator optime' ('For this reason you are the best healer of passions that you yourself have experienced').
12 Among the important studies on the relationship between Augustine and Petrarch, see at least Pietro Paolo Gerosa, *Umanesimo cristiano del Petrarca. Influenza agostiniana, attinenze medievali* (Turin: Bottega d'Erasmo, 1966); Elena Giannarelli, "Petrarca e i Padri della Chiesa," in *Quaderni Petrarcheschi* 9–10 (1992–3): 393–412; Giuseppe Billanovich, "Petrarca, Boccaccio e le 'Enarrationes in Psalmos' di sant'Agostino," in idem, *Petrarca e il primo Umanesimo* (Padua: Antenore, 1996): 68–96; Enrico Fenzi, "Platone, Petrarca, Agostino," in idem, *Saggi petrarcheschi*, 519–552; Roberto Cardini and Paolo Viti, eds., *Petrarca e i Padri della Chiesa: Petrarca e Arezzo* (Pagliai: Polistampa, 2004): 29–100 and 209–305; Roberto Cardini and Donatella Coppini, eds., *Petrarca e Agostino* (Rome: Bulzoni, 2004); and Alexander Lee, *Petrarch and St. Augustine: Classical Scholarship, Christian Theology and the Origins of the Renaissance in Italy* (Leiden: Brill, 2012).
13 Cf. *Secretum*, I:42 where Petrarch states that, when he read the *Confessions*, he would find that it mirrored his own situation. Cf. also *Fam.*, X:3, 56, where, among the Augustinian readings recommended to Monica, the *Confessions* are paired with the *Soliloquium* and *Fam.*, IV:1 about the similarity that Petrarch stated between his existential path and Augustine's.
14 *Proem*, 26: 'illa de singulis in silentio iudicante' ('Truth, who passed silent judgment on every word').
15 *Proem*, 26: 'hunc nempe scribendi morem a Cicerone meo didici; at ipse prius a Platone didicerat' ('I learned this technique from Cicero who in turn had learned it from Plato'). In the *Tusculan Dispu-*

lation of Philosophy and Augustine's *Confessions*, together with the moral writings of Seneca.[16] From the prologue on, Petrarch refers to Augustine's *Soliloquium*[17] as well. As has already been pointed out,[18] the Cassiciaco dialogues were, among Augustine's works, one of the major influences on the character of Francesco in the *Secretum*.[19] Without forgetting the substantial differences between them, these similarities show the importance of assent in the quest for truth and also how, in the *Secretum*, Francesco lacks the final assent that would allow him to take on a new moral path. Further evidence of the influence of the *Soliloquium* on the *Secretum* are the facts that the inner dialogue between Augustine and Ratio also lasts for three days and that Ratio advises Augustine to ask for God's help against the infirmities of sin ('ora salutem et auxilium'). In the *Soliloquium*, the author 'undertakes, and in turn discusses, the difficult path of philosophical reflection, which is aimed at investigating, through reason and evidence, those truths that matter to man and to which he refers to live.'[20] Nevertheless, Augustine, unlike Francesco, recites a long prayer before the actual opening of the dialogue. In the prayer, he turns desire and *voluntas*[21] towards God and begs to be able to reach God's knowledge and that of the soul.[22] Furthermore, he demonstrates his gradual moral elevation, showing his progress[23] and his willing spiritual growth.

---

tations, I:4,8 Cicero acknowledged in turn having drawn inspiration from the Socratic maieutic model, consecrated by Plato.

16 For the classical and medieval models of the *Proem*, see the *ad locum* comments of Rico and Fenzi.

17 *Sol.*, I:1,1: 'Volventi mihi multa ac varia mecum diu ac per multos dies sedulo quaerenti memetipsum ac bonum meum, quidve mali evitandum esset, ait mihi subito sive ego ipse sive alius quis, extrinsecus sive intrinsecus, nescio; nam hoc ipsum est quod magnopere scire molior, ait ergo mihi.'

18 Nicolae Iliescu wrote about the connections between the *Secretum* and the *Soliloquium*, *Il Canzoniere Petrarchesco e Sant'Agostino* (Rome: Società Accademica Romena, 1962): 43: 'His direct model [for the *Secretum*] is the *Soliloquium*, rather than the *Confessions*: because of the same dialogical form, the debate on the many forms of vanity, the character of intimacy (*Soliloquia-Secretum*) and because of the presence of Truth.' See also Francesco Tateo's interesting observations, *Dialogo interiore e polemica ideologica nel 'Secretum' del Petrarca* (Florence, Le Monnier, 1965) now revised in idem, *L'ozio segreto di Petrarca* (Bari: Palomar, 2005): 21–95, esp. 36–38. As for the *Proem*, cf. especially Rico, *Secretum*, 21–41; *ibidem*, 37, n.112 and 38, where the scholar stresses the topic of the *Secretum* as an imitation of the *Soliloquium*.

19 See Rico, *Secretum*, 384; 415–416.

20 Unless otherwise stated, English translations are the author's. Cf. Onorato Grassi in Augustine, *Soliloquia*, ed. Onorato Grassi (Milan: Bompiani, 2002): 7 (introduction): '[L'autore] percorre, e a sua volta ripropone, la difficile strada della riflessione filosofica, volta a indagare, mediante la ragione e secondo il criterio dell'evidenza, le verità che interessano l'uomo e alle quali egli si riferisce per vivere.'

21 On the relationship between *amor* and *voluntas* in Augustine's works, cf. Donatella Pagliacci, *Volere e amare. Agostino e la conversione del desiderio* (Rome: Città Nuova, 2003). For the *Soliloquium* in particular, see the second chapter, *ibidem*, 47–100.

22 *Sol.*, I:1–6.

23 Cf., e.g., *ibidem*, I:10,17.

In the *Proem*, Francesco lies in a situation of error and inner closure; however, at the end of the dialogue, after a long analysis of his conscience, he still wishes—as at the beginning—to take care of his mundane commitments ('mortalia negotia' III:214). Indeed, he does not display a thoroughly manifest will towards the virtuous life, and his master Augustine rebukes him accordingly. In the *Secretum*, Petrarch, through an introspective analysis in the presence of Truth, delineates the project of a virtuous life to be put into practice in Augustine's replies; still, the disciple defers his master's proposals. Francesco's moral progress and the awareness he acquires of his own sin should allow him to shed the *phantasmata* ('imagines rerum visibilium'; 'pestis illa fantasmatum')[24] that make one's spirit numb and paralyses one's actions. Nevertheless, he does not reach an immediate practical goal, but rather a deferred action. This is testified by the master's closing line, where he resignedly joins in with a prayer: 'But so be it, since it cannot be otherwise. I pray to God and beg Him to accompany you on your way, and to grant that your errant footsteps will nonetheless lead you to a place of safety.'[25] Besides, while in the *Soliloquium* Augustine's deferral of an answer opens up the possibility of a broader argumentation, meant to show the moral progress he has achieved,[26] in the *Secretum* Francesco's stalling in heeding his master's call, and so Truth's own call, is due to sloth and to his unwillingness to face the matter and admit his error, or to his persistent dwelling in error itself.

In the first book of the *Secretum*, Augustine bestows upon his disciple the duty of acknowledging his own negligent *voluntas* towards good, impaired by his mundane passions. The saint at once introduces the matters he cherishes the most: the redis-

---

24 Cf. *Secretum*, I:64–66. To explain the meaning of this word, Augustine refers to a passage mistakenly attributed to St. Paul (in truth an excerpt from *Sap.*, IX:15), and Francesco mentions Augustine's *De vera religione* and the influence it had on him; the master then specifies that *De vera religione* was inspired by his reading of Cicero's *Hortensius*, and generally by Plato, Socrates, and Cicero, and quotes with this respect a passage from the *Tusculan Disputations*. On this passage, see Rico, *Secretum*, 11–121; Fenzi, *Secretum*, 314–315, n. 141 and 142 and introduction. For the relationship between *De vera religione* and Petrarch's works, see Rico, "Petrarca y el 'De vera religione'," *Italia medioevale e umanistica* 17 (1974): 313–364. On this theme, see Rino Caputo, *Cogitans fingo. Petrarca tra 'Secretum' e 'Canzoniere'* (Rome: Bulzoni, 1987). Massimo Ciavolella, "La stanza della memoria: amore e malattia nel 'Secretum' e nei 'Rerum vulgarium fragmenta'", *Quaderns d'Italià* 11 (2006): 55–63, examines the *phantasmata* and the role of the faculty of the imagination in the *Secretum* and in sonnets LXXXIII, CVII, CXVI, CXXX of the *RVF*, with respect to the theories of the philosophers and doctors of Scholastic and Arabic traditions tracing back to Aristotle and Galen. Concerning Petrarch's *RVF* and closely relating to Dante's *Vita Nuova*, the topics, vocabulary, and physiological processes determined by the imaginative faculty with respect to the *amor hereos*, with ample reference to philosophical and scientific treatises, were discussed by Natascia Tonelli, *Fisiologia della passione. Poesia d'amore e medicina da Cavalcanti a Boccaccio* (Florence: Edizioni del Galluzzo per la Fondazione Ezio Franceschini, 2015): 125–151.
25 *Proem*, III:214: 'Sed sic eat, quando aliter esse non potest, supplexque Deum oro ut euntem comitetur, gressusque licet vagos, in tutum iubeat pervenire.'
26 E.g. *Sol.*, I:10,17; e.g. Augustine stopped desiring honours: 'Fateor, eos modo ac paene his diebus cupere destiti.'

covery of one's self (*nosce te ipsum*), the awareness of error, the *meditatio mortis*,[27] and the search for happiness through virtue; he then moves on to analysing Francesco's past experiences and his state of spiritual misery. Firstly—in the second book—the saint pressingly questions Francesco about the seven deadly sins, greatly elaborating on sloth, the sin by which Francesco is most tormented. Then, in the third book, Augustine probes the two passions that, for his disciple, are the hardest to get rid of: his love for Laura and his longing for glory.

Augustine's words in Book I echo the strict principles of Stoic morality,[28] which binds together notions of virtue and truth, preaching abstention from passions—thus from richness, earthly love, and the desire for glory—and the primacy of will.

> A: For if virtue alone makes the mind happy, as has been frequently proved with the most convincing arguments by Cicero and many others, then it follows absolutely that nothing removes the mind from happiness unless it is the opposite of virtue [...].
>
> F: Of course I remember: you are directing me back to the teaching of the Stoics, which are contrary to popular opinion and closer to the truth than to general practice. [...] I [...] don't doubt that the maxims of the Stoics are preferable to the errors of the common people [...]. For that reason, even allowing for the Stoic maxim, one can accept that many are unhappy against their will, while grieving and wishing that the contrary were true. [...]
>
> A: I had set about showing you that in order to escape the confines of our mortal condition and to lift ourselves to higher things, the first step, so to speak, consists of meditation on death and human misery; the second is the ardent desire and determination to rise above them.
>
> F: I wouldn't dare to admit that I had set my mind against it. For my esteem for you has so grown since my youth that if my opinion were in any way different from yours, I'd recognize that I was mistaken.[29]

---

27 On the *meditatio mortis* in the *Secretum*, besides the comments of Rico and Fenzi on the many passages of the dialogue where the topic is present, see Sabrina Stroppa, *Petrarca e la morte. Tra 'Familiari' e Canzoniere* (Rome: Aracne, 2014): 59–76.

28 The Stoic morality, as highlighted by Rico, *Secretum*, 53 ff. and Baron, *Petrarch's 'Secretum'*, 34–46, acquires a growing importance for Petrarch right in the 1350s, hence at the same time of the composition of the *Secretum*, and, according to Baron, it determines following additions to the first writing that can be witnessed in several parts of the *Secretum*. On the Stoicism of the *Secretum*, besides the ad locum comments of Rico and Fenzi, see Ugo Dotti, *Secretum*, (introduction): 7–47, idem, *Vita di Petrarca* (Rome-Bari: Laterza, 1987): 154–175.

29 *Secretum*, I:34: 'A: Nam si sola virtus animum felicitat, quod et a Marco Tullio et a multis sepe validissimis rationibus demonstratum est, consequentissimum est ut nichil quoque nisi virtutis oppositum a felicitate dimoveat [...].

F: Recordor equidem; ad stoicorum precepta me revocas, populorum opinionibus aversa et veritati propinquiora quam usui. [...] Quam ob rem, stante licet stoicorum sententia, tolerari potest multos invitos ac dolentes optantesque contrarium esse miserrimos. [...].

A: Id agere tecum institueram, ut ostenderem, ad evadendum huius nostre mortalitatis angustias ad tollendumque se se altius, primum veluti gradum obtinere meditationem mortis humaneque miserie; secundum vero desiderium vehemens studiumque surgendi; quibus exactis ad id, quo vestra suspirat intentio, ascensum facilem pollicebar; nisi tibi forte nunc etiam contrarium videatur.

F: Contrarium michi quidem videri dicere non ausim; ea namque de te ab adolescentia mea mecum crevit opinio ut, siquid aliter michi visum fuerit quam tibi, aberrasse me noverim.'

Francesco complains about the impracticability of the Stoic tenets and confirms the sternness of his will: indeed, despite wanting to, he has not managed to detach himself from human passions. The harsh and abstract dimension of Stoic morality is then mitigated in the second book by the master and disciple's shared proposals, favouring a 'peripatetic moderation'[30] that considers material necessities and the control of passions less severely. Augustine's recommendations and rebukes rest on the fundamental topics of the book: a lack of virtue is the cause of man's unhappiness, and the sole remedy is a sincere and thorough meditation on death. Such a meditation is not merely contemplative, but should be able to drag the mind towards certain spirit-changing thoughts, so that, assisted by the action of a powerful will, they can elevate man from his state of misery and moral anguish. A stern will can hold passions in check and manage the *fluctuationes* and moral inadequacies that cause the breaks, toils, and contradictions that drive man away from happiness and truth. The issue of the *opinionum perversitas*—that is, self-deception as the root of all evil, a Stoic topic tracing back to Seneca and Cicero—is also crucial, and is acknowledged from the beginning of the saint's discourse. [31]

From this first part of the dialogue, one can already grasp how the whole discourse will unravel and how the inner dialectic is driven by the two characters.[32] Francesco is the kind of disciple who objects and answers back to his master, but who is also able to admit his own error, albeit standing by his own beliefs. Augustine is the *pater optime*, redeemed sinner and doctor of the soul, who guides spiritual reflection, examines the disciple, grasps argumentative inspirations from his replies, and points out his inconsistencies and contradictions, compelling him to better define his concepts, words, and possible justifications. The discourse about *voluntas* is a fitting example:

> A: We agreed to set aside the snares of deceit and to devote ourselves with absolute candor to the search for truth. [...].
> F: There'll be no end to this, for I will never say that. For I know, and you are my witness, how often I wanted to, but couldn't, and how many tears I shed to no avail.
> A: I can bear witness to your many tears, but by no means to your will.[33]

---

30 Cf. *Secretum*, II. For this notion, refer to the precise explanation in Fenzi, *Secretum*, 55–77 (introduction); 295, n. 18; 327, n. 68; 331–332, n. 94; 332–332, n. 99; 338, n. 142; n. 348, n. 207 (commentary).
31 Cfr. *Secretum*, I, 36; II, 68 II, 108.
32 These aspects were discussed in Tateo, *Dialogo interiore e polemica ideologica nel 'Secretum' del Petrarca*, passim, and Oscar Giuliani, *Allegoria retorica e poetica nel 'Secretum' del Petrarca* (Bologna: Pàtron, 1977), passim.
33 *Secretum*, I:40: 'A: Conventa sunt, ut fallaciarum laqueis reiectis circa veritatis stadium pura cum semplicitate versemur. [...]
F: Nunquam erit finis; nunquam enim hoc fatebor. Scio quidem, et tu testis es michi, quotiens volui nec potui; quot lacrimas fudi, nec profuerint.
A: Lacrimarum tibi testis sum multarum, voluntatis vero minime.'

Truth is sought by digging deep into the soul, thus laying bare Francesco's miseries, faults, and desires. He tries, sometimes, to escape his own responsibilities through answers meant to defend his literary activity and the two chains that bind him to sin: his love for Laura and his desire for poetic glory. The whole dialogue appears as a critical debate about human behaviour, or more specifically about the vices of Francesco as a man,[34] in a crescendo full of harsh accusations. According to Augustine, *voluntas* manages the very possibility of choice at the Pythagorean crossroads between good and evil. Therefore, he distinguishes between 'one wanting to...' and 'one being able to...' based on a resolve that, for Francesco, is not a longing but a feeble wish (*Secretum*, I:44). This awareness helps to clear the mind from the danger of self-deception and the justification of vice (*Secretum*, I:28). The whole work, indeed, is based on the Augustinian topic of finding oneself,[35] of dedicating oneself to *otium*,[36] understood as an inner quest aimed at perfecting one's morality in a Christian dimension.

A Failing Adhesion

From the first, the dialogue is rich in argumentations pertaining to the foundational question[37] of all the discourse that Francesco addresses to the master: 'What holds me back?'[38] The question is repeated in order to complain that the *meditatio mortis* has not achieved the desired effect (*Secretum*, I:62). There is a further reference to Augustine's *Soliloquium*: 'Why then did I still stay in suspense and will I defer with an astonishing sorrow?'[39] Still, in the Augustinian passage, the author exhibits the longing for knowledge that determines the very meaning of life.[40] This expectation cannot be found in the words of Francesco, for whom vain mortal cares overwhelm the quest for truth and the possibility of living a virtuous life.[41]

Augustine's continuous pleas for the *meditatio mortis*—a pivotal matter for the whole dialogue—which allows us to grasp the value of eternity and to tell what is ephemeral and useless from what is worthy of being pursued, arouse in Francesco,

---

34 E.g. *Secretum*, I:26.
35 Cf. Augustine, *De vera religione*, 39:72: 'Noli foras ire, in te ipsum redi, in interiore homine habitat veritas.'
36 Cf. Teresa Caligiure, "Otium," in *Lessico petrarchesco*, eds. Romana Brovia and Luca Marcozzi (Rome: Carocci, 2016): 220–230.
37 Fenzi, *Secretum*, 309, n. 110. Cf. also the letter to the Ventoso (*Fam.*, IV:I,14).
38 *Secretum*, I:58: 'Quid ergo me retinet?'
39 *Sol.*, I:13, 22: 'Quid ergo adhuc suspendor infelix, et cruciatu miserabili differor?'
40 Cf. *ibidem*: 'Ego autem solam propter se amo sapientiam, caetera vero vel adesse mihi volo, vel deesse timeo propter ipsam; vitam, quietem, amicos.' Cf. also *Acad.*, III:2,4: 'Etenim quia vivo, propterea volo sapientiam, non quod sapientiam desidero, volo vitam.'
41 Cf. Fenzi, *Secretum*, 309.

even on the third day of the dialogue, fears pertaining to the time[42] he ought to dedicate to his activities as a poet and historian. First of all, the impossibility of completing the epic poem *Africa*, aimed at praising Scipio Africanus' heroic deeds and therefore the great history of Rome, a work fiercely reproved by Augustine as a waste of time for the sole scope of mundane glory:

> A: Thus you have dedicated the whole of your life to these two projects (not to mention the many others with which they have been interspersed) wasting your most precious and irreplaceable gift, for as you write about others, you forget yourself. [...] Oh unhappy man, if what you say is true.[43]

Francesco wasted the best years of his life as a historian and poet in dedicating himself to works—*Africa* and *De viris*—which please his friends and will win him immortal glory among the living and in posterity.[44] Human ambition is not worthy of being called 'glory,' and so Augustine warns his disciple that he should rather cultivate virtue: 'virtutem cole, gloriam neglige' (*Secretum*, III:206). For happiness to be long-lasting, it must relate to something permanent and not to something transient and changing, and therefore, real happiness can only be found in God, who is eternal: in fact, the sole hope of permanence is 'in Him who never moves and whose sun never sets.'[45] Happy, hence, is he who finds God. Conversely, Francesco addresses his happiness and his main interests towards what is uncertain: to poetry and the poetic glory he will be granted by the *Africa* that he repeatedly mentions in the third book. When the disciple expresses his worry that he might not be able to complete it and argues that he could hardly forsake a work that has cost him so much labour halfway through, Augustine retorts: 'I know which way you are stumbling. You'd rather abandon yourself than your little books.'[46]

The moral bind between will and time, on which is measured the wisdom of men, resonates in Augustine's accusing appeals to eternal goods, to which Francesco responds, foreshadowing the end of the dialogue: 'I am not abandoning them, but it may be that I'm putting them off.'[47] The consequences of such a statement are dire, inasmuch as it means that he has placed his trust in the *incertum*[48] with the final

---

[42] On the topic of time, crucial in Petrarch's works, and for previous references, see Luca Marcozzi, *Petrarca platonico. Studi sull'immaginario filosofico del canzoniere* (Rome: Aracne, 2011): 73–95 and idem, "Tempo" in *Lessico Petrarchesco*, eds. Romana Brovia and Luca Marcozzi (Rome: Carocci, 2016): 325–332.
[43] *Secretum*, III:192 and 196: 'A: Ita totam vitam his duabus curis ['Africa;' 'De viris'], ut intercurrentes alias innumeras sileam, prodigus preciosissime irreparabilesque rei, tribuis deque aliis scribens, tui ipsius obliviscerís. [...] O te si vera memoras, infelicem!'
[44] Cf. also *Secretum*, I:32.
[45] *Ibidem*, III:208: 'In Eo qui non movetur quique occasum nescit.'
[46] *Ibidem*, III:206: 'Quo pede claudices agnosco. Te ipsum derelinquere mavis, quam libellos tuos.'
[47] *Ibidem*, III:196: 'haud equidem destituo; sed fortassis differo.' Cf. Fenzi, *Secretum*, 402, n. 345.
[48] Cf. *ibidem*: 'Quia rerum certarum avarissimi estis, incertarum prodigi.'

result of forsaking himself.⁴⁹ To the master's stern and well-constructed criticism, the disciple responds with an attempt to invert the order of things, as he states his preference to commit first to mortal things and then to the eternal ones, because the former will naturally be followed by the latter, and, when the latter occur, they will definitively oust the former. His effort to justify his passions concerning writing and his love for Laura, yet still within a journey between *mortalia* and *eterna*, is clear.⁵⁰ By aiming his interest towards what he knows to be transient, Francesco postpones and suspends his acceptance of undertaking a path towards the virtuous life. Indeed, there are several passages of the dialogue in which Augustine rebukes Francesco because of how he continually defers, and rather pursues what is uncertain.⁵¹

As for the passages of the *Secretum* where Augustine reprimands Francesco for the time committed to poetry, the quest for glory, and his literary *curiositas*, suggesting to him a philosophical journey of *meditatio mortis*, soul searching, and contemplation of the divine things, Francisco Rico suggested as a source of inspiration—together with other references that he fittingly signals in his commentary—a few Augustinian passages from *De ordine*⁵² and from *Contra Academicos*,⁵³ the first dialogue that Augustine wrote after he converted. Rico highlights how the Cassiciaco dialogues influenced the composition of the *Secretum*:

> Pero tengo por evidente que la figura de Licencio contribuyó aun más a modelar la situación en que ahora se halla Francesco. Descubrir el paralelismo con el caso de Licencio, así, desvanece cualquier duda que aún pudiera albergar el lector sobre el sentido de la contestación del Santo.⁵⁴

Licentius burns with love for his own poetry and for that of Virgil, and Augustine attempts to draw him closer to the study of wisdom by suggesting that he reads Cicero's *Hortensius*.⁵⁵ If the character of Licentius has somehow helped to mould the figure of Francesco and the situation that the *Secretum* describes, it may be useful to point out

---

49 Cf. *ibidem*, III:206: 'te ipsum derelinquere mavis.' As Augustine retorts with a *reductio ad absurdum*, asking Francesco what would he do if he had an infinite amount of time before him, Francesco answers, with swift certainty, by mentioning the *Africa*, saying that he would then be able to compose a famous, rare, and excellent work ('preclarum nempe rarumque opus et egregium').
50 Cf. *Secretum*, III:198. See Rico, *Secretum*, 397–398; Fenzi, *Secretum*, 403, n. 361.
51 Cf., e.g., *Secretum*, III:186: 'Cogita in hoc uno falli in homines, quod differendum putant quod differi non potest.'
52 *De ordine*, I:III, 6, 8; I:V, 12.
53 Cf. Rico, *Secretum*, 384; 415–416.
54 Rico, *Secretum*, 416: 'But it is evident to me that the figure of Licentius further contributed to shaping the situation in which Francesco now finds himself. The discovery of the parallelism with the case of Licentius, thus, dispels any doubts that the reader might still harbour about the meaning of the saint's answer.'
55 It was the reading of Cicero's *Hortensius* that caused Augustine to become involved in philosophy, cf. *Conf.*, III:4, 7–8.

the passages which, in the *Contra Academicos*,⁵⁶ pertain to the diatribe against the Academics and the sceptics. Augustine first scolds Licentius, who favours the Academics, because of the latter's excessive interest in writing poetry and reading the *Aeneid*—the same *Aeneid* that Francesco has been mentioning at crucial points in the *Secretum* from the *Proem* (I:22) onwards—and then resumes the discourse on Academics and the value of philosophy (*Acad.*, II:IV,10). Immediately afterwards, the discussion moves on to the notion of philosophy upheld by both the ancient and the new Academics beginning from Carneades' definitions, through an argument connecting the search for truth, assent, and what is likely to be (*Acad.*, II:IV,11 ff.). Yet again, in the third book, Augustine, after pointing out that Licentius has composed some verses and is consumed by the love of poetry ('quorum amore ita perculsus est'), returns to the existential importance of philosophy as a necessary and most noble occupation for searching for the truth, compared to poetry and all other activities: 'Negotium nostrum non leve aut superfluum, sed necessarium ac summum esse arbitror: magnopere quaerere veritatem' (*Acad.*, III:1,1). In the last passage individuated by Rico, Augustine finds Licentius toiling to compose his verses and so, to address him a more effective rebuke, he says:

> I hope that someday you will gain mastery of poetics as you desire. Not that this accomplishment pleases me very much! I see that you are so infatuated that you can't escape this love except through tiring of it, however, and it's customary for this to happen readily after one becomes accomplished.⁵⁷

He then calls him back to fruitful philosophy.

In the Augustinian works, the discourse about scepticism begins with Cicero as the unique Latin source, through whom Augustine becomes acquainted with the scepticism born into the Platonic Academy with Arcesilaus and developed by Carneades and Philo. Augustine's polemic against the Academics concerns philosophical research and includes its relationship with Christian religion.⁵⁸ Through a critical

---

56 For a synthesis of the different interpretations of the work with respect to the objective of the Augustinian polemic and the meaning of scepticism in Augustine, see Augustine, *Contro gli accademici*, ed. Giovanni Catapano (Milan: Bompiani, 2005); Giovanni Catapano, "Quale scetticismo viene criticato da Agostino nel 'Contra Academicos'?", *Quaestio* 6 (2006): 1–5.
57 *Acad.*, III:IV,7: 'Opto quidem, inquam, tibi ut istam poeticam quam concupisti, complectaris aliquando: non quod me nimis delectet ista perfectio; sed quod video te tantum exarsisse, ut nisi fastidio evadere ab hoc amore non possis; quod evenire post perfectionem facile solet.' English translation from Augustine, *Against the Academicians and The Teacher*, trans. Peter King (Indianapolis and Cambridge: Hackett Publishing Company, 1995): 58.
58 On the relationship between Christianity and scepticism in the *Contra Academicos*, see Anne-Isabelle Bouton-Touboulic, "Scepticisme et religion dans le 'Contra Academicos' d'Augustin," in *Scepticisme et religion. Constantes et évolutions, de la philosophie hellénistique à la philosophie médiévale*, eds. Anne-Isabelle Bouton-Touboulic and Carlos Lévy (Turnhout: Brepols, 2016): 171–192. For the differences between Academic scepticism and Christianity in the *Enchiridion*, see Giovanni Catapano, "Errore, assenso e fede. La critica dello scetticismo accademico nell'*Enchiridion*' di Agostino," in

examination of several sceptical theses, Augustine defends *scepsis*,[59] exhorting Licentius and his disciples to dedicate themselves to philosophy, enriching the plea with autobiographical elements about his former acquaintance with the Academics' arguments.[60] It is those arguments that had distracted him from seeking the truth in the past, and that is why he now defends the usefulness of philosophising (*Acad.*, III:20,43).[61] The strictly interwoven Cassiciaco dialogues, including the *Soliloquium*, were written by Augustine right after his conversion in order to confront the problem of certainty in the possibility of knowing the truth following his adhesion to the Manichean doctrines and his proximity to the scepticism of the New Academy. Sceptical doubt was an intellectual obstacle to be tackled, and Augustine felt that he had to justify the value of knowledge and to show it to his disciples. Here, the issue of the certainty of truth is bound to that of happiness:[62] if we want to be happy, we have to search for truth.

In the final passage of *Contra Academicos*, Augustine shares his last appeal about the positions of the Academics in an attempt to persuade Licentius and the other bystanders and declares that, while accepting that he is not yet wise and rather thinking of himself as a fool,[63] he is confident about his possibility of reaching the truth;[64] however, in order to do this, which is what the Academics would prevent him from doing, he has to detach himself from those things that mortals deem to be good and rely on the authority of the Christ:

> I've renounced all the other things that mortal men think to be good and proposed to devote myself to searching for wisdom. The arguments of the Academicians seriously deterred me from this undertaking. Now, however, I am sufficiently protected against them by this discussion of ours. Furthermore, no one doubts that we're prompted to learn by the twin forces of authority and reason. Therefore, I'm resolved not to depart from the authority of Christ on any score whatsoever.[65]

Scepticisme et religion. Constantes et évolutions, de la philosophie hellénistique à la philosophie médiévale, 219–233.

59 As for this thesis, I follow Catapano, "Quale scetticismo viene criticato da Agostino nel 'Contra Academicos'?," 12–13.

60 In the period preceding his conversion to Christianity, after having experienced error and having adhered to Manichean doctrines, Augustine had been tempted by scepticism and became close to the New Academy.

61 Catapano, "Quale scetticismo viene criticato da Agostino nel 'Contra Academicos'?," 8–9.

62 *Acad.*, I:II,3.

63 *Acad.*, III:V,12; VIII:17; IX:21; XII:27; XIII:29. I refer to the passages highlighted by Catapano, "Quale scetticismo viene criticato da Agostino nel 'Contra Academicos'?," 12.

64 This proposal includes the idea of a Platonism akin to the Christian sphere and Christ's safe *auctoritas*.

65 *Acad.*, III:20,43: 'Contemptis tamen caeteris omnibus, quae bona mortales putant, huic investigandae inservire proposui. A quo me negotio quoniam rationes Academicorum non leviter deterrebant, satis, ut arbitror, contra eas ista disputatione munitus sum. Nulli autem dubium est gemino pondere nos impelli ad discendum, auctoritatis atque rationis. Mihi ergo certum est nusquam prorsus a Christi auctoritate discedere: non enim reperio valentiorem.'

It is a goal to be achieved in due time,⁶⁶ and one that Augustine connects with the figure of Christ, proclaiming the urgency of forsaking mortal things. His final message is radical, inasmuch as he expresses his confidence in the search for truth based on Christian *auctoritas*, and stresses the need to turn away from mortal things. Francesco, instead, when Augustine calls on him to answer for himself, declares his commitment to the *res humanae*. Augustine has just begged him not to make his words vain:

> 'The whole life of a philosopher is nothing more than a preparation for death.'⁶⁷ It is indeed this thought that will teach to scorn mortal deeds [...]. I'll reply that you do not need lengthy instructions [...]. There's no need to think about it at length. [...] You must not hesitate a moment longer. [...] For the rest, since our discussion has ranged so widely, if you liked anything I said, I'd ask you not to let it whiter away through idleness and neglect; if there was anything you found harder to swallow, then do not take it amiss.⁶⁸

Francesco replies as follows:

> I shall attend to myself as best I can and will gather together the scattered fragments of my soul and will dwell diligently upon myself. But as we speak there are definitely many important matters awaiting my attention, even if they are still mortal ones.⁶⁹

After the master's broad argumentations—accusing the disciple of loving mundane things for their own sake and not as works of God, and of sinning out of weakness of will—Francesco, even while accepting the truth of Christian principles, avoids a completely moral resolve. He suspends his moral choice and does not give that assent which, in Augustinian terms, would allow him to set off on a completely Christian path, notwithstanding the fact that he has conceived of and somehow made this assent his own. The argumentations present in the works dating back to the Cassiciaco period, still considering the complexity of the Augustinian works and the substantial differences between them, seem to have left a mark on Petrarch's dialogue and also in the debated ending. The time and zeal that Licentius devotes to poetry in Au-

---

66 Indeed, he contends he is just 33 and must not lose hope of achieving it (*Acad.*, III:20,43). On the topic of time in Augustine, see Pasquale Porro, "Agostino e il 'privilegio dell'adesso'," in *Interiorità e intenzionalità in S. Agostino*. Atti del I e del II Seminario Internazionale del Centro di Studi Agostiniani di Perugia, ed. Luigi Alici (Rome: Institutum Patristicum "Augustinianum," 1990): 177–204.
67 Quoting Cicero from the *Tusculan Disputations*, I:30,74.
68 *Secretum*, III:210–212: 'Tota philosophorum vita commentatio mortis est. Ista, inquam, cogitation docebit te mortalia facta contemnere [...]. Respondebo tibi longis te monitionibus non egere [...]. Non longis deliberationibus opus est. [...] Non est ulterius hesitandum. [...] Ceterum, quia satis multa contulimus, queso, siquid ex me gratum accepisti, ne patiaris situ desidiaque marcescere; siquid autem asperius, ne moleste feras.'
69 *Secretum*, III:214: 'Adero michi ipse quantum potero, et sparsa anime fragmenta recolligam, moraborque mecum sedulo. Sane nunc, dum loquimur, multa me magnae, quamvis adhuc mortalia, negotia expectant.'

gustine's *Contra Academicos* closely resonate with the character of Francesco; some of the arguments in favour of philosophy from the Cassiciaco dialogues are the same ones that Augustine employs to persuade Francesco to abandon poetical and historical works and the pursuit of that *inanis gloria* that sways him from what is true and eternal; thus Francesco's final answer emerges in stern opposition to Augustine's conclusive message in *Contra Academicos*. Many of Augustine's arguments in the *Secretum* attempt to dissuade Francesco from his desire to dedicate the precious span of his life to poetry and the quest for poetic glory, connecting to the main topics of the work, such as the *ruit hora*, the meaning of life, and the *meditatio mortis*, the ultimate goal of philosophy.

In the *Secretum*, the 'sceptical' aspect (if it can be called this) consists in not choosing correctly and in not adhering to moral pagan teachings and to the Christian truth proposed by Augustine in the present time. Francesco's attitude is therefore sceptical, given his suspension and the deferral of a choice after the many convincing and heartfelt pleas coming from Augustine that should seem to elicit a clear answer. Instead, even if the success of the dialogue lies in the future promise that can be assumed from the words 'Adero michi [...] sedulo,' at the practical level, the answer is a different one.[70]

Francesco does not consider the master's teachings as urgent as Augustine suggests several times that they are, and he accepts them only to delay them; in other words, he does not 'accept' them in the totality of the meaning that also includes the category of time: the teachings are true, but to be applied in the future, after attending to what he actually cherishes more. What is still lacking is a strong motivation, an aware resolve to put the precepts into action.

The indecisions and the ambiguities of this failure to make a practical choice clearly show through at the end of the dialogue, which it is important to quote:

> I'm really very grateful to you for this threeday conversation as well as for many other things, for you have wiped the mist from my eyes and have dispelled the thick surrounding cloud of error. But how I can thank the lady who as sat through our long discussion to the end without becoming bored by them? If she had turned her face away from us we would have been wrapped in darkness, wandering down sidetracks, and you would have had nothing concrete to say, nor I anything concrete to learn. But now, since your home is in heaven and my stay on earth is not yet at an end I don't know how long it will last (indeed as you can see I am in a state of suspended anxiety about this), I beg you both not to abandon me, even if I am far distant from you. Without you, dear Father, my life would be unpleasant, but without her it would be nothing.[71]

---

[70] Cf. Fenzi, *Secretum*, 417 n. 442; 418, n. 445.

[71] *Secretum*, III:212: 'Ego vero tibi, tum pro aliis multis, tum pro hoc triduano colloquio magnas gratias ago, quoniam et caligantia lumina detersisti et densam circumfusi erroris nebulam discussisti. Huic autem quas referam grates, que, multiloquio non gravata, usque nos ad exitum expectavit? Que si usquam faciem avertisset, operti tenebris per devia vagaremur, solidumque nichil vel tua contineret oratio, vel intellectus meus exciperet. Nunc vero, quoniam sedes vestra celum est, michi autem terrena nondum finitur habitatio, que quorsum duratura sit nescio et in hoc pendeo anxius, ut vides,

Francesco's final praise of Truth and of the saint whose advice he has declined to follow seem to belittle the long arguments for the necessity of a strong will which had extended over the three-day dialogue. For Augustine, the seat of Truth is unintelligible, to be found in God and the eternal; the *res humanae* are transient, and therefore the time of man becomes meaningful only if it becomes the time of God. Still, in order to do this, one has to avoid the wastage caused by human miseries, and must neither love the creatures more than their Creator nor prefer the quest for glory to the quest for virtue.

Notwithstanding the master's timely and persuasive argumentations, and even after Francesco has admitted his limits and his sin, if there is a final prayer, it is not by Francesco, as one could expect, but by Augustine himself, who prays to God that He may save his disciple during his journey.

Francesco never questions the truthfulness of Christian principles, nor the teaching of Augustine, in which he firmly believes. He often repeats how fundamental the master's works were for him. Moreover, Francesco often calls on Truth as a witness to his moral commitment[72] and to his wish to transcend his spiritual misery. He is eager to talk to his master and to listen to his arguments, thanks to which he becomes aware of the temptation of self-deception, the moral value of time, the necessity of a complete *voluntas*, and the potential rewards of an 'acerrima meditatio mortis.'[73] Francesco seems quite often to shake out of his numbness,[74] and acknowledges the benefits he received from his encounter with Truth, who, since the beginning, has already made him a little wiser ('doctior factus sum,' *Proem*, 24) and without whose help both he and Augustine would have wandered aimlessly in the dark (III:212). Nonetheless, the conversion does not take place.[75]

Rather, a subtle strategy emerges from Francesco's words, delineating the wish to postpone the moral project and the attempt to justify the possibility of combining his actual *negotia* with the concern for eternity. In this case, the function of doubt, understood within the Augustinian heritage as the origin of the dialogue between man and truth, despite leading Francesco to some self-awareness, does not trigger the clear acceptance of taking on a journey to rediscover his interiority and the presence of Christ in his soul.

Francesco, despite acknowledging the truthfulness of the Scriptural message and his own human weaknesses, escapes a full moral decision, still bound—even as he dialogues with the master—to his moral and literal cares. This aspect widens

---

obsecro ne me, licet magnis tractibus distantem, deseratis. Sine te enim, pater optime, vita mea inamena, sine hac autem nulla foret.'
72 Cf. *Secretum*, I:36; I:142–144.
73 *Secretum*, I:54.
74 Cf., e. g., *Secretum*, I:68. Right after the digression about the soul-corrupting *phantasmata*, at the end of the first day, Augustine exclaims: 'Bene habet! Torpor adcessit,' so Francesco admits and acknowledges the numbness of his soul.
75 See Fenzi, *Secretum*, 60 (introduction).

the gap between contingency and immanence, increasing the inner turmoil, existential doubt, and unease of the ego.[76] But what are thoughts and good intentions good for, if they are not put in action? This passage is crucial to understand the movements of one who adheres, but defers. After all, Augustine had already pointed this out about the literary *curiositas*: 'What use was all that reading? How much of the many things that you have read has remained implanted in your mind, has taken root, has borne timely fruits?'[77]

'In antiquam lite relabimur'

In the end, after his pressing exhortations (III:212), the saint abstains from adding further theoretical elements to his discourse ('respondebo tibi longis monitionibus non egere'), expecting a practical answer from his disciple. Francesco's final response recalls his initial situation, when he still dwelled in error and Truth urged him to open his soul and lift his gaze from mortal things to follow the eternal ones. The following lines mirror the alternating voices of conscience, the impulses of the soul ('impetum animi'), which can be either contemptible or beautiful and which, in the latter case, lead to the good ('ad honesta pulcerrimus est'):

> I agree. And the only reason why I'm now so eager to hurry up and attend to the others is so that I can have done with them and come back to these, even if aware that—as you said a short while ago—it would be much safer for me to concentrate on this single line of study and, without deviating, to set off on the road that leads straight to salvation. But I haven't got the strength to curb my desire.[78]

And the master's answer highlights this return[79] to the initial situation—'We are back where we started our argument'[80]—calling out the main 'default' of the disciple: 'You describe your will as weakness.'[81] Francesco, as we have seen, does not follow the Augustinian principle of divine time, but rather a mundane one that favours his mortal occupations. The dialectical match reaches an apparently unexpected conclusion, but, as Enrico Fenzi[82] explained, it is the only one which fits the discourse of the

---

76 Francesco Petrarca, *Mi secreto. Epístolas (selección)*, ed. Rossend Arqués Corominas, transl. Rossend Arqués Corominas and Anna Saurí (Madrid: Cátedra, 2011): 22–27.
77 *Secretum*, II:72: 'Lectio autem ista quid profuit? Ex multis enim, que legisti, quantum est quod inheserit animo, quod radices egerit, quod fructum proferat tempestivum?'
78 *Secretum*, III:214: 'F: Fateor; neque aliam ob causam propero nunc tam studiosus ad reliqua, nisi ut, illis explicitis, ad hec redeam: non ignarus, ut paulo ante dicebas, multo michi futurum esse securius studium hoc unum sectari et, deviis pretermissis, rectum callem salutis apprehendere. Sed desiderium frenare non valeo.'
79 As correctly defined by Fenzi, *Secretum*, 5–77 (introduction).
80 'In antiquam litem relabimur.'
81 'Voluntatem impotentiam vocas.'
82 Fenzi, *Secretum*, 418, n. 448.

whole book. This conclusion, which Bortolo Martinelli deemed as insignificant,[83] has provoked different interpretations. Nicolae Iliescu[84] comments on it by referring to a passage of the *Confessions* (III:2,21) where Monica, to avert her son from the Manichean doctrines, addresses a bishop who, knowing Augustine's stubbornness and his intelligence, tells her to pray, because Augustine will discover his error on his own precisely by reading those Manichean books ('Tantum roga pro eo Dominum; ipse legendo reperiet, quis ille sit error et quanta impietas'). According to Illiescu, the *Secretum* repeats the same message of trust displayed by the prayer through which Francesco is entrusted into God's care. But Fenzi rightly objects that 'the suggestion is attractive, and certainly enriches our reading of this conclusion. But it is not conclusive, if only because the bishop's words are not found at the end of the Confessions, but at the beginning.'[85] In the view of Francesco Tateo, 'the return to history and literature is not a relapse, if it is indeed conceived as a transition. [...] Perhaps we should not seek any coherence in the character, or give too much weight to his incoherence. He does not represent the actual Petrarch.'[86] Rico stresses the previous passage and Francesco's adhering answer ('adero michi...sedulo'), which represent the acceptance of the saint's invitation to 'live for one's own sake' as is proper for a philosopher ('ut philosophum decet').[87] He comments that Francesco is hence eager to realise the programme of the *Soliloquium* and of *De vera religione*, namely to seek for the truth inside of himself, and that he has learned the correct order of the hierarchy of values and a clear awareness of the 'inanis gloria': this is—he argues— the last and perhaps the greatest of Augustine's triumphs.[88] According to Ugo Dotti: 'Such self-analysis does not lead to any concrete resolution and this is, in the end, the most important result, the one that does not reveal so much the writer's incapacity to choose between two equally true paths, but rather his resolve in escaping the choice itself.'[89] According to Oscar Giuliani, Francesco refuses to adhere to the saint's invitation, but accepts the essential guidelines in his proposals to delay them as far as his writings are concerned.[90]

Before ending our discourse, it should be remembered that the ending of the *Secretum* is somewhat anticipated in *Parthenias*,[91] in the first eclogue of the *Bucolicum carmen* composed in 1347 after Petrarch had visited his brother Gherardo, who was a monk at the Chartreuse de Montrieux. In this composition, Silvio (that is, Petrarch),

---

83 Martinelli, *Il Secretum conteso*, passim.
84 Iliescu, *Il Canzoniere Petrarchesco e Sant'Agostino*, 65.
85 Fenzi, *Secretum*, 419, n. 448.
86 Tateo, *Dialogo interiore e polemica ideologica nel 'Secretum' del Petrarca*, 92–94.
87 Rico, *Secretum*, 444–446.
88 Rico, *Secretum*, 449.
89 Dotti, *Vita di Petrarca*, 158.
90 Giuliani, *Allegoria retorica e poetica nel 'Secretum' del Petrarca*, 189–201.
91 On the relationship between *Parthenias* and *Secretum* see Martinelli, "Il finale del 'Secretum'," *Revue de études italiennes* 29 (1983): 70–71, and recently the comprehensive essay by Enrico Fenzi, "Verso il 'Secretum': 'Bucolicum Carmen' I, 'Parthenias'," *Petrarchesca* 1 (2013): 13–54.

and Monico (his brother Gherardo) represent the contrast between the classical and profane poetry of Homer and Virgil, revered by Silvio, and sacred poetry, the Psalms of David, praised by Gherardo. The eclogue, too, begins with the matter of unhappiness caused by one's own will. When Silvio describes himself as unhappy and wandering among thorny hills and woods, Monico answers him that there is no one forcing him, but that Silvio himself is the cause of his own ill ('cunctorum vera laborum / ipse tibi causa es. Quis te per devia cogit?' 6–7). Monico proposes the possibility of a monastic life to his brother and a poetical ideal inspired by David's psalms. Silvio's answer is elusive, as he is now busy with things he cannot defer: 'Experiar, si fata volent; nunc ire necesse est' (110). And, as Monico questions him as to what hurries him so much and where ('Quo precor? Aut quis te stimulus, que cura perurget?' 111), Silvio answers that what urges him is the love of poetry ('urget amor muse,' 112) and the wish to sing the great story of Rome and of humanity; that is, to dedicate himself to the *Africa*. In the *Secretum*, unlike in the eclogue, the contrast between pagan and classical culture is absent. Francesco, indeed, does not contrast his cultivated literary activity with the possibility of writing holy texts: as claimed by Umberto Bosco, 'his intimate estrangement is conceived within Christianity.'[92]

Hence, the reason for the return to the initial situation, stressed in the words of the saint, and the coherence of the conclusion with the rest of the dialogue, are to be sought, following Fenzi's reading—highlighting the strict bond between the dialogue and Petrarch's other works—in the literary and practical necessities Petrarch was experiencing at that time. According to Fenzi, in the *Secretum* Petrarch exhibits the idea of stopping work on the *Africa*, which was taking too much time away at a historical moment when many things had changed for him.[93]

A series of radical changes had altered his vision of history, personal and universal, and affected the conception, evolution, and drafting of his later works: the death of Laura and many friends from the plague of 1348, his decision to distance himself from Cola di Rienzo's endeavour, his final break-up with the Colonna family, and the ever-shrinking possibility of remaining in Avignon. As Fenzi explains, these are vital needs transposed into the literary dimension, but they manifest a crisis and a need for change. In the *Secretum*, the author, approaching old age, sheds light on the moral inadequacy of old poetical and cultural commitments and the want of a 'change of life and values' mirroring the need to save himself, to 'go back to himself.'[94] In this sense, the adhesion to the words of the saint is present, but it will take place in the future, while for the moment Francesco will provisionally return to the old commitments that will not last for long. This interpretation partially follows Baron's interpretation of the *Secretum*, as he reads it as an autobiographical tes-

---

92 Umberto Bosco, *Francesco Petrarca* (Bari: Laterza, 1961): 90–91.
93 Fenzi, *Secretum*, 5–77 (introduction).
94 Ibidem.

timony referring to the problems and the dynamics that authors were really experiencing in those years.

The figure of Francesco, therefore, fits a precise literary design, modelled on the Augustinian example of the truth-questing sinner, which will appear in the later works in which Petrarch portrays himself as finally free from the adamantine chains described in the *Secretum*, committed to the writing of new works. Therefore, the conclusion and the entire book should be read as the expression of a crisis and of an 'intimate evolution of the author,'[95] who transforms facts into an idealised biography[96] to be handed down to posterity.

The deferral of the master's project will in fact find a later development in the 'sparse rhymes' of the *RVF* and in other great moral works, until the more mature *De suis ipsius et multorum ignorantia*,[97] in which Petrarch, in a later period of his life, presents himself as a moral philosopher, considering his previous words, and hence his previous works, as outdated: 'recedant vetera de ore meo' (II:35–36).

Therefore, the *Secretum* hands us the moral and intellectual portrait of a man experiencing a growing conflict, a phase he eventually transcended in later works. So, in 1360 Petrarch writes to Francesco Nelli:

> I have loved Cicero, I admit, and I have loved Virgil; I was taken by their style and genius more than by anything else [...]. Nor am I just beginning, and from my graying hair I can see that I began none too soon. Now my orators shall be Ambrose, Augustine, Jerome, and Gregory, my philosopher shall be Paul and my poet David, whom, as you know, many years ago in the first eclogue of my *Bucolicum carmen* I compared to Homer and Virgil so as to leave the victory undecided. Until the present the old power of deeply rooted habit has stood in the way, yet personal experience and the glowing revelation of truth allow no room for doubt.[98]

---

[95] Ivi: 55 ff.
[96] On this theme, see Marco Santagata, *I frammenti dell'anima. Storia e racconto nel Canzoniere di Petrarca* (Bologna: Il Mulino, 1992).
[97] On this work see Fenzi's introduction to and impressive commentary on the text in Francesco Petrarca, *De Ignorantia. Della mia ignoranza e di quella di molti altri*, ed. Enrico Fenzi (Milan: Mursia, 1999)
[98] *Fam.*, XXII:10,5–8: 'Amavi ego Ciceronem, fateor, et Virgilium amavi, usqueadeo quidem stilo delectatus et ingenio ut nichil supra [...]. Sed iam michi maius agitur negotium, maiorque salutis quam eloquentie cura est; legi que delectabant, lego que prosint; is michi nunc animus est, imo vero iampridem fuit, neque enim nunc incipio, neque vero me id ante tempus agere coma probat albescens. Iamque oratores mei fuerint Ambrosius Augustinus Ieronimus Gregorius, philosophus meus Paulus, meus poeta David, quem ut nosti multos ante annos prima egloga Bucolici carminis ita cum Homero Virgilioque composui, ut ibi quidem victoria anceps sit; hic vero, etsi adhuc obstet radicate consuetudinis vis antiqua, dubium tamen in re esse non sinit victrix experientia atque oculis se se infundens fulgida veritas.' I quote from Francesco Petrarca, *Letters on Familiar Matters. Rerum Familiarum Libri*, XVII-XXIV, vol. 3, trans. Aldo S. Bernardo (Baltimore and London: Johns Hopkins University Press, 1985).

Conclusion

Petrarch has indeed presented a phase of his life in the *Secretum*, examining some of his literary and moral projects through the dialogue. The dialogic *fictio* sets out the different positions of Augustine and Francesco and offers a piece of the idealised autobiography that Petrarch builds across his writings. The references to the Cassiciaco dialogues and to the character of Licentius allow us to understand how Augustine's early Christian writings influenced some aspects of the development of the figure of Francesco, his final deferral, and his failure to assent to the dedication of his life to *otium*. Petrarch will further develop the topic of inner recollection, delineated in the *Secretum* and modelled in the tradition of Plato, Seneca, Cicero, and Augustine, in later works, always in relation to the issue of the quest for happiness through the practice of virtue, in a line of thought which, beginning with the *Secretum* and unravelling through other works, arrives at *De ignorantia*, the most comprehensive manifesto of his understanding of philosophy, written between 1367 and 1371, almost a decade after the 1358 final rereading of the *Secretum*.[99] In *De ignorantia*, Petrarch challenges the authority principle, against scholastic Aristotelianism that tends to reduce human culture to the limits of physical and logical problems.[100] The quarrel is indeed recalled in the *Secretum* (I:42; I:52), where it concerns the garrulity of the dialectics ('dyaleticorum garrulitas'), that is of the terminist logicians of the Ockhamian tradition whose ideas, rooted in Oxford and Paris, would reach Italy in the middle of the fourteenth century.[101] Rather than being against Averroism, Petrarch's blows are aimed at Aristotelism,[102] at the dogmatism of the *ipse dixit* stalwarts[103] and of those who reject the multiplicity of perspectives and doctrines with respect to the method of attaining the truth.[104] As Eugenio Garin explains, 'here, the attitude is radical, and it displays, in the clear critical orientation, the teaching of the *Cicero scepticus*, that is, the questioning not only of an encyclopaedia, but of an epistemology.'[105] Petrarch, who owned Cicero's *Academica*,[106] would rely on several sceptical

---

99 Cf. note 3.
100 Eugenio Garin, *Il ritorno dei filosofi antichi. Ristampa accresciuta del saggio 'Gli umanisti e la scienza'* (Naples: Bibliopolis, 1994): 23.
101 Cf. Rico, *Secretum*, 86, n. 112; see also: 138–139; 233, 239–240; Fenzi, *Secretum*, 297, n. 32; 300–301, n. 53; 304–305, n. 78.
102 Cf. Paul O. Kristeller, "Petrarch's 'Averroists.' A note on the History of Aristotelianism in Venice, Padua and Bologna," *Bibliotèque d'Humanisme et Renaissance* XIV (1952): 59–65.
103 On this issue, see Luca Bianchi, "'Aristotele fu un uomo e poté errare': sulle origini medievali della critica al "principio di autorità," in idem, *Filosofia e teologia nel Trecento. Studi in ricordo di Eugenio Randi* (Louvain: Institut d'Études médiévales, 1994): 509–533.
104 Garin, *Il ritorno dei filosofi antichi. Ristampa accresciuta del saggio 'Gli umanisti e la scienza'*, 24–25.
105 *Ibidem*, 25: 'Qui veramente l'atteggiamento è radicale, e svela nel chiaro orientamento critico il magistero del *Cicero scepticus*, ossia di quella messa in discussione non solo di una enciclopedia, ma di una epistemologia.'

strategies as he argued against Scholasticism, especially in *De Ignorantia*.[107] He urges paying more attention to the principle of *ratio* than to that of *auctoritas*: 'I believe that Aristotle was a great man and a polymath. But he was still human and could therefore have been ignorant of some things, or even of many things.'[108] In many passages of the treatise, Petrarch openly states that Aristotle, an unquestioned authority for many 'stultos aristotelicos' and for an 'insanum et clamosum scolasticarum vulgus,'[109] did not grasp the principles on which knowledge should be based.

Petrarch argues in a polemic against four Venetian Aristotelians who accuse him of being a good man, but an ignorant one.[110] His discourse attacks the *Nicomachean Ethics*, which completely fails in its claim of teaching how to reach happiness; in fact, after having read it, we understand what happiness is, but not how to reach it. The Aristotelian treatise, therefore, lacks a practical goal inasmuch as, after having read Aristotle, we may know something more about virtue, but we will not have improved ourselves. This polemical work, linked to a complex series of matters relating both to the historical and cultural context of the time and to the author's biographical issues,[111] represents—together with other works—a closing of the circle. In *De ignorantia*, Petrarch, relying on the richness of a soul inclined towards *otium*, proposes himself as a master and a *philosophus* who, investigating his own self, has the duty of

---

106 Petrarch inserts Cicero's *Academica* into the list of 'libri mei peculiares,' but he initially thought it to be Cicero's *Hortensius*. In fact, it was *Academica Priora*, book 2 (*Lucullus*). He realised this later, in 1343 (*Seniles*, 16:1). Cf. Martin McLaughlin, *Petrarch and Cicero: Adulation and Critical Distance*, in *Brill's Companion to the Reception of Cicero*, ed. William H. F. Altman (Leiden and Boston: Brill, 2015): 19–20. Petrarch refers to Cicero's sceptical attitude in *Secretum*, III:156.

107 Cf. Charles B. Schmitt, *Cicero Scepticus: A Study of the Influence of the 'Academica' in the Renaissance* (The Hague: Martinus Nijhoff, 1972): 45–46. For Cicero's influence in Petrarch, see McLaughlin, *Petrarch and Cicero: Adulation and Critical Distance*, 19–38. Cf. also Diego Pirillo, "Philosophy", in *The Cambridge Companion to the Italian Renaissance*, ed. Michael Wyatt (Cambridge: Cambridge University Press, 2014): 260–275, particularly the entry "Ancient Skepticism and Renaissance Doubt," 273–275.

108 *Ign.* IV:63: 'Ego uero magnum quendam uirum ac multiscium Aristotilem, sed fuisse hominem, et idcirco aliqua, imo et multa nescire potuisse arbitror.' I quote from Marsh's excellent translation in Francesco Petrarca, *De suis ipsius et multorum ignorantia/On His Own Ignorance and That of Many Others*, in idem, *Invectives*, ed. and trans. David Marsh (Cambridge, Mass.: Harvard University Press, 2003): 222–363.

109 *Ign.*, IV:152; 155.

110 *Ign.*, II:17.

111 On these matters, see Andreas Kamp, *Petrarcas philosophisches Programm. Über Prämissen, Antiaristotelismus und 'Neues Wissen' von 'De sui ipsius et multorum aliorum ignorantia'* (Frankfurt am Main, Bern, New York, and Paris: Lang, 1989) and idem, "Petrarch," in *Encyclopedia of Medieval Philosophy: Philosophy Between 500 and 1500*, vol. 2, ed. Henrik Lagerlund (Heidelberg: Springer, 2011): 968–973; see especially Fenzi's introduction in Francesco Petrarca, *De Ignorantia. Della mia ignoranza e di quella di molti altri*, ed. Enrico Fenzi: 5–104. The issue is also carefully discussed by Ruedi Imbach, "Virtus illitterata. Il significato filosofico della critica della Scolastica nel 'De sui ipsius et multorum ignorantia' di Petrarca," in *La sfida laica, per una nuova storia della filosofia medievale*, eds. Ruedi Imbach and Catherine König-Pralong (Rome: Carocci, 2016): 115–128.

teaching the love of truth rather than its knowledge: a thoroughly Augustinian lesson. Opposing a cold and list-like science and openly arguing against Aristotle's supporters, Petrarch presents himself not as a cultivated man, but rather as a good man who teaches us how to be virtuous.[112]

Such a perspective shows a different portrait of the author to that depicted in the *Secretum*, characterised by an ethical scepticism that would prevent Francesco from practising virtue. After a few pages dedicated to Petrarch's scepticism[113] and prudent interest in the Academics,[114] with respect to *De ignorantia* and the Petrarchan conception of philosophy, Pietro Paolo Gerosa writes: 'the profession of true philosophy cannot therefore be divided from the Christian practice, because it is such only when to the knowledge of God, one also adds his worship. [...] Did [Petrarch] always do this? Alas no; and he is forced to confess this in the conclusion of the *Secretum*.'[115]

Therefore, in the treatise, philosophy becomes for Petrarch a positive and practical lifestyle, and the search for truth finds its foundation in an intimate reconnection with Christ (Ign. IV:147). The tenets of Christian morality, which in the Latin dialogue were defended and proposed by Augustine, are now the reasons that Petrarch defends[116] in order to rediscover himself and to be an example for others.

---

112 *Ign.*, IV:148. Cf. also the invitation addressed to Antonio Albanzani in *Sen.*, XI:7.
113 Gerosa, *Umanesimo cristiano del Petrarca. Influenza agostiniana, attinenze medievali*, 270–275.
114 *Ibidem*, 270. Gerosa quotes with this respect a passage from *Rer. mem.*, IV:31, 1–3: 'Nobis autem eatenus modestus Achademie mos placeat: verisimilia sequi ubi ultra non attingimus, nichil temere dampnare, nichil impudenter asserere. Veritas ergo suis locis maneat; nos ad exempla pergamus.'
115 Gerosa, *Umanesimo cristiano del Petrarca. Influenza agostiniana, attinenze medievali*, 233–234: 'La professione della vera filosofia non è perciò separabile dalla pratica cristiana poiché è tale sol quando alla conoscenza di Dio ne unisca anche il culto [...] L'applicò egli [Petrarca] sempre? Purtroppo no; ed è costretto a confessarlo nella conclusione del *Secretum*.'
116 *Ign.*, IV:64.

Bill Rebiger
Sceptical Strategies in Simone Luzzatto's Presentation of the Kabbalists in his *Discorso*[1]

Introduction

In the sixteenth consideration of his *Discorso circa il stato degli Hebrei* ('Discourse on the State of the Jews')[2] entitled *Circa l'applicatione de studii, e varie classi di dottori appresso gli Hebrei* ('Regarding the Jews' Application to Their Studies and the Various Classes of Sages'), the Venetian Rabbi Simone Luzzatto (?1583–1663) included a rather long section focusing on the kabbalists as the third group of Jewish sages. The other two groups presented in the sixteenth consideration are the rabbis or talmudists and the philosophising theologians.[3] According to Luzzatto's view, these three groups were literarily active 'during the long period of the Nation's captivity, when not every spark (of knowledge) was completely extinguished.'[4] While the kabbalists are characterised more specifically as those who 'profess mysteries,'[5] they, together with the other two groups, also belong to the realm of literature and knowledge. However, only the other two groups are explicitly acknowledged from a

---

[1] I would like to thank the staff and fellows of the Maimonides Centre for Advanced Studies at the University of Hamburg, especially Michela Torbidoni, Guido Bartolucci, Felix Papenhagen, Stephan Schmid, and Giuseppe Veltri, for the many inspiring discussions we have had concerning Simone Luzzatto.
[2] Simone Luzzatto, *Discorso circa il stato degli Hebrei et in particolare dimoranti nell'inclita Città di Venetia* (Venice: Giovanni Calleoni, 1638). This text is included in the recently published edition of Luzzatto's two main Italian works; see Simone Luzzatto, *Scritti politici e filosofici di un ebreo scettico nella Venezia del Seicento*, ed. Giuseppe Veltri (Milan: Bompiani, 2013): 3–106. An English translation of the *Discorso* will be published by Giuseppe Veltri and Anna Lissa (Berlin: De Gruyter, 2018). All translations from the *Discorso* quoted in this article are theirs. I am very grateful to them for providing me with the results of their work in advance.
[3] The source for Luzzatto's typology is very likely Giovanni Pico della Mirandola, *Opera omnia* (Basel, 1557), 180 (*Apologia*). Pico in turn relied on Abraham Abulafia; cf. Saverio Campanini, "Talmud, Philosophy, and Kabbalah. A Passage from Pico della Mirandola's *Apologia* and its Source," in *"The Words of a Wise Man's Mouth are Gracious" (Qoh 10,12): Festschrift for Günter Stemberger on the Occasion of his 65th Birthday*, ed. Mauro Perani (Berlin and New York: De Gruyter, 2005): 435 and 440–443. According to Bonfil, this typology was introduced by Profiat Duran in the early fifteenth century; cf. Robert Bonfil, "A Cultural Profile," in *The Jews of Early Modern Venice*, eds. Robert C. Davis and Benjamin Ravid (Baltimore and London: The Johns Hopkins University Press, 2001): 170–172. However, Luzzatto in fact adds another, fourth, group: the Karaites; see his *Discorso*, 84r-85r.
[4] Cf. Luzzatto, *Discorso*, 75v.
[5] *Ibidem*; cf. *ibidem*, 80v: The kabbalists 'were given mysterious expositions of the Scripture.'

Jewish perspective. Concerning the first group, the passage describing them ends as follows:

> To these sages, all the Jews in every place and at all times assented, strictly following their instruction as to the fulfilment of rites and precepts, and especially ceremonials. [...] In fact, the Jews believe the rabbis to be the trustworthy and sincere reporters of the rites and ceremonies executed in ancient times.[6]

The passage on the second group, the philosophising theologians, ends with:

> The Jews are respectful to the above-mentioned [learned men] as far as opinions and dogmas pertaining to the articles of their religion are concerned. [They also rely on them] as far as morality and ways of conversing and behaving in society and civil life, with whatever people or nation, are concerned.[7]

I would like to emphasise that the third group, the kabbalists, is, in contrast, excluded from this kind of appreciation at the end of the passage which describes them. Thus, from the very beginning, Luzzatto degrades the rank of the kabbalists. The subsequent passage concerning them was brought back to scholarly attention by François Secret, who produced an edition of the Italian text with some annotations.[8] However, it has only been analysed by Giuseppe Veltri.[9] In contrast to the few lines on Simone Luzzatto written by Moshe Idel, where he came to the conclusion that Luzzatto 'is not to be considered either as a Kabbalist or as an opponent of this lore,'[10] I would like to emphasise in the following that Luzzatto was indeed an opponent of the Kabbalah–certainly less strikingly than, e.g., his Venetian colleague Rabbi Leon Modena (1571–1648),[11] but in a more elegant and subtle manner.[12]

---

6 *Ibidem*, 77v.
7 *Ibidem*, 79v.
8 François Secret, "Un texte mal connu de Simon Luzzatto sur la kabbale," *Revue des etudes juive* 118 (1959–1960): 121–128. By mistake, Secret dated the first edition of the *Discorso* to 1629; cf. *ibidem*, 121. For earlier presentations of the *Discorso* before Secret's article, cf. the Latin translation of the sixteenth to eighteenth considerations by Johann Christoph Wolf, *Bibliotheca Hebraea*, vol. 4 (Hamburg: Theodor Christoph Felginer, 1733): 1115–1135; the complete Hebrew translation of the *Discorso* prepared by Dan Lattes and published together with a biography of Luzzatto written by Moshe A. Shulvass and an introduction by Riccardo B. Bachi, see Simone Luzzatto, *Ma'amar 'al Yehudei Veneşia* [Hebrew] (Jerusalem: Mosad Bialik, 1950); and the excerpts from the *Discorso* translated into English by Felix Giovanelli, including the sixteenth consideration, see idem, "Learning Among the Hebrews. A 17th-Century Report. Simone Ben Isaac Luzzatto," *Commentary* 13 (1952): 589–593.
9 Giuseppe Veltri, *Renaissance Philosophy in Jewish Garb: Foundations and Challenges in Judaism on the Eve of Modernity* (Leiden and Boston: Brill, 2009): 33–36 and 213–214; cf. also the summary in Cristiana Facchini, "The City, the Ghetto and Two Books. Venice and Jewish Early Modernity," *Quest. Issues in Contemporary Jewish History. Journal of Fondazione CDEC* 2 (2011): 38–40.
10 Moshe Idel, *Kabbalah. New Perspectives* (New Haven, London: Yale University Press, 1988): 5.
11 Cf. Yaacob Dweck, *The Scandal of Kabbalah. Leon Modena, Jewish Mysticism, Early Modern Venice* (Princeton: Princeton University Press, 2011).

This can be seen in Luzzatto's use of what I call sceptical strategies in the passage on the kabbalists, which I want to present and discuss in the following.

In contrast to ancient scepticism, topics such as knowledge, certainty, and doubt are essential in early modern scepticism.[13] In particularly, questioning the certainty of traditional sources of knowledge and doubting the established authorities became more and more common in early modern times, even in discourses outside the philosophical school tradition. In this non-philosophical context, the posing of questions of certainty and the casting of doubt on authorities were realised by means of sceptical strategies in a broader sense, as will be defined now. In short, sceptical strategies are a set of literary or rhetorical means intended to induce doubts, questions, and intellectual uneasiness. Eventually, when successful, the use of these sceptical strategies will result in undermining the reliability or trustworthiness of (any) authority as a source of knowledge. In contrast to argumentation based mainly on formal logic, these strategies are more content-related insofar the foundations and presuppositions of various claims are questioned. Hence, the application of sceptical strategies, as understood here, has to be distinguished from the ancient philosophical tradition of scepticism in the strict sense of the term—either in the Pyrrhonian or in the Academic school—and we can call it 'subversive scepticism.' Of course, philosophical scepticism uses these (and other)[14] sceptical strategies as well, but it goes, at least in Pyrrhonian scepticism, one step further, finally leading to equipollence (*isostheneia*) concerning the validity of different and contradicting statements and

---

12 Cf. Heinrich Graetz, *History of the Jews, vol. 5: From the Chmielnicki Persecution of the Jews in Poland (1648 C.E.) to the Period of Emancipation in Central Europe (c. 1870 C.E.)* (Philadelphia: Jewish Publication Society, 1895): 81: 'Simone Luzzatto did not suffer himself to be ensnared by Kabbalistic delusions,' and *ibidem*, 84: 'One of his disciples relates of him that he ridiculed the Kabbalists.' In line with this, cf. Gershom Scholem, *Sabbatai Ṣevi: The Mystical Messiah* (Princeton: Princeton University Press, 1973): 77; Bernard Septimus, "Biblical Religion and Political Rationality in Simone Luzzatto, Maimonides and Spinoza," in *Jewish Thought in the Seventeenth Century*, eds. Isadore Twersky and Bernard Septimus (Cambridge, Mass.: Harvard University Press, 1987): 416, n. 76; and David B. Ruderman, "Science and Skepticism. Simone Luzzatto on Perceiving the Natural World," in idem, *Jewish Thought and Scientific Discovery in Early Modern Europe* (New Haven and London: Yale University Press, 1995): 159–160. It is now evident that Luzzatto was indeed involved in a discussion with Count Charles de Valliquierville, a libertine visiting the Ghetto of Venice in 1646, on theological speculations including Kabbalah and in selling Hebrew books to him, but, nevertheless, this is no proof of any alleged sympathy in Luzzatto towards Kabbalah; cf. Evelien Chayes, "Visitatori libertini del Ghetto: Ismaël Boulliau e Charles de Valliquierville," in *Oltre le mura del Ghetto. Accademie, scetticismo e tolleranza nella Venezia barocca*, eds. Giuseppe Veltri and Evelien Chayes (Palermo: New Digital Press, 2016): 133–136.
13 Cf. Katja Vogt, "Ancient Skepticism," The Stanford Encyclopedia of Philosophy (Winter 2016 Edition), ed. Edward N. Zalta, https://plato.stanford.edu/archives/win2016/entries/skepticism-ancient: 'The core concepts of ancient skepticism are belief, suspension of judgment, criterion of truth, appearances, and investigation. Important notions of modern skepticism such as knowledge, certainty, justified belief, and doubt play no or almost no role.'
14 Obviously, the tropes are most relevant in this respect; see Sextus Empiricus, *Outlines of Pyrrhonism*, I:13–17.

therefore to suspension of judgement (*epoché*) and possibly even tranquillity (*ataraxia*). Sceptical strategies, in the sense defined here, are especially fruitful when the participants do not share the same discourse and/or logic of argumentation and proofs, as is expressed in the Latin maxim *contra principia negantem non est disputandum*. In the present case, the argumentation against certain claims is less important than the strategy of undermining the certainty, authority, or legitimacy of a text, person, or institution as a source of knowledge. In this way, there is at least a chance that a certain person approached by sceptical strategies will lose their certainty and confidence, cast doubts in the future, and not continue to follow their teachers or leaders and the claims they make.[15]

Simone Luzzatto employs these sceptical strategies—in the sense defined above—in the framework of his general philosophical scepticism, which aims at questioning authority (*auctoritas*) on two levels. Firstly, on an epistemological level, he targets our confidence in sources of knowledge (e.g. reason or revelation); secondly, on a social level, Luzzatto's doubts address people (e.g. prophets or sages). Both levels of his scepticism have already been dealt with elsewhere.[16] In the case of the *Discorso*, it is rather difficult to detect Luzzatto's personal position, because the book is primarily addressed—at least apparently—to a Christian audience and, even more importantly, because it is an apologetic text.[17] However, his general philosophical scepticism is obvious throughout his writings. So, e.g., in the passage on kabbalists, Luz-

---

15 My definition of sceptical strategies owes much the popular but nevertheless intriguing book on subversive thinking written by the Austrian philosopher Hubert Schleichert, *Wie man mit Fundamentalisten diskutiert, ohne den Verstand zu verlieren. Anleitung zum subversiven Denken* (Munich: Beck, 1999). A more elaborated presentation of my definition of sceptical strategies will be published separately in the near future.
16 In this regard, Luzzatto's other Italian book, *Socrate overo dell'humano sapere* (Venice: Tomasini, 1651), is especially decisive. This work was also included in the recently published edition of Luzzatto's works; see Luzzatto, *Scritti politici e filosofici*, 107–400. An English translation of the *Socrate* will be published by Giuseppe Veltri and Michela Torbidoni (Berlin: De Gruyter, 2018). On Luzzatto's scepticism, cf. Ruderman, "Science and Skepticism," 153–184; Ariel Viterbo, "Socrate nel ghetto: lo scetticismo mascherato di Simone Luzzatto," *Studi Veneziani* 38 (1999): 79–128; Giuseppe Veltri, "Principles of Jewish Sceptical Thought, The Case of Judah Moscato and Simone Luzzatto," in *Rabbi Judah Moscato and the Jewish Intellectual World of Mantua in the 16th-17th Centuries*, eds. Giuseppe Veltri and Gianfranco Miletto (Leiden and Boston: Brill, 2012): 17–19 and 27–35; Giuseppe Veltri and Michela Torbidoni, "Alcune considerazioni sulla sospensione del giudizio e il silenzio nella tradizione ebraica scettica," in *Seconda navigazione, Omaggio a Giovanni Reale*, eds. Roberto Radice and Glauco Tiengo (Milan: Bompiani, 2015): 753–756; Michela Torbidoni, "Il metodo del dubbio nel *Socrate*," in *Filosofo e Rabbino nella Venezia del Seicento. Studi su Simone Luzzatto con documenti inediti dall'Archivio di Stato di Venezia*, ed. Giuseppe Veltri (Ariccia: Aracne, 2015): 183–245; and Giuseppe Veltri, "Un accademico scettico: Simone Luzzatto," in *Oltre le mura del Ghetto. Accademie, scetticismo e tolleranza nella Venezia barocca* eds. Giuseppe Veltri and Evelien Chayes (Palermo: New Digital Press, 2016): 147–173; see also the article by Michela Torbidoni in this volume.
17 Cf. Ruderman, "Science and Skepticism," 154.

zatto explicitly acknowledges the epistemological scepticism of Sextus Empiricus (c. 160 – c. 210):

> This is what Sextus Empiricus demonstrated, i.e. that every phenomenon and object is mixed and involved in five kinds of relations. Proceeding in his examination, he even demonstrated that it is almost impossible to grasp anything about objects other than their relation.[18]

Furthermore, I would like to stress the point that a text is not only read by its addressees, but also by readers not explicitly envisaged by its author. Therefore, these sceptical strategies sometimes only deploy their effectiveness in their later reception history.

In this article, I want to present and discuss five particular sceptical strategies used by Luzzatto in the passage concerning the kabbalists. These strategies are, to a certain degree, intertwined, and include 1) relativisation, 2) objectification, 3) historicisation, 4) indictment of heresy, and finally, 5) delegitimation.

1 Relativisation

Relativisation as a sceptical strategy refutes the claim of the uniqueness and essential importance of a certain statement or idea in contrast to others. Through this strategy, the claim will become only one among others, thus losing its original entitlement.[19] Another case would be the marginalisation of a claim formerly acknowledged as central. Here, the strategy of relativisation is interpreted only in a synchronic perspective, in contrast to the diachronic perspective of the strategy of historicisation presented below. In fact, relativity constitutes the highest category in the tropes described by Sextus Empiricus in his *Outlines of Pyrrhonism*.[20] Accordingly, a specific result of this strategy would be the well-known sceptical state of equipollence in the face of contradicting statements. However, the Pyrrhonian trope of relativity is not used by Luzzatto in this passage, but only relativisation, as described in the following examples.

According to Luzzatto's first sentence in the present passage, the Kabbalah was only approved by some Jews, especially Jews from the Levant and Poland.[21] It is very likely that Luzzatto is alluding here to Sephardic Jews expelled from Spain and to Ashkenazic Jews stemming from Polish centres such as Cracow and Lublin. Thus, he suggests that Kabbalah is not only a minor phenomenon, but also one that is

---

18 Luzzatto, *Discorso*, 82r; cf. Sextus Empiricus, *Outlines of Pyrrhonism*, I:15 ('The Five Tropes').
19 Cf. Schleichert, *Wie man mit Fundamentalisten diskutiert*, 30–32 and 147–150.
20 See Sextus Empiricus, *Outlines of Pyrrhonism*, I:14.39.
21 Cf. Scholem, *Sabbatai Ṣevi*, 77, n. 113: 'A similar statement was made in 1624 by the kabbalist Aaron Berakhya Modena in his *'Ashmoreth ha-Boqer* (Mantua, 1624), fol. 247b.'

somewhat foreign or even alien from an Italian perspective.²² Regarding the dissemination of Kabbalah in Italy, especially as a centre for printing kabbalistic books, and its deep influence on the thinking of numerous Italian Jews (and also non-Jews), this suggestion can easily be disproved from a historical perspective.²³ This is important insofar as Luzzatto wrote his *Discorso* in Italian addressing first and foremost a non-Jewish readership but probably not intending to exclude Jewish readers at all.²⁴ However, the borderline he defines at this point is not between Jews and non-Jews, but between Italians and non-Italians, in terms of linguistic abilities. Furthermore, Luzzatto does not acknowledge Kabbalah as a central and essential concept or system of Jewish tradition or even as a secret Jewish lore at all. In line with this strategy of relativisation and marginalisation, he emphasises that the acceptance of Kabbalah is not mandatory for Jews.

2 Objectification

The sceptical strategy of objectification consists in objectifying a certain phenomenon that is originally related to insiders, that is, believers, adepts, or followers—as marking their identity—but not to scholars. That is, in our case, Kabbalah is not presented as an auratic tradition of which the author is a part, but as the usual topic of a scholarly endeavour from a distant outsider perspective. In short, kabbalists depict their own statements in the literary mode of scriptural exegesis or as a narration, e.g., a Midrash or a vision, referring to scriptural verses as proofs. In contrast, the strategy of objectification presents kabbalistic claims in a purely descriptive way,

---

22 Luzzatto's presentation of the Karaites sounds very similar; see Luzzatto, *Discorso*, 84v-85r.
23 Concerning the history, characteristics, and varieties of the Kabbalah in Italy until the time of Simone Luzzatto, cf. above all the seminal studies by Moshe Idel, e.g., idem, *Kabbalah in Italy 1280–1510: A Survey* (New Haven and London: Yale University Press, 2011); idem, "Italy in Safed, Safed in Italy: Toward an Interactive History of Sixteenth-Century Kabbalah," in *Cultural Intermediaries: Jewish Intellectuals in Early Modern Italy*, eds. David B. Ruderman and Giuseppe Veltri (Philadelphia: University of Pennsylvania Press, 2004): 239–269; idem, "Kabbalah in Italy in the 16th Century: Some New Perspectives," *Materia giudaica* 15–16 (2010–11): 309–317; idem, "Major Currents in Italian Kabbalah between 1560 and 1660," in *Essential Papers on Jewish Culture in Renaissance and Baroque Italy*, ed. David B. Ruderman (New York and London: New York University Press, 1992): 345–368; and idem, "Differing Conceptions of Kabbalah in the Early Seventeenth Century," in *Jewish Thought in the Seventeenth Century*, eds. Isadore Twersky and Bernard Septimus (Cambridge, Mass.: Harvard University Press, 1987): 137–200.
24 In this case, he would exclude those Jews who were not able to read Italian, such as, ironically, many Jews from the Levant and Poland living in Venice in his time. Concerning the question of Italian literacy among the Venetian Jews in this time, cf. Ruderman, "Science and Skepticism," 155. Regarding the addressed readership of non-Jews as well as Jews, cf. Bonfil, "A Cultural Profile," 170 and Ariella Lang, "The Double Edge of Irony in Simone Luzzatto's *Discorso*," *Jewish Social Studies: History, Culture, Society* n.s. 15 (2009): 116. Concerning the latter, I am not totally convinced that Lang's 'ironic' reading of the *Discorso* is plausible throughout this book.

without rhetorical embellishment or Scriptural reasoning.[25] Thus, the change in the mode of presentation and the outsider perspective as given by the strategy of objectification can already lead to sceptical questions concerning the validity and certainty of kabbalistic truth claims.

This strategy describes Luzzatto's general approach throughout his treatise very well, and in the following I would like to present various examples of it. He begins his presentation of the Kabbalah with a rather modern scientific approach that discusses terminology and etymology. Thus, he reduces the widespread fascination of this phenomenon to the literal meaning of the term 'Kabbalah' which is simply 'reception' in the sense of a tradition which the student receives from his master. Regarding the 'secrets' alleged by many, not only followers but also enthusiasts, to belong to the Kabbalah, the sceptical strategy of objectification also results in demystifying the phenomenon because it focuses only on the reduced essence of pure statements. However, in the early stage of the scholarly discussion of Kabbalah presented by Luzzatto, the kabbalistic use of a symbolic language that tries to express what is beyond the sphere of expression was not acknowledged as such.

After his terminological clarifications, Luzzato gives a systematic description of Kabbalah: the well-established division of Kabbalah into two parts, the first practical and the second theoretical and scientific, i.e. the theosophical Kabbalah.[26] The practical Kabbalah, i.e. *qabbalah ma'aśit* in Hebrew, he characterises as follows:

> It deals with some odd combinations of letters, calculations of numbers and certain forms of the Hebrew characters. For even the crown of a letter is considered by them with wonderful explanation. They mainly devote themselves to the names of God.[27]

In fact, the afore-mentioned hermeneutical techniques were already present in rabbinic literature in Late Antiquity. However, in medieval Judaism, these techniques were used obsessively and became a hallmark of various mystical and magical trends, e.g., in the writings of the German Pietists (*Ḥasidei Ashkenaz*) and of the ec-

---

[25] On the change of rhetorical genre in the sixteenth consideration, as can be seen in the descriptive manner in which Luzzatto presents Judaism, cf. Veltri, *Renaissance Philosophy in Jewish Garb*, 213.
[26] See already e.g., Abraham Abulafia, *We-zot li-Yehudah*, in idem, *Ḥayye ha-'Olam ha-Ba* [Hebrew] (Jerusalem: Amnon Gross, 1999): 25 or Pico della Mirandola, *Opera omnia*, 107–108 (*Conclusiones*); cf. Gershom Scholem, "Zur Geschichte der Anfänge der christlichen Kabbala," in *Essays Presented to Leo Baeck on the Occasion of his Eightieth Birthday*, eds. Norman Bentwich et al. (London: East and West Library, 1954): 164, n. 1; Moshe Idel, *Kabbalah. New Perspectives*, XI-XII; idem, "The Magical and Neoplatonic Interpretations of the Kabbalah in the Renaissance," in *Jewish Thought in the Sixteenth Century*, ed. Bernard D. Cooperman (Cambridge, Mass.: Harvard University Press, 1983): 197; and Campanini, "Talmud, Philosophy, and Kabbalah," 438–440.
[27] Luzzatto, *Discorso*, 80v.

static kabbalist Abraham Abulafia (1240 – after 1291) as well as in the Jewish magical traditions.[28]

Luzzatto introduces the theoretical Kabbalah by showing that he was quite familiar with its basic kabbalistic concepts and ideas. Besides the kabbalistic adaptation of the Neoplatonic concept of emanation, Luzzatto deals especially with the kabbalistic concept of the ten Sefirot, but without mentioning this specific term. He defines the Sefirot as 'ten fundamental principles,'[29] adopting the typical kabbalistic images of the Sefirot as described in classical kabbalistic texts,[30] when he writes:

> It [i.e. the theoretical Kabbalah] considers the dependence of this corporeal world on the spiritual one, disembodied and archetypal. They [i.e. the kabbalists] believe that there are some principles and origins that are the seeds of all perceptual things. They are like ever-flowing fountains, which, like aqueducts and canals, can receive the influx of divine power and energy directed at this corporeal world of ours.[31]

This passage continues as follows:

> They [i.e. the kabbalists] count ten fundamental principles assigned to the performance of this task—like also the Pythagoreans happened to set the number ten when they had to decide on the number of their own principles—but [according to the kabbalists], they [i.e. the principles] are to be duplicated according to the distinguishing principle of good and evil.[32]

Due to the ambiguous syntactical structure used by Luzzatto here, it is difficult to understand the real intention of this passage. In particular, it is unclear whether the Pythagoreans or the kabbalists duplicate the ten principles with regard to the distinction between good and evil.[33] In fact, the Italian used here allows both interpretations in terms of the language. According to Aristotle,[34] the Pythagoreans are ascribed a 'table of ten opposites' including ten pairs such as odd/even, right/left, male/female, light/darkness, good/evil, and others.[35] However, this kind of doubling of the ten principles does not follow an overall partition between good and evil as Luzzatto describes it. Therefore, the English translation presented here instead prefers the

---

28 Cf. Joshua Trachtenberg, *Jewish Magic and Superstition. A Study in Folk Religion* (New York: Behrman's Jewish Book House, 1939; reprinted Philadelphia: University of Pennsylvania Press, 2004): 78–103; Moshe Idel, *Language, Torah, and Hermeneutics in Abraham Abulafia* (Albany: State University of New York Press, 1989): 82–124; and Daniel Abrams, "From Germany to Spain: Numerology as a Mystical Technique," *Journal of Jewish Studies* 47 (1996): 43–63.
29 Luzzatto, *Discorso*, 81r.
30 Cf. Gershom Scholem, *Kabbalah* (Jerusalem: Keter, 1988): 116.
31 Luzzatto, *Discorso*, 80v-81r.
32 *Ibidem*, 81r.
33 In contrast to my view, Dan Lattes remarks in his Hebrew translation of the *Discorso* that Luzzatto does not refer to the ten Sefirot of the *Siṭra Aḥra*; cf. Luzzatto, *Ma'amar*, 171, n. 194.
34 Aristotle, *Metaphysics*, I:5 (986a22–26).
35 Cf. Walter Burkert, *Lore and Science in Ancient Pythagoreanism* (Cambridge, Mass.: Harvard University Press, 1972): 51.

other possible interpretation³⁶ that Luzzatto is very likely alluding to the specific kabbalistic doctrine that indeed duplicates the system of ten Sefirot when it comes to the question of the existence of evil. This doctrine can already be found in the *Sefer ha-Zohar*, where the evil side is called *Siṭra Aḥra* in Aramaic.³⁷ The Christian kabbalist Johannes Reuchlin (1455–1522) generally identified Kabbalah with Pythagoreanism in his *magnum opus De arte cabalistica* (Hagenau, 1517), and he considered himself a *Pythagoras redivivus*.³⁸ However, Luzzatto's comparison of kabbalistic concepts with those of the Pythagoreans also refers at the same moment to the sceptical strategy of historicisation, as will be discussed below.

Another kabbalistic concept is described as follows:

> But the kabbalists [...] observed that all mundane things share a close and proximate gradation of short, distinct intervals. [...] All the other things are differentiated subordinately without admitting peculiar lapses. Instead, they are linked and joined together in a very gradual manner. In the same way, in the transition from the infinite, the One, immutable and incorporeal, to the finite, composite, mutable, and corporeal, we should similarly interpose some other essences. These essences are supposed to have a partial correspondence with the eminent infinity of God by means of their spirituality and excellence, and [on the other hand] they are also supposed to bear similarity and sympathy with mundane creatures because of their being dependent and created.³⁹

This concept is based on Plato's doctrine of the necessary plenitude of the world as well as on the Aristotelian principle of continuity or infinitesimal gradation in nature. Both ideas were combined in Neoplatonism and reinterpreted as the conception of the universe as a 'Great Chain of Being' throughout the Middle Ages and the Renaissance until the eighteenth century.⁴⁰ The Neoplatonic idea of emanation from the

---

36 The difficulty is to which 'principii' the verb 'erano dupplicati' refers—to the principles of the Pythagoreans, or to those of the kabbalists? Actually, the Italian used here allows both interpretations. In my interpretation, it refers to the principles of the kabbalists, because the duplication of the ten Sefirot with regard to the good and the evil side is known from kabbalists but not from Pythagoreans. Thus, the parenthesis concerning the Pythagoreans begins with 'como anco' and ends with 'li loro principii.' The following 'ma erano dupplicati' refers back to the 'a tale fontione applicati,' which in addition is marked by the two rhyming verbs.
37 Cf. Gershom Scholem, *On the Mystical Shape of the Godhead: Basic Concepts in the Kabbalah* (New York: Schocken Books, 1991): 56–87; idem, *Kabbalah*, 123.
38 Johann Reuchlin, *On the Art of the Kabbalah. De arte cabalistica*, trans. Martin and Sarah Goodman (Lincoln and London: University of Nebraska Press, 1993); cf. Moshe Idel, "Introduction to the Bison Book Edition," in *ibidem*, XI-XVI; Wilhelm Schmidt-Biggemann, *Geschichte der christlichen Kabbala, vol. 1: 15. und 16. Jahrhundert* (Stuttgart-Bad Cannstatt: Frommann-Holzboog, 2012): 164–207.
39 Luzzatto, *Discorso*, 82v-83r.
40 Cf. the classic study by Arthur O. Lovejoy, *The Great Chain of Being: A Study of the History of an Idea* (Cambridge, Mass.: Harvard University Press, 1966). Concerning the Jewish tradition, cf. David Blumenthal, "Lovejoy's Great Chain of Being and Medieval Jewish Tradition," in *Jacob's Ladder and the Tree of Life: Concepts of Hierarchy and the Great Chain of Being*, eds. Marion L. Kuntz and Paul G. Kuntz (New York: Peter Lang, 1987): 179–190.

divine sphere down to earthly matters was also accepted by many Jewish and Christian kabbalists.⁴¹

In the following passage, Luzzatto again shows his detailed knowledge of the kabbalistic system of the Sefirot:

> Some of them adhere to the severity of justice, others to mercy, and others to a tempered clemency. They differ from the angels, whose function is to contemplate and carry out the voluntary commandments of God, sometimes by assuming corporeal form in order to appear to men.⁴²

In this sentence, Luzzatto is apparently referring to the fourth to sixth Sefirot, *ḥesed* ('mercy'), *din* ('judgment'), and *raḥamim* ('compassion'). Furthermore, he emphasises the fundamental difference between the Sefirot and the angels. In the continuation, Luzzatto mentions another kabbalistic concept:

> [The kabbalists] believe that these ideas exist in four distinct ways: the worthiest are emanated or inspired, the second created, the third shaped, the fourth and last made and completed. Each is subordinate to the other in a regulated hierarchy.⁴³

In this passage, Luzzatto summarizes a kabbalistic concept known as early as the *Tiqqunei Zohar* or the writings of Isaac of Acre in the late thirteenth and early fourteenth century, namely, the concept of four worlds: *aṣilut* ('emanation'), *beri'ah* ('creation'), *yeṣirah* ('formation'), and *'aśiyyah* ('making'). From the sixteenth century onwards, this fourfold concept became quite widespread in the kabbalistic tradition.⁴⁴

To quote one last example in this line, Luzzatto writes:

> Moreover, the kabbalists placed an essence between the soul and the body, by means of which the soul becomes capable of passions and sentiments, and this they supposed to be the spirit of a most subtle body, similar to the vehicles asserted by Platonists. They maintain that it accompanies the soul after its departure from the body, by means of which it suffers tormenting punishments on account of the sins committed.⁴⁵

In this passage, Luzzatto is very likely alluding to the Neoplatonic and kabbalistic concept of an astral body that was identified with the divine image (*ṣelem* in Hebrew) in some kabbalistic texts such as the *Sefer ha-Zohar*.⁴⁶

---

41 Cf. Scholem, *Kabbalah*, 96–105.
42 Luzzatto, *Discorso*, 83r.
43 Ibidem.
44 Cf. Scholem, *Kabbalah*, 118–119; Moshe Hallamish, *An Introduction to the Kabbalah* (Albany: State University of New York Press, 1999): 194–195.
45 Luzzatto, *Discorso*, 83v.
46 Cf. Scholem, *On the Mystical Shape of the Godhead*, 262.

3 Historicisation

Historicisation is deeply interwoven with the afore-mentioned sceptical strategies of relativisation and objectification. On the one hand, historicisation as a sceptical strategy refutes the claim of the uniqueness and essential importance of a certain statement or institution, and on the other, it presents the typical scholarly manner of objectifying a certain phenomenon. In a more specific sense, the sceptical strategy of historicisation focuses diachronically on terms denoting time in reconstructing the genealogy and interdependence of certain ideas and concepts, thus dismantling categories such as revelation or secret wisdom.[47] To historicise a phenomenon means to explain it by reconstructing its development from its origin throughout history. This results in simultaneously dissolving mythical and theological categories such as 'divine creation', 'history of decay' or 'Last Judgment'. In general, the temporal concept of historicisation does not make any ontological difference between past, present, and future.[48] Thus, with regard to the acceptance of sources of knowledge, categories such as 'ancient revelation' or 'old secret wisdom' are denounced as simply metaphysical by this strategy.

Historicisation is probably the most effective of Luzzatto's sceptical strategies in the passage dealing with the kabbalists. After the systematic presentation of the two different types of Kabbalah, Luzzatto focuses on the broader historical context of kabbalistic concepts and ideas, including Greek, Latin, and Arabic authors. It is very striking that Luzzatto devotes two-thirds of the passage on kabbalists to the presentation of non-Jewish philosophers and their ideas. By doing this, he not only compares Kabbalah with the philosophies of Plato, Aristotle, Sextus Empiricus, Philo, Avicenna, Dante, and others, but he also places it as one of the many extant ideas in the history of philosophy. Therein Luzzatto mirrors the characteristics of Italian Kabbalah, which generally shows a positive attitude towards philosophy, including various syntheses of both traditions.[49] It is worth mentioning that the promulgator of Lurianic Kabbalah, Israel Saruq,[50] who was active in Venice in the years after 1590, also interpreted Kabbalah as a kind of philosophy for his Italian audience.[51]

---

[47] Cf. Schleichert, *Wie man mit Fundamentalisten diskutiert*, 42–43.
[48] Cf. Glenn W. Most, "Preface," in *Historicization – Historisierung*, ed. Glenn W. Most (Göttingen: Vandenhoeck & Ruprecht, 2001): VIII.
[49] Cf. Idel, "Major Currents in Italian Kabbalah," 345–349; idem, "Italy in Safed, Safed in Italy," 243; idem, "Differing Conception of Kabbalah," 155–157; and idem, "Kabbalah in Italy in the Sixteenth Century," 316.
[50] According to his own signature in Ms Oxford, Bodleian Library, Neubauer 1624, fol. 35, this is the correct spelling and not the formerly known Sarug; see Ronit Meroz, "Contrasting Opinions among the Founders of R. Israel Saruq's school," in *Expérience et écriture mystiques dans les religions du livre*, eds. Paul B. Fenton and Roland Goetschel (Leiden: Brill, 2000): 191, n. 1.
[51] Cf. Leon Modena, *Ari Nohem*, ed. Nehemiah S. Libowitz (Jerusalem: Darom, 1929): 53 [= (Jerusalem, 2012), 88]: 'And I have also heard from the mouth of the kabbalist R. Israel Saruq, a distinguish-

However, Christian kabbalists such as Giovanni Pico della Mirandola (1463–94) or Francesco Giorgio Veneto (also known as Zorzi, 1466–1540) also depicted Kabbalah in a philosophical way.[52] By presenting Kabbalah as philosophy, the often-alleged mystical and visionary aspect of it would be neglected. Very similarly to Leon Modena,[53] Luzzatto goes an important step further when he implicitly suggests by his strategy of historicisation that Kabbalah has no Jewish origin. Thus, historicisation is related to the sceptical strategies of indictment of heresy and delegitimation which will be discussed below.

In the same way, he mentions the Pythagoreans again—see above—when dealing with the topic of transmigration of the soul:

> The said kabbalists believed in the Pythagorean transmigration [of the soul], which the talmudists did not.[54]

Again, according to Luzzatto, the kabbalists follow non-Jewish sources, such as the Pythagoreans, and not the presupposed genuine Jewish tradition as alluded to by the talmudists. Probably the first Jewish scholar to explicitly connect Pythagoras with kabbalists with regard to the transmigration of the soul (*metempsychosis*) was the Aristotelian philosopher Moses ben Samuel ha-Cohen Ashkenazi (second half of the fifteenth century).[55] Accordingly, Luzzatto's colleague Leon Modena also attributed this idea to Pythagoras.[56] Both Venetian rabbis were involved in the debate on this topic in Amsterdam in 1635–6, where Modena's former student, Rabbi Saul Levi Morteira (1596–1660), preached against the concept of the transmigration of the soul (and the Kabbalah as well).[57]

---

ed student of Luria, blessed be his memory, who said that there is nothing between Kabbalah and philosophy.'

52 Cf., e.g., Chaim Wirszubski, *Pico della Mirandola's Encounter with Jewish Mysticism* (Jerusalem: The Israel Academy of Sciences and Humanities, 1989); Francesco Zorzi, *L'Armonia del Mondo*, ed. Saverio Campanini (Milan: Bompiani, 2010); and Schmidt-Biggemann, *Geschichte der christlichen Kabbala, vol. 1*, 70–130 and 384–449.
53 Cf. Idel, "Major Currents in Italian Kabbalah," 360.
54 Luzzatto, *Discorso*, 84v.
55 On the genealogy of this topos, cf. the summary presented by Brian Ogren, *Renaissance and Rebirth. Reincarnation in Early Modern Italian Kabbalah* (Leiden, Boston: Brill, 2009): 270–297.
56 Cf. Howard E. Adelman, *Success and Failure in the Seventeenth Century Ghetto of Venice: The Life and Thought of Leon Modena, 1571–1648* (PhD dissertation, Brandeis University, 1985): 480; Dweck, *Scandal of Kabbalah*, 140; and Idel, "Differing Conceptions of Kabbalah," 158–162. Concerning Modena's general approach of historicisation, cf. Bezalel Safran, "Leone da Modena's Historical Thinking," in *Jewish Thought in the Seventeenth Century*, eds. Isadore Twersky and Bernard Septimus (Cambridge, Mass.: Harvard University Press, 1987): 381–398.
57 Cf. Adelman, *Success and Failure*, 727.

4 Indictment of heresy

The strategy of indicting an idea or concept as heretical is well known, especially in polemics. Luzzatto uses indictment of heresy as a sceptical strategy in a way that is embedded in the broader framework of his sceptical strategy of historicisation. The evidence of Jewish kabbalistic texts which were already translated into Latin by Christian kabbalists—he mentions Giovanni Pico della Mirandola and his main work in this regard, the *Conclusiones*,[58] in the beginning of the passage dealing with Kabbalah[59]—is, for Luzzatto, of double importance. Firstly, it is directed to his Christian audience and their supposed familiarity with this topic, especially when they are also sceptical towards Kabbalah. Secondly, it is an admonition regarding the dangers to Jewish people inherent in this fact, even when they are kabbalists themselves. Indeed, the very existence of Christian Kabbalah evoked a heavy discussion among Jewish scholars at that time.[60] In general, Luzzatto tends to play down the differences between Christians and Jews throughout his *Discorso*, where he presents both of them as equally useful citizens of the *Serenissima*.

By relating kabbalists to 'the Valentinians and the gnostics and other ancient heretics,'[61] Luzzatto decries the former and also indicts Kabbalah as heresy. Heinrich Cornelius Agrippa of Nettesheim (1486–1535) was probably the first to emphasise the gnostics' assumed dependence on Kabbalah.[62] However, Luzzatto was seemingly influenced by Sixtus of Siena (also know as Senensis, 1520–69), who also wrote about this relationship in his *Bibliotheca sancta*.[63]

However, gnosticism was not only a topic of Late Antiquity, but also a contemporary phenomenon in Luzzatto's time in some trends of the Kabbalah. Regarding gnostic features in Kabbalah, one may acknowledge the dissemination of Lurianic Kabbalah in Italy by Israel Saruq in the last decades of the sixteenth century as a probable evoking factor, because many mythical and gnostic elements can be detect-

---

58 See the *editio princeps* Pico della Mirandola, *Conclusiones nongentae* (Rome, 1486). Actually, the *Conclusiones* by Pico include two sets of kabbalistic theses but no translations of kabbalistic texts into Latin; cf. Wirszubski, *Pico della Mirandola's Encounter with Jewish Mysticism*, 19–52 and 133–200. However, a whole library of kabbalistic texts was indeed translated for Pico by the convert Flavius Mithridates; cf. Giulio Busi, ed., *The Kabbalistic Library of Giovanni Pico della Mirandola*, 5 vols. (Turin: Nino Aragno, 2004–2012).
59 Cf. Luzzatto, *Discorso*, 80v.
60 Cf. Moshe Idel, "Jewish thinkers versus Christian Kabbalah," in *Christliche Kabbala*, ed. Wilhelm Schmidt-Biggemann (Ostfildern: Jan Thorbecke, 2003): 49–65; Dweck, *Scandal of Kabbalah*, 154–169.
61 Luzzatto, *Discorso*, 83r.
62 See Heinrich Cornelius Agrippa of Nettesheim, *De incertitudine et vanitate scientiarum liber* (Frankfurt am Main, 1693): 178–185 (chapter 47: De Cabala).
63 Sixtus of Siena, *Bibliotheca sancta* (Venice, 1566): 227; cf. Secret, "Un texte mal connu de Simon Luzzatto sur la kabbale," 125, n. 1.

ed in Isaac Luria's (1534–72) cosmogony.[64] However, Luzzatto's silence concerning Luria's ideas is striking here because they were accepted by several Italian kabbalists in his lifetime, especially by the most important one: Rabbi Menaḥem Azariah da Fano (1548–1620).[65] However, selectivity and neglect are in fact rhetorical strategies, but not stringently sceptical strategies as defined here.[66]

5 Delegitimation

As we have already seen above, Luzzatto denounces the Kabbalah by suggesting its non-Jewish origin and heretical character. The sceptical strategies presented so far culminate in the one that I would like to call 'delegitimation.' This strategy is extremely important in the case of refuting kabbalistic statements because the Kabbalah first and foremost consists of a tradition that relies on genealogy, filiation, and authority. Thus, the legitimacy of Kabbalah will be undermined by arguing that the chain of genealogy is broken somewhere and that the venerated authorities are somehow not trustworthy. Accordingly, Luzzatto clearly emphasised the pseudepigraphic character of the alleged authorship of the *Sefer ha-Zohar* by calling it an attribution: he did not explicitly mention the name of the fictitious author, Shimon bar Yoḥai, and therefore did not acknowledge him, but instead marginalised him by use of the phrase 'one of the ancient rabbis.'[67] Despite the fact that the *Sefer ha-Zohar* was printed for the first time in Italy, the Italian kabbalists themselves were quite indifferent to this central text of the Spanish trend of theosophical Kabbalah.[68] In contrast, Christian kabbalists were much more interested in the *Zohar,* as can be seen by the efforts made by Guillaume Postel (1510–81) to translate large portions of it into Latin.[69]

---

[64] Cf. Gershom Scholem, *Major Trends in Jewish Mysticism* (New York: Schocken Books, 1946; reprinted, New York: Schocken Books, 1995): 260–280; Isaiah Tishby, "Gnostic Doctrines in Sixteenth-Century Jewish Mysticism," *Journal of Jewish Studies* 6 (1955): 146–152; Idel, "Italy in Safed, Safed in Italy," 252–256; and Dweck, *Scandal of Kabbalah*, 127–147.
[65] Cf. Idel, "Major Currents in Italian Kabbalah," 356–357 and Robert Bonfil, "Halakhah, Kabbalah, and Society: Some Insights into Rabbi Menahem Azariah da Fano's Inner World," in *Jewish Thought in the Seventeenth Century*, eds. Isadore Twersky and Bernard Septimus (Cambridge, Mass.: Harvard University Press, 1987): 39–61.
[66] The rhetorical strategies of selectivity and neglect will be elaborated elsewhere.
[67] Luzzatto, *Discorso*, 84v.
[68] Cf. Idel, "Italy in Safed, Safed in Italy," 253.
[69] Cf. Schmidt-Biggemann, *Geschichte der christlichen Kabbala, vol. 1*, 597–616 and 638–657; Judith Weiss, "Guillaume Postel's Introduction to His First Latin Translation and Commentary on the Book of Zohar" [in Hebrew], in *And This Is for Yehuda: Studies Presented to Our Friend, Professor Yehuda Liebes*, eds. Maren R. Niehoff, Ronit Meroz, and Jonathan Garb (Jerusalem: The Bialik Institute, 2012): 254–280; Idel, "Kabbalah in Italy in the Sixteenth Century," 315; and Boaz Huss, "Translations of the Zohar: Historical Contexts and Ideological Frameworks," *Correspondences* 4 (2016): 87.

Luzzatto includes another reference to the printed edition of the *Sefer ha-Zohar* ('The Book of Splendour') when he writes that there is an 'extremely large volume on the five books of Moses called the *Splendour*.'[70] The designation of this book as an 'extremely large volume' very probably refers[71] to the edition published in one large-format volume by Christians and converted Jews in Cremona in 1558–60, whereas the almost contemporaneous Mantua edition was printed by several Jews in a smaller format in three volumes.[72] Accordingly, only those parts of the multipartite *Sefer ha-Zohar* are referred to here, i.e. those parts which were arranged in the Cremona edition within the literary framework of a commentary on the weekly portions of the Torah. Thus, other parts of zoharic literature, including the *Tiqqunei Zohar* (*editio princeps* Mantua, 1558) and the *Zohar Ḥadash* (*editio princeps* Salonica, 1597), are not considered by Luzzatto despite the fact that they were already easily accessible in printed editions.

However, Luzzatto does not use the sceptical strategy of delegitimation concerning all relevant matters. For instance, he did not explicitly reject the alleged old age of the *Sefer ha-Zohar* as others had done before him.[73] In addition, Luzzatto acknowledges the Hebrew *Sefer Yeṣirah* ('Book of Creation') as the most important kabbalistic book.[74] Thus, he apparently shared the self-image of the kabbalistic tradition regarding this text. In fact, and despite the pre-kabbalistic origin of this book, many basic features and terms, such as the Sefirot and the concept of the creation of the world through God's use of the Hebrew letters, are provided for the development of Kabbalah. Furthermore, there are dozens of kabbalistic commentaries on the *Sefer Yeṣirah*. This work was printed for the first time in two versions together with four commentaries (Mantua, 1562).[75] The first Latin translation, prepared by Guillaume Postel, had

---

[70] Luzzatto, *Discorso*, 84v: '[...] un altro volume grandissimo sopra li cinque libri de Moise nominato Il Splendore.'
[71] Though the only other edition of the *Zohar* published prior to the time Luzzatto wrote his *Discorso* is that printed in Lublin in 1623–1624, which indeed follows the *Vorlage* of the Cremona edition, it is in my view more likely that Luzzatto knew the former.
[72] Cf. Boaz Huss, *The Zohar. Reception and Impact* (Oxford: The Littman Library of Jewish Civilization, 2016): 99–106 and Daniel Abrams, *Kabbalistic Manuscripts and Textual Theory: Methodologies of Textual Scholarship and Editorial Practice in the Study of Jewish Mysticism* (Jerusalem: Magnes Press and Los Angeles: Cherub Press, 2010): 232–245.
[73] Among the philosophers who criticised the Kabbalah, cf., e.g., Samuel ibn Seneh Zarza, *Sefer Meqor Ḥayyim* (Mantua 1559), fol. 118b (*Parashat Ki Teṣe*) or Elijah Delmedigo in his *Sefer Beḥinat ha-Dat*, see the edition prepared by Giovanni Licata, *La via della ragione. Elia del Medigo e l'averroismo di Spinoza* (Macerata: Edizioni Università di Macerata, 2013): 324–325 (§28); cf. Kalman P. Bland, "Elijah del Medigo's Averroist Response to the Kabbalah of Fifteenth-Century Jewry and Pico della Mirandola," *Journal of Jewish Thought and Philosophy* 1.1 (1991): 43. Concerning criticism on the *Sefer ha-Zohar*, cf. also Huss, *The Zohar*, 239–255 and Dweck, *Scandal of Kabbalah*, 59–100.
[74] Luzzatto, *Discorso*, 84v.
[75] Cf. Saverio Campanini, "On Abraham's Neck. The Editio Princeps of the Sefer Yetzirah (Mantua 1562) and Its Context," in *Rabbi Judah Moscato and the Jewish Intellectual World of Mantua in the*

already been printed ten years earlier (Paris, 1552), later followed by two other Latin translations, one by Johannes Pistorius (Basle, 1587) and one by Johann Stephan Rittangel (Amsterdam, 1642).[76] Thus, when Luzzatto wrote his *Discorso*, the *Sefer Yeṣirah* was already well known and studied by Jewish and Christian audiences. Since Luzzatto mentions the title as *De Creatione*, he is very likely referring to Pistorius' Latin edition of it included in his collection *Ars Cabalistica* from 1587.

The only kabbalist Luzzatto mentions by name is Moses Gerondi, i.e. Naḥmanides (1197–1270), to whom he attributes a 'very sharp mind.'[77] The reason why Luzzatto only refers to Naḥmanides is probably because the Geronese kabbalist was widely acknowledged, especially in Italy[78] and also by Christians, as a halakhic and exegetical authority who restricted the dissemination of Kabbalah either to personal instruction in a small circle of students or by alluding only with caution and rather rarely to kabbalistic lore in his writings. If this was indeed the reason why Luzzatto praised Naḥmanides, then it would be an elegant critique of the rather widespread printing and reception of kabbalistic books, particularly in Italy.[79] Likewise, it must be emphasised that Luzzatto ignored or neglected contemporary phenomena of Kabbalah, such as, e.g., the Italian kabbalists of his time, the prevailing influence of Moses Cordovero's (1522–70) writings on kabbalists in Italy,[80] or, as already mentioned above, the emergence of Lurianic Kabbalah and its fiery adept Israel Saruq, who was active in Venice before 1600.

Summary

To sum up, the main characteristic of Luzzatto's subversive scepticism in the passage on kabbalists is the perpetual inquiry into various topics in a distancing, scholarly way, striving for the final goal of undermining their authority and tradition as a source of knowledge. However, in contrast to Pyrrhonian scepticism, Luzzatto does not want to evoke equipollence of contradicting statements in order to suspend judgment and reach a state of tranquillity. He does not want to judge whether Kabbalah in general or kabbalistic statements in particular are true or not. He does not look for

---

16th-17th Centuries, eds. Giuseppe Veltri and Gianfranco Miletto (Leiden and Boston: Brill, 2012): 253–278.
76 Cf. Wilhelm Schmidt-Biggemann, "Das Buch Jezira in der christlichen Tradition," in *Das Buch Jezira. In der Übersetzung von Johann Friedrich von Meyer*, eds. Eveline Goodman-Thau and Christoph Schulte (Berlin: Akademie Verlag, 1993): 45–64.
77 Luzzatto, *Discorso*, 84v.
78 Cf. Idel, *Kabbalah in Italy*, 98–99, and see *ibidem*, 220 concerning the 'good' kabbalistic books recommended by Rabbi Yehudah Ḥayyat—who was expelled from Spain and came to Italy in the late fifteenth century—in the introduction to his *Minḥat Yehudah*: 'and the secrets of Naḥmanides should be written upon the table of your heart.'
79 Concerning the debate about the printing of the *Sefer ha-Zohar*, cf. Huss, *The Zohar*, 191–205.
80 Cf. Idel, "Kabbalah in Italy in the Sixteenth Century," 313.

counter-arguments or contradicting statements at all. Instead of this, he uses various sceptical strategies—as defined above—in order to induce doubts, questions, and intellectual uneasiness. The sceptical strategies discussed here, such as relativisation, objectification, historicisation, indictment of heresy, and, finally, delegitimation, are tightly intertwined and could eventually result in crushing the backbones of adherents of the Kabbalah. The subversive character of these sceptical strategies can be seen in the way that the reader is not immediately aware that he is attacked because Luzzatto's presentation of the Kabbalah is written in an erudite and objective way without any kind of direct attack or polemic.

Luzzatto is probably the first Jewish non-kabbalist to present the Kabbalah in this way. The innovative and likewise early modern approach of Luzzatto can be seen in the lack of either explicit polemic against the Kabbalah or sharp attack on it typical of its earlier opponents.[81] This becomes even more obvious if Luzzatto's presentation of Kabbalah is compared with another example written by a contemporary Jew. In 1639, only one year after the publication of the *Discorso*, his above-mentioned Venetian colleague, Leon Modena, wrote the first full-fledged critique of Kabbalah in his *Ari Nohem* ('Roaring Lion'), which is devoted exclusively to this topic.[82] It is very likely that Luzzatto was alluding to his colleague's work-in-progress when he ended his passage on Kabbalah with the following sentence:

> At the moment, I have nothing else to say about the kabbalists, since to explain their doctrines properly would require a volume in itself.[83]

Modena collected and quoted all the authors and arguments against the Kabbalah with which he was familiar. While Modena's presentation of the Kabbalah is actually intended as a harsh attack against it, Luzzatto's strategy is completely different.[84] Instead of evaluating the Kabbalah from a personal perspective, he decided to present a rather systematic and historical survey of these pages without any explicit polemical tone. Although the style of his presentation is elegant and subtle, the effect of his

---

81 Cf. Bill Rebiger, "The Early Opponents of the Kabbalah and the Role of Sceptical Argumentations: An Outline," in *Yearbook of the Maimonides Centre for Advanced Studies 2016*, eds. Giuseppe Veltri and Bill Rebiger (Berlin: De Gruyter, 2016): 39–57. Concerning the disappearance of the Christian *theologia polemica* since the seventeenth century, cf. Ernestine van der Wall, "Ways of Polemicizing: The Power of Tradition in Christian Polemics," in *Religious Polemics in Context*, eds. Theo L. Hettema and Arie van der Kooij (Assen: Royal Van Gorcum, 2004): 404–409.
82 See Leon Modena, *Ari Nohem*; cf. Adelman, *Success and Failure*, 791–815; Moshe Idel, "Differing Conceptions of Kabbalah," 142–190; and Dweck, *Scandal of Kabbalah*; concerning Luzzatto's attitude to Kabbalah, see *ibidem*, 20–21.
83 Luzzatto, *Discorso*, 84v; cf. Adelman, *Success and Failure*, 796. However, Pico della Mirandola wrote something very similar in his *Apologia* concerning a sufficient presentation of Kabbalah: 'specialem librum exigeret;' see idem, *Opera omnia*, 181; cf. Campanini, "Talmud, Philosophy, and Kabbalah," 436.
84 A comparative study of both authors, Leon Modena and Simone Luzzatto, and their critique of Kabbalah will be published soon.

sceptical strategies in undermining a kabbalist's self-confidence is probably even more destructive.

The systematic presentation of several main topics of Kabbalah clearly shows Luzzatto's familiarity with these matters. The sources of his kabbalistic knowledge have not been completely identified thus far, but according to Secret it seems that he mainly relied on texts by Christian kabbalists. The Christian perspective can also be seen in another point. Thus, Luzzatto's presentation of Kabbalah as a kind of philosophy is in line with the view of Italian kabbalists as well as Christian kabbalists. However, the Italian kabbalists were usually quite indifferent towards the theosophical-theurgical branch of the Kabbalah as presented first and foremost by Sephardic kabbalists and their central source—the *Sefer ha-Zohar*—because of its mythical and anthropomorphic orientation. In contrast, the zoharic Kabbalah was only interpreted as a kind of philosophy by the Christian kabbalists—and Luzzatto.

The mode of Luzzatto's presentation evokes an almost scientific distance between the scholar and his topic. The strategy of soberly and systematically describing the basic features of Kabbalah results in disenchanting its fascinating character of supposed secret wisdom. According to Luzzatto, fascination is generally suspect because it plays with emotions, passions, and illusions, but not with reason.[85] The printing of kabbalistic books provided every potential reader with kabbalistic claims even when he or she was otherwise without any access to kabbalistic teachers and circles. In other words, Kabbalah no longer correlates with its etymological meaning as a 'tradition' or 'reception.' Instead of being an esoteric lore taught only to close disciples, in this way Kabbalah could become a rather accessible topic of scholarly study. Thus, Kabbalah is only one set of ideas among many others without any superiority or uniqueness.

Luzzatto's main aim in employing the sceptical strategy of historicising the Kabbalah is twofold: on the one hand, he seeks to avoid a debate about the truth and certainty of kabbalistic claims, and, on the other, he aims at disenchanting the fascination of the Kabbalah as a genuine revealed wisdom by presenting the genealogy of certain kabbalistic ideas and their subsumption into learned Christian and non-Christian (Egyptian, Greek, Roman, Hellenistic etc.) traditions. Thus, against the kabbalistic self-confidence, he denounces Kabbalah as non-Jewish in its very origin. In contrast to the kabbalistic concept of eternal and absolute truths—similar to the Renaissance and Baroque concepts of a *prisca theologia* or a *philosophia perennis*[86]— which are revealed only to dignified adepts, the historicisation of Kabbalah emphasises the dynamics and innovations of claims and ideas throughout history and their

---

85 Cf. Luzzatto, *Socrate*, 276 and 290 (I owe many thanks to Michela Torbidoni who provided me with these references).
86 Cf., e.g., Wilhelm Schmidt-Biggemann, *Philosophia perennis: Historical Outlines of Western Spirituality in Ancient, Medieval and Early Modern Thought* (Dordrecht: Springer, 2004).

entanglement with other intellectual trends.[87] For the Christian audience, Luzzatto emphasises the heretical implications of the kabbalistic tradition with regard to gnosticism. Historicisation of the Kabbalah by means of asserting a dependency on already disqualified historical phenomena such as gnosticism can serve as a subversive strategy of undermining the legitimacy and credibility of kabbalistic authorities and sources. Eventually, this leads to a devastating delegitimation of kabbalistic claims, at least in later generations. However, the reception history of Luzzatto's passage on kabbalists in his *Discorso* is still a scholarly *desideratum*.

---

87 Cf. Wilhelm Schmidt-Biggemann, "Die Historisierung der 'Philosophia Hebraeorum' im frühen 18. Jahrhundert. Eine philosophisch-philologische Demontage," in *Historicization – Historisierung*, ed. Glenn W. Most (Göttingen: Vandenhoeck & Ruprecht, 2001): 103–128.

Michela Torbidoni
The Italian Academies and Rabbi Simone Luzzatto's *Socrate*: the Freedom of the *Ingenium* and the Soul

1 Introduction

Simone Luzzatto, chief rabbi of the Jewish community of Venice, a highly talented classicist conversant with Latin and Greek literature as well as a passionate reader of medieval Italian culture, was the author of the well-known apologetic treatise *Discorso circa il stato degli Hebrei et in particular dimoranti nell'inclita città di Venetia* ('Discourse Concerning the Condition of the Jews, and in Particular Those Living in the Fair City of Venice'), published in Venice in 1638, and also of *Socrate overo dell'humano sapere* ('Socrates or on Human Knowledge'), which appeared in Venice in 1651. The scope and purpose of this latter work are indicated in the book's extended title: *Esercitio seriogiocoso di Simone Luzzatto hebreo venetiano. Opera nella quale si dimostra quanto sia imbecile l'humano intendimento, mentre non è diretto dalla divina rivelatione* ('The Serious-Playful Exercise of Simone Luzzatto, Venetian Jew. A Book That Shows How Incapable Human Intelligence Can Be When It Is Not Led by Divine Revelation'). Thus, the work is meant as a demonstration of the limits and weaknesses of the human capacity to acquire knowledge without being guided by revelation. Luzzatto achieved this goal by offering an overview of the various and contradictory gnosiological opinions disseminated since ancient times: he analyses the human faculties, namely the functioning of the external (five) senses, the internal senses (common sense, imagination, memory, and the estimative faculty), the intellect, and also their mutual relation.[1] In his work, Luzzatto gave an accurate analysis of all these issues by getting to the heart of the ancient epistemological theories. The divergence of views, to which he addressed the most attention, prevented him from giving a fixed definition of the nature of the cognitive process. This obliged him to come to the audacious conclusion of neither affirming nor denying anything concerning human knowledge, and finally of suspending his judgement altogether. Luzzatto's intention contains the promise of a genuinely sceptical investigation into the validity of human certainties, to which he opposed the solidity of the divine truth.

This work unfortunately had little success in Luzzatto's lifetime, and was subsequently almost forgotten. Only a few copies existed before it was republished in

---

[1] See Harry Austrin Wolfson, "The Internal Senses in Latin, Arabic and Hebrew Philosophic Texts," *The Harvard Theological Review* 28 (1935): 69–133.

2013,[2] for the first time since 1651. The absence of evidence from Luzzatto's contemporaries and that of his epistolary have thus increased the difficulty of tracing not only its legacy in the history of philosophical thought, but also of understanding the circumstances surrounding the writing of his *Socrate*.[3]

The present contribution is a preliminary study aiming to shed some light on the still-obscure intellectual context of Luzzatto's philosophical commitment. Therefore, it will point out some traces which may strengthen the hypothesis that Luzzatto's work may be read in line with the literature of the Italian Academies,[4] and, more precisely, with the innovative and bizarre compositions of the *Accademia degli Incogniti*

---

2 Simone Luzzatto, *Scritti politici e filosofici di un rabbino scettico nella Venezia del Seicento*, ed. Giuseppe Veltri (Milan: Bompiani, 2013).
3 Although there are some references to Luzzatto's book in scholarly literature, a complete study of the entire work has not yet been carried out. Besides a mention in the Christian Hebraist Giulio Bartolocci's *Bibliotheca Magna Rabbinica* (Rome: Typographia Sacrae Congregationis de Propaganda Fide, 1693) and in Johann Christoph Wolff's *Bibliotheca Hebraea*, vol. 3 (Hamburg: Christophorus Felginer, 1727): 1115–1135, brief references to Luzzatto's *Socrate* appeared in some works during the nineteenth century: in Giovanni Bernardo De Rossi, *Dizionario*, vol. 2 (Parma: dalla Reale Stamperia, 1802): 16 and in Moritz Steinschneider, *Die Italienische Literatur der Juden* (Frankfurt a. M.: Kauffmann, 1901): 418–419. A still-more-detailed description may be found in Isidor Busch, *Kalender und Jahrbuch für Israeliten*, vol. 6 (Wien: Schmid, 1866): 106–108; Heinrich Graetz, *Geschichte der Juden*, vol. 10 (Leipzig: Oskar Liener, 1868), Chap. 5: die Wühler (1620–1660): 148–153; and Samuel David Luzzatto, *Autobiografia* (Padova: Crescini, 1882). In the 1930s, Jehuda Bergmann published an article entitled "Sokrates in der jüdischen Literatur," *Monatsschrift für Geschichte und Wissenschaft des Judentums* 80 (1936): 3–13, in which he traced the history of Socrates' appearance in the Jewish tradition, including Luzzatto's book. According to his interpretation, the main issue raised by Luzzatto was the necessity that neither reason nor authority should have supremacy, but that both should be equally honoured, because only by completing and limiting one another could they best rule human life. There have only been four more recent contributions to research on Luzzatto's *Socrate*. The first is David Ruderman, "Science and Skepticism Simone Luzzatto on perceiving the Natural World," in *Jewish Thought and Scientific Discovery in Early Modern Europe*, ed. David Ruderman (New Haven: Yale University Press, 1995): 153–184. Ruderman analysed Luzzatto's deep involvement in the naturalistic and scientific studies of his time by focusing on his appreciation of and proficiency in mathematics and astronomy. Furthermore, cf. the dissertation by Ariel Viterbo, written in Hebrew and partly published in Italian in 1999: idem, "Lo scetticismo mascherato di Simone Luzzatto," *Studi Veneziani* 38 (1999): 79–128. Viterbo describes the text's contents and proposes interpreting it as an intellectual autobiography of Luzzatto. The most recent contributions to research on *Socrate* were published by Giuseppe Veltri in his edition of Simone Luzzatto, *Scritti politici e filosofici* (Milan: Bompiani, 2013) and the volume edited by him entitled *Filosofo e rabbino nella Venezia del Seicento* (Rome: Aracne, 2015). Veltri highlighted the importance of Simone Luzzatto's work as the only Jewish example of sceptical thought in the early modern period. In an essay published in the last of the above-mentioned volumes, Michela Torbidoni analysed Luzzatto's practice of doubt in *Socrate* by examining the influence and role of Sextus Empiricus' *Outlines of Pyrrhonism* on the entire structure of *Socrate*; cf. Michela Torbidoni, "Il metodo del dubbio nel *Socrate*," in *Filosofo e rabbino nella Venezia del Seicento*, ed. Giuseppe Veltri (Rome: Aracne, 2015): 183–245.
4 On the historical reconstruction of the relationships between the Jews and the Academies, see Giuseppe Veltri and Evelien Chayes, *Oltre le mura del Ghetto. Accademie, scetticismo e tolleranza nella Venezia barocca* (Palermo: New Digital Press, 2016).

founded by the Venetian aristocrat Giovan Francesco Loredan (1607–1661), the author of several playful and provocative writings as well as the editor of the collective works of his Academy.[5]

In order to achieve this goal, I intend to proceed by giving first a brief overview of the main features of the *Incogniti*'s writings by stressing the pivotal role of their anti-dogmatism and their celebration of the free exercise of reason and then discussing how this tendency was displayed in a new literary genre, that of the *imprese*. Secondly, I will present some evidence gathered from both the frontispiece and the content of Luzzatto's *Socrate* recalling the unique literature produced by the Academicians. Thirdly, I will present how the issue of free inquiry cannot be detached from that of the soul both in the framework of the mission of the Academies and in Luzzatto's *Socrate*. Finally, I will explain why the free and sceptical inquiry carried out by Luzzatto must be considered to be in continuity with God's revelation.

2 The *Accademia degli Incogniti* and the Freedom of *Ingenium* against Dogmatism

The fall of gnosiological certainties during the seventeenth century motivated a new interest in free investigation and literary experiments. The freedom of the *ingenium* became a new means for the intellect to inquire and penetrate into the inner and changeable nature of things in this time. From the sixteenth to the seventeenth century, learned Academies[6] became the epicentre of a very lively culture in Italy; they promoted discussions in a wide range of disciplines from literature and philosophy to astronomy or medicine. As an alternative institution to the official universities, they attracted the attention of a different kind of scholar and promoted an intellectual exchange among them that stands out in terms of topics and issues. They were associations or groups of learned people motivated by the desire to freely advance their innovative scholarly arguments and to perform poetry and plays which were sometimes marked by ludicrous, bizarre, and libertine traits.[7]

Among them, the *Incogniti*, which included important Venetian and foreign intellectuals, future senators, and even some members of the Church, played the role of an unofficial seat of political power in Venice for almost thirty years. Thanks to their

---

5 There is a very rich bibliography on Giovan Francesco Loredan and his Academy, cf. Davide Conrieri, *Gli Incogniti e l'Europa* (Bologna: Emyl di Odoya, 2011); Clizia Carminati, "Giovan Francesco Loredan," in *Dizionario Biografico degli Italiani* 65 (2005); Monica Miato, *L'Accademia degli Incogniti* (Florence: Olschki, 1998); and Michele Maylender, *Storia delle Accademie d'Italia* (Bologna: Cappelli Editore, 1926–1930).
6 Cf. Michele Battagia, *Delle Accademie Veneziane: Dissertazione storica* (Venice: G. Picotti-G. Orlandelli Editore, 1826).
7 Cf. Monica Miato, *L'Accademia degli Incogniti* (Florence: Olschki, 1998): 8–10.

wide range of publications, including moral essays, novels, and opera librettos,[8] the *Incogniti* deeply influenced the cultural and political affairs of the Venetian Republic. From a philosophical point of view, the Academy was influenced by the teachings of Cesare Cremonini (1550–1631),[9] professor of philosophy at the University of Padua, well known for his rigorous interpretation of Aristotle's philosophy and, at the same time, for his heterodoxy in religion. He was therefore suspected of heresy and often denounced to the Inquisition. Many future members of the *Accademia degli Incogniti* were his students. He taught them the necessity of questioning all accepted dogma by promoting Aristotelian arguments and a sceptical approach concerning the immortality of the soul in favour of a materialistic conception of life. The members of the Academy were thus used to debating several topics in their meetings, from very serious philosophical topics such as what kind of relation, if any, exists between body and soul, the connection between being and not-being, and nothingness,[10] to ludicrous treatments of everyday and even meaningless things. Any topic, even the less important and serious ones, became subject to debate in order to sharpen and demonstrate their rhetorical skills, which needed to be performed for *pro* and *contra* arguments independently of the position held by the speaker. The discourses of the *Incogniti* are mainly directed towards the search for originality in order to extend the borders of knowledge. The only way to attain this goal was to create the conditions for complete freedom of thought and expression. As already highlighted by many scholars,[11] the institution of the Academy was initially intended to be free of any restrictions, as testified by the Academician Luigi Manzini (1604–1657), a former Benedictine monk and prelate in the Roman Curia,[12] in his commendation of nothingness,[13] where freedom is assumed as an essential condition of the discourses in the *Accademia*. This enabled them to open a wider perspective above any dogmatic assertion:

---

[8] Cf. Ellen Rosand, *Opera in Seventeenth-Century Venice: the Creation of a genre* (Berkeley-Los Angeles and Oxford: University of California Press, 2007).

[9] On Cesare Cremonini, cf. Charles Schmitt, "Cesare Cremonini," in *Dizionario Biografico degli Italiani* 30 (1980); Luigi Olivieri, ed., *Aristotelismo veneto e scienza moderna* (Padova: Hoepli, 1983) and Charles Schmitt, "Cesare Cremonini, un aristotelico al tempo di Galilei," *Centro Tedesco di Studi Veneziani* 16 (1980): 3–21.

[10] Cf. Carlo Ossola, *Le antiche memorie del nulla. Con versioni e note a cura di Linda Bisello* (Rome: Edizioni di Storia e Letteratura, 1997).

[11] Cf. Jean-François Lattarico, "Sous l'autorité du bizarre. Le discours académique des Incogniti, entre tradition et subversion," *Cahiers du Celec* 6 (2013): 1–12; http://cahiersducelec.univ-st-etienne.fr/index.php?option=com_content&view=article&id=31%3Acahiersducelec6&Itemid=2.

[12] On Luigi Manzini, cf. Luigi Matt, "Luigi Manzini," in *Dizionario Biografico degli Italiani* 69 (2007); Stanislas Breton, *La pensée du rien* (Kampen: Peeters Publisher, 1992).

[13] Luigi Manzini, *Il Niente [...] Recitato nell'Accademia degl'Incogniti di Venezia, a Ca' Contarini* (Venice: Andrea Baba, 1634).

Your excellent Lords, it will be novel, but it will be true, if I say that the glorious abundance of wits, which felt nauseated by the most common maxims, is now wandering among innovative schools in freedom.[14]

Thanks to their discourses, the members of the *Accademia degli Incogniti* seemed to incline towards a genre based only on pure rhetoric to the detriment of any philosophical and scholarly assumptions, since, as noted by Loredan—who considered them as 'veils which cast a shadow over the truth'—[15] they offer only illusions and uncertainties. Together with Loredan, Manzini defined philosophy as 'hoary and rank,'[16] and, against the authority of science, he also aimed to free the mind from any dogmatic restriction. He accused dogmatic intellects of being betrayers of reason, as of one's own wife:

That libidinous wit, which repudiated its wife—which is Reason—and loves the concubine—which is Authority—, must be condemned for adultery.[17]

It is also known that the discourses or discussions generally held by the members of the Italian Academies were usually called *imprese* (literally 'endeavours'), devices or exercises that must be considered a proper literary genre of the time. According to several authors of the sixteenth and seventeenth centuries who wrote compendiums (also called 'teatri,' literally 'theatres') on this issue, an Academician's choice of a specific image together with a motto qualified a literary work as an *impresa*.

To mention some of the many among both the clergy and laypeople who wrote anthologies about this genre, we may refer to Monsignor Paolo Giovio, whose *Dialogo dell'imprese militari e amorose* (1559), which was held in high esteem by all subsequent authors of this kind of work, delivered some rules for shaping a perfect *impresa*. According to him, it should fulfil five conditions:

Firstly, to respect the correct correlation between soul and body. Secondly, not to be unclear concerning its goal; it must not need a Sybil's interpretation in order to be understood, nor it must be so clear as to be understood by any plebeian. Thirdly, it must look good and appear very cheerful by involving stars, suns, moons, fire, water, green trees, mechanical instruments, bizarre animals, and fabulous birds. Fourthly, it must not select any human shape. Fifthly, it needs a motto, which is the soul of the body and must commonly be in a language different from that of the person undertaking the *impresa* [...]. It must be brief, but not so much that it becomes doubtful; if made of merely two or three words, it would be very good [...].[18]

---

14 Carlo Ossola, ed., *Le antiche memorie del nulla*, 96 (my translation): 'Sarà nuovo, ma sarà vero, VV. Illustrissimi, s'io dirò che 'lusso glorioso degli ingegni, fatt'ormai nauseante delle massime più dimestiche, va peregrinando per le scuole innovatrici della libertà.'
15 *Ibidem*, 96, (my translation): 'veli che adombrano la verità.'
16 *Ibidem*, (my translation): 'canuta and rancida.'
17 *Ibidem* (my translation): 'Condannasi per adultero quell'ingegno libidinoso, che ripudiando la sposa ch'è la Ragione, ama la concubine ch'è l'Autorità.'
18 Paolo Giovio, *Dialogo dell'imprese militari e amorose* (Venice: Gabriel Giolito de' Ferrara, 1559), ed. Maria Luisa Doglio (Rome: Bulzoni, 1978): 6–7 (my translation): 'Sappiate adunque M. Lodovico mio,

A similar description is also given by Abbot Giovanni Ferro in his *Teatro d'imprese*, published in 1623, which is a wonderfully detailed encyclopaedia of all the *imprese* of the time with their symbols and mottos respectively.[19]

One may gather from this short description that the symbol and the motto must anticipate at least part of the content of the book, and also that the motto must be written in a different language from that spoken by the author of the *impresa*.[20]

3 The Oracle of Delphi and the Frontispiece of *Socrate* as Revelatory of Luzzatto's *impresa*

This brief overview of the *Accademia*'s world provides us with significant details with which to initiate a comparison with the genre of and the issues featuring in Luzzatto's *Socrate*. The hypothesis of placing Luzzatto's philosophical work alongside the mission of the Italian Academies, and more precisely the most well-known Academy, the *Accademia degli Incogniti*, may be strengthened by the many exchanges of the noble Venetian Giovan Francesco Loredan and the members of the *Accademia* with some Jews.[21] This interaction between Christians and Jews within the framework of the Academy is proved, for instance, by the connection of Sara Copio Sullam with both Ansaldo Cebà and Baldassarre Bonifacio[22] and by Rabbi Leon Modena's correspondence with Count Maiolino Bisaccioni, Giovanni Argoli, and many other non-

---

che l'Invenzione overo Impresa, s'ella deve havere del buono, bisogna ch'abbia cinque condizioni. Prima, giusta proporzione d'anima e di corpo. Seconda, ch'ella non sia oscura di sorte, c'habbia mestiero la Sibilla per interprete à volerla intendere; né tanto chiara ch'ogni plebeo l'intenda. Terza che sopra tutto habbia bella vista, la qual si fa riuscire molto allegra, entrandovi stelle, soli, lune, fuoco, acqua, arbori verdeggianti, instrumenti mecanici, animali bizzarri, e uccelli fantastici. Quarta, non ricerca alcuna forma umana. Quinta richiede il motto, che è l'anima del corpo, e vuole essere comunemente d'una lingua diversa dall'Idioma di colui, che fa l'impresa, perché il sentimento sia alquanto più coperto. Vuole anco esser breve, ma non tanto che si faccia dubbioso; di sorte che di due o tre parole quadra benissimo; eccetto che fusse in forma di verso, ò integro, ò spezzato.'

19 Cf. Giovanni Ferro, *Teatro d'Imprese* (Venice: Sarzina, 1623): 6: 'L'impresa è una invention dell'ingegno dell'uomo composta di giusta proportione d'anima e di corpo, cioè di brieve motto diverso dall'idioma di colui fa l'impresa, e di vaghe figure fuori dell'humana forma in modo però che né per lo corpo oscura, né per le parole dubbiosa rimanga, per significare parte de' generosi pensieri che in se egli ritiene.'

20 On this topic, see also Giuseppe Veltri and Evelien Chayes, *Oltre le Mura del Ghetto*, 59–62.

21 Cf. *ibidem* and Gaetano Cozzi, "Società veneziana, società ebraica," in *Gli Ebrei e Venezia secoli XIV-XVIII*, ed. Gaetano Cozzi (Milan: Edizioni di Comunità, 1987): 333–374; see also Giuseppe Veltri and Gianfranco Miletto, "Difesa inedita del senatore veneziano Loredan in favore degli ebrei nel 1659–60, basata sul *Discorso* di Simone Luzzatto," in *Filosofo e Rabbino nella Venezia del Seicento. Studi su Simone Luzzatto con documenti inediti dall'Archivio di Stato di Venezia*, ed. Giuseppe Veltri (Rome: Aracne, 2015): 253: '[...] per esser buon Catolico Cristian, è necessario esser perfettamente Ebreo.'

22 Umberto Fortis, *La "bella ebrea": Sara Copio Sullam poetessa nel ghetto di Venezia del '600* (Turin: Silvio Zamorani editore, 2003).

Academicians, who were in contact either with the *Incogniti* or with Leon Modena.[23] Furthermore, we should not neglect to mention a letter from Loredan, which recommended Rabbi Salomon Vita Serravale to Signor Andrea Bradadino in Udine,[24] thus a persuasive demonstration of his attempt to protect a Jew. In the specific case of Rabbi Simone Luzzatto, since we have not yet found documents or correspondence enabling us to prove this exchange directly,[25] most of what we may put forward is suggested by his writings, predominantly by his book *Socrate overo de l'humano sapere*.

Before coming to the issue of the frontispiece of *Socrate*, it would be useful to reflect on the many pieces of information collected in the book's hermetic prose, which might also illuminate Luzzatto's intellectual environment. To mention only some of them, in the opening pages, Luzzatto portrays the fictional image of the foundation of a new Academy in Delphi intended to reform human knowledge. He specifies that the meeting of the Academicians took place in the temple of Apollo and became a pole of attraction for many people coming from many different locations:

> The establishment of an Academy in Delphos was intended to reform human knowledge. In the temple of Apollo,[26] where the assembly [of the Academy] was held, the claim made by Reason that she was imprisoned and oppressed by human Authority could be found in writing.[27]

And a few pages later, Luzzatto repeated:

> Many people from diverse countries came to Delphi for the occasion of the opening of the new Academy, which had the purpose of reforming human knowledge. Some of them were interested in being part of such a noble company, others intended to emend doctrines considered to be absurd. Many of them came just to watch the development and the success of such a useful project. […].[28]

---

23 Cf. Howard Tzevi Adelman, Abstract online: https://www.academia.edu/14931471/Leon_Modena_and_Sarra_Copia_Sullam_and_lAccademia_degli_Incogniti.
24 Cf. Giuseppe Veltri and Evelien Chayes, *Oltre le Mura del Ghetto*, 70–71.
25 The closing statement pronounced in Venice in favour of the Jews and based on the *Discorso* of Simone Luzzatto is unfortunately not yet proof of this, since the speaker, Senator Loredan, defined himself as very young, and thus he cannot be the famous Giovan Francesco Loredan, who at that time was already 64 years old; cf. Giuseppe Veltri and Gianfranco Miletto, "The Difesa inedita del Senatore veneziano Loredan in favore degli ebrei nel 1659–1660," 249–274.
26 Cf. Plutarch, *Moralia, vol. 5: The E at Delphi* (Cambridge, Mass.: Harvard University Press, 1936).
27 Luzzatto, *Scritti politici e filosofici*, 111: 'Essendosi instituita in Delfo Accademia, il cui impiego era la riforma dell'humano sapere, congregatasi nel tempio di Apolline, si ritrova scrittura che per parte della ragione finta carcerata.'
28 *Ibidem*, 112–113: 'Aperta che fu in Delfo l'Accademia reformatrice dell'humano sapere, non pochi di varie nationi vi concorsero. Alcuni per arrolarsi in sì nobile compagnia, altri per procurare emenda ad alcune dottrine a loro parere alquanto assorde. E molti vi si condussero per semplicemente osservare il progresso e riuscita di tanto proficuo proponimento. In quel tempo avenne, che fattasi assemblea nel tempio di Appoline per dar essordio a tal nobile intrapresa, ritrovossi ivi scrittura, che fingendosi colà dalla carcerata ragione inviata, in questo tenore favelava.'

The choice of Apollo's temple in Delphi as a starting point of *Socrate* seems to be consistent with Luzzatto's decision to perform both a Socratic and a sceptical investigation. The temple was indeed the place where the Pythia stated that none was wiser than Socrates (Plato, *Apology* 21a), who, by following one of the famous phrases carved into the entrance of the temple, 'know yourself,' came to the conclusion that the wisest person is the one who becomes aware of not knowing anything. The Delphic exhortation to know himself and the attainment of it as an acknowledgement of human ignorance take on the meaning of a commitment to a persistent inquiry and search for answers. It reproduces in society the ritual manner in which people would deal with the oracle. According to Plutarch's dialogue *On the 'E' of Delphi*, among the famous inscriptions appearing at the entrance of the temple was an enigmatic 'E.' Among the three interpretations that he gave was one which suggested identifying the letter with εἰ ('if') as a fundamental part of the ritual phrase with which one consulted the oracle. Apollo, according to Plutarch, solves the problems of our practical lives on the one hand and on the other is the god who raises intellectual doubts and offers them to whomsoever is naturally a philosopher by inspiring his soul to search for the truth.

The long legacy of the Delphic Oracle over the centuries is also demonstrated by the existence of the Delphic Academy, or Gussonia, in seventeenth-century Venice, founded in 1647 by Francesco Gussonio.[29] It is noteworthy that the little surviving information concerning this Academy suggests that we should consider it as an affiliation of the Academy of *Incogniti*.[30] The latest edition of the book *Cento novelle amorose de Signori Accademici Incogniti*, edited by Maiolino Bisaccioni (1582–1663), a poet and professor of rhetoric at the University of Ferrara and secretary of the Academy at that time, demonstrates that this collection of poems was dedicated to the Delphic Academy, of which many of the *Incogniti* were also members.[31] Furthermore, to confirm that Apollo's temple became a *topos* among the Venetian Academies, and more precisely for the *Incogniti*, there is evidence left in *Le glorie degli Incogniti*

---

[29] The *Accademia Delfica* was hosted in Francesco Gussonio's palace, Grimani a San Fosca, located in the *sestiere* of Cannaregio.

[30] Cf. Francesco Sansovino, *Venezia città nobilissima et singolare, descritta in XIIII libri, con aggiunta di tutte le cose notabili della stessa città, fatte et occorse dall'anno 1580 fino al presente 1663* (Venice: Curti, 1663): 396 and Michele Maylender, *Storia delle Accademie d'Italia*, vol. 2 (Bologna: Cappelli, 1927): 156–157.

[31] *Cento Novelle amorose de Signori Accademici Incogniti* (Venice: Guerigli, 1651): 3r–v: 'A chi altro, che alla nobilissima Accademia de i Delfici convenivansi le fatiche gentilissime della incognita? Gran parte de' nostri Illustrissimi lumi sono stelle del vostro Delfico Cielo. I nostri incogniti vengono a palesarsi tra vostri oracoli e, se qui hanno sensata e teneramente ammoreggiato, così esserciteranno la maestà de' più dotti ragionamenti e de i più vivi sentimenti dell'anima.' A partial translation of this collection was published in England in 1652 with the title *Choise Novels and Amorous Tales, written by the most refined Wits of Italy. Newly translated into English* (London: T.N. for Humphrey Moseley at the sign of the Prince's Arms in St. Paul Churchyard, 1652).

(1647),³² written by Giovan Francesco Loredan. This work, intended to celebrate the results of the collective work of the Academy, also contains a treasury of information for an entire reconstruction of the scene of the Academy itself, namely characters, topics, and even meeting places. Indeed, when Loredan referred, among others, to the poet, jurist, and co-founder of the *Incogniti* Guido Casoni di Serravalle (1561–1642),³³ he did not neglect to mention his house, because it was a lively meeting point for many intellectuals and scholars. What is surprising is that Casoni's house was described by Loredan as being like a new temple of Apollo:

> [...] in order to appease his spirit, he [i.e. Guido Casoni] came to Venice. Here, his house became a new Temple of Apollo and of the Muses, which every day gathered all the greatest intellects who were in this marvellous city at that time.³⁴

This reference may resolve many doubts concerning the fictional place chosen by Luzzatto as the opening scene of his book. It is revealed indeed to have been inspired by an event that was perhaps known or even directly experienced by Luzzatto himself. In addition to this, the hypothesis that he was related to an Academy is strengthened by the image and motto appearing on the frontispiece of *Socrate*, namely the image of a silkworm emerging from its cocoon accompanied by the motto *L'ordito lacero*, which in the vernacular³⁵ means either 'I lacerate the weft' or 'the lacerated weft' (even if the first solution is more plausible, as it also accords with the image of the silkworm in the action of emerging from the cocoon and thus lacerating something originally unbroken).

In the encyclopaedia published by the aforementioned Giovanni Ferro, among the many images and symbols adopted by the Academicians we also find that of the silkworm. Ferro described it as a small worm, the maker of a very fine weft in which it remains rashly imprisoned. Ferro specified that only after many days of captivity does the silkworm emerge from it and that this act of freeing itself might either be seen as a 'rising again' or as a 'rebirth,' depending on the way in which one interprets the cocoon, either as a grave or as a cradle. According to Ferro, the fact that the silkworm's new form is that of a butterfly makes this insect a most suitable metaphor for the human soul, compelled to remain within the body and then, after its death, becoming free to fly up to the sky thanks to the Platonic wings of truth and good,

---

32 Giovan Francesco Loredan, *Le Glorie degli Incogniti overo gli uomini illustri dell'Accademia de' Signori Incogniti di Venetia* (Venice: Francesco Valvasense, 1647).
33 On Guido Casoni, cf. Claudio Mutini, "Guido Casoni," in *Dizionario Biografico degli Italiani* 21 (1978).
34 Loredan, *Le Glorie degli Incogniti*, 293–294 (my translation): 'per tranquillarsi l'animo si ridusse in Venetia, dove la sua casa divenne un novello Tempio d'Apollo, e delle Muse, riducendo egli ogni giorno tutti i più begli spiriti che si trovassero allhora in questa meravigliosa Città.' It was indeed Guido Casoni who suggested to Loredan in 1626 that they should change the name of the Academy from '*Academia Loredana*' to '*Accademia degli Incogniti*.'
35 Which is not surprising, considering what Giovanni Ferro pointed out in his explanation.

formerly lost within the body. [36] Marsilio Ficino's account of the Platonic myth reverberates in Ferro's description. In Ficino's account, on leaving the body, the soul aimed to reach truth and good thanks to its wings, intellect, and will.[37] The two wings of the soul were a recurring topic in the discourses of the *Incogniti*, animated by the longing to catch the truth of things by means of their debunking spirit. Marin Dall'Angelo, in the *Discorsi academici de' Signori Incogniti*, wrote that:

> According to the Platonists, it [i.e. the soul] always maintains the image of its knowledge, to which it is aroused by a continuous longing for the highest good, to understand the truth of things. From this, the Academicians will be persuaded to lift both wings: the desire for the truth and the natural inclination to the good.[38]

The silkworm leaving the cocoon therefore became an allegory of the soul, which, according to Ferro, expressed a different meaning depending on how the silkworm was represented, either as leaving its cocoon, being enclosed in it, or even remaining on the mulberry[39] (*Morus*) tree. To each of those possibilities, there is an alternative corresponding motto, each with a specific meaning.[40] Among these examples, there is also the allusion to some well-known scholars of the time, such as Giovan Battista Della Porta (c. 1535–1615) and Scipione Bargagli (1540–1612), who adopted the

---

36 Cf. Ferro, *Teatro d'Imprese*, 117: 'Baco, o Verme da seta, Ruga: Nasce da picciolo, e quasi non veduto seme minutissimo Verme, il quale à poco à poco pascendosi di frondi di Gelso bianco, cresce alla grandezza di menomissimo dito, e venuto ad età di operare, traspare fuor della pelle il pregio del suo lavoro. Indi fatto di cibo satollo, più à quello non bada, ma comincia à fabricare à se stesso di sottilissimo filo, e di finissima seta, che con la bocca del suo corpicciolo ne trahe stanza, e ricetto. Et è sì fattamente all'opera intento, et à scaricare le ricche merci, che inavedutamente nell'intrecciato, et intessuto artificio resta cattivo, e prigione, e quindi rimane per giorni racchiuso non so se mi dica vivo, ò sepolto. Quindi n'esce poi, né so bene se da culla, ò da tomba, se risorto, ò pur nato, ben diverso da quello di prima, e di verme di terra, n'esce fatto uccelletto dell'aria, à cui d'intorno volando s'aggira. Rassembra un tal animaletto nel mondo, ch'esce dalla boccia, l'anima nostra; che rattenuta nel corpo, quindi col morire ne parte, e dirizza al Cielo il volo con l'ale di Platone, che sono i due naturali desideri del vero, e del bene, perduti da lei nell'unirsi alle membra secondo la loro opinione, riacquistati poi per lo scioglimento di morte. Il che volse intender Dante quando disse: "Non vi accorgete voi, che noi siam vermi/ Nati à formar l'angelica farfalla; / Che vola alla giustitia senza schermi" (Dante, *Purgatory*, X, 124–126).'
37 Cf. Marsilio Ficino, *Platonic Theology*, trans. Michael Allen, ed. James Hankins (Cambridge, Mass.: Harvard University Press, 2006): 6 (Book XVII, Chap. II, 24–27): 'Pythagoreans and Platonists call the soul a chariot and assigns it two wings, the instinct of the intellect for Truth itself and of the will for the Good itself; a charioteer, namely the mind.'
38 Loredan, *Discorsi Academici de' signori Incogniti* (Venice: Sarzina, 1635): 269 (my translation): '[l'anima] conserva però ella sempre secondo I platonici l'immagine del suo sapere, che l'eccitano una continua brama al sommo bene, ad intendere la verità delle cose, da che resteranno persuasi gli accademici ad impennar le due ali. Il desiderio del vero, l'istinto al buono.'
39 Mulberry leaves, especially those of the white mulberry, are indeed the sole source of food for the silkworm.
40 Cf. Ferro, *Teatro d'Imprese*, 118.

image of the silkworm in connection with a motto that seems to be similar to that of Luzzatto: the former wrote *et feci, et fregi* ('I made it and I destroyed it'), and the latter wrote *construxi destruxi* ('I constructed it and I destroyed it').

Even if the images and mottos of Della Porta and Bargagli have different goals, as explained by Ferro's encyclopaedia,[41] they certainly help us by delimiting the range of interpretation of *Socrate*'s frontispiece message. This discovery seems to harmonise elements that have until now appeared disparate, preventing us from having a plausible overview of the meaning and intention of Luzzatto's book.

4 The Soul

Giovanni Ferro's guidelines suggest that the frontispiece is responding to a rhetorical motif, that of the silkworm emerging from its cocoon depicting the soul leaving the prison of the body after death, after which it is finally free to attend again to truth and good. The corresponding motto adopted by Luzzatto, *L'ordito lacero* ('I lacerate the weft'), clearly plays with the image of the silkworm lacerating its cocoon. Luzzatto's symbol and motto reflect his *impresa*, his commitment to sceptically deconstructing any assumed knowledge and dogmatic belief built up by the human intellect, like the weft made by the silkworm. Human intellect, like a silkworm, is imprisoned in its own construction and aims to destroy it in order to search for the truth. The idea of the intellect and the will as the two wings of the soul may explain why the issue of the soul cannot, in the literature of the *Incogniti* or in Luzzatto's *Socrate*, be detached from that of the free investigation of reason in the search for the truth above any dogma. Throughout the entire work, Luzzatto plays with the metaphor of a mind entangled in the ropes of human doctrines. In the very first lines of *Socrate*, Luzzatto clarified that:

> [...] the ambition to release the human mind from the ropes in which it was entangled by the arrogant and too-pretentious knowledge must not be seen as a purpose too daring for a man of my status, as Aesop's mouse managed to free the generous and ferocious lion with its mere gnawing.[42]

Being ensnared in mistakes while being unaware of them is considered by the author as the highest level of ignorance,[43] but likewise, those who persistently inquire and

---

41 Cf. *ibidem*, 119.
42 *Ibidem*, 110: 'Né paia ad alcuno troppo ardita intrapresa ad homo della mia conditione, l'attentare la libertà dell'animo humano inviluppato da lacci, con quali l'ardito e troppo pretendente sapere lo tiene legato e stret|to, poiché l'esopico topo, con il suo minuto rodimento, già sciolse generoso e feroce leone.' He is referring to Aesop, *Fables*, 150 (Perry): 'The Lion and the Mouse.'
43 Cf. *ibidem*, 139: 'Per il vero il sommo dell'ignoranza stimarei che fosse, il ritrovarsi irretito et inviluppato nelli errori, e tutavia non avedersene, per il che pregoi che mi rendi avisato di tale mia inadvertentia, e schiochezza.'

Figure 1. Simone Luzzatto, *Socrate overo Dell'humano sapere* (Venice: Tomasini, 1651): frontispiece. Courtesy of the Ministero dei Beni e delle Attività Culturali e del Turismo—Biblioteca Nazionale Marciana (copyrights)

BACO, O VERME DA SETA, RVGA.

Figure 2. Giovanni Ferro, *Teatro d'Imprese* (Venice: Sarzina, 1623), 118.

debate in search of the truth end up in unsolvable difficulties, like ropes winding around their minds.[44] A human being's intended state is that of being entangled in the ensemble of the alleged human knowledges and not being able to overcome them because of other insurmountable issues, according to Luzzatto, as they are the infinite, the indivisible minimum, the eternal motion, the time (which consumes everything), and the vacuum.[45]

Socrate must be thus conceived as a sapiential path of the mind or the soul, also confirmed by the variety of characters, such as the philosophers, poets, and politicians of ancient Greece who appear during Socrates' wandering and questioning in his report to the judges; this Dantesque atmosphere is also emphasised by the decision of someone like Theaetetus, who is persuaded by Socrates's arguments to follow him in his inquiry[46] even though he then disappears without officially taking

---

44 Cf. *ibidem*, 294: 'Ma in tali salebri et inviluppi ci conducemo per cagione dell'immoderato dibatimento che circa l'investigatione della Verità praticamo.'
45 Cf. *ibidem*, 318.
46 Concerning Theaetetus cf. *ibidem*, 295–296: 'Yet Theaetetus, endowed with a more noble nature and generous spirit, decided to put effort into this inquiry with me. Besides, he did not want to affirm or deny his judgment concerning any dogma in the future before having resolved this investigation.

leave of Socrates. What Socrates reports is indeed an *itinerarium mentis*; it is a tale that covers his entire life. In the beginning, he presents himself at a very young age (*alla mia età alquanto giovanile*)⁴⁷ and then, in the middle of the book, he defines himself as 'old aged' (*della mia senile età*).⁴⁸ This thesis is also consolidated by the occurrence of the expression 'my mental journey' (*mio mental viaggio*)⁴⁹ or 'mental path' (*mentale cammino*),⁵⁰ through which Socrates describes his commitment to investigating knowledge throughout his life. Just as the soul, by leaving the prison of the body, can finally attain the truth, so too Socrates' free investigation, as an exercise of his *scepsis*, must be understood as a process of deconstructing human doctrines in favour of the only truth, that of God. Together with an evident Platonic dualism of mind and body, one may also acknowledge in Luzzatto's work traces of the Aristotelian tradition, in which 'mind' (*nous*) is also rendered as 'intellect' or 'reason' and thus as the part of the soul by which it knows and understands.⁵¹ Luzzatto indeed identified the issue of the intellect with that of the soul by bringing the debate towards the question of its immortality on a purely gnosiological level. This is confirmed by the fact that the terms 'mind,' 'intellect,' 'reason,' '*animus*' and '*anima*' are used interchangeably for the same intellectual faculty. Once he comes to the examination of the intellect, Socrates proposed proceeding in the following way:

> Firstly, to investigate what the intellect is.
> Secondly, whether there is one being or many beings at the helm of our government.
> Thirdly, what its actions and functions are.
> Fourthly, to what it addresses its operations.
> Fifthly, in which part of us it resides and dwells.
> Sixthly, how much time it requires for its ordinary actions.
> Seventhly, by what means it carries out its actions.
> Eighthly, by which order it rules and practices its discourses.
> Ninthly, in which way it carries out its decisions.
> Tenthly, the goal of so much work, and what it is attempting to achieve and obtain.⁵²

As soon as Socrates begins his inquiry, he encounters the same difficulty experienced in any field of knowledge, namely the existence of different and conflicting opinions. The investigation into the essence of the intellect becomes, of course, an examination of the many views expressed in the history of ancient philosophy about the soul. Luzzatto therefore provides an overview that ranges from ancient theories, as reported in Aristotle's *On the Soul*, to modern positions, such as that of the

---

He considered the presumption of knowing the condition of anything while one is ignorant of what that same knowledge is to be an unreasonable claim.'
47 *Ibidem*, 153.
48 *Ibidem*, 194.
49 *Ibidem*, 265; 322.
50 *Ibidem*, 340; 249.
51 Aristotle, *On the soul*, III 4 (429a9–10); cf. III 3 (428a5); III 9 (432b26); III 12 (434b3).
52 Luzzatto, *Scritti politici e filosofici*, 228.

soul as the pilot of a ship, put forward by Giordano Bruno in his *Cause, Principle and Unity* (1584) through the words of Teofilo:

> [...] while I was searching for the essence of the intellect, on which all its other conditions depend, I encountered the same difficulties that had already arisen when dealing with the ancient principles of things. I found opposing and discordant opinions as much towards the former [i.e. the intellect] as the latter [i.e. the principles of things]: indeed, the authors asserted the soul to be like their asserted principles of things. Rather, there were those who considered it [i.e. the soul] as a feeble and very thin spirit, namely a compound of blood mixed with air;[53] others [considered it] as a fragment of world's universal soul,[54] a source of life for it [i.e. the world] [...]. Others [considered it] as simple power borne by an internal material organ.[55] Others, in general, uttered that this illustrious faculty called the soul was perfectly placed in a part of the body. Yet others spread around that it was like a coachman in a chariot,[56] or like the helmsman of a ship,[57] who assists and leads his mobile abode and portable dwelling. Others said that it had originated from a certain agent intellect; [the soul is] not separated from it, but also not identical to it.[58] Others declared that it is nothing other than a portion of the excellent magnet,[59] induced to say this by the correspondence of aversions and inclinations between the mind and the magnet. But I would be too prolix if I wanted to meticulously refer to all [the opinions]. And, in conclusion, there was also someone who, with daring recklessness, declared that the intellect was a name without a subject and merely a simple activity produced by the combination and separation of the already-perceived relics of sensations. Yet others considered, with more grounded reason, that it was an immortal essence dwelling in the body.[60]

It must be pointed out that to present such a variety of opinions is part of Luzzatto's sceptical strategy for showing that there is no certain and unquestionable knowledge even concerning the soul. Although he qualified the position of those who defended the immortality of the soul and its transitory dwelling in the body as 'more reasonable,' he nevertheless specified his intention in the following way:

> I have collected and presented all these opinions not because I am inclined to assent to them, but in order to demonstrate the scale of the incapacity of our understanding in acknowledging its own and essential nature, while on the contrary it dares to discover the most hidden and remote causes of the universe.[61]

---

53 Cf. Aristotle, *On the Soul*, A (405b 5–10): he was referring to Critias's opinion.
54 This is the Stoic position.
55 Luzzatto seems to be referring to Aristotle's concept of passive or potential intellect (*On the Soul*, III, 4).
56 Cf. Plato, *Phaedrus*, 246 a-b.
57 Cf. Giordano Bruno, *Causa, principio et uno* (Venice: 1584); idem, *Cause, Principle and Unity*, ed. Richard J. Blackwell (Cambridge: Cambridge University Press, 1998), 2nd dialogue.
58 Luzzatto seems to be referring to the Averroistic position, which defends the separation of the agent intellect and passive intellect respectively from the individual soul, but also as two separated substances, as two aspects of one same substance.
59 Cf. Aristotle, *On the Soul*, A2 (405a 20–22): reference to Thales.
60 Luzzatto, *Scritti politici e filosofici*, 229. In the last passage, Luzzatto is referring to the Pythagorean and Platonic opinions.
61 *Ibidem*.

Even if Socrates allows the reader to briefly believe that he inclines to the opinion of those who profess the immortality of the soul, Luzzatto comes to undermine what he has previously affirmed and does so by means of the 'serious-playfulness.' Indeed, he begins to mock the same theory through which Plato supported the thesis of the immortality of the soul, namely that of the *anamnesis* developed in the dialogues *Meno*, *Phaedo*, and partially in *Phaedrus*. In his book, Luzzatto recalls, in a humorous way, the famous scene from *Meno* in which Socrates employs maieutics to demonstrate that even a slave boy who knows nothing about geometry can solve a geometrical issue only by remembering what he has merely forgotten. The theory of *anamnesis* is presented ironically by Socrates as a simple figure of speech which he once playfully expressed but which was then taken seriously by the majority of the people and subsequently spread and was accepted by many learned men.[62] Luzzatto continues playing with the metaphors of the soul offered by Plato's dialogues: he recalls, for example, the tripartite human soul presented in the dialogue *Phaedrus*, in which the soul is represented allegorically as a chariot driven by a charioteer, which is the rational part, and pulled by two horses, which represent respectively the irascible and concupiscent parts of the soul.[63] Furthermore, he also provides us with another classical image, that of the oyster bound to its shell, as a symbol of the soul's relation to the body, originally adopted by Plato in his *Phaedrus*[64] and then taken up, with some variations, among Stoic, Neoplatonic, and early Christian thinkers.[65] Luzzatto focuses on a specific aspect of this metaphor, namely the static nature of the mollusc, with its shell permanently attached to the stone. Through this image, he clearly summarised the position of those who believe in the passivity of our intellect and claimed that the activity of knowing must be reduced to that of receiving the influences of the external senses:

> For this reason, the author of such a dogma considers the intellect similar to an oyster, which, remaining fixed on a stone, is endowed only with the faculty of opening and closing itself.[66]

It cannot be overlooked that the soul represents a very significant and sensitive topic in the philosophical and theological debates of the seventeenth century, in which ecclesiastical and university authorities did not tolerate those who denied its immortality or even those who put forward ideas leading to such a conclusion. This topic had been widely discussed since the Fifth Lateran Council (1512–1517), especially after the publication of the treatise by Pietro Pomponazzi (1462–1525) entitled *On the Immortality of the Soul* in 1516, in which he dealt for the first time (following the meth-

---

62 Cf. *ibidem*, 270.
63 Plato, *Phaedrus*, 246a-254e.
64 *Ibidem*, 250c.
65 Cf. Erminio Caprotti, "La metafora dell'ostrica e la condizione umana," *Bollettino Malacolologico* 45.2 (2009): 99–104.
66 Luzzatto, *Scritti politici e filosofici*, 236: 'l'autore di tal dogma, ad ostrica marina, che stando affissa ad un sasso di altra facoltà non si trova dotata che d'aprirsi e rachiudersi.'

ods of Aristotelian philosophy) with an issue that up until that time had belonged only to the theological sphere. The questions that Pomponazzi raised on this topic were certainly decisive for the ensuing debate concerning human free will and the dialectic between the intellect and the will, which was the origin of a lively discussion and investigation in the Italian Academies from the second half of the sixteenth century.

The Jewish commitment to this topic must be considered symptomatic of a response to—or an attempt at dialogue with—the Christian world. Indeed, Jews did not spontaneously engage in any controversy on this issue, nor did they directly write on the immortality of the soul, but when they did, they did so either in Latin or in their vernacular language and not in Hebrew,[67] and only because of the need to defend themselves, as in the well-known case of Sara Copio Sullam and Baldassare Bonifaccio, or to look for support among the Christian side, as was the case for Menasseh ben Israel.[68]

Thus, Luzzatto too, probably under the influence of tendencies dominating the *Accademia degli Incogniti* where the discussion on the soul was very lively, seems to pursue this issue to the extent that it does not end up in a new dogmatic position. He built the entire framework of his *Socrate* on the grounds of a traditional outline, that of the soul imprisoned in the body, but only as a metaphor of both the contemporary condition of the human mind and the necessity of breaking down the prison in which that same mind had trapped itself over the centuries. The exercise of doubt in *Socrate* indeed does not come to a halt even before this crucial topic, and it continues further up until the suspension of judgement. Luzzatto took shelter from any criticism thanks to the title of his work, in which is clearly stated not only his aim of showing the 'incapability of human intelligence when it is not led by divine revelation,' but also that he will play with the ambiguous borderline between what is permitted and what is not, thanks to the expression 'serious-playful exercise.' Through the 'serious-playfulness,' he invites the readership not to take what he intends to present entirely seriously. In this way, Luzzatto enables himself to freely investigate and bring into question all human knowledge traditionally accepted as true.

5 Free Inquiry and Revelation in Luzzatto's *Socrate*

In accordance with these tendencies, philosophy, as a collection of alleged truths, is described throughout *Socrate* as an abyss, which, instead of increasing and motivating the advancement of learning, has blinded Socrates' reasoning:

---

[67] Cf. Alessandro Guetta, "The Immortality of the Soul and an Opening to the Christian World: A Chapter in Early Modern Jewish-Italian Literature," in *Hebraic Aspects of the Renaissance: Sources and Encounters*, eds. Ilana Zinguer, Abraham Melamed, and Zur Shalev (Leiden and Boston: Brill, 2011): 105.
[68] *Ibidem.*

> I think that you well know, Lord Judges, that in my youth I devoted myself to the exercise of philosophy with much diligence and solicitude, without of course disregarding those arts such as painting, sculpture, arithmetic, music, and the like, which are held in high regard and esteem by us Greeks. But while I was advancing in the latter, I obtained different, rather contrary success in the former. The more I entered into the above-mentioned arts, the more I profited from them, but the deeper I delved into philosophy, the more I encountered inextricable difficulties which made my mind so confused and upset that the vertigo produced by the irreconcilable altercations and opposed and balanced opinions blinded the light of my reason, and almost extinguished it.[69]

The development of Luzzatto's entire inquiry is thus a result of an 'exercise of the free intellect,' namely a demonstration of the wandering of the mind when it is not restricted by the limits imposed by the authority of what is traditionally and dogmatically accepted as the truth. Throughout the work, Socrates reproaches himself repeatedly for having held the authority of ancient wisdom, which was at the origin of the consolidation of errors, in too high an esteem. An example can be seen in a passage in which Socrates is debating with Gorgias concerning *ens*:

> Now, therefore, persuaded by your instances, I would judge that it is possible to obtain cognition as much of being as of non-*ens*, since apprehensibility is common to both of them. Thus, our apprehension will turn out to be our internal affection rather than the image of an external object. This is a thought very different from the one that I so rashly had before, while I held the authority of the ancient wise men in too much veneration: indeed, I uttered that *ens* was the only object that correctly matched the wide content of the mind.[70]

The opinions coming from the past, which established our traditional knowledge, represent the limit which Luzzatto, with his sceptical inquiry, aims to overcome. For this reason, his free intelligence and deconstructive power now celebrate the freedom of thought and inquiry. The text is rich in praise for any performances produced by the free exercise of the wit. It is no coincidence that *Socrate*'s incipit was

---

69 Luzzatto, *Scritti politici e filosofici*, 123: 'Stimo non esservi affatto occulto, Signori Giudici, con quanta applicatione et urgenza d'animo, nella mia giovenile età m'impiegai nelli esercitii della filosofia, non trascurando n'anco quelle arti che in maggior pregio e stima appo noi Greci si ritrovano, come la pittura, scultura, aritmetica, musica, e simili, onde progredendo in queste et in quella, diverso anzi contrario successo incontrai. Nell'arti predette quanto più m'inoltravo, tanto maggiormente profitavo, ma nella filosofia, alquanto in essa internandomi, in difficoltà inestricabili mi conducevo, onde a tal segno divenne la mia mente confusa e turbata, che la vertigine delle irreconciliabili altercationi e contraposte et equilibratte opinioni il lume del discorso di essa mi abbagliò, e quasi affatto spense. Il che tanto più mi turbò, osservando io che circa li primi principii dell'universal esser delle cose, tanto varii e repugnanti ritrovansi li pareri delli più insigni cultori della filosofia.'
70 *Ibidem*, 144: 'Giudicarei hora dunque, persuaso dalle tue instanze, che tanto dell'esser quanto del non ente si possa ottener|ne cognitione, essendo l'apprensibilità comune tanto all'uno quanto all'altro. Onde perciò l'apprendimento piuttosto nostro resentimento interno che imagine di oggetto esterno riuscirà. Pensiero assai diverso da quello già inavedutamente stimavo, tenendo per inanzi in troppo veneratione l'autorità delli antichi sapienti, mentre pronontiai, che l'ente solamente fosse l'aggiustato oggetto, che all'ampla continentia della mente corispondesse.'

found in a letter which was supposed to have been written by Reason, who claimed that she had been oppressed by her daughter Authority with the help of Fame and Custom and then hidden in a prison by Felony. Reason describes the behaviour of Authority and begs the Academicians to free her from her isolation:

> Hence since this dishonest one [i.e. Felony] began to take despotic control of human matters, mankind has stopped investigating and discussing the purpose towards which men must proceed and the goal towards which it is worthwhile to address their actions, but instead only takes care that a numerous crowd moves in this direction; indeed, Authority established that it was not the weight of opinions, but only a large number of supporters that was the wisest demonstration of the truth. Furthermore, Felony also ungratefully attempted to deny her lineage from me [i.e. Reason], pretending to have been derived from some other external principles and foreign origins. Yet what really offended me most was her arbitrary manipulation and upheaval of everything, even though she is not even armed with mediocre virtues, nor even decorated with powerful weapons, nor provided with other instruments; indeed, she has only illusory appearances and false arts. Indeed, she put forward her position only by means of sumptuous dresses, authoritative postures, wrinkled foreheads, intimidating glances, narrowed eyes, concise and ambiguous words, brief and reluctant conversations, contemptuous and delusory manners, obstinate and inflexible assertions, shameless boasting, and affected acclaim from a vulgar and impudent group of indolent satellites, and every other thing attributed to her by deceitful Fame and confirmed by obstinate Custom, both of them promoters of her acclaim and commendation. In this way, she has continued to oppress mankind. Since then, an infinite number of mad people have followed her, and a smaller number of wise men are destined to succumb to those who are more powerful and numerous. Hence, her violence is so tyrannical that I ask and implore Your magnanimous and generous virtues to take immediate charge of restraining such an inhuman traitor. If the perfidious one is defeated by Your great merit and I am restored to my original position, I promise that I will grant the doctrines their former glory so that mankind can retrieve its lost decorum.[71]

---

71 *Ibidem*, 114: 'Da quindi è che havendo la iniqua occupato il despotico dominio delli affari humani, non più s'indaga e consulta, a qual scopo incaminare li omini si devono, et a qual fine il traino delle loro attioni dirigere li con|venga, ma solamente è ricercato se numerosa folla, e turba a quella volta viaggi, essendo dall'autorità decretato, che non il peso de pareri, ma il copioso loro satelitio sia il saggio cimento della verità. E per non lasciare alla ingratitudine che desiderare, già ardisce negare da me trahere li suoi natali, pressumendo da strani principii et alieni esordii dedurre la sua genealogia. E quello che più mi offende, che non essendo pur anco di mediocre virtù armata, né da vigorose arme decorata, nondimeno il tutto a suo arbitrio ragira e sconvolve, né de altri adminicoli rimane provista, che de illusorie apparenze, e falaci arti, havendosi cotanto avanzata solamente con l'aiuto di pomposi vestiti, gravi portamenti, rugosa fronte, torva vista, accigliati occhi, concise et ambigue parole, scarsa e ritrosa conversatione, sprezzanti e delusorii trattamenti, ostinate et inflessibili assertioni, inverecondi milantamenti, affettate acclamationi di volgari e sfrontato satelitio di scioperati, e di tutto quello che le tiene attaccato et ingionto, la bugiarda fama, e confirmato le ha la contumace consuetudine, de' suoi applausi e comendationi promotrici. Questi sono li mezzi con che essa tiene oppresso il genere umano, ché essendo come che infiniti li pazzi che la seguono, conviene a' savii di minor numero, soccombere a più potenti, e numerosi. Hor dunque essendo a tal segno giunta la tirannica violenza di costei, invito et imploro la magnanima e generosa Vostra virtù che alla depressione della dishumanata proditrice, con presentaneo provedimento vi accoriate, ché se giamai per il Vostro egregio valore rimanesse la perfida debelata, et io al pristino stato ridonata, promettovi restituire alle dottrine il perduto loro splendore, et al vostro genere lo smarrito decoro.'

According to this narrative fiction, the new Academicians define this letter as the 'product of ingenuity, which is free and without limit'[72] and, after a long discussion, they agree to free her and to pull Authority down from her conquered throne.

Only at this moment is Socrates, charged with having attempted to subvert traditional knowledge, called to defend himself. His defence cannot be conceived otherwise than as an expression of free thought and speech beyond the limit of what one is officially allowed to say. Socrates and all his interlocutors in this long inquiry are aware that they are in a highly sensitive field, namely that of questioning and doubting, which has the potential to destroy what is defined as the 'admirable framework of human knowledge' or even to dismantle its very foundations. Nevertheless, the fictional deposition of Authority from her office creates the perfect scene for the free expression of Socrates, who claimed to have devoted his whole life to free reasoning, which is the sole foundation on which his charge can be based.[73] All the characters who demonstrated the courage to speak out against any dogmatic knowledge during Socrates' questioning are commended for this freedom: to mention only one of them, we see Theophrastus, presented by Luzzatto as a critic of the syllogism of Aristotle:

> 'I consider that this was Aristotle's approach to human knowledge. Since he was completely informed of the incapability and weakness of human knowledge and fruitlessly devoted so much study to finding the truth, he proposed this syllogism, full of so many difficulties and arduous circumstances that one could never solve it. Hence, some intelligent men simply attributed the difficulty to their own ineptitude and not to the impossibility of the matter, and held undamaged the esteem they had for the author of this syllogism. A most evident sign of this was that he [i.e. Aristotle] has never formed a syllogism that could fulfil all the numbers and the many conditions he put forth through so much speculation. Similarly, a clue to this was that he exemplified his syllogism by appealing to our Greek alphabet. Therefore, he did not represent his syllogisms using appropriate examples, because if he had represented them in real terms, we would have immediately recognised the invalidity of such a structure.' Here ended Theophrastus' examination. I commended him for being an untangled and free intellect, and, despite the familiarity he had with Aristotle, for not having acquired that obstinacy which is peculiar to his [i.e. Aristotle] followers.[74]

---

72 *Ibidem*, 115.
73 *Ibidem*.
74 *Ibidem*, 307–308: 'A questo modo apunto stimo che Aristotele si diportasse circa il saper humano, che ritrovandosi appieno informato dell'imbecilità e fiachezza dell'humano sapere, et havendo infrutuosamente consumato molto studio per rinvenire la verità, propose tale silogismo pieno di tante difficoltà et ardue circonstantie, a modo tale che giamai a capo di esso devenire non si potesse, onde l'homini d'ingegno semplice attribuendo la difficoltà alla loro propria inettia, e non alle impossibiltà del fatto, conservassero appo loro illesa la conceputa stima dell'autore di tal silogismo. Segno evidentissimo di ciò mi fu che giamai nel corso di tante sue speculationi non formasse silogismo tale, che adempiuto havesse tutti li suoi numeri, e che tante conditioni possedesse, quante che da esso proposte furno. Indicio di ciò parimente mi fu, che essemplificando egli tal suo silogismo ricorse al nostro greco alfabeto, onde con non proprii essempii rappresentò suoi silogismi, ché se con termini reali rafigurati l'havesse, immediate riconosciuta si harebbe l'invalidità di tali machine". Havendo qui fatto fine Teofrasto al suo divisare, lo comendai d'ingegno sciolto e libero, e che la famigliarità che tenne con Aristotele non li arrecò quella tenacità che proprio è di suoi seguaci.'

Another one is Timon, the renowned misanthrope of ancient Greece who entertained Socrates with his argumentations, which bravely despised the supposed wisdom of mankind. In this case, Socrates also takes his leave by expressing his appreciation for Timon's free speech.[75]

Yet in order to acquire an overview of this very complex work, it will be necessary first to explain a potential solution to the problem of combining the two facets of Luzzatto's commitment, namely that of the religious thinker and that of the natural philosopher,[76] highly praised by Rabbi Josef Delmedigo in his *Sefer Elim* for his great expertise in natural sciences such as mathematics and astronomy.[77] In this regard, it will be useful to view the relationship between God's omnipotence and human freedom of inquiry in Luzzatto's work.

Even if the references to God throughout the text are few, and although the majority of them invoke his name in order to express hopes and wishes, nevertheless, the few remaining mentions are very significant, because they strengthen the position of God as an essential concept of *Socrate*. God, as divine revelation, appears in the title of the book as a leader of human intelligence. He is also identified as a harbour of truth[78] and as the one who, together with providence, persists in our minds against the ravages of time;[79] he dispenses wisdom to humans,[80] and finally, Luzzatto writes, he finds his true temple in the mind or soul of the wise man.[81] God must thus be considered as the author of the whole architecture of this theatre, namely the load-bearing component of all the inquiry performed by Luzzatto in his work. Nevertheless, the presence of God does not impede Luzzatto from developing his reckless investigation by stressing the capacity of reason through the sceptical method: the expression 'serious-playful' appearing in the title helps him to repel criticism coming from outside, from hasty readers, as a result of misunderstanding some passages of *Socrate*, but with God, Luzzatto does not need any stratagem.

Luzzatto, whom we might even consider as a precursor of the Jewish Haskalah, in agreement with Isaac Barzilay's study,[82] does not doubt his faith by questioning traditional knowledge, the so-called 'truth'; he knows that this right belongs to

---

75 *Ibidem*, 393.
76 Cf. Ruderman, "Science and Skepticism. Simone Luzzato on Perceiving the Natural World," 154.
77 Cf. Josef Delmedigo, *Sefer Elim* (Odessa, 1865): 131; cf. Ruderman, "Science and Skepticism: Simone Luzzato on Perceiving the Natural World," 156.
78 Luzzatto, *Scritti politici e filosofici*, 322.
79 *Ibidem*, 358.
80 *Ibidem*, 341.
81 *Ibidem*, 397.
82 Cf. Isaac Barzilay, "The Italian and Berlin Haskalah (Parallels and Differences)," *Proceedings of the American Academy for Jewish Research* 29 (1960–1961): 21: 'as late as the middle of seventeenth century, when the liberal tradition of Renaissance days was already past history, and the Ghetto system a universal institution in most Italian cities, it was still the view of the Rabbi Simone Luzzatto of Venice, that the pursuit of secular learning was vital for the Jews as a means in their struggle for survival.'

him and that it was granted by the same God. What might only be supposed by reading *Socrate* is rather confirmed by one of the author's earlier writings, a brief introduction composed for the *Ṣafnat Pa'neaḥ* ('Revealing Enigmas') in 1640 written by Samuel ha-Cohen of Pisa and published in 1656 in Venice at the Martinelli printing house. In a few pages of text, written in Hebrew, Luzzatto developed the defence of Job, accused of having denied resurrection after death. Thanks to rhetorical strategies, Luzzatto argued for clemency for Job throughout the introduction and concluded by saying:

> It is also part of God's mercy and goodness toward His creatures that He has permitted them to inquire into and examine the way in which the world is governed and [the way in which] His ways are balanced (*hashva'at middotav*) in his glorious order [...]. And just as choice flows from the will [so that] a man may incline it toward whatever he turns and decides, so the intellect is free, according to each and every man's level, to consider and explore any subject he wishes.[83]

In addition to this, he also clarifies another relevant aspect, namely that if our will is free, then our intellect will be even more so, and that it will push its exploring, wandering, and searching far beyond the limits of what is necessary, according to its own capacities.[84] Luzzatto adopts Hebrew verbs such as *lehaśkil* ('to intelligise') and *latur* ('to explore,' 'wandering in search') in order to define this specific freedom granted by God to human beings. Although we are still in the sphere of what is permitted by God, nevertheless Luzzatto does not fail to point out that the human being who intelligises and explores strengthens a specific freedom—human curiosity—which, as is known, is limitless and thus it cannot be foreseen how far it may go. Luzzatto seems to share here not only the Aristotelian statement according to which the desire to know is an innate characteristic of human beings,[85] but also, and especially, the spirit of an entire age; the Baroque, in which the literary work is an innovative and provocative product of the mind. It is meant as an exercise of the intelligence in connecting images from different semantic levels as expressions of a new concept of time and space dominated by the awareness of the caducity of life and the constant changes of nature. This new perspective, as a consequence of scientific discoveries which on the one hand had enlarged the human horizons of nature and on the other had thrown into crisis what was once an unquestionable system of knowledge, is reflected in Luzzatto's work in the sense of confusion and uncertainty concerning the human ability to know:

---

83 Samuel ha-Cohen, *Ṣafnat Pa'neaḥ* (Venice: Martinelli, 1656): 2v-4r. The translation is from Bernard Septimus, "Biblical Religion and Political Rationality in Simone Luzzatto, Maimonides and Spinoza," in *Jewish Thought in the 17th Century*, eds. Isadore Twersky and Bernard Septimus (Cambridge, Mass.: Harvard University Press, 1987): 399–400.
84 Cf. Samuel ha-Cohen, *Ṣafnat Pa'neaḥ*, 4r.
85 Cf. Aristotle, *Metaphysics*, I (980a-980b).

Yet if human intellect must apply itself to the cognition of natural things, at all times it remains embroiled, among the other torments, in five cruel and constantly tormenting objects: the infinity, which distracts it [i.e. the intellect]; the divisible minimum, which compresses it; motion, which agitates it; time, which consumes it; and space or the vacuum, which reduce it to nothing. They are such thorny matters that the one who presumes to finally intelligise them will be certainly unhappy, if he is entangled in them. And what is even worse is that another disaster also occurs to us, namely that just as the sea is commanded and beaten by contrary winds and does not know which one it should obey, so the mind, distracted many times by contrary evidence and differently influenced by opposite instances, does not know how to decide which of them to believe or to accept.[86]

6 Conclusion

It is not surprising that Luzzatto chose Socrates as the leader of his inquiry: this legendary figure perfectly embodies the human desire for knowledge, and, since the earliest theological controversies, has symbolised the first authentic free thinker as well as a victim of intolerance.[87] Luzzatto's aim is to demonstrate the limits of the human capacity to know without the guidance of divine revelation as the only source of truth; nevertheless, he does not renounce the right to investigate, and sets his desire to know free to operate against dogmatism as a sign of free thought and expression. The whole book must be conceived as an 'exercise in free thinking' against previously established knowledge. Socrates maintains that he was pushed to put forward what he defines as his inquiry towards knowledge by 'the curiosity and restlessness of his wit.' His goal is to appease the human soul by freeing it from false opinions, which are, according to Luzzatto, those unquestionable doctrines delivered by tradition. His subversive aim, of which his *Socrate* is strong evidence, may be better understood only by placing it alongside the Academic mission.

From this contribution, it follows that Luzzatto shared many traits with the Academic world and, more particularly, with the *Incogniti*. First of all, the frontispiece of the book reveals his adherence to the genre of the *imprese*: Luzzatto, according to the

---

[86] Luzzatto, *Scritti politici e filosofici*, 318: 'Ma se alla cognitione delle cose naturali l'humano intelletto incombe, fra li altri tormenti a cinque oggetti crudeli e sempre flagellanti egli si comette: all'infinito che lo distrahe, al minimo indivisibile che lo comprime, al motto che l'agita, al tempo che lo consuma, et al loco over vacuo che l'inanisce, materie tanto piene di spinosità ch'infelice per il certo è colui mentre che in esse invilupato, presume venire a capo della loro intelligenza. E quello è peggio che altro disastro ci occorre, che siccome il mare da contrarii venti comandato e percosso, non sa a qual di essi obedire, così la mente molte fiatte distratta da contrarie evidenze, e da repugnanti instanze diversamente raguagliata, non sa né può deliberare a quale di esse prestare debba la sua credenza et assenso.'

[87] On Socrates' legacy, cf. Michael Trapp, ed., *Socrates from Antiquity to the Enlightenment and Socrates in the Nineteenth and Twentieth Centuries* (Aldershot: Ashgate, Centre for Hellenic Studies, 2007) and Sara Ahbel-Rappe and Rachana Kamtekar, eds., *A companion to Socrates* (Hoboken: Blackwell Pub, 2009).

aforementioned rules laid down by some of his contemporaries, chose an image and a motto for his work, namely that of the silkworm emerging from the cocoon and the motto of *L'ordito lacero*, written in the vernacular. Secondly, the modes of playful expression, parody, and ambiguity through which he treated some extremely crucial issues of his time, such as the topic of the immortality of the soul, is another fundamental clue framing Luzzatto's work in a specific context. The expression *serio-giocoso* ('serious-playful') announced in the title indeed demonstrates that Luzzatto's work should be viewed as participating in the tradition of *serio ludere* ('to play seriously'), very popular in the Renaissance and early modern period.[88] Thirdly, Luzzatto seems to share the anti-authoritarian tendency of the *Incogniti*. He criticises the authority of established and traditional knowledge, of which philosophy is a part, in favour of freedom of thought and expression, and he achieves this goal through a specific sceptical rhetoric formed by the alternation of questions and answers and an eclectic adoption of an Aristotelian epistemological language, as well as through metaphors gathered from Plato's dialogues together with his dualistic metaphysics. The entire book may be considered a wise defence and celebration of the free production of ingenuity beyond any dogmatic restriction.

---

[88] Cf. Maria V. White, *Serio Ludere: Baroque* Invenzione *and the development of the Capriccio* (unpublished doctoral thesis, Columbia University 2009).

Guido Bartolucci
Jewish Thought vs. Lutheran Aristotelism: Johann Frischmuth (1619–1687) and Jewish Scepticism[1]

The history of Jewish scepticism is articulated within a series of definitions and principles that are often not easily distinguishable. If scepticism has, in fact, been part of the history of Jewish tradition, the central issue has to be whether this phenomenon was due to the fact that it was influenced by ancient scepticism or whether this philosophical and strategic ability was already part of the history of Jewish thought.[2]

Some scholars, for example, in reading the works written by Jewish intellectuals who lived between the second half of the sixteenth century and the first half of the seventeenth century, have noticed a particular Jewish interest in classical sceptical philosophy. The Venetian rabbi Simone Luzzatto was one of the main figures of Jewish scepticism. Between 1638 and 1651, he published two works in Venice which collected important references to classical scepticism.[3] Luzzatto's use of this particular philosophy can be interpreted in different ways. On the one hand, we can argue that Luzzatto was imitating the Christian apologetics (such as Giovan Francesco Pico della Mirandola) who used sceptical tools to delegitimise classical philosophical knowledge. On the other hand, a second possible interpretation is that the Jewish rabbi wanted to show a relationship between scepticism and Jewish tradition, particularly with the Talmud, which used doubt as one of its main strategies of argumentation.[4]

---

[1] This paper is the preliminary result of research into Jewish scepticism as viewed through the eyes of Protestants, which Giuseppe Veltri and I will develop in the next few years. My contribution, therefore, must be read together with Veltri's.

[2] Giuseppe Veltri, "Principles of Jewish Skeptical Thought. The Case of Judah Moscato and Simone Luzzatto," in *Rabbi Judah Moscato and the Jewish Intellectual World of Mantua in 16th-17th Centuries*, eds. Giuseppe Veltri and Gianfranco Miletto (Boston and Leiden: Brill, 2012): 15–36; idem, "Maharal against Azaria de Rossi: The other side of Skepticism," in *Rabbinic Theology and Jewish Intellectual History: The Great Rabbi Loew of Prague*, ed. Meir Seidel (Oxford: Oxford University Press, 2012): 65–76; and idem, "Do/Did the Jews Believe in God? The Skeptical Ambivalence of Jewish Philosophy of Religion," in *Envisioning Judaism: Studies in Honor of Peter Schäfer on the Occasion of his Seventieth Birthday*, vol. 2, eds. Ra'anan Boustan et alii (Tübingen: Mohr Siebeck, 2013): 717–733.

[3] Simone Luzzatto, *Discorso circa lo stato degli Hebrei et in particolar dimoranti nell'inclita città di Venezia*, (Venice: Gioanne Calleoni, 1638) and idem, *Socrate overo dell'Humano sapere* (Venice: Tomasini, 1651).

[4] On Luzzatto, see Simone Luzzatto, *Scritti politici e filosofici di un rabbino scettico nella Venezia del Seicento*, ed. Giuseppe Veltri (Milan: Bompiani, 2013); Giuseppe Veltri, ed., *Filosofo e Rabbino nella Venezia del Seicento: Studi su Simone Luzzatto con documenti inediti dall'Archivio di Stato di Venezia* (Rome: Aracne, 2015); and Giuseppe Veltri and Evelien Chayes, *Oltre le Mura del Ghetto: Accademie, scetticismo e tolleranza nella Venezia barocca* (Palermo: New Digital Press, 2016).

The study of Jewish tradition, however, is not the only useful way to analyse the link between Judaism and scepticism. An interesting point of view is the Christian interpretation of Judaism, particularly from the sixteenth century onward. In fact, at the beginning of this period, the combination of philological knowledge of the sources (first promoted by Lorenzo Valla and then by Erasmus of Rotterdam) and the Lutheran *sola scriptura* stimulated the study of Hebrew and spread it throughout Europe.[5] This new field of research became one of the main areas in which different religious confessions and political ideas began to challenge one another. Biblical and post-biblical literature became, therefore, one of the tools used by different Christian confessions in theological, political, and philosophical struggles, especially in the seventeenth century. One of the strategies for legitimising the use of these sources was to interpret them through the classical tradition, namely by finding political models comparable to Aristotle's philosophy within the history of the Jewish people.[6] During the English Revolution, for example, political references to Jewish tradition were more common than references to Aristotle, Plato, or Roman republicanism in legitimising the main turning points of the struggle between the monarchy and Parliament, including the beheading of King Charles I.[7] The European debate on Oliver Cromwell's victory and the reaction to the killing of the king were thus partly focused on the role played by Jewish history in justifying the parliamentary victory. The theological, philosophical, and political debates on Judaism and its political use also deeply transformed the traditional image of Judaism itself among Christians, and it is in this context that a new idea of Jewish scepticism emerged.

The German Lutheran world, strongly grounded in Aristotelian philosophy, reacted against the use of Judaism made by the Calvinist tradition in England and the Netherlands. The study of Jewish tradition within the Lutheran academies and universities ended up, as we will see, weakening its affinity with classical thought,

---

[5] On the origin and history of Christian Hebraism, see François Secret, *Les kabbalistes chrétiens de la Renaissance* (Paris: Dunod, 1964); Jerome Friedman, *The Most Ancient Testimony: Sixteenth-Century Christian-Hebraica in the Age of Renaissance Nostalgia* (Athens: Ohio University Press, 1983); Frank E. Manuel, *The Broken Staff: Judaism through Christian Eyes* (Cambridge, Mass.: Harvard University Press, 1992); Saverio Campanini, "Die Geburt der Judaistik aus dem Geist der Christlichen Kabbalah," in *Gottes Sprache in der philologischen Werkstatt: Hebraistik vom 15. bis zum 19. Jahrhundert*, eds. Giuseppe Veltri and Gerold Necker (Leiden: Brill, 2004): 135–241; and Paul F. Grendler, "Italian Biblical Humanism and the Papacy, 1515–1535," in *Biblical Humanism and Scholasticism in the Age of Erasmus*, ed. Erika Rummel (Leiden: Brill, 2008): 227–276. For a comprehensive bibliography, see Stephen G. Burnett, *Christian Hebraism in the Reformation Era (1500–1660): Authors, Books, and the Transmission of Jewish Learning* (Leiden: Brill, 2012).

[6] For example, Carlo Sigonio (1523?-1584), a Catholic historian, wrote a tractate on the Hebrew republic in 1582 in which he maintained that the regime instituted by God and Moses was comparable with the aristocratic constitution described in Aristotle's *Politics*; see Carlo Sigonio, *De republica Hebraeorum libri VII* (Bologna: Giovanni Rossi, 1582); cf. Guido Bartolucci, *La repubblica ebraica di Carlo Sigonio. Modelli politici dell'età moderna* (Florence: Olschki, 2007) and idem, "The *De republica Hebraeorum* of Carlo Sigonio: a Re-evaluation," *Hebraic Political Studies* 3.1 (2008): 19–59.

[7] See note 13.

and in particular with Aristotelian philosophy, by ascribing some features to it that had previously been acknowledged as belonging to sceptical strategies. In accordance with this tendency, series of short treatises were published which investigated the Jewish tradition in depth: the *dissertationes*.

The *dissertatio* is an important document for understanding the teaching activity within the Lutheran academies and universities. During the second half of the seventeenth century, the *dissertatio* changed its form, shifting from the two-page work of the sixteenth century to a short treatise of twenty to thirty pages. Because of this transformation, the *dissertatio* became an important but simple tool for the circulation of ideas, as well as for showing the university's academic orientation. The formal structure of the *dissertationes* consists of a *praeses*, a professor who had the role of presenting the work, and a *respondens*, usually a student, who defended the thesis in public and theoretically had to be the author of the work. Usually, however, the author of the *dissertatio* was the professor himself, while the student had the role of assisting him.[8] The authors of the *dissertationes* were not always Hebraists or theologians, but were also philosophers and jurists: the target of these writings, thus, was not scholarly knowledge of Jewish antiquities, or exclusive religious controversies (against the Jews or other confessions), but also, and perhaps above all, the political use of Judaism.[9] Yet the professors of holy languages did not remain indifferent to this controversy, and they put their extensive knowledge of Hebrew and rabbinic literature at the service of Lutheran political debate. In the second half of the seventeenth century, one of the most important figures attempting to think about Judaism in a new way was Johann Frischmuth (1619–1687).

---

[8] On the *Dissertationes* on Jewish topics, see Valerio Marchetti, "Sulla degiudaizzazione della politica. In margine alla relazione di Horst Dreitzel," in *Aristotelismo politico e ragion di stato* (Atti del convegno internazionale di Torino 11–12 Febbraio 1993), ed. Artemio Enzo Baldini (Florence: Olschki, 1995): 349–358; idem, "An Pythagoras proselytus factus sit," *Dimensioni e problemi della ricerca storica* 2 (1996): 111–121; idem, "Aristoteles utrum fuerit Iudaeus. Sulla degiudaizzazione della filosofia europea in età moderna," in *Anima e paura. Studi in onore di Michele Ranchetti*, ed. Anna Scattigno (Macerata: Quodlibet, 1998): 249–266; idem, "Il teologo Johann Franz Budde (1667–1729) e la filosofia ebraica," in *L'interculturalità dell'ebraismo*, ed. Mauro Perani (Ravenna: Longo, 2004): 299–314; and Giuseppe Veltri, "Academic Debates on the Jews in Wittenberg. The Protestant Literature on Rituals, the Dissertationes and the Writings of the Hebraists Theodor Dassow and Andreas Sennert," *European Journal of Jewish Studies* 6 (2012): 123–146.

[9] The main *dissertationes* published in these years on Jewish political topics are: Hermann Conring, *De Republica Hebraeorum dissertatio* (Helmstedt: Henning Mueller, 1648); Johannes Vorst, *De Synedriis Hebraeorum brevis dissertatio academica* (Rostock: Richelius, 1651); Michael Wendeler, *Disputatio Politica Artes Pacis Exemplo Salomonis* (Wittenberg: Johannes Röhner, 1650); idem, *Disputatio Politica De Republica Hebraeorum* (Wittenberg: Johannes Honter, 1655); and idem, *Disputatio Politica de Magno Iudaeorum Synedrio* (Wittenberg: Johannes Haken, 1659). Hermann Conring (1606–1681) was a jurist and historian and Johannes Vorst (1623–1676) was a theologian and Hebraist, while Michael Wendler (1610–1671) was a philosopher and theologian.

Frischmuth was born in Wertheim in 1619 and grew up in a bourgeois Lutheran family.[10] In 1636, he moved to the University of Altdorf, where he became particularly interested in religious matters and began to study oriental languages: Hebrew, Aramaic, Syriac, and Arabic. At this time, his professor was Theodoricus Hackspan, one of the great Hebraists of the period, who in 1649 published the Jewish edition of *Sefer Niṣṣaḥon*, an anti-Christian treatise written by Rabbi Yom Tov Lipmann ben Solomon Muehlhausen at the end of the fourteenth century.[11] Frischmuth, under the guidance of his professor, focused mainly on the study of rabbinic literature, in which he became a specialist. In 1645, he was called to the University of Jena, where he taught holy languages until his death in 1687. During his life, he published remarkable works devoted to investigating the relationship between the Bible and the Jewish exegetical interpretations, particularly the rabbinic interpretations. As his contemporaries have emphasised, Frischmuth's main task was to point out the dangers of rabbinic interpretation, especially for those scholars who considered it a faithful analysis.[12] However, as we will see, his work did not only have a theoretical or theological purpose, but also, and especially, a political agenda. In these years, he published several treatises on different topics and decided to spread his work using the model of the *dissertatio*. Frischmuth had already discussed two *dissertationes* with Hackspan when he still was a student in Altdorf: one on the names of angels and demons and the other on the interpretation of Psalm 110.[13] He then moved to Jena, where he began his production of *dissertationes* with two works on the seven pre-

---

[10] On Frischmuth's life, cf. Johannes Simon Ponickau, *Oratio in memoriam et honorem viri celeberrimi Ioannis Frischmuthii professoris de Academia Ienensi optime meriti* (Jena: Golneriana, 1698); Gustav Moritz Redslob, "Frischmuth, Johann," in *Allgemeine Deutsche Biographie* 8 (1878) (https://www.deutsche-biographie.de/sfz17628.html); and Johann Zeumer, *Vitae professorum Theologiae, Iurisprudentiae, Medicinae et Philosophiae qui in illustri Academia Ienensi ab ipsius fundatione ad nostra usque tempora vixerunt et adhuc vivunt* (Jena: Johannes Felix Bielck, 1711): classis IV, 101–104.

[11] Yom Tov Lipmann Muehlhausen, *Liber Nizachon, conscriptus anno a Christo nato MCCCXCIX diuque desideratus, nec ita pridem fato singulari e Iudaeorum manibus excussus, oppositus Christianis, Sadducaeis atque aliis. Editus typis Academicis, curante Theodorico Hackspan* (Nuremberg: Wolfang Endter, 1644). Yom Tov Lipmann ben Solomon Muehlhausen lived in Bohemia, Poland, and Austria between the fourteenth and the fifteenth century. On this work, see Ora Limor and Israel J. Yuval, "Scepticism and Conversion: Jews, Christians and Doubt in *Sefer ha Nizzahon*," in *Hebraica Veritas?: Christian Hebraists and the Study of Judaism in Early Modern Europe*, eds. Allison Coudert and Jeffrey S. Shoulson (Philadelphia: University of Pennsylvania Press, 2004): 159–179.

[12] Ponickau, *Oratio*, C2v: 'Praesertim in id collocaverat operam, studium, atque cogitationes suas, ut e rabbinorum commentariis bona haut secus ac rosas rariores inter spinas collecta, ad usum publicum transferret, spinas vero contereret et ignea tela, quae subinde inter Iudaicas doctrinas tanquam pestilentissimo veneno infecta, micant, incautos vulnerant, extincta in adversariorum ora dirigeret.'

[13] Johann Frischmuth, *De Angelorum Daemonumque Nominibus. Disputatio publice proposita a Theodorico Hackspan, [...] respondente M. Johanne Frischmuth* (Altdorf: Scherfius, 1641) and idem, *Disputatio in Psalmum 110 philologica [...] sub praesidio Theodorici Hackspan, Johannes Frischmuth (respon.)* (Altdorf: Scherfius, 1644).

cepts of Noah.¹⁴ In these early works, Frischmuth developed his idea of studying—and, above all, understanding—Jewish tradition. First of all, he chose a subject: the Noachide laws, which at that time were at the centre of the debate on natural right, especially after John Selden's publication of *De iure naturali* in 1640.¹⁵ The use of Jewish sources made by some authors, mostly Calvinists, was the reason for Frischmuth's critique of the rabbinic tradition in these early works. Such a strategy is manifest, for example, in what he claims in the introduction to the second *dissertatio* on Noah's laws. He explicitly rejects any usefulness of rabbinical literature for political or juridical purposes by contesting authors such as Joseph Scaliger and Isaac Casaubon, who, on the other hand, had supported the utility of their study.¹⁶ In this introduction, Frischmuth shows his attitude to Jewish tradition, which was far from the interests of Calvinist Hebraists whose works were published in the Netherlands and England. Frischmuth employed a controversial religious strategy inherited from the medieval and Lutheran anti-Jewish tradition, and he indeed used his knowledge of Jewish language and rabbinic tradition as an instrument against the Jews in order to demonstrate the truth of the Christian religion. Yet the interpretation of Judaism also played an important role in the religious dispute against Calvinism

---

14 Johann Frischmuth, *De septem Noachi praeceptis dissertatio, pubblice ventilationi submittunt Johannes Frischmuth et Michael Goechaeus* (Jena: Sengwald and Freyschmid, 1646) and idem, *De septem Noachi praeceptis dissertatio II. Praeside Johanne Frischmuth, Johannes Hilpert (resp.)* (Jena: Georg Sengenwald, 1647).
15 John Selden, *De iure naturali et gentium iuxta disciplinam Ebraeorum libri septem* (London: Richard Bishop, 1640). On this work, see Gerald J. Toomer, *John Selden. A Life in Scholarship*, vol. 1 (Oxford: Oxford University Press, 2009): 490–562. On the diffusion of Selden's theory in Germany, see Martin Mulsow, "John Selden in Germany: Religion and Natural Law from Boecler to Buddeus (1665–1695)," in *For the Sake of Learning: Essays in Honor of Anthony Grafton*, eds. Ann Blair and Anja-Silvia Goeing, vol. 1 (Leiden and Boston: Brill, 2016): 286–308. Cf. also Gianni Paganini, "Da Jean Bodin a John Selden: il modello Noachide della Repubblica delle lettere," *Bruniana e Campanelliana* 1.9 (2003): 83–107.
16 *De septem Noachi praeceptis dissertatio II*, A2: 'Equidem, cui aliquid operae in Rabbinis collocare volup' est, vera istos duumviros dixisse comperiet. Tametsi enim vel nascendi sorte, vel alio quodam fato, deploratae sortis mortales, saepenumero impingant: experimento tamen didicimus, eos non omnimodo aberrare a scopo, sed ipsis Christianorum placitis quandoque docere gemella, ac veritati testimonium perhibere longe gratissimum.' Frischmuth writes, for example, about Casaubon: 'Nec abiectius de iisdem sensit Isaacus Casaubonus: "Equidem" inquiens "non dubio multa in Sacris literis ex Iudaeorum scriptis posse, atque adeo debere illustrari." Quin ipsemet, qui et quantus vir! Suam in has literas *ormen* non obscure profitetur, dum ait: "Si studiorum socium haberem, non leviter me in libros Rabbinorum immergerem, quos aliquando coeperam diligenter evolvere, sed me aliae curae revocarunt."' (Frischmuth, *De septem Noachi praeceptis dissertatio II*, A2r). On Casaubon's study of Hebrew, see Anthony Grafton and Joanna Weinberg, *"I Have Always Loved the Holy Tongue". Isaac Casaubon, the Jews, and a Forgotten Chapter in Renaissance Scholarship* (Cambridge, Mass., and London: Harvard University Press, 2011).

and Catholicism: the Lutheran theologians recognised, particularly in the latter, the main defects of Judaism, such as the formal observance of ceremonies.[17]

Frischmuth, however, did not focus his attacks on Judaism, only within the narrow fence of theology. In 1653, he published a treatise of over 180 pages in which he analysed the right of kings in accordance with chapter 17 of Deuteronomy.[18] This work could be confused with a scholarly study of Jewish sources on monarchy. Yet from the very beginning, the analysis of the sources on the Jewish king became part of the huge debate on the monarchical institution, which began in 1649 after the beheading of Charles I at the end of the English Revolution.[19] Frischmuth's main purpose was to show that Jewish sources could not legitimise the superiority of the other institutions, such as the Sanhedrin, over the king's authority. He harshly criticised the work of Schickard, Selden, and Milton, who had supported the supremacy of assemblies and magistrates over the sovereign by using rabbinic sources. Frischmuth employs a very peculiar strategy to demonstrate the inconsistency of Jewish interpretation; in fact, he contrasts the sources adopted by his opponents by quoting another Jewish author, Isaac Abravanel.[20] The starting point of the discussion is Deuteronomy 17:14, in which God has given the people of Israel the opportu-

---

[17] On the Protestant critique of the ceremonial laws, cf. Giuseppe Veltri, *Renaissance Philosophy in Jewish Garb: Foundations and Challenges in Judaism on the Eve of Modernity* (Leiden and Boston: Brill, 2008): 169–194.

[18] Johann Frischmuth, *De rege eligendo et deponendo discursus, ex Deuteronomio cap. XVII ac Ebraeorum commentariis Christianorum manibus haut ita tritis conscriptus* (Jena: Casper Frenschmied, 1653).

[19] For the use of the Jewish sources in the debate on monarchy, see Eric Nelson, *The Hebrew Republic: Jewish Sources and the Transformation of European Political Thought* (Cambridge, Mass.: Harvard University Press, 2010).

The main works that participated in the debate on the Jewish king in this period were: Wilhelm Schickard, *Mishpat haMelech, ius regum Hebraeorum a tenebris Rabbinicis erutum et Luci donatum* (Strasbourg: Lazarus Zetzner, 1625); *Defensio regia pro Carolo I ad Serenissimum Magnae Britanniae regem Carolum II filium natu maiorem, heredem et successorem legitimum* (s.l.: Sumptibus regis, 1649); John Milton, *Pro populo anglicano defensio contra Claudii anonymi, alias Salmasii defensionem regiam* (London: Du Gardianis, 1651); and John Selden, *De Synedriis et Praefecturis iuridicis Veterum Ebraeorum libri tres* (London: Flesher, 1650–1655). Schickard's work was a treatise on the figure of the king according to Jewish sources, which was written in a part of the Lutheran world that at that time was considering the constitution of the German Empire and that was at the same time reacting to the absolutist principles spread by Bodin's work, particularly regarding the indivisibility of sovereignty. The main exponents of this current were Christoph Besold and Henning Arnisaeus; cf. Julian H. Franklin, *Sovereignty and the Mixed Constitution: Bodin and his Critics*, in *The Cambridge History of Political Thought, 1450–1700*, ed. James H. Burns (Cambridge: Cambridge University Press, 2008): 323–328. Schickard's work, even if it was published twenty years before King Charles' execution, deeply influenced the debate on the monarchical constitution during the English revolution.

[20] Isaac Abravanel was a Jewish author who was well known by Christian scholars in this period, although we do not yet know why, or in particular why his work was used against the rabbinical tradition.

nity to establish a king.²¹ The main political problem was the interpretation of the first verses on the meaning of the establishment of a king. According to some scholars, such as Schickard and Cunaeus, the passage referred to the people's opportunity to elect the king. The two authors, in order to confirm their statement, argued that the famous episode described in the First Book of Samuel, which presented a violent criticism of monarchy, was evidence that the people had violated God's law by asking for a king (as all the other nations had) and not by electing one.²² This idea was the result of a series of interpretations that Christian authors summarised from rabbinical literature, above all from Maimonides. Frischmuth responded to his opponents by presenting the authority of Abravanel, who, on the contrary, interpreted Samuel's passage by maintaining the interpretation of an unelected king. Frischmuth's use of Jewish sources is always instrumental: even an author such as Abravanel, who had shown an open position against the monarchical institution in his writings, becomes in Frischmuth's treatise a faithful ally against the enemies of monarchical absolutism.²³ In counterpoising various Jewish interpretations, Frischmuth seems to present the Jewish tradition as a realm in which opposing views could coexist together within the same passage, a hermeneutical method that cannot catch the real truth. This implicit critique of Judaism in Frischmuth's work is linked to a much more gen-

---

21 Deuteronomy 17:14: 'When you come to the land which the Lord your God is giving you, and possess it and dwell in it, and say: "I will set a king over me like all the nations that are around me," you shall surely set a king over you whom the Lord your God chooses.'

22 Frischmuth, *De rege eligendo*, A1v-A2r: 'Multi et magni nominis viri, cum Christiani tum Iudaei persuasum habent, his verbis Israelitas accepisse mandatum eligendi regis, quod devictis demum hostibus et terra Canaan occupata debuerint exequi. [...] Ex Christianis non dubitarunt quidam a Schaligero et Casambono divinis laudibus ornati Maimonidis sententiam amplecti. Ita enim W. Schikardus pag. 6 *De Iure Regio Ebraeorum* disserit: "Quod Samuelem attinet, non is populum increpabat, quia regem peterent, sed quia non legitime peterent, ut cordatus noster Maimonides prudenter explicat." Petrus quoque Cunaeus: "Permultis," ait, "mirati sunt, cur indigne tulerit Deus summam rei a Samuele ad regem aliquem transferri, siquidem illud et probaverat antea et futurum pro indole sacri populi dixerat, sed illis crudite respondit Maimonides, atque indignationem Numinis ex eo esse ortam ait, quia regem concupissent per ambiguas querelas sectiosasque voces, non uti legis praeceptum peragerent, sed quod displicebat ille sanctissimus vates Samuel." Lib. I *de Rep. Ebraeorum* cap. 14.' The second reference is to Petrus Cunaeus, *De republica Hebraeorum libri tres* (Leiden: Elvevirium, 1617).

23 Frischmuth, *De rege eligendo*, A2r-v: 'Non placet haec interpretatio Abravaneli, cum aliis de causis tum maxime hisce. [...] His inquam rationibus motus Abravanel ipsi Maimonidi dicam scribere non veretur et examinatis aliorum quoque sententiis, novam expositionem molitur, eamque tam apte deducit, ut si Scaligero, Casaubono, Schickardo, Cunaeo aliisque oculis eam usurpare contigisset, haud dubie dicturi fuerint prae Maimonide eum inter Iudaeos ineptire desiisse.' On the debate on monarchy in Jewish tradition and especially in Maimonides and Abravanel, see David Polish, *Give Us a King: Legal-Religious Sources of Jewish Sovereignty*, (Hoboken, New Jersey: Ktav Publishing House, 1989); Yair Lorberbaum, *Disempowered King. Monarchy in Classical Jewish Literature* (New York and London: Continuum, 2011); and Michael Walzer, Menachem Lorberbaum, and Noam, J. Zohar, eds., *The Jewish Political Tradition*, vol. 1 (New Haven and London: Yale University Press, 2000): 108–165.

eral discussion on the role of Jewish political tradition in comparison with that of classical thought.

Frischmuth often quotes Hermann Conring's *De republica Hebraeorum*, which was published as a *dissertatio* in 1648.[24] Conring, a German jurist and historian, wrote this work together with his student Martin Müller in order to criticise the Calvinist treatises on the Jewish political institutions. He maintained that the Jewish tradition was unrelated to Aristotelian political thought because the Jewish constitutional model could not be included among the definitions Aristotle gave in his *Politics* (monarchy, aristocracy, or democracy), but was rather a theocracy. Political power, Conring continued, was not managed by human beings, but directly by God, and therefore the Jewish model could not be discussed within the framework of the current political debate.[25]

---

[24] Conring, *De Republica Hebraeorum dissertatio*. On his political interpretation, see Marchetti, "Sulla degiudaizzazione della politica. In margine alla relazione di Horst Dreitzel." On political Aristotelism, see Horst Dreitzel, *Absolutismus und ständische Verfassung in Deutschland: ein Beitrag zu Kontinuität und Diskontinuität der politischen Theorie in der frühen Neuzeit* (Mainz: von Zabern, 1992). On Conring's political thought, see Michael Stolleis, ed., *Hermann Conring: (1606–1681). Beiträge zu Leben und Werk* (Berlin: Duncker & Humblot, 1983); Costantin Fasolt, "Political Unity and Religious Diversity: Hermann Conring's Confessional Writings and the Preface to Aristotle 'Politics' of 1637," in *Confessialisation in Europe, 1555–1700: Essays in Honor and Memory of Bodo Nischan*, eds. John M. Headley, Hans J. Hillerbrand, and Anthony J. Papalas (Aldershot: Ashgate, 2004): 319–345; and Martin van Gelderen, "Aristotelians, Monarchomachs and Republicans: Sovereignty and *respublica mixta* in Dutch and German Political Thought, 1580–1650," in *Republicanism: A Shared European Heritage*, vol. 1, eds. Martin van Gelderen and Quentin Skinner (Cambridge: Cambridge University Press, 2002): 195–217.

[25] Conring, *De Republica Hebraeorum dissertatio*, A4: 'Tria adeo fuerint in quibus summa potestas, quantam nimirum cunque in politiis observare possumus, maxime est conspicua: leges condere, bellum indicere, magistratus constituere. IIX. Porro horum omnium in republica Hebraeorum penes ipsum Deum arbitrium fuit.' *ibidem*, D2v: 'Primum nulla ex formis rerumpublicarum quas Aristoteles nobis descripsit, reipublicae Hebraeorum, quae ante regis fuit, satis convenire deprehenditur. Omnes illae formae tales sunt, ut *to kurion* sive summa potestas rerum agendarum fuerit penes homines. At in Hebraeorum republica *to kurion* diu mansit penes ipsum Deum. Apparet idipsum ex maiestatis iuribus, quae maiora vocant, legum sanctione, magistratuum institutione, bellorum indictione, quae Deus sibi servarat.' His analysis, however, was focused on the first period of Jewish history, from Moses to Samuel, when, according to Calvinist thought, the aristocratic model was founded. Conring had a different idea of the Jewish monarchy and its political legitimation, even if he also considered this institution as not completely part of Aristotelian thought; cf. *ibidem*, F2r: 'Quod antea diximus de regum Hebraeorum potestate, id patebit etiam amplius, si iura maiestatis expenderimus, quomodo se illa regum aevo habuerint. Iura autem maiestatis nobis hodie sunt ipsum *to kurion*. Cuius quasi partes sunt potestas ferendarum et abrogandarum legum, ius belli et pacis, potestas magistratuum et iudiciorum istituendorum, facultas iudicandi tam in publice quam privatis reipublicae negotiis. Haec nimirum omnia penes reges Hebraeorum fuerunt. LXXI. Ut autem de poteste ferendarum et abrogandarum legum primo dicamus, dubium (fateor) cui videri possit, an ea penes reges Hebraeorum fuerit. [...] Debuerunt igitur divina scita in Hebraeorum republica manere rata, etiam tum cum reges imperarunt, neque regibus illa immutare aut abrogare fuit integrum.'

Frischmuth probably had this idea of Jewish tradition in mind when he published the *dissertatio De loco Deuteronomio XVII v. 8 et seqq. et quae ad illum moveri solet questione: An Ebraei statuant, idem simul posse esse et non esse* in 1658, combining it with the idea that different and contradictory interpretations could coexist within the rabbinical tradition.[26] The treatise is different from all his other works, which are focused on political or theological issues; indeed, here he deals directly with a philosophical question, more precisely with one of the main statements of Aristotelian philosophy, namely the principle of non-contradiction. The *dissertatio* begins with the assertion that the Jews used to pull the false out from the true, a statement that Frischmuth employs to demonstrate the untrustworthiness of rabbinic biblical exegesis.[27] At the heart of his reasoning is a passage from Deuteronomy 17 which discusses a judge's conduct when he is uncertain about the sentence. According to Deuteronomy, in fact, the judge had to appeal to a higher authority chosen by God who would suggest the verdict to him and from whose decision the judge could not depart.[28] Starting from this passage, Frischmuth develops an articulated discussion on the principle of authority in Jewish tradition by dividing his examination into two distinct parts, one mainly linked to religious dispute, the other connected to philosophical speculation. The starting point of his analysis is the assertion that Jews hold the authority of their rabbis in such high reverence that they are inclined to disregard the principle of non-contradiction even when faced with a clear and obvious reason to adopt it.[29]

To confirm his assumption, he quotes the works of two Lutheran scholars, the Helmstedt theologian Konrad Hornejus and the Jena philosopher Daniel Stahl,

---

[26] Johann Frischmuth, *De loco Deuteronomio XVII v. 8 et seqq. et quae ad illum moveri solet questione: An Ebraei statuant, idem simul posse esse et non esse exercitium academicum*, Johannes Leonartus Will (resp.), (Jena: Samuel Krebs, 1658).

[27] Frischmuth, *De loco Deuteronomio XVII*, A2r: 'Ex ipsa veritate falsum eligere Ebraeos, saepenumero deprehendunt Christiani.'

[28] Deuteronomy 17:8–11: 'If there arise a matter too hard for thee in judgment, between blood and blood, between plea and plea, and between stroke and stroke, being matters of controversy within thy gates: then shalt thou arise, and get thee up into the place which the Lord thy God shall choose. And thou shalt come unto the priests the Levites, and unto the judge that shall be in those days, and enquire; and they shall shew thee the sentence of judgment: And thou shalt do according to the sentence, which they of that place which the Lord shall choose shall shew thee; and thou shalt observe to do according to all that they inform thee: According to the sentence of the law which they shall teach thee, and according to the judgment which they shall tell thee, thou shalt do: thou shalt not decline from the sentence which they shall shew thee, to the right hand, nor to the left.' On the meaning of this passage for the construction of the authority of the Sanhedrin, see *infra* Giuseppe Veltri's contribution.

[29] Frischmuth, *De loco Deuteronomio XVII*, A2r: 'Maxime vero omnium oculos in se convertunt Iudaei, dum dictamini rectae rationis haud obscure obniti et nimia doctorum suorum reverentia fascinati, illud in omni materia certissimum et irrefrenabile principium "impossibile est idem simul esse et non esse," prorsus non agnoscere perhibentur.'

who stated that Jewish authority was founded on absurd principles.[30] Frischmuth made use of the works of these two German scholars, especially of Stahl's treatise, to link his analysis to the authorities of Johannes Buxtorf and Martin Luther. The first author, Buxtorf (1564–1629), was one of the most important Hebraists of the sixteenth century. He wrote several works on Judaism, but he was best known for his anti-Jewish work entitled *Synagoga Judaica*, published in German in 1603 and then in Latin in 1604. In the first chapter of this work, the Christian Hebraist wrote:

> If two rabbis contend amongst themselves and struggle, issuing contradictory sentences, it is nevertheless to be believed that both of them obtained their doctrine from Moses, each sentence being the word of the living God—which is a supreme blasphemy.[31]

Frischmuth, then, introduces the words of Luther, who argued in his work on the Hebrew name of God, *Shem ha-mephorash*, that the Jews blindly believed in the authority of their rabbis even beyond the rationality of their words.[32]

By quoting Luther and Buxtorf, Frischmuth inserts his treatise into the Lutheran tradition of polemical writings against the Jews. The first part of his treatise is a development of Luther's (and Buxtorf's) claim about the authority of rabbis within Jewish communities. Frischmuth's analysis thus has the purpose of confirming the Lutheran position by adding a number of Jewish sources such as the Talmud, Maimonides, Abravanel, and Lipmann's *Sefer Niṣṣaḥon*, which, as we have seen,

---

30 Konrad Hornejus, *De processu disputandi liber* (Frankfurt: Conrad Eifrid, ²1633): 68–69 and Daniel Stahl, *Regulae philosophicae sub titulis XXII comprensae* (London: F. Redmayne, 1672).

31 Frischmuth, *De loco Deuteronomio XVII*, A2v: 'Nimirum si duo Rabbini inter se contendant et pugnent, ac sermones contradicentes proferant, non minus credendum esse utrumque suam doctrinam a Mose accepisse, immo (quae summa est blasphemia) utramque sententiam verbum Dei viventis esse.' I am quoting from Frischmuth's work, which quoted Stahl's tractate. For the original quotation, see Joannes Buxtorf, *Synagoga Judaica* (Basel: Ludovicus König, 1641): 61–64. Buxtorf comments the same passage of Deuteronomy 17:11. For Buxtorf's life and work, see Stephen G. Burnett, *From Christian Hebraism to Jewish Studies: Johannes Buxtorf (1564–1629) and Hebrew Learning in the Seventeenth Century* (Leiden, New York, and Köln: Brill, 1996).

32 Frischmuth, *De loco Deuteronomio XVII*, A2v: 'Beatus quoque Lutherus [...] Iudaeis exprobrat, quod Rabbinis dextram sinistram et sinistram dextram vocantibus credendum esse asserant.' Cf. Martin Luther, *Vom Schemhamphoras: und vom Geschlecht Christi. Matthei am I. Capitel* (Wittenberg: Raw, 1543): 8v: 'Wie ists beschlossen [...] das alles was die Rabinen sagen, sol ein Jude gleuben, und nicht davon weichen. Dahersagen sie nu, Sie mussen iren Rabinen gleuben wenn die selben gleich sagten, die rechte hand were die lincte, und die lincte were die rechte, wie Purchetus schreibt.' Luther took this idea from Porchetus de Salvaticis, *Victoria adversus impios Hebraeos* (Paris: Aegidius Gourmont et Franciscus Regnault, 1520). Luther's copy of Porchetus' work is now in Karlsruhe, Badische Landesbibliothek, RH (42B 297 RH). On Luther and Judaism, see Thomas Kaufmann, "Luther and the Jews," in *Jews, Judaism and the Reformation in Sixteenth-Century Germany*, eds. Dean P. Bell and Stephen G. Burnett (Leiden and Boston: Brill, 2006): 69–104.

was edited some years before by Hackspan.³³ In this first part, he repeats the same scheme used in the previous works: he reproduces a dialogue between the various Jewish sources and he often ascribes a superior authority to Abravanel compared to the Talmud and Maimonides.³⁴

Frischmuth's first effort was to neutralise the Catholic interpretation of the passage from Deuteronomy. The Church of Rome had indeed legitimised the Pope's infallibility in judging religious matters precisely through the interpretation of the role of the Sanhedrin.³⁵ The German Hebraist, on the other hand, maintained that Moses wanted to invest the Senate (that is, the Sanhedrin) with the role of resolving those cases which were particularly difficult to judge.³⁶

After presenting some sources, particularly Abravanel's commentary, to illustrate his statement, Frischmuth begins to discuss the problem at the centre of his analysis, namely the issue of obedience. As soon as the lower judges have to follow the judgment of the Sanhedrin literally, he acknowledges that all the Jews can do is obey the authority of the rabbis (who are the Sanhedrin's heirs) without having the opportunity to question their judgment, even if it seems to be unreasonable.³⁷ And at the conclusion of the first part of the treatise, he maintains:

> We think that they [i.e. the Jews], after the prophets ceased to appear and the oral tradition finally took up space, said that for this reason the opinions of the masters found greater truth among the people and their authority grew immensely, since their opinions, even if they departed from the judgment of reason and senses, were nevertheless to be received as holy. The same

---

33 Frischmuth, *De loco Deuteronomio XVII*, C2v: 'Revera non tam ad sententias, quae in iudiciis sub ratione iusti feruntur, quam ad Doctorum quaevis sub ratione veri acceptanda placita veteres spectasse, ex R. Lipmanno patescit numero 321 libri *Nizzachon*.'

34 *Ibidem*, B3v: 'Caeterum tale quid veteres Iudaeos voluisse innuere, prorsus non fit verisimile ob illas rationes, quas infra sumus adducturi. Neque unquam eum in modum quo R. Nissim conatur, eos excusare vel duriora verba sic emollire quisquam est conatus. Unde R. Abarbenel ab eo non tantum facit divortium, sed his verbis explicationem eius impugnat.'

35 *Ibidem*, A3r: 'Ad nauseam usque haec verba, quae tamen Ebraico textui minime respondent, urgere solent Pontificii demostraturi Romani Pontifici infallibilitatem.'

36 *Ibidem*, A3r-v: 'Sane qui totum contextum sine praeiudicio perpendit, is animadvertit minime de religionis hic agi negotio, neque de causis, quae proprie videri possint sacerdotales, nedum ut Romani Pontificis in controversiis fidei infallibiliter definiendis confirmetur autoritas. Potius in eo occupatur legislator sapientissimus, ut doceat, iudici oppidano in causa ambigua et obscura haerenti [...] adeundum et consulendum esse Senatum illius loci, quem ad publicos conventus habendos Dominus elegerit et a quo ad alium appellare non liceat.'

37 *Ibidem*, B1v-B2r: 'Acquiescendum omnino fuisse Iudicibus minoribus sententia Synedrii, velut omnis ulterioris provocationis expertis, clare patescit cum ex poena quam immorigero interminatur, tum mandato: "et facies quaecuque dixerint, et docuerint te iuxta, sequeris sententiam eorum, nec declinabis ad dextram neque ad sinistram." Quae verba ex usu scripturae non nisi obedientiam significat. [...] Paulo aliter R. Gerundensis: "[...] Etiamsi tibi persuaseris eos errare et in oculis tuis id tam evidens appareat, quam liquidum est discriminen inter dextram et sinistram, tamen facias oportet, quae illi praeceperint".'

blind obedience [...] is demanded by the Church of Rome, which in many respects is similar to Judaism, like an egg is the same as another egg.³⁸

Frischmuth thus attacked both Judaism and Catholicism. Yet while the latter was condemned, above all because of Pontifical primacy, as we have already seen, the former was subjected to a more radical criticism, which he developed in the second part of the treatise.

Frischmuth shifts his analysis from a controversial religious point of view to a philosophical one: he compared the principle of authority in the rabbinical tradition directly with Aristotelian thought by reaching far more extreme results. In doing so, he makes explicit what was still hidden in his other works, namely that Judaism was grounded on anti-Aristotelian principles of reasoning. This interpretation brings Jewish tradition further from classical philosophy and closer to sceptical strategy, and thus turns it into a threat to Christian society.³⁹

---

38 Frischmuth, *De loco Deuteronomio XVII*, C2r: 'Arbitramur eos postquam Prophetae cessarunt, et locum tandem invenit oralis traditio, idcirco ita loquutos esse, ut eo maiorem fidem apud populum invenirent magistrorum sententiae et horum autoritas in immensum augeretur, quippe quorum responsiones, quantumvis rationis sensuumque iudicio repugnent, nihilominus velut sanctae recipiendae sint. Eiusmodi coecam obedientiam [...] Romana quoque exigit Ecclesia, quae Iudaica in pluribus tam similis est, quam ovum ovo.'

39 On the reception of sceptical thought in Germany in the early modern period, see Martin Mulsow, "Eclecticism or Skepticism? A Problem of the Early Enlightenment," *Journal of the History of Ideas* 58.3 (1997): 465–477; Jean-Robert Armogathe, *Early German Reactions to Huet's* Censura in *Skepticism in the Modern Age: Building on the Work of Richard Popkin*, eds. José R. Maia Neto, Gianni Paganini, and John Christian Laursen (Leiden and Boston: Brill, 2009): 297–308; and Martin Mulsow and Helmut Zedelmaier, eds., *Skepsis, Providenz, Polyhistorie. Jakob Friedrich Reimmann (1668–1743)* (Tübingen: Max Niemeyer, 1998). An important source for the study of scepticism in this period is Johann Franz Buddeus, *Dissertatio Philosophica De Scepticismo Morali* (Halle and Magdeburg: Christian Henckel Publisher, 1698). For the second part of Frischmuth's tractate and its connection to scepticism, see *infra* Giuseppe Veltri's contribution.

Giuseppe Veltri
Negotiating the Principle of (Non)-Contradiction: Johann Frischmuth on the Rabbinic Dialectic Discussion

The principle of contradiction (αρχή τῆς ἀντιφάσεως) first appears in Aristotle's *Metaphysics* IV. Perhaps no other passage of Aristotelian philosophy is as controversially debated as the fundamental binary logical incompatibility between true and false, the foundation of the principle of contradiction (commonly called the principle or law of non-contradiction, PNC). Three formulations of it are given in the fourth chapter of the *Metaphysics*:[1]

> 1. It is impossible for the same attribute at once to belong and not to belong to the same thing and in the same relation (τὸ γὰρ αὐτὸ ἅμα ὑπάρχειν τε καὶ μὴ ὑπάρχειν ἀδύνατον τῷ αὐτῷ καὶ κατὰ τὸ αὐτό); [2]
> 2. It is impossible to hold (suppose) the same thing to be and not to be (ἀδύνατον γὰρ ὁντινοῦν ταὐτὸν ὑπολαμβάνειν εἶναι καὶ μὴ εἶναι);[3]
> 3. Opposite assertions cannot be true at the same time (ἀδύνατον καὶ τἀναντία ὑπάρχειν ἅμα).[4]

The intention of Aristotle's formulations is to offer a fundamental proposition of ontological, psychological, and logical craft[5] in order to avoid an infinite recourse to the proof (*apodeixis*). Discussions of Aristotle's different formulations and their origin and logical consistency have been the object of many commentaries from antiquity until recent times.[6] It is not my intention to repeat, reformulate, or reinforce the valid and probable objections to the PNC or even to defend it against its opponents or detractors.[7] My purpose is only to introduce the reader to a seventeenth-century debate which originated in the Protestant University of Jena in Germany. The *appa-*

---

[1] Here I am following Paula Gottlieb, "Aristotle on Non-contradiction," *The Stanford Encyclopedia of Philosophy* (Summer 2015 Edition), ed. Edward N. Zalta, https://plato.stanford.edu/archives/sum2015/entries/aristotle-noncontradiction. The reader may find the literature on this topic there.
[2] Aristotle, *Metaphysics* IV:3 (1005b19–20), according to the Loeb Classical Library; Perseus: 'It is impossible for the same thing to belong and not to belong at the same time to the same thing and in the same respect.'
[3] Aristotle, *Metaphysics* IV:3 (1005b24; cf. 1005b29–30).
[4] Aristotle, *Metaphysics* IV:6 (1011b13–20).
[5] Gottlieb, "Aristotle on Non-contradiction," but cf. also the controversy on this formulation in Jean-Louis Hudry, "Aristotle on Non-Contradiction: Philosophers vs. Non-Philosophers," *Journal of Ancient Philosophy* 7 (2013): 51–74.
[6] See the recent work by Enrico Berti, *Contraddizione e dialettica negli antichi e nei moderni* (Brescia: Morcelliana, 2015).
[7] See John Woods, "Dialectical Considerations on the Logic of Contradiction: Part I," *Logic Journal of the IGPL* 13 (2005): 231–260.

rent intention of this debate was to present Jewish thought as an anti-Aristotelian tradition; its *real* purpose was to undermine the principle of the reception of the Dual Torah.

This discussion is imperative for the modern scholar not only because of its author's attempt to qualify a religion as illogical and as pretending to be true while contradicting the principle of non-contradiction, but also, and perhaps much more intriguingly, because of his attempt to judge Jewish scholars as blasphemous in their real or alleged attribution of logical contradictions to the first principle, i.e. God. We will first examine the cause of the discussion. Then, we will follow the attempts to resolve the question from a rabbinic point of view. Finally, we will attempt to discuss the diverse hypothesis of a fruitful discussion of or inquiry into the question of whether the truth can be negotiable in a system of thought that defines it.

Casus disputandus: *elu we-elu divre elohim ḥayyim*

In 1658, Johann Frischmuth (1619–1687), professor of 'holy language' at the University of Jena in Germany, together with his student Johannes Leonart Will, presented and defended a *dissertatio*[8] on *An Hebraei statuant idem posse esse et non esse* ('Whether the Jews Can Claim That the Same Thing Both Can and Cannot Exist [at the Same Time]').[9] The booklet presents two arguments with the strategy of disavowing any connection between Judaism and Aristotelianism: the foundation of rabbinical authority[10] and the Jewish 'principle' of contradiction. In both cases, the rabbis—according to Frischmuth are so impertinent and sacrilegious as to derive their own authority from God and supreme blasphemy to attribute the origin of two contradictory positions to him, or in his own words:

> If two rabbis contend amongst themselves and struggle, issuing contradictory sentences, it is nevertheless to be believed that both of them obtained their doctrine from Moses, each sentence being the word of the living God which is a supreme blasphemy.[11]

---

8 For the format of the *dissertatio*, see Giuseppe Veltri, "Academic Debates on the Jews in Wittenberg. The Protestant Literature on Rituals, the Dissertationes and the Writings of the Hebraists Theodor Dassow and Andreas Sennert," *European Journal of Jewish Studies* 6 (2012): 123–146.
9 Johann Frischmuth and Johannes L. Will, *De Loco Devt. XVII. v. 8. seqq. et quæ ad illum moveri solet, quæstione: An Ebræi Statuant, Idem Simul Posse Esse Et Non Esse, Exercitium Academicum, Præside Dn. M. Johanne Frischmuth, Lingg. Sacr. Prof. Publ. Famigeratissimo, & Facultatis Philosophicæ h.t. Decano spectabili, Publicè ventilandum exhibet M. Johannes Leonartus Will* (Jena: Krebsius, 1658) [Jena, Univ., Phil. Disp., 1658].
10 This argument is treated by Guido Bartolucci in this issue of the Yearbook.
11 *De Loco Devt. XVII*, A2v: 'Si duo Rabbini inter se contendant & pugnent, ac sermones contradicentes proferant, non minus credendum esse, utrumque suam doctrinam a Mose accepisse, immo (quae summa est blasphemia) utramque sententiam verbum Dei viventis esse.'

The reader of Frischmuth's dissertation may be deceived by this formulation, believing that he is approaching a controversy of philosophical importance. On the contrary: Frischmuth is abusing a philosophical topic of Aristotelian logic to combat rabbinic authority based on Oral Torah. Therefore, he begins with Deuteronomy 17:8, already quoted in the title of the *dissertatio*, where the main problem is the foundation of the Sanhedrin and the Torah as the supreme constitutional authorities (a court system and a religious and political document) of the Jewish way of life,[12] interpreted in the light of Exodus 23:2 (according to which the Halakhah follows the majority).[13]

Yet let us begin at the beginning. The blasphemy against God consists of attributing internally contradictory assertions because they are controversially disputing (*contendant & pugnent*) to the doctrine of Moses and hence basing their opposing authority on God himself (*credendum esse [...] utram sententiam verbum dei viventis esse*). This rabbinic position indeed occurs in some texts, of which the most famous is a quotation from the Babylonian Talmud, *Eruvin* 13b, to which Frischmuth expressly and directly refers. It must be stated at the outset that his rendition does not come from the text of the Babylonian Talmud, but is a direct quotation from the anti-Christian *Sefer Niṣṣaḥon* ('Book of the Triumph')[14] by Rabbi Yom Tov Lipmann Muehlhausen (fourteenth-fifteenth century), a philosopher and controversialist:

> For three years, the House of Hillel and the House of Shammay debated. One said: 'The Halakhah is in accordance with our opinion.' The other objected: 'The Halakhah is in accordance with our opinion.' The voice of God rang out (and entered into the discussion), saying: 'Both the one and the other are the word of the living God. The Halakhah, however, follows the words of the House of Hillel.'[15]

Also, another text from the Babylonian Talmud, *Hagigah* 3b, is, according to Frischmuth who follows also here Yom Tov Lipmann, relevant to the question because it describes a 'rabbinic discussion' as a *perennially* controversial status:

---

[12] On this topic, see Steven D. Fraade, "'If a Case is Too Baffling for You to Decide...' (Deut 17:8–13): Between Constraining and Expanding Judicial Autonomy in the Temple Scroll and Early Rabbinic Scriptural Interpretation," in *Sibyls, Scriptures, and Scrolls: John Collins at Seventy*, eds. Joel S. Baden, Hindy Najman, and Eibert J. C. Tigchelaar, Supplements to the Journal for the Study of Judaism 175 (Leiden and Boston: Brill, 2016): 409–430.

[13] See Giuseppe Veltri, "The limit of scepticism and tolerance," *Bollettino della Società Filosofica Italiana N.S.* 221 (2017): 37–55, spec. 51–54.

[14] Yom Tov Lipmann Muehlhausen, *Liber Nizachon Rabbi Lipmanni, conscriptis anno à Christo nato M. CCC. XCIX.: diuq[ue] desideratus: nec ita pridem, fato singulari, è Judæorum manibus excussus. Oppositus Christianis, Sadducæis atque aliis. Editus typis academicis curante Theodori Hackspan ... Accessit tractatus de usu librorum Rabbinicorum, prodromus apologiæ pro Christianis adversus Lipmannum triumphantem* (Nuremberg: Wolfgang Endter, 1644): 176 (§321); see Ḥaninah Ben-Menaḥem and Shimshon Eṭinger, eds., *Sugyot ba-mishpaṭ ha-'Ivri* [Hebrew], vol. 1 (Ra'ananah: ha-Universiṭah ha-Petuḥah, 2006): 148–150.

[15] See previous footnote; the text is quoted by Frischmuth, *De Loco Devt. XVII*, §15.

> 'The masters of assemblies' (בעלי אסופות): these are the disciples of the wise, who sit in manifold assemblies and occupy themselves with the Torah, some pronouncing unclean and others pronouncing clean, some prohibiting and others permitting, some disqualifying and others declaring fit.[16]

The Talmud gives a commentary on Qohelet 12:1, where the words of the wise are explained as goads, firmly fixed like 'nails by the masters of assemblies.' Frischmuth also adds the talmudic comments that 'they have been transmitted by one shepherd and one shepherd received them, one leader.' He did not directly quote the version of the talmudic discussion, which, according to the current version, reads:

> Should a man say: 'How in these circumstances shall I learn Torah?' Therefore, the text says: 'All of them are given from one Shepherd.' One God gave them [the interpretations of the words/opinion]; one leader uttered them from the mouth of the Lord of all creation, blessed be He; for it is written: *And God spoke all these words* (Exodus 20:1).[17]

This is a rendition of the *Sefer Niṣṣaḥon* by Rabbi Yom Tov Lipmann Muehlhausen, who substituted e*l* ('God') with 'Shepherd' in the sentence 'All of them are given from one Shepherd. One Shepherd gave them,' omitting 'from the mouth of the Lord of all creation, blessed be He; for it is written: *And God spoke all these words*.'

Lippmann adds his comment:

> That is a thing which is difficult to understand: the House of Shammay declared it as pure, the House of Hillel declared it as impure. How can it be possible that they are both the word of God? And how could Moses, freedom be upon him, receive both of them from the Almighty? If he received it pure, he could not receive it impure. If he received it impure, he could not receive it pure.[18]

With this quotation, the Protestant theologian wanted to emphasise that Jewish scholarship was conscious of the problem and made efforts to resolve the contradiction (*ad tollendam contradictionem*) because the principle of truth is of universal validity.

The whole discussion is tactically interesting because Frischmuth and his student present the reader with a melange of rabbinic texts in the original language with Latin translations interspersed with short commentaries, most of which are summaries of the rabbinic texts or insults to the Jews: liars, blasphemers, defenders

---

16 Herz's translation quoted in Judah J. Slotki, Israel Brodie, and Isidore Epstein, eds., *The Babylonian Talmud: Translated into English with notes, glossary and indices* (London: Soncino Press, 1952). **17** "בעלי אסופות" – אלו תלמידי חכמים שיושבין אסופות אסופות ועוסקין בתורה, הללו מטמאין והללו מטהרין, הללו אוסרין והללו מתירין, הללו פוסלין והללו מכשירין. שמא יאמר אדם: היאך אני למד תורה מעתה? תלמוד לומר: כולם "נתנו מרועה אחד" – אל אחד נתנן, פרנס אחד אמרן מפי אדון כל המעשים, ברוך הוא, דכתיב: "וידבר אלהים את כל הדברים האלה" (שמות כ, א). אף אתה עשה אזניך כאפרכסת וקנה לך לב מבין לשמוע את דברי מטמאים ואת דברי מטהרים, את דברי אוסרין ואת דברי מתירין, את דברי פוסלין ואת דברי מכשירין.
18 See above n. 14; the text is quoted by Frischmuth, *De Loco Devt.* XVII, §15.

of absurdities, etc. The tactic behind it is rhetorical, focussed on formulating, verifying with rabbinic texts, and then disseminating the idea that rabbinic and Jewish tradition is nothing but contradiction itself. Seen from the rabbinic point of view, with the message of the quoted texts, it is almost clear that the entire dissertation is based on a clear syllogism: if two rabbinic schools have different *and contradictory* conclusions of capital importance, and if they have based their argumentation on the Torah of Moses, then their conclusions should be considered to have originated with the divine authority even when they are contradictory. I will now present the tactics and logic of rabbinic debate and the (ab)use that Frischmuth made of them.

Frischmuth's Tactics of Argumentation

Frischmuth analyses what a controversy (*maḥloqet*) is, the value and persistence of this controversy, and the divine origin of the results of the contradictory debates. All of these points are introduced and presented after some rabbinic texts, primarily taken from the treatise entitled *Pirqei Avot* and its later commentaries. *Pirqei Avot* is a rabbinic treatise (probably composed between the second century BCE and the second century CE)[19] which is unique in its genre, because although it belongs to the Mishnah (the first main legal collection of the body of rabbinic literature, constitutive of that which is called the Oral Torah), it mirrors a wisdom text with religious, sapiential, and philosophical ideas rather than a typical Mishnaic halakhic composition. Yet this text is fundamental for rabbinic identity, because it presents the chain of tradition from Moses to the rabbinic period.

Maḥloqet le-shem shamayim

Maḥloqet is a postbiblical term for division, controversy, contradictory dispute, or dissent. The reader of talmudic passages would immediately acknowledge that the word was tantamount to ominous disunion. Because of the lack of a central authority capable of settling a dispute, *maḥloqet* was not synonymous with a peaceful dialectic discussion. Over the course of the centuries, it became a warning reminder of a violent episode in talmudic times, in which the students of the House of Shammay killed those of Hillel. This terrible anecdote is important for us because of the importance of both schools and their debates. According to the Babylonian Talmud:

> They [House of Shammay] thrust a sword into the study house and declared: 'Whoever wants to enter may enter, but no one may leave!' And on that day Hillel sat in submission before Sham-

---

19 The dating of rabbinic texts is a tremendous undertaking because of their nature as part of a literature of tradition, not of authors. Scholars consider the age of the Mishnah to be between the second century BCE and the second or third century CE.

may, like one of the disciples, and it was as wretched for Israel as the day on which the [golden] calf was made.[20]

More precisely, the Jerusalem Talmud reported:

> It was taught in the name of Rabbi Yehoshua Oniya: The students of the House of Shammay stood below them and they were killing the students of the House of Hillel. It was taught: Six of them ascended and the others stood over them with swords and lances.[21]

The historical frame of this episode is not clear; however, it is certain that the serious discussion could have led to a violent altercation because of the vital topic they were discussing. As a contrast, we can recall a passage of the Jerusalem Talmud that reports a nostalgic time in which there had been no diversity of opinion, no *maḥloqet*, because of the existence of the Sanhedrin, which settled them.[22] Although the local Sanhedrin could be places of peaceful discussion and judgement, the passionate temperament and vital necessity of debating were and remain characteristic of Jewish religion and life.

The debates between the Houses or Schools of Hillel and Shammay were of a particular nature. Rabbinic literature considers them a kind of *maḥloqet*, described as *le-shem shamayim*, that is, 'for the sake of heaven'; this dispute ends with an *aporia*, i.e. culminating in endless contradiction. The dispute between the Houses of Hillel and Shammay is endless because it is 'for the sake of Heaven' (*le-shem shamayim*), as stated in Mishnah, *Avot* 5:17:

> All controversies (*maḥloqet*) which are for the sake of Heaven will never cease to exist (סופה להתקיים); but one that is not in the name of Heaven will cease to exist. What [kind of] controversy is for the sake of Heaven? Such as was the controversy between Hillel and Shammay. What was an argument that was not for the sake of heaven? That of Korach and his congregation.

What is a *maḥloqet*? Frischmuth quotes the Sefardic philosopher Isaac Abravanel, who wrote a commentary on the treatise *Avot* in the fifteenth to sixteenth century.[23] According to him, a *maḥloqet* is not a play of dialectical value in order to overcome

---

[20] Babylonian Talmud, *Shabbat* 17a; English translation by Daniel Roth, "The Ninth of Adar: the Day Constructive Conflict Turned Destructive," *Pardes* 4 (2013), from http://pcjcr.pardes.org/wp-content/uploads/2013/02/JDCC-Occasional-Paper-2013.pdf.

[21] Jerusalem Talmud, *Shabbat* 1:4 (3c).

[22] Jerusalem Talmud, *Sanhedrin* 1:4 (19c): א"ר יוסי בראשונה לא היתה מחלוקת ישראל אלא סנהדרין של שבעים ואחד היתה יושבת בלשכת הגזית. On *maḥloqet*, see Moshe Sokol. "What Does a Jewish Text Mean? Theories on Elu ve-Elu Divrei Elohim Hayim in Rabbinic Literature," *Da'at* 32–33 (1994): 22–31 and Shaul Magid, "The Intolerance of Tolerance: Makhloket and Redemption in Early Hasidism," *Jewish Studies Quarterly* 8 (2001): 326–368.

[23] *Pirqei Avot. 'im perush ... Mosheh Ben Maimon we-'im perush naḥalat Ya'aqov meha-sar ha-gadol rabbenu don Yiṣḥaq Abarbanel* [Hebrew] (New York: D. Silberman, 1952–1953): 357; available online at http://www.mdz-nbn-resolving.de/urn/resolver.pl?urn=urn:nbn:de:bvb:12-bsb10933939-3.

one's counterpart, but a negotiation as the premise of how the truth comes to light and secret things are revealed,[24] according to his own words:

> (The *maḥloqet* is meant) for people to discuss, but not to prevail one against the other, although it is for the sake of Heaven, i.e. to let the truth come to light and to reveal the secret of the things which become known through the negotiation which is in the discussion.[25]

Frischmuth did not understand the texts and translated מתוך המשא והמתן אשר במחלוקת as *id quod fiat interventu deliberationis in disceptatione* ('to facilitate the decision in the discussion'). It is absolutely true that discussion can contribute to resolving the question, but he missed the point of how this is reached. He misunderstood the important reference to negotiation, which produces explanations or revelations of the secrets of the words. I actually do not know whether Abravanel was the first to compare the dialectic of discussion to a negotiation. However, Saadiah Gaon had already compared the search for the truth of the senses to a test of genuine and counterfeit coins.[26]

However, the idea of negotiation is a typical attitude of rabbinic Halakhah, similar to every legal system. Also, according to the Tosefta, *Sanhedrin* 13:3, the dead will be judged on every act of their lives: there will be the fully righteous, the fully evil, and those in-between, the *benonim* or *shequlim* ('equivalent' or 'equipollent'). Hence, a situation of equipollence of evil/good and true/false can also exist and its result, if any, will be negotiated.

Yet the idea of a negotiation of the truth is also present in Islamic philosophy, according to the work of Dominique Raynaud published in 2013.[27] He writes: 'During the course of a controversy, truth is temporarily suspended and replaced by an exchange of arguments of uncertain statute.'[28] His point of departure is the Persian savant Shams al-Dīn Al-Samarqandī (c. 1250 to c. 1302). He wrote some books on logic, mathematics, and astronomy and four treatises on the rules to be followed in the conduct of a scholarly controversy, of which only three are extant: *Risāla fī adāb al-baḥth* ('Epistle on the Rules and Etiquettes of Debate'), *Qusṭās al-afkār* ('The

---

24 Georg Ursinus, בית הישיבה והמדרש *Seu Antiquitates Hebraicæ Scholastico-Academicæ. In Quibus Scholarum & Academiarum Judaicarum historia tam intra quam extra Scripturam, Forma earundem, Docentium & Discentium officia, Ritus, Dimissio è Schola, Promotio, Promotionum Tituli, Distincti Professorum Ordines & Facultates, Methodus Disputandi, Studia, Statuta, Privilegia & Stipendia continuo, ubi fieri potuit, S. Scripturæ & monumentorum Rabbinicorum concentu eruta leguntur* (Copenhagen: Lieben, 1702): 287.
25 לקנטר ולא להתגבר זה על זה כי אם לשום שמים ר"ל להוציא האמת לאור ולגלות מצפוני הדברים אשר יודעו מתוך המשא והמתן אשר במחלוקת; see n. 14 and n. 23 above and Frischmuth, *De Loco Devt. XVII*, §16.
26 See Giuseppe Veltri, "Testing Genuine and Counterfeit Coins: The Subject's Error in Saadya's Argument of True Knowledge against Scepticism" (in preparation).
27 Dominique Raynaud, "Al-Samarqandī. Un précurseur de l'analyse des controversies scientifiques," *Al-Mukhatabat* 7 (2013): 8–25, now in idem, *Scientific Controversies: A Socio-historical Perspective on the Advancement of Science* (New Brunswick: Transaction, 2015): 163–182.
28 Raynaud, *Scientific Controversies*, 164.

Weighing of Ideas'), and *al-Muʿtaqadāt* ('The Convictions'), composed between 1291 and 1302. This is not the right place to explain the rules of rhetoric and dialectic debate which he settled and developed out of his knowledge of law and jurisprudence (*uṣūl al-fiqh* and *furūʿ*). Yet Al-Samarqandī's contribution to the dialectic and rhetoric of the debate is the careful analysis of the settlement of controversies, introducing the innovation of the 'signs of defeat' (*dalāʾil al-inqitāʿ*), the indication of the moment when one 'of the parties to the debate has [...] emerged as the victor or the vanquished.'[29] The signs are: inconsistency (the conclusion is not proportional to the premises or is self-contradictory); *reductio ad absurdum*; silence; distinction (necessary for the chain of reasoning); incapacity (to respond to a question); digression (a break in the continuity of reasoning); commensurability (non-conformity to the case); deviation (a response to a different question); appeal to the crowd (appealing to the listeners signifying a lack of arguments); or stubbornness (refutation of objections).

The expression 'sign of defeat' is a rhetorical tool for referring to a negotiation which ends in a result, expected at a certain point when the adversary shows signs of weakness. We have a similar situation in a chess game, which, according to the seventeenth-century philosopher Simone Luzzatto, is a symbol or metaphor of controversy, and fundamental to the understanding of philosophical (sceptical) debates:

> Some idle men promulgated other absurdities concerning this [i.e. the original principles of the world], but it would be too inopportune now to attempt to summarise them. Yet by observing these arguments and controversies about the ancient principles of things, I began to have suspicions about the imbecility of human knowledge. According to the probable, I therefore argued that if the disagreements concerning the principles are so complex and numerous, then the difficulties in the development of the discourse will be even more inexplicable. Just like lines that go from the centre to the circumference, when they [i.e. lines] are close to their origin, there is only a little distance between them, but as soon as they advance, they increasingly shift in different directions.
>
> Hence, I likewise started to suspect that as human beings we are indeed not endowed with sufficient organs and faculties to apprehend and acknowledge the truth. Besides, the early bases and foundations from which the edifice of human knowledge rises are indeed not fixed and stable, but arbitrary and laid at our whim, as is usually the case with games, especially with chess, where similarly, while deductions and consequences are necessary, the first positions are indeed contingent and voluntary.[30]

The game is over when the 'signs of defeat' are visible, unchallengeable as a consequence of the debate. According to Al-Samarqandī, they are valid only for controversies concerning philosophy, logic, astronomy, and mathematics. However, what is the purpose of controversies of vital religious importance? Is 'silence' a sufficient reason

---

29 Here I am summarising Raynaud, *Scientific Controversies*, 175–176.
30 Simone Luzzatto, *Scritti politici e filosofici di un ebreo scettico nella Venezia del Seicento*, introduced, commented, and edited by Giuseppe Veltri in cooperation with Anna Lissa and Paola Ferruta (Milan: Bompiani, 2013): 129.

to end the discussion, for example? Or a controversial point of view? The thesis of a legal negotiation cannot obscure the fact that this Islamic philosophical movement is affected by the same tendency present in the debate on the first principle of contradiction: to demonstrate the validity of a principle which cannot be invalidated. That is the reason why the contradiction of the Halakhah disputation will be settled in the end. However, what is the end?

End or Persistence of a Controversy (*sofah lehitqayyem*)?

The negotiability is not the end of the controversy, and that is the problem. Frischmuth quotes the Jewish exegete Obadiah of Bertinoro, who stated that 'he who can discuss exists and has not perished.' This is a reference to Korach's debate in the Bible, also quoted from *Pirqei Avot,* because it was not *le-shem shamayim* ('for the sake of Heaven'). The biblical personage of Korach was the leader of a rebellion against Moses in Numbers 16, along with 249 co-conspirators. He and his congregation were punished by fire from heaven. According to the rabbinic exegesis, Korach had a *maḥloqet* with Moses for private reasons; therefore, he was destroyed, according to both the Bible and Obadiah.

Obadiah also transmits the tradition according to which *sofah* ('her/its end') is not the end but the 'intended purpose' (*takhlit*) of the discussion, namely to reach the truth via debate (*maḥloqet*). The word *sof* (*finis*) became the 'purpose' of finding the truth, which is for the sake of Heaven, as in the case of Hillel and Shammay.[31] The *maḥloqet* in the case of Korach was not *le-shem shamayim*, but rather an intention to dominate (*serarah*), being a desire to overcome (*ahavat ha-niṣṣaḥon*).

Word of the Living God?

The question remains unsolved, according to Frischmuth, because the statement of why true and false should go back to the living God (*elu we-elu divre elohim hayyim*) is unsolved. Frischmuth's quoting of Abravanel on *Pirqei Avot* 5:17 confirms that *only* by debating can one establish which is the true opinion and which is the false. The truth can be established *only* by analysing the positions of the negotiations of both houses, and therefore the words of both houses are the word of the living God.

Here Frischmuth quotes Lipmann, who quotes[32] the anonymous *Sefer Ḥayyim*, which states that intention is the decisive argument for qualifying the schools of

---

31 אני שמעתי פרוש, סופה תכליתה המבוקש מעניינה, והמחלוקת שהיא לשם שמים, התכלית והסוף המבוקש מאותה מחלוקת, זה מתקיים כמ"ש מתוך הויכוח מתברר האמת." (פרק ה משנה ו בפרוש שם). See http://www.daat.ac.il/encyclopedia/value.asp?id1=1169. I am not sure that Obadiah is deconstructing the text, as Dov Landau put it.
32 Yom Tov Lipmann Muehlhausen, *Liber Nizachon*, 289.

both Hillel and Shammay as acting for the sake of Heaven (*le-shem shamayim*). However, Frischmuth objected to putting the question of whether a good will (*bona intentio*) is sufficient reason to qualify them with such a splendid title (*Ecquid vero bona intentio conferre postet ad id, ut illa tam splendido titulo insigniantur?*). Of course not: only conformity to the truth accords with the divine will. Nobody affirms, so Frischmuth says, that God's will is the contradiction of licit and illicit, pure and impure, unless he convinces himself that there is a known authority figure, like the Jews, who state such 'absurdity.' Yet Lipmann, the author most quoted by Frischmuth, stated that the controversial point is to be found in the explanation and not in the body of the commandment. And so we have the real enemy of the Protestant theologian: the Oral Torah, the explanation of the written text, and hence the authority of the rabbinic schools.

This is not the right place to discuss the Oral Torah as an unwritten teaching (like Plato's?) in contrast to or in consonance with the written text (or the dogmas of Greek philosophy). Frischmuth stigmatises the arch-enemy of the Protestant Reformation, the oral authoritative tradition, as the source of every evil in (the Church's) history. False and true, the dichotomy cannot be in the Written Torah and cannot be in God, but can only be among the alleged authority of the Jews with their absurd commentaries.

The Jewish Sceptical Attitude

There are many contradictory statements in the Jewish tradition, beginning with the book of Qohelet and continuing throughout rabbinic literature. Frischmuth quotes abundant material from the Talmud, the Midrash, and contemporary scholarly literature, such as the much-quoted Ashkenazic Lipmann Muehlhausen and Sephardic Isaac Abravanel. Yet the interesting aspect of such a position against Judaism is that he only quotes from authors and works that confirm his thesis of sceptical Judaism, leaving out the considerable number of treatises on Aristotelian logic quoted, translated, and commented on by medieval Jewish authors. A century later, in 1766, the scholar Johann Jakob Baur published an examination of the Jewish concern with philosophy, *Strictura quaedam ex philosophia Hebraeorum* ('A Stricture of Jewish Philosophy'), a chapter of which is devoted to logic (*Strictura quaedam ex logica*).[33] He sustains that nothing is extant from the ancient Jewish preoccupation with logic and that what rabbinic academies used were rules of hermeneutics which were based on logic such as *argumentum a maiore ad minus, analogia*, etc. Against Frischmuth's position, he quoted Maimonides,[34] who stated that impossible

---

[33] Johann Jakob Baur, *Stricturae Quaedam Ex Philosophia Hebraeorum, Maxime Recentiorum Cum Moderna Philosophandi Ratione Conformi. Speciatim Ex Logica Atque Metaphysica* (Tübingen: Schramm, 1766).
[34] *Moreh Nevukhim* III:15, Baur, *Stricturae*, XXXIII.

things are excluded from the power of God (*Res impossibiles sive contradictoria ab ipsa potentia Dei O.M. excludi monet*), or, according to Friedlander's translation of this passage:

> We have thus shown that according to each one of the different theories there are things which are impossible, whose existence cannot be admitted, and whose creation is excluded from the power of God, and the assumption that God does not change their nature does not imply weakness in God, or a limit to His power. Consequently, things impossible remain impossible, and do not depend on the action of an agent. It is now clear that a difference of opinion exists only as to the question to which of the two classes a thing belongs; whether to the class of the impossible, or to that of the possible.[35]

Frischmuth claims that the negation of principle is not only a philosophical position, but also a typical characteristic attributed to the Jewish temperament (*Sed nunc alia adhuc adducenda sunt, ex quibus patescet, hactenus Iudaeis nihil nos tribuisse, quod ab illorum indole sit alienum*).[36] The reader cannot avoid inferring that the Protestant theologian is looking for an argument for disqualifying Jewish philosophy, as such making it appear to be a 'natural attitude' to contradiction. In attributing a sceptical attitude to Jews, he is carrying on Protestant theology's policy of negating any relationship of the Jewish tradition to philosophy, a project initiated with the Reformation and developed throughout the seventeenth and eighteenth centuries.

To the already known attempt I have presented elsewhere,[37] I would like to add another here. Some years later, in 1704,[38] an anonymous article was published in issue VIII of *Observationes selectae* in Halle, with the title *An Salomon fuerit Scepticus* ('Could It Be That Solomon Was a Sceptic?'). As Martin Mulsow proved, the author of this text was the Lutheran theologian and philosopher Jakob Friedrich Reimann,[39] who, protected by the anonymity of the Halle journal, experimented with 'unorthodox ideas,' as Mulsow stated. His intention is clear: to deny the philosophical characterisation of a biblical figure, or, in his own words: 'It is ridiculous to make philosophers of all the Hebrew Patriarchs' (*ridiculum est ex omnibus Patriarchi Hebraeorum facere philosophos*). 'Philosophers,' for Reimann, means being 'dogmatic.' He treated the book and the figure of Job as prototypes of scepticism because of Job's enquiries into the origin of evil, whether God is to be considered good, his negation of the presence of wisdom and knowledge on earth (very similar to *nil sciri*), etc. He concentrat-

---

[35] Online: https://en.wikisource.org/wiki/The_Guide_for_the_Perplexed_(Friedlander)/Part_III/Chapters.
[36] *De Loco Devt. XVII*, §15: C4r.
[37] See the first part of my *Sapienza Alienata. La Filosofia ebraica tra mito, scienza e scetticismo* (Rome: Aracne, 2017): 31–147. An English version with additions will be published in 2018.
[38] Jakob Friedrich Reimmann, "An Salomo fuerit Scepticus?," *Observationes selectae ad rem litterariam spectantes* 8 (1704): 327–367.
[39] Martin Mulsow, "Eclecticism or Skepticism? A Problem of the Early Enlightenment," *Journal of the History of Ideas* 58.3 (1997): 466, n. 5.

ed his attention on Solomon, considering him an Ephectic (ἐφεκτικός, from ἐπέχειν). According to him, Solomon (of Proverbs, the Song of Songs, and of course Qohelet) is by no means a philosopher of the *universalia* (that is, a dogmatic), but of particular things, basing all things on experience and not on logical deductions and inferences. Reimann's real intention is not primarily to characterise the biblical tradition of Solomon as sceptical, but to justify or support scepticism on the basis of biblical exempla. Scepticism is not only the foundation of the modern sciences, but also originates from a new conception of the divinity, which is much more preoccupied with human life than with celestial dogmas. Furthermore, according to him, Judaism is not a philosophy, but it is sceptical in the main.

Conclusion

The logic of rabbinic discussion is based on a dogma, like the dogma of PNC: the Principle of the Reception of Torah (PRT):

PNC: either false or true   PRT: either received or not

Neither is demonstrable. The debate on the plausibility of PNC or PRT is not proof of the validity of either of them. The discussion will last forever, according to the rabbinic mind, because nobody can claim to resolve the *aporia* of a Written and Oral Torah that is on earth and no longer in Heaven.

God (G) gave the Written and the Oral Torah (OT & WT), i.e. the text and its logical/interpretational rules and tradition at Sinai (legislative moment). He therefore gave every tool for solving every problem. If Rabbi Hillel (RH) and Rabbi Shammay (RS) reached opposite conclusions (C1 and -C1) on the same problem (P), then there are three possible explanations for the opposition, the first two of which were developed by Saadiah Gaon in another context.[40]

- The opposition is because of RH and RS: this is excluded because they are not acting for themselves, but *le-shem shamayim* ('for the sake of Heaven'). They do not have any personal reason for a conflict of interest.
- They are incapable of deciding on or are ignorant of OT & WT: this is also excluded because, according to the rabbinic mind, both the schools of RH and RS and the fundament of rabbinic authority are excellent.
- The contradiction is to be included in OT & WT, i.e. in the work of the lawgivers.

The everlasting debate is, therefore, to be interpreted as an everlasting *aporia*, the impossibility of finding a definitive solution to the problem. The Jewish scholars made a great effort to find a solution to the *aporia* of the everlasting debating be-

---

40 See my article quoted in n. 24.

tween the rabbinic schools. Obadiah of Bertinoro interpreted *sofah lehitqayyem* as 'the purpose of the truth will be reached,' in contrast to the philological and philosophical arguments. However, *sofah lehitqayyem* really means 'at its end (the discussion) will persist.' The discussion is not a premise of a veritable conclusion, of which there can only be one—the truth—, but it will still exist at its end. The negotiation is only a temporary pause in the process of human life. This would at least explain why both contradictory positions are 'words of the living God.' The God of the Jews vividly interferes in the debate, but only the majority can offer a temporary solution to the everyday dilemmas, and 'temporary' means that the debate will also be everlasting.

Libera Pisano
Silence, Translation, and Grammatical Therapy: Some Features of Linguistic Scepticism in the Thought of Rosenzweig and Wittgenstein

In this essay, I will attempt to investigate the different approaches of Rosenzweig and Wittgenstein as two manifestations of the constellation of *Sprachskepsis*, which—despite their apparent divergences—can be seen as the common thread linking these two very different authors. I will try to show how the importance of the apophatic moment, reflection about the limits of language, a critical attitude towards dogmatism and essentialism, and the concept of philosophy as therapy—features that we can find in the thought of both Rosenzweig and Wittgenstein—stem from a *sprachskeptische Horizontbildung* present in the cultural debate of that time.

Rosenzweig and Wittgenstein: a Forgotten Dialogue

The link between these authors has almost been forgotten, and in fact, with the exception of Hilary Putnam—who does not consider the linguistic matter—and an important article written by Paul Franks,[1] there is no critical study which gives a thorough investigation of the theoretical connection between Franz Rosenzweig (1886–1929) and Ludwig Wittgenstein (1889–1951). This is also due to the inadequate attention paid to the *Sprachskepsis*, which has always been considered a poetic and literary phenomenon.[2] However, it also has a pivotal role in philosophical debate—start-

---

[1] Hilary Putnam, *Jewish Philosophy as a Guide to Life* (Bloomington and Indianapolis: Indiana University Press, 2008); idem, "Introduction" to the English translation of Franz Rosenzweig, *Understanding the Sick and the Healthy*, trans. Nahum Glatzer (Cambridge, Mass.: Harvard University Press, 1999): 1–20; and Paul Franks, "Everyday speech and revelatory speech in Rosenzweig and Wittgenstein," *Philosophy Today* 50.1 (2006): 24–39. There are some suggestions in a book by Reza Hosseini, a paper by Cora Diamond, and an article by William Franke; see Reza Hosseini, *Wittgenstein and Meaning in Life: In Search of the Human Voice* (Basingstoke, UK, and New York: Palgrave Macmillan, 2015) and Cora Diamond, "Wittgenstein on Religious Belief: The Gulfs Between Us," in *Religion and Wittgenstein's Legacy*, eds. Dewi Zephaniah Philipps and Mario von der Ruhr (Aldershot: Ashgate, 2005): 99–138. Diamond thinks that Wittgenstein made significant progress with the revelatory uses of language, a problem that can be clarified with the help of Rosenzweig. Furthermore, see William Franke, "Franz Rosenzweig and the Emergence of a Postsecular Philosophy of the Unsayable," *International Journal for Philosophy of Religion* 58 (2005): 161–180.
[2] See Katherine M. Arens, "Linguistic Scepticism: Towards a Productive Definition," *Monatshefte* 74.2 (1982): 145–155 and George Steiner, *Language and Silence* (New York: Athenaeum, 1970); Franco Rella, *Il silenzio e le parole* (Milan: Feltrinelli, 1984).

ing from Fritz Mauthner[3]—because it reveals the break between word and world by turning language into one of the main topics discussed in philosophy.

The dialogue between these two authors illuminates Rosenzweig's connection with the so-called *Sprachkrise* at the turn of the last century;[4] if Wittgenstein's relationship with the specific constellation of *Sprachkrise*, which developed in Vienna, has already been stressed by different scholars,[5] critical study of Rosenzweig has not paid due attention to his connection with this phenomenon.

It is undeniable that Rosenzweig and Wittgenstein were two of the most important philosophers of language of the last century, with two distinct approaches. It is worth saying that their books, namely Rosenzweig's *The Star of Redemption* and Wittgenstein's *Tractatus*, are somehow a product of war, because they were written at the front during World War I. Without any doubt, Rosenzweig's theological and transcendental thread is completely different from the linguistic immanence of Wittgenstein's approach.[6] Their philosophies manifest two opposite movements: a vertical transcendence and a horizontal commonality. However, even if the former's theological aura could have been considered the opposite of Wittgenstein's critique of linguistic enchantments, there are some elements that allow us to develop an original and serious opposition between them. In my view, both attempts can be interpreted within the wider phenomenon of *Sprachskepsis*, which entails a denial of an absolute foundation of knowledge, a delimitation of human understanding, and a re-thinking of the philosophical task.

By trying not to oversimplify the complexity of these authors, let me make some methodological remarks. My essay is a hermeneutical attempt to shed light on the affinity between these two authors in order to analyse some elements of linguistic scepticism. In doing so, it is not my purpose to follow the critical debate between the different readings of Wittgenstein scepticism[7] or to reduce Rosenzweig's religious

---

3 Cf. Libera Pisano, "Misunderstanding Metaphors: Linguistic Scepticism in Mauthner's Philosophy," in *Yearbook of the Maimonides Centre for Advanced Studies 2016*, eds. Giuseppe Veltri and Bill Rebiger (Berlin and Boston: De Gruyter, 2016): 95–122.

4 Leora Batnitzky maintains that Rosenzweig's hermeneutic sensibilities stem from the epistemological and existential crises of the twentieth century; cf. Leora Batnitzky, "Foreword," in Franz Rosenzweig, *Cultural Writings*, trans. Barbara Galli (New York: Siracuse University Press, 2000): IX.

5 Engelmann stressed the influence of Viennese culture at the turn of the century, particularly the work of Kraus and Loos, on his friend Wittgenstein. See the masterful work by Allan Janik and Stephen Toulmin, *Wittgenstein's Vienna* (New York: Touchstone, 1973) and William W. Bartley, *Wittgenstein* (Philadelphia and New York: J.B. Lippincott Company, 1973).

6 Cf. Franks, "Everyday speech and revelatory speech in Rosenzweig and Wittgenstein," 30: 'Wittgenstein [...] sees language as natural to the human-life form, perhaps therefore as God's gift to the human being. But he does not see language as God's word to the human being,' as Rosenzweig does.

7 In his *Pyrrhonian Reflection on Knowledge and Justification*, Fogelin makes a distinction between two diametrically opposed approaches in Wittgenstein's later writings: a Pyrrhonian approach (Diamond, Conant, later Baker) according to which Wittgenstein aims to persuade us to give up all philosophical views, and anti-Pyrrhonian readings (Hacker, Hintikka, Pears, von Savigny), which replace

(and perhaps dogmatic) depth. Furthermore, I will not go into the debate about the different phases of Wittgenstein's thought.[8] In the analysis of his philosophy, I based my research on the work of Cora Diamond, David Stern, and Pierre Hadot;[9] in particular, the reading of the latter, who considers philosophy as a way of life, is the hermeneutic ground for my interpretation of scepticism. It is worth noting that Hadot's interpretation of Wittgenstein is a nonconformist reading; in fact, it was neglected and overlooked by the critics, even if his account of ancient philosophy as an ethical praxis contributed to opening up new readings of Wittgenstein.[10]

Moreover, I will point out some features of linguistic scepticism in the *Tractatus* and in the *Philosophical Investigations*, particularly—as we will see—the issue of silence and the sceptical metaphor in the former and the problem of translation alongside grammatical therapy in the latter. As is well known, the most striking difference between the early and later phases of Wittgenstein's philosophy concerns his concep-

---

the critique of certain traditional theories with a positive philosophical position in Wittgenstein's works; cf. Robert J. Fogelin, *Pyrrhonian Reflection on Knowledge and Justification* (Oxford and New York: Oxford University Press, 1994): 205–222; see also the reconstruction of this debate made by David Stern, *Wittgenstein's Philosophical Investigations: An Introduction* (Cambridge: Cambridge University Press, 2004): 33–36, 168–170. As is well known, there is also another struggle among Wittgenstein's interpreters: the debate between the 'quietist' (Diamond, Putnam, McDowell) who believes that the binomial 'form of life' is not the basis for a pragmatist theory of meaning and praxis, and the 'anti-quietist,' who defends the opposite position. Furthermore, I will not deal with the topic of rule-following scepticism discussed by Saul A. Kripke in his important work *Wittgenstein on Rules and Private Language* (Cambridge, Mass.: Harvard University Press, 1982), where he contends the conjunction between scepticism and rules, because—according to a Wittgensteinian approach—it is impossible to prove whether a rule was followed in a correct way. Kripke stated that the rule-following paradox is 'the most radical and original sceptical problem that philosophy has seen to date' (*ibidem*, 60). According to him, following a rule means doing as the community does. On the debate about sceptical traits in Wittgenstein's notion of a rule, cf. Michael Dummett, "Wittgenstein's Philosophy of Mathematics," *Philosophical Review* 68 (1959): 324–348; Henry Staten, *Wittgenstein and Derrida* (Lincoln: University of Nebraska Press, 1984); Colin McGinn, *Wittgenstein on Meaning* (Oxford: Blackwell, 1984); Simon Blackburn, "The Individual Strikes Back," *Synthese* 58 (1984): 281–303; Peter Winch, *The Idea of Social Science and its Relation to Philosophy* (London: Routledge & Kegan Paul, 1958); and Norman Malcolm, *Nothing is Hidden: Wittgenstein's Criticism of his Early Thought* (Oxford: Blackwell, 1986).

8 I will follow David Stern, who saw continuities and contrasts 'between the Tractarian logical atomism, the "logical holism" of the 1929–34 period, and the "practical holism" of the later 1930s,' cf. Stern, *Wittgenstein's Philosophical Investigation: An Introduction*, 27. On the different interpretations of the two phases of Wittgenstein's thought, see Paul Feyerabend, "Wittgenstein's Philosophical Investigations," *Philosophical Review* 64 (1955): 449–483; Cora Diamond, *The Realistic Spirit: Wittgenstein, Philosophy and the Mind* (Cambridge, Mass.: MIT Press, 1991); and Anthony Kenny, *Wittgenstein* (Cambridge, Mass.: Harvard University Press, 1973).

9 See Diamond, *The Realistic Spirit: Wittgenstein, Philosophy and the Mind*; David Stern, *Wittgenstein's Philosophical Investigations: An Introduction*; idem, *Wittgenstein on Mind and Language* (Oxford: Oxford University Press, 1966); and Pierre Hadot, *Wittgenstein et les limites du langage* (Paris: Vrin, 2004).

10 See Sandra Laugier, "Pierre Hadot as a Reader of Wittgenstein," *Paragraph* 34.3 (2001): 322–337.

tion of language: if, in the *Tractatus*, Wittgenstein deals with a quest for the general form of propositions, an *a priori* order of the world shared by word and thought and a logical definition of language, in the later *Philosophical Investigations*, he points out a variety of language uses or language games. In my view, the passage from the explanation to the description—from a strict theory of meaning to the impossibility of formulating a definition by referring to family resemblances—is the meaningful change in Wittgenstein's thought. One can say that the passage from the *Tractatus* to the *Philosophical Investigations* is a shift in focus from *reductio ad unum* to the plurality of the games.

On the other hand, regarding Rosenzweig's philosophy, I will attempt to give an account of some elements of his linguistic scepticism by analysing *The Star of Redemption*, the *New Thinking*, his preface to his translation of Jehuda Halevi's poems, and his short book *Understanding the Sick and the Healthy*.

Sprachkrise as Hermeneutic Horizon

The sceptical atmosphere in which I will situate Rosenzweig and Wittgenstein is the *Sprachkrise*; that is, radical scepticism towards the language's capability to grasp reality and disclose the truth at the turn of the twentieth century. This constellation of crises was the premise for a renewed interest in the philosophy of language in many different approaches; on the other hand, it is also the tool which allows us to understand the connection between these authors.

Even if this binomial is not so common in the history of thought, linguistic scepticism can be broadly defined as philosophical doubts about the communicative, epistemological, and ontological value of language, which constitutes one of the most extensively discussed problems in Western philosophy. Certainly, at the beginning of the twentieth century with the so-called *Sprachkrise*—a complex phenomenon of language critique diffused in the philosophical and literary debate among poets and intellectuals before World War I—language attracted special attention, especially among German-Jewish thinkers.

Considering the boundaries of language was the specific trait of the theoretical constellation of *Sprachkrise* that was characterised by a general distrust of words and a struggle against the linguistic cage. Many writers, poets, and thinkers—for instance von Hofmannsthal, Schnitzler, Mombert, Rilke, Zweig, Kafka, Kraus, and many others—dealt with the crisis of a whole set of values, with the failure of the teleological concept of history, and with the collapse of language as a epistemological, logical, and ontological tool.[11] This phenomenon was interpreted as more literary than phil-

---

[11] Cf. Franke, "Franz Rosenzweig and the Emergence of a Postsecular Philosophy of the Unsayable," 161: 'A particularly dense and destiny-laden nodal point in the midst of this history is Viennese culture at the turn from the 19th to the 20th century, pivoting on figures such as Hofmannsthal, Wittgen-

osophical, but—in my view—its role is crucial for at least two reasons: firstly, the *Sprachkrise* helps us to better understand how the critique of language became the focus of philosophical thought at the beginning of the last century long before the linguistic turn; secondly, this phenomenon acquired special attention, especially among German-Jewish thinkers. In fact, since all these authors have a double mother tongue in common, or better, a double belonging both to Jewish tradition and to German philosophy, their sceptical attitudes or critical distance towards language also have their premises in autobiographical factors.

Thanks to the mediation of Mauthner, whose work was the *trait d'union* between literature and critical thought, the phenomenon of *Sprachskepsis* spread throughout the milieu of German-Jewish philosophy; in fact, it involves the whole generation of thinkers whose elective affinities were analysed by Löwy, i.e. Landauer, Benjamin, Buber, Scholem, Bloch, and others, who linked together language, messianism, libertarian utopias, and Romanticism.[12] Among these authors, it is worth mentioning Eugen Rosenstock, who had a strong influence on Rosenzweig's philosophy thanks to the elaboration of his 'grammatical approach' according to which language is a bridge between men.[13]

The *Sprachkrise* had a wide variety of aspects and was the epiphenomenon of a deep crisis of meaning, starting from Nietzsche's philosophy and a *Zeitgeist* characterised by the collapse of classical reason. One feature of this phenomenon was a kind of 'apophatic crisis,'[14] namely a paradoxical apophatic *koine* which combined the Neo-Platonic and mystic traditions with Jewish thought. In fact, it is not by chance that the *Sprachkrise* is also connected with the reinterpretation of mysticism, namely the *Neue Mystik* that was developed in Germany at the turn of the twentieth century by poets and writers such as Julius and Heinrich Hart, Wilhelm Bölsche,

---

stein, Musil, Rilke, Klimt, Kraus and Schoenberg. The catastrophe of an entire historical epoch was here felt in all its extremity and was expressed with the utmost acuteness and oftentimes pathos too.'
12 Cf. Michael Löwy, *Redemption and Utopia: Jewish Libertarian Thought in Central Europe*, trans. Hope Heany (London: Verso, 1992); Elke Dubbels, *Figuren des Messianischen in Schriften deutsch-jüdischer Intellektueller 1900–1933* (Berlin and Boston: De Gruyter, 2011); and Gerd Mattenklott, *Gustav Landauer. Ein Portrait*, in Gustav Landauer, *Werkausgabe*, vol. 3, eds. Gert Mattenklott and Hanna Delf (Berlin: Akademie Verlag, 1997): VII-XXII.
13 In his *Angewandte Seelenkunde*, published in 1916, Rosenstock defined language as the essential part of the human soul which plays a pivotal role in the creation of a linguistic community. He spoke of the 'grammar of the soul' that has its origin in religion and precedes logic formal thinking; cf. Eugen Rosenstock-Huessy, *Angewandte Seelenkunde* (Darmstadt: Röther-Verlag, 1916). Concerning the influence of Rosenstock on his thought, Rosenzweig wrote: 'Without Eugen I would never have written the *Star of Redemption*,' quoted by Alexander Altmann, "Franz Rosenzweig and Eugen Rosenstock-Huessy an Introduction to Their 'Letters on Judaism and Christianity,'" *The Journal of Religion* 24.4 (1994): 267; cf. Corinna Kaiser, *Gustav Landauer als Schriftsteller. Sprache, Schweigen, Musik* (Berlin and Boston: De Gruyter, 2014): 12–13.
14 Cf. Franke, "Franz Rosenzweig and the Emergence of a Postsecular Philosophy of the Unsayable," 162; Janik and Toulmin, *Wittgenstein's Vienna*; Rella, *Il silenzio e le parole*.

Willy Pastor, Rainer Maria Rilke, Alfred Mombert, Bruno Wille, etc.[15] This new kind of mysticism does not deal with the traditional idea of a mystic union between God and the soul, but rather with an awareness of a connection between the individual and the community, the present and the past. This kind of secularised mysticism combines aesthetical-linguistic aspects—it is not by chance that most of these authors were writers and poets—with a political and social idea of the regeneration of humankind.[16] The act of doubting our knowledge, our language, our representations of the world, and our political institutions is not a mere theoretical exercise, but rather is connected to a political purpose.

The *Sprachkrise* is not a mere refusal of language *tout court*, but rather a questioning of some uses of language through a permanent linguistic critique which becomes the task of philosophy itself. The critical consideration of language in its political, epistemological, and aesthetical role is at the heart of this new way of thinking. Many aspects are involved, such as the relationship between ordinary language and philosophical vocabulary, the role of silence, and the theoretical conjunction between community and linguistic practice. Therefore, the comparison between Rosenzweig and Wittgenstein will be structured into four deeply connected paths: the apophatic thought of Rosenzweig's *The Star of Redemption* and the mysticism at the end of Wittgenstein's *Tractatus*; the question of translation and the problem of understanding; the grammatical therapy for philosophical illness which also concerns a critique of essentialism; and the sceptical metaphors for a redefinition of philosophy.

I Boundaries of Language: Apophatic Grammar and Mystic Silence

Rosenzweig's and Wittgenstein's philosophies wrestle with the boundaries of language. If, according to the former, speaking means staying in touch with the unsay-

---

[15] The connection between a new idea of community and a particular idea of language was also experienced at that time by the organisation called 'Neue Gemeinschaft,' formed by a group of artists and writers who shared the ideas of Heinrich and Julius Hart, two brothers known for their literary criticism. Their attempt was to offer a revitalisation of society in accordance with a reform of literature, and their spiritual guide was the metaphysical and religious ideas of Julius Hart, explained in his works such as *Der neue Gott* and *Die neue Welterkenntnis*.

[16] Cf. Walther Hoffmann, Neue Mystik, in *Die Religion in Geschichte und Gegenwart*, vol. 4, eds. Friedrich M. Schiele and Leopold Scharnack (Tübingen: Mohr, 1913): 608–611; Uwe Spörl, *Gottlose Mystik in der deutschen Literatur um die Jahrhundertwende* (Paderborn: Schöningh, 1997); Martina Wagner-Egelhaft, *Mystik der Moderne. Die visionäre Ästhetik der deutschen Literatur im 20. Jahrhundert* (Stuttgart: Metzler 1989); and Anna Wolkowicz, *Mystiker der Revolution. Der utopische Diskurs um die Jahrhundertwende* (Warsaw: WUW, 2007). In my view, the new conception of mysticism passes through the translation of Meister Eckhart by Landauer, who rethinks mystic desire as an afflatus to a harmonic union of community in a kind of social mysticism.

able otherness, in Wittgenstein's *Tractatus*, silence is the ethical boundary of language. Both authors consider the religious element within a linguistic perspective by dealing with its modality of expressions. However, Wittgenstein does not consider the positive content of religious revelation as an articulation of the inexpressible, as Rosenzweig does.[17]

In *The Star of Redemption*, Rosenzweig stated that:

> [...] there is nothing more deeply Jewish than a final suspicion of the power of the word ['Misstrauen gegen die Macht des Wortes'] and a heart-felt confidence in the power of silence ['Zutrauen zur Macht des Schweigens'].[18]

The apophatic gesture of Rosenzweig consists of a deep reconsideration of human existence on the basis of the negativity of knowledge as constitutive of human discourse. It could seem paradoxical to speak of an apophatic tendency in Rosenzweig's thought; however, in *The Star of Redemption*, not only do silence and gesture play a

---

[17] This comparison can help us to shed light on the Jewish aspect of Wittgenstein's notion of language; in fact, the unsayability of religious belief could be interpreted as a deep-rooted Jewish attitude, in which the prohibition of pronouncing the Tetragrammaton turns silence into a theological element. In particular, the relevance of silence connected to the element of religion is particularly interesting if one reads it in line with the Jewish tradition. We should not underestimate the fact that Engelmann claimed that Wittgenstein's attitude towards language was typically Jewish. Actually, as Stern stated, the debate on the relationship between Judaism and Wittgenstein is also controversial because it is difficult to give a unique definition of Judaism or Jewishness, firstly because Wittgenstein was not a religious man—even if, in a letter to his student Drury, he defined himself as 'one hundred percent Hebraic' and in 1931 he spoke of himself as a Jewish thinker—and secondly because the reception of his thought was almost always in the context of analytic philosophy. However, the connection between silence and the unsayable and religious belief, the Talmudic traits of his arguments, and explicit references to the Kabbalah play an important role in his thought. Moreover, the interpretation of language in connection with the praxis and form of life—which will be analysed as follows—could be interpreted in the wake of the Jewish tradition. Cf. Paul Engelmann, *Letters from Ludwig Wittgenstein with a Memoir* (Oxford: Basil Blackwell, 1967) and David Stern, "Was Wittgenstein a Jew?" in *Wittgenstein: Biography and Philosophy*, ed. James C. Klagge (Cambridge: Cambridge University Press, 2001): 237. See in particular the work of Brian F. McGuinness, "Wittgenstein und Judentum," in *Paul Engelmann (1891–1965) Architektur Judentum Wiener Moderne*, ed. Ursula A. Schneider (Vienna: Folio Verlag, 1999); Ray Monk, *Ludwig Wittgenstein: The Duty of Genius* (New York: The Free Press, 1990); Bela Szabados, "Autobiography after Wittgenstein," *The Journal of Aesthetics and Art Criticism* 50 (1992): 1–12; idem, "Was Wittgenstein an Anti-Semite? The Significance of Antisemitism for Wittgenstein's Philosophy," *Canadian Journal of Philosophy* 29 (1999): 1–28; Donatella Di Cesare, "Ethik als Lebensform. Jüdische Spuren bei Wittgenstein," *Wittgenstein-Studien* 4 (2013): 249–264; Ranjit Chatterjee, *Wittgenstein and Judaism. A Triumph of Concealment* (Frankfurt am Main: Lang Verlag, 2005); and idem, "Judaic Motifs in Wittgenstein," in *Austrians and Jews in the 20th Century*, ed. Robert S. Wistrich (Basington, UK, and New York: Palgrave Macmillan, 1992): 142–161.

[18] Franz Rosenzweig, *The Star of Redemption*, trans. Barbara E. Galli (Madison: Wisconsin Press, 2005): 321.

crucial role, but there is also a kind of linguistic scepticism towards knowledge which crosses human experience.

In the first part of the *Star*, Rosenzweig deals with the issue of how we can speak of the pre-world, seen as an amorphous magma in which God, Man, and World cannot be distinguished and thence, named. In fact, these three elements—God, World, and Man, connected through creation, revelation, and redemption—are articulated in relation to one another, but in themselves, they remain pure enigmas and ineffable mysteries. Through the unspoken original words 'Yes,' 'No,' and 'And,' the edifice of logos is built. In the transition from creation to revelation, from the night of these proto-words to the day of words, Rosenzweig wrote precious pages on his philosophy of language, or better his philosophy of the name that 'is not sound and smoke, but word and fire.'[19] According to Rosenzweig, language is the dynamic bridge between men, but it always copes with the border of the unsayable and with a nothingness that cannot be grasped, even if it constitutes the ground, or rather background, of our discourses. From beyond all manner of verbal determinations, which constitute human experience, language can recall the unsayable abyss of nothing.[20]

The third part of the *Star* deals with divine ineffability and the fact that—in Rosenzweig's view—redemption is both beyond names and beyond language:

> [...] the progress of Redemption in the world happens in the Name and for the sake of the Name. But the end is nameless, above all name. The sanctification of the Name itself happens so that the Name one day may become silent. Beyond the word—and what is the name other than the completely concentrated word?—beyond the word the silence gives light.[21]

The word, even the word of God, is always penultimate because it is a permanent anticipation of everything that follows; therefore, the final redemption must be silent:

> [...] in eternity the word ceases to exist in the silence of the harmonious gathering—for we are united only in silence; the word unites, but those who are united grow silent.[22]

However, the silence of redemption is opposed to the silence of creation, or better, it is its fulfilment.[23] In the *Star*, one can distinguish at least two different forms of silence: in the first part of the book, the silence of the tragic hero corresponds to the

---

19 Cf. *ibidem*, 202.
20 See Franke, "Franz Rosenzweig and the Emergence of a Postsecular Philosophy of the Unsayable," 170: 'Precisely this Nothing is the ground, or rather the background, to which Rosenzweig constantly recalls attention in expounding the elements of his new linguistic thinking.'
21 Rosenzweig, *The Star of Redemption*, 406.
22 *Ibidem*, 317.
23 In my reading of *The Star of Redemption*, its movement and structure are deeply Hegelian and, like his *Science of Logic*, the being at the end of the book is the fulfilment of the being of the beginning.

isolated gesture of one who is separated from his community; on the other hand, at the end of the book, there is the 'full' silence of liturgy, rites, and prayers, which is the shared silence of redemption where every single man acknowledges himself in his silent community. If the first is an abstract silence which belongs not only to the hero but also to the mathematic symbols, the second is an ultra-linguistic silence, beyond all possible misunderstandings and varieties of languages.

In his *Tractatus*, written while he was a soldier, Wittgenstein connects world and word through a kind of axiomatic logic based on a picture theory of meaning, according to which human thoughts or mental representations are expressed in propositions whose content is the truth condition of their correspondence to reality. In the first years after its publication, the *Tractatus* was usually seen as a work of logic and as a contribution to the Vienna Circle's[24] verificationists, especially regarding his attempt to put end to nonsensical language and metaphysical speculation. However, as is well known, Wittgenstein refused to be part of this philosophical circle, and when he was invited to explain his cryptic theory of meaning and representation, he preferred to read Tagore's poems instead of answering their questions. In the 1950s, scholars interpreted the metaphysical aspects of the *Tractatus* that the positivists had not taken into account; for instance, the distinction between *Sagen und Zeigen*, namely what we can say in words and what we can only show.

In the *Tractatus*, Wittgenstein's attempt to axiomatise knowledge, to communicate the truth, and to achieve a correct analysis of language is based on an isomorphism between world and language. According to his view, propositions—the elementary propositions which correspond to some atomic facts[25]—are a sort of picture of reality; in fact, both share a logical form with the thing they represent, and they are not false or true *a priori*, but rather their falsity or truth can only be verified by their comparison with facts in the world.

As Diamond stated, the main difficulty in this work consists in Wittgenstein's understanding of the limits of the expression of thoughts and nonsense.[26] In Wittgenstein's *Tractatus*, if a proposition does not conform to the general conditions that are met by a meaningful discourse, it is taken to be nonsensical; namely, a proposition that cannot be verified by comparison with reality.[27] However, according to Wittgenstein, there are some cases in which we do not need to look at the state of things to

---

[24] The Vienna Circle was composed of philosophers and scientists who shared a logical empiricism or logical positivist position. Among its members were Schlick, Waismann, Carnap, Neurath, Gödel, etc.

[25] See Ludwig Wittgenstein, *Tractatus Logico-Philosophicus*, trans. David F. Pears and Brian F. McGuinness (London: Routledge & Kegan Paul, 1974): 36 (4.22–4.2211).

[26] Cora Diamond, "Ethics, imagination and the method of Wittgenstein's Tractatus," in *The New Wittgenstein*, ed. Alice Crary and Rupert Read (London: Routledge, 2000): 151.

[27] Even scepticism is defined by Wittgenstein as nonsensical since it calls into question what is unquestionable: a doubt exists if there is a question and a question exists if there is an answer. One can say that scepticism is somehow an attempt to wrestle with the limits of our language. See Wittgenstein, *Tractatus Logico-philosophicus*, 88 (6.51).

say whether a proposition is true or false; for instance, this is the case for logical propositions, namely tautologies, which are always true, and contradictions, which are always false. These logical propositions do not correspond to the facts of the world, but show the logical form of a reality that is nonsensical because it cannot be true or false. Even if these propositions are nonsensical, Wittgenstein defines logic as a 'mirror-image of the world,'[28] because it shows the possibility of language itself. In the last pages of his work, logic and ethics are defined as transcendent and therefore nonsensical, because a meaningful 'proposition can express nothing that is higher.'[29]

Wittgenstein's adjective 'nonsensical' must be interpreted as that which exceeds the ordinary logic of correspondence on which a meaningful proposition is based. What is 'Unaussprechliches'—which could be logical or ethical—lies beyond any language, but shows itself in language. Thence, there are some things that cannot be said but can only be shown. Wittgenstein connects this manifestation to the realm of mysticism and the unsayable: 'There are, indeed, things that cannot be put into words. They *make themselves manifest*. They are what is mystical.'[30] Among what cannot be said are the fields of aesthetics, religion, art, culture, and the meaning of life, and in the face of these, logical sense collapses. If the 'sense of the word must lie outside the word,'[31] it must be outside the limits of our language.

As Russell stated in his introduction to Wittgenstein's book, language considered as a whole is nonsensical, because it cannot express itself.[32] Furthermore, there are some ethical truths that exceed the logical space and that cannot be said because 'they *make themselves manifest*.'[33] In this impossibility lies the philosophical paradox of the *Tractatus*, which deals not only with the communication of the truth, but also with what escapes our linguistic understanding.

The apophatic feature of the *Tractatus* was emphasised by Wittgenstein not only in a letter to Russell of 1919—in which he writes

> The main point is the theory on what can be said by propositions [...] and what cannot be expressed by propositions, but only shown, which I believe is the cardinal problem of philosophy.[34]

---

[28] *Ibidem*, 87 (6.43).
[29] *Ibidem*, 86 (6.42).
[30] *Ibidem*, 89 (6.522).
[31] *Ibidem*, 86 (6.41).
[32] Bertrand Russell, "Introduction," in *ibidem*, XXIII: 'Everything, therefore, which is involved in the very idea of the expressiveness of language must remain incapable of being expressed in language, and is, therefore, inexpressible in a perfectly precise sense.'
[33] *Ibidem*, 89 (6.522).
[34] Ludwig Wittgenstein, *Cambridge Letter*, 124, quoted by Stern, *Wittgenstein's Philosophical Investigation: An Introduction*, 41. As is well known, Russell, in his "Introduction" to Wittgenstein's *Tractatus*, also stressed the mystic traits of the book.

–, but also in the famous letter to the editor Ludwig von Ficker, in which he explains the way his book is to be interpreted by stressing the ethical point and the question of silence:

> My work consists of two parts: the one presented here plus all that I have not written. And it is precisely this second part that it is the important one [...]. In short, I believe that where many others today are just babbling, I have managed in my book to put everything firmly in place by being silent about it.[35]

This interpretation based on the relevance of silence in Wittgenstein's work leads to an ethical-religious reading; in fact, even later in his *Lecture on Ethics*, he described the tendency to speak or write on ethics or religion as a hopeless experience of 'running against the walls of our cage,'[36] i.e. the boundaries of our language. The *Lecture on Ethics* help us to clarify his interpretation of ethics seen as nonsensical utterances based on a misuse of language, but on the other hand as a human tendency to extend the boundaries of our linguistic faculties.

> My whole tendency and I believe the tendency of all men who ever tried to write or talk Ethics or Religion was to run against the boundaries of language. This running against the walls of our cage is perfectly, absolutely hopeless. Ethics so far as it springs from the desire to say something about the ultimate meaning of life, the absolute good, the absolute valuable, can be no science. What it says does not add to our knowledge in any sense. But it is a document of a tendency in the human mind which I personally cannot help respecting deeply and I would not for my life ridicule it.[37]

The most important part of the *Tractatus*—which remains one of the most enigmatic works in the history of philosophy—is a remnant that resists assimilation: the realm of the unsayable, which are the fields of aesthetics, religion, art, culture, and the meaning of life. In the face of these, logical sense collapses: 'There are, indeed, things which cannot be put into words.'[38] In fact, these spheres cannot exist within logical space and cannot be expressed within logical language, which is composed of logical propositions as mere expressions of facts. However, far from refuting this unsayability, Wittgenstein claims that some nonsense could illuminate those truths which cannot be said. In this desperate attempt to say what cannot be said, he speaks of a mystically illuminating experience which can reveal the unsayable. As Hadot stated, the word 'mystic' is used by Wittgenstein in at least three ways that reflect the same impossibility of giving meaning to the world seen as a whole: the feeling of human existence, the idea of delimited totality, and the experience of

---

35 Ludwig Wittgenstein, "Letters to Ludwig von Ficker," ed. Allen Janik and trans. Bruce Gillette, in *Wittgenstein: Sources and Perspectives* (Hassocks, Sussex: Harvester Press, 1979): 82–98.
36 Ludwig Wittgenstein, "Lecture on Ethics," *The Philosophical Review* 74.1 (1965): 11.
37 *Ibidem*.
38 Wittgenstein, *Tractatus Logico-philosophicus*, 89 (6.522).

the 'unsayable,' which wrestles with the boundaries of language.[39] The utterance at the end of the *Tractatus*—'What we cannot speak about we must pass over in silence'[40]—could be interpreted as a mystic call for silence.[41] Following Hadot, I would like to give an account of the ethical silence in the *Tractatus* within the framework of sceptical tradition, i.e. an interior *epoché* of any value judgments.[42] The link between ethics and silence is a form of sceptical exercise which deals with a redefinition of philosophy itself.

I suggest that the importance of silence—in both thinkers—is connected to the religious and ethical boundaries of language and should be interpreted as a feature of their linguistic scepticism. As we have seen, this phenomenon was deeply connected to a new form of mysticism in which silence is linked to a religious, ethical, and aesthetical experience.[43]

II Limits of Translation. Limits of Understanding

The second path of this study concerns the issue of translation, which plays an important role in the context of *Sprachkrise*[44] and—albeit with some variations—also concerns the boundaries of human language and the limits of our understanding in the thought of Rosenzweig and Wittgenstein. Although this issue was discussed by philosophers for the first time in German Romanticism (Schleiermacher, Humboldt, and Hamann) and the diversity of languages was considered as a set of different articulations of the word, one can say that the crucial contributions on this matter came from the philosophy of the last century.

---

[39] Hadot sees a link between Wittgenstein's idea of mysticism and Schopenhauer's conception of knowledge liberated from the willing; cf. Hadot, *Wittgenstein et les limites du langage*, 20–26. On the conception of mysticism in Wittgenstein, see also Jacques Bouveresse, *Wittgenstein. La rime et la raison* (Paris: Éditions de Minuit, 1973): 21–72 and Ewald Wasmuth, "Das Schweigen Ludwig Wittgensteins: über das Mystische im Tractatus logico-philosophicus," *Wort und Wahrheit* 7 (1952): 315–322.
[40] Wittgenstein, *Tractatus Logico-philosophicus*, 89 (7).
[41] There are many discussions on the autobiographical and mystical aspects in Wittgenstein's thought. Cf. Brian F. McGuinness, "The Mysticism of the Tractatus," *The Philosophical Review* 75 (1966): 305–328 and Monk, *Ludwig Wittgenstein: the Duty of Genius*.
[42] See Pierre Hadot, Sandra Laugier, Arnold Davidson, "'Qu'est-ce que l'éthique?' Interview with Pierre Hadot," *Cités* 1.5 (2001): 134, trans. by Laugier, "Pierre Hadot as a Reader of Wittgenstein," 328: 'Thus, this silence can have a sceptical meaning according to the ancient meaning of the term. That is that it is a sceptical attitude consisting in living like everyone else but with total interior detachment, which implies the refusal of any value judgment. This represents a form of wisdom.'
[43] See also Adela Curtis, *Die Neue Mystik. Schule des Schweigens* (Heidelberg: Kampmann, 1923).
[44] On the theoretical conjunction between *Sprachkrise* and translation studies, cf. Alice Leal, "Linguistic Scepticism and the Jung-Wien: Towards a New Perspective," *Translation Studies, Trans-kom* 7.1 (2014): 99–114.

Despite a coincidence between speaking and translating in line with the Romantic tradition, Rosenzweig admits that true translation is impossible; Wittgenstein states that translation, as an interruption of the *continuum* of language games, is a border experience which elucidates human understanding. For both authors, translation is a hermeneutic operation which characterises the inter- and intra-linguistic process.⁴⁵

As one of the major figures of Jewish hermeneutics, Rosenzweig deals with both an interlinguistic theological translation and an intralinguistic practical one: if the former is a dialogue between the holy tongue and other languages, the latter is at the core of the process of speaking and understanding.⁴⁶ If the first form has an eschatological and messianic value connected to the exile of the Jewish language that coincides with the exile of the Jewish people, the second form deals with speech, in which there is always a kind of estrangement.

The interstitial space between holy languages and the other tongues turns translation into a theological question in line with the original vocation of the *Torah*, which—according to Rosenzweig—has to be translated. Referring to the gap between holy and profane tongues, he defines Hebrew as a treasure whose traces of brightness are to be found in other languages.⁴⁷ Therefore, far from being a substitution of label words, translation has an eschatological and messianic value because it is responsible for a silent dialogue between different languages which forces the mother tongue to rethink itself.

However, there is also an intra-linguistic translation that coincides with the mechanism of linguistic practice; in fact, Rosenzweig agrees with Hamann by stating that speaking is translating and translation is connected to every communicative act. Seen as a mode of linguistic operation, translation becomes the precondition for the dialogue and, therefore, for human understanding.⁴⁸ This intra-linguistic movement of translation is at the root of every language and allows openness to the dialogical dimension. However, this turns translation into an impossible attempt: there is a radical difference between the speakers and human understanding is always a paradoxical bet;⁴⁹ in fact, we cannot be sure of the commonality of the meaning of our words

---

45 On Wittgenstein's reading of translation, cf. Dinda L. Gorlée, *Semiotics and the Problem of Translation* (Amsterdam: Rodopi, 1994): 88–112 and eadem, *Wittgenstein in Translation* (Berlin and Boston: De Gruyter, 2012).
46 Cf. Franz Rosenzweig, "Scripture and Luther," in *Scripture and Translation*, eds. Martin Buber and Franz Rosenzweig (Bloomington: Indiana University Press, 1994) and idem, *Franz Rosenzweig and Jehuda Halevi. Translating, Translations and Translators*, ed. Barbara E. Galli (Montreal and London: McGill-Queen's University Press, 1995).
47 Franz Rosenzweig, "Classical and Modern Hebrew," in *Franz Rosenzweig: His Life and Thought*, ed. Nahum N. Glatzer (New York: Schocken, 1953): 263–270.
48 See Leora Batnitzky, *Idolatry and Representation. The Philosophy of Franz Rosenzweig Reconsidered* (Princeton: Princeton University Press, 2000): 108–109.
49 Cf. Donatella Di Cesare, *Utopia of Understanding*, trans. Niall Keane (Albany: Suny Press, 2012): 35–78.

or of certain comprehension. The possibility of misunderstanding crosses all human discourse: language is face to face with the unsayable; the otherness that cannot be truly translated and, thence, said.

Concerning Wittgenstein's interpretation of translation, one can say that this issue has received very little attention from critics because we are lacking a deep analysis of translation in his work and there are only a few remarks on it. In the *Tractatus*, Wittgenstein briefly mentions the issue of translation by stating that it does not involve the whole proposition, but the constitutive part of it,[50] while in his *Philosophical Investigations*, Wittgenstein gives many examples of linguistic activities in order to describe language games, among which he mentions the act of 'translating from one language into another.'[51] He radicalises the conventionality of language by admitting that between all speakers there is a kind of deal which consists of a pre-comprehension. However, when understanding is suspended, we are forced to interpret, namely to 'see as,' and—according to Wittgenstein—this interpretation is an inter-linguistic translation of signs.

This border experience reveals the operating principle of language and sheds light on the ongoing process of understanding connected to what Wittgenstein called 'perspicuous representation,'[52] namely a method of understanding a particular phenomenon through a network of similarities with other phenomena. It is not a logical procedure based on means-end or on causal links, but instead it is analogical, based on family resemblance ('Familienähnlichkeit'), or better, the specific features that one can recognise in some members of the same family. If we do not understand a sign, we translate it into another one or we look for other connections, and this movement of translation crosses language itself. Misunderstanding is the premise for translation, but, at the same time, it discloses the web of signs on which human understanding, which cannot do without this ongoing game of references, is based. However, if translation is an interruption of language, it is an extra-linguistic movement; in fact, it recalls gesture and the unsayable. Thence, since interpretation stems from misunderstanding, translation is an experience of alienation that shows the limit of our linguistic understanding.

---

[50] Cf. Wittgenstein, *Tractatus Logico-philosophicus*, 25–26 (4.025–4.027).

[51] Wittgenstein, *Philosophical Investigations*, 12 (§23).

[52] The notion of 'perspicuous representation' ('übersichtliche Darstellung') is at the core of his interpretation of ritual used for the first time in his *Remarks on Frazer's Golden Bough*. In his *Philosophical Investigations*, Wittgenstein argues: 'A main source of our failure to understand is that we do not command a clear view of our use of words. Our grammar is lacking in this sort of perspicuity. A perspicuous representation [portrayal] produces just that understanding which consists in seeing connections,' cf. Ludwig Wittgenstein, *Philosophical Investigations*, trans. Gertrude. E.M. Anscombe, (Oxford: Blackwell, 1958): 49 (§122). In my opinion, this attempt at analogical definition that is not a true definition is quite similar to what Vico defined as *ingenium*, which we can broadly define as a human practical and theoretical capacity to see connections; this topic is, in my view, very interesting even if it has received very little attention from critics.

In addition to this, it is worth saying that the issue of translation seems to me paradoxical from the perspective of the *Philosophical Investigations*, according to which Wittgenstein reads ceremonies as a form of language and a form of life based on shared habits and common rules.[53] Wittgenstein's later interpretation of language as a concrete praxis similar to a rite and a habit[54] calls into question the idea of translation itself. If the act of speaking is similar to the understanding of a ritual and is impossible to found theoretically, if 'the *speaking* of language is part of an activity, or of a form of life,'[55] if it is merely something that we cannot explain, think, or define, if it is only something shared and lived, how then is it possible to translate it, aside from the correct pronunciations of the sounds and following the grammatical rules? Is it possible to translate a *Lebensform*?

III Grammatical Therapies for Philosophical Illness

The third path concerns the similarities between Rosenzweig's criticism of philosophy and Wittgenstein's later approach, particularly in the *Philosophical Investigations*, concerning their use of grammatical thought against the metaphysicians' quest and the Socratic quest for essence. In his later book, Wittgenstein admits that 'the philosopher treats a question like an illness,'[56] and his therapy aims to dissolve the philosophers' puzzles and consists of attention to ordinary language, while Rosenzweig, in his *Understanding the Sick and the Healthy*, stresses the relevance of common sense,[57] interpreted as an everyday use of language against abstractions. In both attempts, there is a grammatical therapy at work aiming to save us from philosophical illness.

In his *Büchlein*, Rosenzweig described the traditional quest for essence that must go beyond experience, the reductionism of philosophy, and the nature of illness that causes it to be distanced from ordinary life.[58] He wrote this little book—which was

---

[53] They could be even considered in their political dimension; cf. Di Cesare, "Ethik als Lebensform," 249: 'Die Lebensform ist kein – wenn auch ethisches – Schicksal des Einzelnen. Wie die Sprache ist sie vielmehr die Gemeinschaft, der gemeinsame Spielraum, in dem die Menschen übereinstimmen.'
[54] In my view, the key concept of 'form of life' in Wittgenstein's late work arises from his confrontation with these kinds of ritual practices.
[55] Wittgenstein, *Philosophical Investigations*, 11 (§23).
[56] *Ibidem*, 91 (§255).
[57] Even if first Aristotle and then Epictetus gave a classical description of common sense (*koinòs vous*) as the use of common faculties, this term is usually associated in the eighteenth century with Thomas Reid and his critique of Hume's epistemological radicalism and Berkeley's immaterialism. In opposing them, Reid speaks of instinctive original principles and beliefs (such as the notion of an external world) that are our common sense, more trustworthy than analytical philosophies. A philosophical research project into scepticism and common sense would be very useful.
[58] Cf. Luca Bertolino, *Il nulla e la filosofia: idealismo antico e esperienza filosofica in Franz Rosenzweig* (Turin: Trauben, 2005).

published posthumously—in July 1921, in order to make his position expressed in *The Star of Redemption* more understandable. In these pages, he uses medical metaphors about paralysis of philosophy and sickness of reason, which is quite odd because the first symptoms of his muscular degenerative disease appeared in 1922. According to Rosenzweig, the dissolution of experience, the abstraction of the subject, and the disappearance of the world, which are the main features of philosophy, are symptoms of a sickness of the understanding. The philosopher should be cured through a correct understanding of language as a bridge which connects creation, revelation, and redemption. In the new thinking, language, seen in its concrete practices, is the horizon in which human lives are understood.

In direct opposition to the abstractions, common sense is a healthy understanding that deals with ordinary life, individual existences, and concrete practices. Even if the philosopher renounces common sense, he cannot ignore it in practice. As Rotenstreich stated, Rosenzweig considers 'the common sense approach intrinsically superior to all others since it is not an abstraction of man's essential features but an acknowledgment of his actual existence.'[59] By criticising the permanent quest for essence, Rosenzweig stated:

> 'Essential' [*eigentlich*]—no one but a philosopher asks this question or gives this answer. In life the question is invalid. He is scarcely interested in knowing what half a pound of butter costs 'essentially.' The terms of life are not 'essential' but 'real;' they concern not 'essence' but 'fact.'[60]

The later phase of Wittgenstein's thought could be interpreted as a grammatical therapy.[61] In fact, Wittgenstein renounced a logical systematisation of language by rethinking the role of philosophy itself as a permanent linguistic critique. The vagueness of ordinary speech does not have to be eliminated, but is rather a sceptical strategy towards philosophical abstractions. The relevance of everyday language could be interpreted as a strategy for converting philosophy into a praxis, or better, a form of life. In the *Philosophical Investigations*, Wittgenstein claims that his task is to bring the words back from metaphysics to their everyday use. Since philosophical

---

59 Nathan Rotenstreich, "Common Sense and Theological Experience on the Basis of Franz Rosenzweig's Philosophy," *Journal of History of Philosophy* 5.4 (1967): 356.
60 Rosenzweig, *Understanding the Sick and the Healthy*, 41.
61 By referring to the therapeutic interpretation of Wittgenstein's thought, I follow the positions contended by Diamond; cf. Diamond, *The Realistic Spirit: Wittgenstein, Philosophy and the Mind* and eadem, "Ethics, Imagination, and the Method of Wittgenstein's *Tractatus*," in *Bilder der Philosophie*, eds. Richard Heinrich and Helmuth Vetter (Vienna: Oldenbourg, reprinted in Crary and Read 2000): 55–90. According to her, in order to reject traditional philosophy, the therapeutic role of Wittgenstein's approach consists in a struggle against linguistic bewitchment and in a return to ordinary language. However, as Stern stated, in the *Philosophical Investigations* there is inevitably a 'proto-philosophical theorization about the everyday,' see Stern, *Wittgenstein's Philosophical Investigation: An Introduction*, 51.

problems arise 'when language *goes on holiday*,'⁶² namely from a confusion induced by language, the only way to resolve them is—paradoxically—to use ordinary language as a tool to unmask abstract superstitions.

Like Mauthner, Wittgenstein speaks of a permanent linguistic critique,⁶³ and the therapeutic point of his thought is in line with a redefinition of the task of philosophy as a 'battle against the bewitchment of our intelligence by means of language.'⁶⁴ His injunction—'Don't think, but look'⁶⁵—is the sign of a sceptical strategy to resist the idea of inner or private language and, thence, of private understanding that is a *contradictio in adjecto* because the words are always products of shared uses. Through a radical scepticism towards interior privacy, Wittgenstein turns the grammar of inner feelings into a public grammar.

In a conversation with Waismann in 1929, Wittgenstein distances himself from a separation of a primary phenomenological language from a secondary everyday language, which he distinguished as two different systems:

> I think that essentially we have only one language, and that is our everyday language. We need to invent a new language or construct a new symbolism, but our ordinary language already is the language, provided we rid it of the obscurities that lie hidden in it.⁶⁶

In fact, philosophy should not deal with a meta-language or a meta-world, but rather with everyday life and phenomena. In a Hegelian wake—according to which the familiar is not understood precisely because it is familiar⁶⁷—in his *Philosophical Investigations*, Wittgenstein stated that 'we must stick to the subjects of our every-day thinking, and not go astray and image that we have to describe extreme subtleties.'⁶⁸

---

62 Wittgenstein, *Philosophical Investigations*, 19 (§38).
63 He speaks of a mythology deposited in our language, namely a set of propositions that function as rule for our representation and practices. In his last notes, collected with the title *On Certainty*, Wittgenstein points towards some grammatical propositions that compose our world-picture and function as channels for other propositions; they can be defined as types of fluid guidelines, but Wittgenstein considers them as mythology: 'The propositions describing this world-picture might be part of a kind of mythology. And their role is like that of rules of a game; and the game can be learned purely practically, without learning any explicit rules,' cf. Ludwig Wittgenstein, *On Certainty*, eds. Gertrude E.M. Anscombe and Georg H. Von Wright, trans. Gertrude E.M. Anscombe and Denis Paul (Oxford: Blackwell, 1969): 15e (§95).
64 *Ibidem*, 47 (§109).
65 *Ibidem*, 31 (§66).
66 See Friedrich Waismann, ed., *Ludwig Wittgenstein and the Vienna Circle*, trans. by Brian F. McGuinness and Joachim Schulte (New York: Barnes & Noble Books, 1979): 45.
67 Hegel's famous sentence in the preface of the *Phenomenology of the Spirit* is: 'Das Bekannte überhaupt ist darum, weil es *bekannt* ist, nicht *erkannt*.' Cf. Georg W.F. Hegel, *Phänomenologie des Geistes*, in idem, *Werke*, vol. 3 (Frankfurt am Main: Suhrkamp, 1986): 35.
68 Wittgenstein, *Philosophical Investigations*, 47c (§106).

In this sense, the task of his philosophy is to liberate our language from bewitchment, confusions, and traps.[69] However, it is worth noting that Wittgenstein's account of philosophy in the *Philosophical Investigations* is twofold:[70] on the one hand, it is a product of a distorted use of language and philosophical issues are pseudo-problems; on the other, philosophy is a grammatical therapy for our language.

This two-sided account of philosophy reflects the role of language as *pharmakon*, in its ancient double meaning of cure and poison. In the second phase of Wittgenstein's thought, there is a kind of permanent auto-therapy of the philosophy which can heal him from his disease. Whether this therapy, described in the *Philosophical Investigations*, is the aim of philosophy or just another articulation of philosophy itself is a much-debated question. As a medical treatment, Wittgenstein writes prescriptions to save us from metaphysical essentialism through a return to everyday language. However, the tension between philosophy as permanent therapy and philosophy as a theory, between *pars construens* and *pars destruens*, is at the heart of scepticism itself and is also to be found in the *Philosophical Investigations*, where 'examples of how "ending philosophy" and "doing philosophy" are interwoven.'[71]

In the therapeutic redefinition of philosophy—which is to be found in both Rosenzweig and Wittgenstein—there is a strong critique of philosophical essentialism. One can say that a *topos* that these two thinkers have in common is an anti-Socratic approach and a refusal of the *ti esti* question. They criticise the way in which philosophical problems have been raised; in fact, Rosenzweig speaks of the timeless artificiality of the question regarding essence, while Wittgenstein is critical not only of philosophical answers, but also of philosophical questions.[72]

In his *Büchlein*, Rosenzweig affirms that:

> What is it? What is it in essence? is inevitably raised. And so once again the question is repeated. The answer to this question is always the same: whatever it is, it is not what it appears to be.[73]

According to Rosenzweig, the desperate search for essence denies particular experience and paralyses the act of thinking. If common sense is a healthy understanding, the philosophy that goes beyond it and ventures to criticise it is the sick one. This metaphor, as well as his grammatical therapy to cure the sick philosophical essenti-

---

69 See *The Big Typescript: TS 213*, trans. Grant Luckhardt and Maximilian Aue, in a facing-page English-German edition (Oxford: Blackwell, 2004): 312e: 'Language has the same traps for everyone; the immense network of easily trodden false paths.'
70 See Nyiri, "Wittgenstein and Common-Sense Philosophy," 242: 'Wittgenstein continues to use the word philosophy in two different, contrasting senses: in the sense of systematically confused thinking misled by the grammar of language; and in the sense of philosophical therapy redeeming us from our linguistic confusions-common-sense philosophy in a tenable sense of the word.'
71 Stern, *Wittgenstein's Philosophical Investigation: an Introduction*, 54.
72 Cf. Franks, "Everyday speech and revelatory speech in Rosenzweig and Wittgenstein," 26.
73 Rosenzweig, *Understanding the Sick and the Healthy*, 66.

alism, are the sceptical features in Rosenzweig's philosophy. Ordinary life and common sense are seen as the horizons where the theoretical abstractions end up.

The Socratic approach sealed the catastrophic fate of Western philosophy, from Ionia to Jena, with its reductionist approach that was distant from real life. This path from essence to factuality, from theory to praxis, is the therapy that Rosenzweig prescribes in his short book. Far from being a theoretical object, language is a relationship, a concrete bridge between men that deals with time and otherness, but the philosopher—according to Rosenzweig—gives up common sense the instant he believes that philosophising is necessary. Common sense does not care about the essence of things and places its trust in the power of existence.

In order to stress the difference between the first and second phases of his thought, Wittgenstein—in a conversation in 1931 that was noted by Waismann—spoke out against two dangerous philosophical mistakes which he made in the *Tractatus*, namely dogmatism and the subordination of philosophy to natural science, according to which there is a logical clarification of thought based on a correspondence between answers and questions.[74] He described dogmatisms as the 'craving for generality'[75] and as attempts to reach the essence, seen as an ideality beyond time and space. Since Socrates, the illness of essentialism characterised the history of philosophy and also affected Wittgenstein's *Tractatus*. In fact, there is a parallelism between the answer to the *ti esti* question and Wittgenstein's first attempt to define the essence of language. The strategy Wittgenstein later uses in order to reject essentialism is the refusal of a definition of language itself through games; in fact, instead of one precise characteristic that strictly defines them, the games have many resemblances to one another in common.

There is no single essence, but only crisscrossing and interwoven patterns of similarities and dissimilarities, like in a family or in the case of games. While Rosenzweig condemned the philosophical quest for essence that makes the philosopher sick, Wittgenstein writes that instead of searching for thorough explanations, it would be useful to settle for a description. His therapy moves from metaphysical explanation to a description of language games and he argues that there are some phenomena—for instance, a musical theme or the smell of coffee—that do not need any further explanation.

As is well known, in his *Philosophical Investigations*, Wittgenstein does not explain or define, but rather describes by stating similarities between phenomena:

> Consider for example the proceedings that we call 'games.' I mean board-games, card-games, ball-games, Olympic Games, and so on. What is common to them all?—Don't say: 'There must be something common, or they would not be called "games"'—but look and see whether

---

74 See Luigi Perissinotto, *Wittgenstein. Una guida* (Milan: Feltrinelli, 2008): 69–80.
75 Ludwig Wittgenstein, *The Blue and the Brown Books* (Oxford: Blackwell, 1958): 18.

there is anything common to all.—For if you look at them you will not see something that is common to all, but similarities, relationships, and a whole series of them at that.[76]

One can say that—according to Wittgenstein—it is necessary to remove one's Socratic glasses; in fact, beyond general definitions and explanations, there are many different elements that escape this generalisation. Thence, there is no such thing as *the* definition, *the* explanation, *the* theoretical fundament, but a variegated set of different language games.

IV Conclusion: Sceptical Metaphors for a *Lebensphilosophie*

The last path concerns the transformation of the theoretical approach towards language into a practical one. Their anti-theoretical approach is clear in the primacy of praxis.[77] Both thinkers propose two practical linguistic ways to go beyond metaphysics and philosophical abstractions. Quoting Goethe, Wittgenstein claimed that 'language is a refinement, "in the beginning was the deed."'[78] Rosenzweig's and Wittgenstein's reflections on language turn the ordinary use of words into a critical path towards a new redefinition of philosophy as a way of life, which is at the core of ancient scepticism.[79]

To avoid the risk of turning their thought in dogmatism, they use sceptical strategies.[80] Going beyond the book, this is the main trait of their scepticism, which is

---

[76] Ludwig Wittgenstein, *Philosophical Investigations*, 31 (§66).
[77] Cf. Putnam, "Introduction," 3: 'Both Wittgenstein and Rosenzweig direct us away from the chimera of a philosophical account of the 'essence' of this or that to the ordinary use we make of our words.'
[78] 'Im Anfang war die Tat' is a quotation taken from Goethe's *Faust*. It would be valuable to analyse the different ways in which Rosenzweig and Wittgenstein constantly use Goethe, especially concerning his conception of language. On Goethe and *Sprachkrise*, see Christian Mittermüller, *Sprachskepsis und Poetologie* (Tübingen: Niemeyer, 2008). In many different places in this work, Goethe calls into doubts the communicative role of language: just think of his aphorism 'Sobald man spricht, beginnt man schon zu irren.'
[79] My interpretation is directly opposed to Hosseini's idea, according to which the therapy provided by Wittgenstein and Rosenzweig aims to cure the sceptical approach seen as indifference (Wittgenstein) or fear of living (Rosenzweig); cf. Hosseini, *Wittgenstein and Meaning in Life: In Search of the Human Voice*, 111–113. Furthermore, I do not agree with Cavell, who claims that Wittgenstein's return to ordinary language is a 'formidable attack on scepticism,' cf. Stanley Cavell, "The Ordinary as the Uneventful," in idem, *Themes Out of School* (San Francisco: North Point Press, 1984): 184–194.
[80] On Sextus's philosophy of language, cf. Emidio Spinelli, *Questioni scettiche. Letture introduttive al pirronismo antico* (Rome: Lithos, 2005): 114–130. On the influence of Sextus's conception of language on contemporary philosophy, see Lorenzo Corti, *Scepticisme et langage* (Paris: Vrin, 2009). On the ladder metaphor in the history of philosophy, see Dimitri Gakis, "Throwing Away the Ladder Before Climbing it," in *Papers of the 33rd IWS*, eds. Elisabeth Nemeth, Richard Heinrich, and Wolfram Pichler (Kirchberg am Wechsel: ALWS, 2010): 98–100.

deeply connected to their critique of philosophy. This transition from theory to a linguistic praxis could be seen as a sceptical movement, due also to some metaphors that may be found in the works of both authors. Most of all, the famous image of the ladder that Wittgenstein took from Sextus thanks to the mediation of Mauthner, one of the few authors quoted in his *Tractatus*. As is well known, the first person to use the ladder metaphor was Sextus, together with the images of fire and the purgative by describing the sceptical strategy used to prevent the risk of dogmatic arguments.[81]

The 'final solution of the philosophical problems'[82] that arises out of a misunderstanding of the logic of our sentences is nothing but the drawing of a boundary to language and philosophy; in this attempt lies the 'anti-philosophical aim'[83] of Wittgenstein's book. The *Tractatus* should not be used as a ladder that must be climbed and then discarded,[84] but rather—as Hadot stated—every discourse on this book will be a useless ladder, an ancient sceptical purgative that aims at silence.

However, the ladder offers different meanings and, not least, develops an idea of progress that is misleading and was later rejected by Wittgenstein himself.[85] The act of climbing a ladder is much closer to an old philosophical approach, which seeks a clear view of the word from one's special standpoint. This idea of a privileged perspective is strongly rejected by the later Wittgenstein in order to show how philosophies are nothing but peculiar language games based on our ordinary position in the word. Furthermore, the symbol of the ladder refers to the idea of progress and to a teleological idea of history that Wittgenstein denied.[86]

---

81 See Sextus Empiricus, *M* VIII 481: 'And again just as it is not impossible for the man who has ascended to a high place by a ladder to overturn the ladder with his foot after his ascent, so also it is not unlikely that the Sceptic after he has arrived at the demonstration of his thesis by means of the argument proving the non-existence of proof, as it were by a step-ladder, should then abolish this very argument.'
82 Wittgenstein, *Tractatus Logico-Philosophicus*, 4.
83 Stern, *Wittgenstein's Philosophical Investigations: An Introduction*, 32.
84 Cora Diamond reads the image of throwing away the ladder as the key to understanding the *Tractatus* as an anti-philosophical strategy. However, we have to be careful, because the image of the ladder suggests an idea of progress that Wittgenstein rejects. As Stern stated: 'instead of climbing a ladder in order to get a clear view of our predicament, he now thought the task of the philosopher was to describe where we currently stand, in a way that would make ladder-climbing unattractive,' cf. Diamond, *The Realistic Spirit: Wittgenstein, Philosophy and the Mind*, 19; Stern, *Wittgenstein's Philosophical Investigations: An Introduction*, 48.
85 Cf. Ludwig Wittgenstein, *Culture and Value*, ed. Peter Winch (Oxford: Blackwell, 1998): 10: 'I might say: if the place I want to reach could only be climbed up to by a ladder, I would give up trying to get there. For the place to which I really have to go is one that I must actually be at already. *Anything that can be reached with a ladder does not interest me*" (the emphasis is mine),' and further *ibidem*, 38: 'You write about yourself from your own height. You don't stand on stilts or on a ladder but on your bare feet.'
86 It is worth noting that the motto of the *Philosophical Investigations*, a quotation by Nestroy's *Der Schützling*, was: 'Anyway the thing about progress is that it looks much greater than it really is,' quot-

In order to define the sceptical strategy against dogmatism, I find the last passages of *The Star of Redemption* more interesting, in which Rosenzweig stresses the necessity of going beyond the book and beyond his own work. His active engagement in turning theological problems into lived philosophy and human terms could be accomplished only by an overcoming of theory itself. This is at the core of his new thinking that is distant from theory and develops an epochal change between logical and grammatical thinking:

> In the old philosophy, 'thinking' means thinking for no one else and speaking to no one else (and here, if you prefer, you may substitute 'everyone' or the well-known 'all the world' for 'no one'). But 'speaking' means speaking to some one and thinking for some one. And this some one is always a quite definite some one, and he has not merely ears, like 'all the world,' but also a mouth.[87]

Instead of abstractions, Rosenzweig's grammatical thought is based on pronouns and the concrete practice of speech. The 'speaking thinking' ('das sprechende Denken') is directly opposed to 'thinking thinking' ('das denkende Denken'); whereas the latter knows its own thought before its expression, the former does not know in advance where it will end up and is touched by time and otherness.

As we have seen in the first path of this study, in *The Star of Redemption*, Rosenzweig suggests a kind of sacrifice of the word in order to reach the shared gesture and silence of community. His word could be seen as a ladder that has to be climbed in order to reach the silence of redemption:

> For where a man expresses himself entirely in his gesture, there, the space that separates man from man sinks away in a 'wondrously quiet' emotion; there the word evaporates that had thrown itself headfirst into the dividing space in between in order to fill it in with its own body and thus become through this heroic self-sacrifice a bridge between man and man.[88]

I believe that this gesture summarises his scepticism towards language; moreover, as language in this redemption must evaporate into silence, the *Star* has to go beyond itself. In fact, the conclusion of the *Star* is an invitation to go through the gate on which the following words are written:

---

ed by Stern, *Wittgenstein's Philosophical Investigations: An Introduction*, 7–8. On the relevance of Nestroy as part of Austrian culture, see John R.P. McKenzie, "Nestroy's Political Plays," in *Viennese Popular Theatre: A Symposium*, eds. William E. Yates and John R.P. McKenzie (Exeter: University of Exeter, 1985): 123–138. On the important mediation of Krauss, which led a revival of Nestroy with his "Nestroy und die Nachwelt," *Die Fackel*, 349/350 (1912): 1–23, see Jacques Bouveresse, "The Darkness of This Time: Wittgenstein and the Modern World," in *Wittgenstein: Centenary Essays*, ed. Allen P. Griffiths (Cambridge: Cambridge University Press. 1992): 33.

87 Franz Rosenzweig, "The New Thinking," in *Franz Rosenzweig: His Life and Thought*, 200.
88 Rosenzweig, *The Star of Redemption*, 394.

> [...] the words are above the gate, the gate that leads out from the mysterious, wonderful illumination of the divine sanctuary where no man can remain alive. But whither do the wings of the gate open? You do not know? INTO LIFE.[89]

Therefore, since language—as scepticism—is a concrete praxis and a form of life which allows us to make the changeover from a philosophy of essence to an *erfahrende Philosophie*, the return to a healthy understanding is a sceptical strategy towards traditional dogmatism, which acquired a performative role for philosophy itself. One can say that—according to Rosenzweig—the promise of the success of his linguistic therapy deals with the sceptical jump beyond the book, word, and theory in order to reach a form of life that could save us from the sick abstractions of thought.

Against the essentialism of philosophical traditions, in my view, Rosenzweig and Wittgenstein offer two different strategies in order to recall the importance of life and everyday speech through which they worked for a (dis)solution of previous philosophies. As we have already seen, language is the *pharmakon* for doing or undoing philosophy, namely the danger and the salvation of thought. The grammatical therapy of both authors leads to a philosophical path which deals with life (Rosenzweig) or with a form of life (Wittgenstein). The rehabilitation of everyday linguistic praxis as the hermeneutic horizon is—following Hadot's vision—the space of the conversion/transformation of philosophy, which characterised ancient thinkers and scepticism as well. I believe that this form of 'philosophical exercise' is also to be found in Rosenzweig and Wittgenstein. If there is an aim in their attempt, it is not to advance abstract theories, but rather to work out of philosophical abstractions and linguistic misuses. However, far from being an anti-philosophical approach, this kind of *Lebensphilosophie* is based on a sceptical rejection of essentialism, a critique of dogmatism, and a necessary quest for a living form of thought by coping at the same time with the boundaries of language and, thence, with the finiteness of the human being.

---

89 *Ibidem*, 447.

Harald Bluhm
Was Leo Strauss a Zetetic Political Philosopher?

I

In recent years, the ideas of Leo Strauss have received a great deal of attention. They have also been a source of controversy. Strauss's concept of political philosophy and his interpretation of canonical philosophical texts gained influence in the 1950s with the emergence of the Straussian school and spread over the following decade as former students took teaching jobs at major American universities. Several years after Strauss's death in 1973, the academic writings of his disciples triggered the first wave of Straussianism. The wave's swell was amplified by the entry of Straussians into top-level government circles during the first Reagan administration, where they served as political advisors, particularly in the State Department. In 1987, Straussianism became known to the wider public through *The Closing of the American Mind*, the best-selling work by Allan Bloom, Strauss's most illustrious student.[1] As surprising as this public resonance was, Strauss's teachings would rise to even greater prominence two decades later during the heated debate about the pivotal role Straussians were alleged to have played in George W. Bush's decision to invade Iraq.

Amid the ongoing disputes between Straussians, their opponents, and some more measured voices, contemporary scholars have begun to take a closer look at Strauss's political philosophy. Volumes such as *The Cambridge Companion to Leo Strauss* (2009) and *Brill's Companion to Leo Strauss' Writings on Classical Political Thought* (2015) have since secured Strauss a place in the academic pantheon. 'Among the great philosophers of the twentieth century,' Heinrich Meier, a leading interpreter and the editor of Strauss's collected works in German, wrote in 2014, 'political philosophy had only one advocate.'[2] Whether this assessment of Strauss is justified—and whether his political philosophy is a mere product of idiosyncratic readings of other philosophers—will not be discussed here. Rather, I am interested in a specific vein among the great variety of interpretations of Strauss:[3] the view that

---

[1] Allan Bloom, *The Closing of the American Mind* (New York: Simon & Schuster, 1987). The book grew out of an article he wrote for *National Review* in 1982; see http://www.nationalreview.com/article/218808/our-listless-universities-williumrex.
[2] Heinrich Meier, "How Strauss became Strauss," in *Reorientation: Leo Strauss in the 1930s*, eds. Martin D. Yaffe and Richard S. Ruderman (New York: Palgrave Macmillan, 2014): 13.
[3] In addition to the usual distinctions between East Coast, Midwest, and West Coast Straussians, Michael Zuckert also identifies rationalist, decisionist, zetetic, faith-based, Aristotelian, and Platonic

he is a sceptic, or, in Grecophile terms, a zetetic, philosopher. Stephen B. Smith, Catherine and Michael Zuckert, Daniel Tanguay, Thomas Pangle, Leora Batnitzky, Laurence Lampert, and other scholars have sought to define exactly what constitutes scepticism and zeteticism in Strauss's thought.[4] Moreover, they have used the label 'zetetic' label to distinguish him from the Straussians in the reception history of his work.

In examining the aptness of this label, I will primarily consider *On Tyranny* (first published in 1948) and Strauss's correspondence with Alexandre Kojève, because these sources contain the few passages in which Strauss addresses zeteticism directly.[5] I will argue that Strauss's zeteticism is an insufficiently elaborated form of scepticism that builds on ancient models but whose philosophical jumping-off point lies in the philosophy of Nietzsche, Heidegger, and Husserl. The enduring motifs of those philosophers are for the most part hidden in Strauss's work, and as such can only be staked out, not systematically investigated.[6] Like Nietzsche and Heidegger, Strauss was sceptical of modern philosophy and the philosophical tradition, which he thought sclerotic and stale.[7]

I will begin by describing the meaning of 'zetetic' in antiquity and its use in latter-day approaches (II). After taking an interlude to sketch out some of Strauss's key ideas (III), I will turn to the role of the 'zetetic' in his interpretation of Xenophon (IV). I will then discuss several passages in which Strauss uses the terms 'zetetic' and

---

approaches; see idem, "Straussians," in *The Cambridge Companion to Leo Strauss*, ed. Steven B. Smith (Cambridge: Cambridge University Press, 2009): 267.

4 See Steven B. Smith, *Reading Leo Strauss: Politics, Philosophy, Judaism* (Chicago: University of Chicago Press, 2006); Catherine H. Zuckert and Michael Zuckert, *The Truth about Leo Strauss* (Chicago: University of Chicago Press, 2006); Daniel Tanguay, *Leo Strauss: An Intellectual Biography* (New Haven: Yale University Press, 2005); Thomas Pangle, *Leo Strauss* (Baltimore: Johns Hopkins University Press, 2006); Leora Batnitzky, *Leo Strauss and Emmanuel Levinas: Philosophy and the Politics of Revelation* (Cambridge: Cambridge University Press, 2006); and Laurence Lampert, *The Enduring Importance of Leo Strauss* (Chicago: University of Chicago Press, 2013).

5 See Viktor Gourevitch, "Philosophy and Politics," *The Review of Metaphysics: A Philosophical Quarterly* 22.1 (1968): 59; and idem, "Philosophy and Politics, II," *The Review of Metaphysics: A Philosophical Quarterly* 22.2 (1968): 281–325.

6 For a discussion of these motifs, see Stanley Rosen, *Hermeneutics as Politics* (Oxford: Oxford University Press, 1987) and Michael Zank's seminal "Introduction" to Leo Strauss, *The Early Writings (1921–1932)*, trans. and ed. Michael Zank (Albany: State University of New York Press, 2002): 3–49.

7 In 1930, Strauss wrote: 'The tradition has been shaken at its roots by Nietzsche. It has altogether forfeited its self-evidence,' see idem, "Die religiöse Lage der Gegenwart," in idem, *Gesammelte Schriften*, vol. 2, ed. Heinrich Meier (Stuttgart: J.B. Metzler, 1997): 389; translated in Leo Strauss, "Religious Situation of the Present," in *Reorientation: Leo Strauss in the 1930s*, 234. On the relationship between Strauss and Heidegger, see Richard L. Velkley, *Heidegger, Strauss, and the Premises of Philosophy: On Original Forgetting* (Chicago: University of Chicago Press, 2011) and Rodrigo Chacón, "Reading Strauss from the Start: On the Heideggerian Origins of 'Political Philosophy'," *European Journal of Political Theory* 9.3 (2010): 287–307.

'sceptic' in order to better understand Straussian scepticism and its limits (V) before drawing some conclusions about the kind of philosopher Strauss was (VI).

II

Zétesis (ζήτησις) is an ancient Greek word meaning 'open inquiry.' Its most precise definition can be found in Sextus Empiricus' *Outlines of Pyrrhonism*, in which four variants of scepticism are distinguished:

> The Sceptic School, then, is also called 'zetetic' from its activity in investigation and inquiry, and 'ephectic' or suspensive from the state of mind produced in the inquirer after his search, and 'aporetic' or dubitative either from its habit of doubting and seeking, [...] and 'Pyrrhonian' from the fact that Pyrrho appears to us to have applied himself to scepticism more thoroughly and more conspicuously than his predecessors.[8]

Sextus Empiricus describes scepticism as:

> An ability, or mental attitude, which opposes appearances to judgements in any way whatsoever, with the result that, owing to the equipollence of the objects and reasons thus opposed, we are brought firstly to a state of mental suspense and next to a state of 'unperturbedness' or quietude.[9]

Two features of the ancient understanding of scepticism are striking from today's perspective. For one, it is primarily practical, not epistemological, and hence strongly associated with a way of life.[10] For another, many thinkers of antiquity, the Middle Ages, and the early modern era understood Socrates as a sceptic without much differentiation between his statements in the early aporetic dialogues and the later ones containing Platonic doctrines. 'Zetetic' was a known term in modern bourgeois philosophy—Kant, for instance, would occasionally use it in his lecture announcements[11]—but over time, it became obsolete. It was not until the late twentieth century that scholars took a renewed interest in the idea. In his 1990 monograph *Zetetic Skepticism*, Stewart Umphrey provides a broader account of the term and argues

---

[8] Quoted in Richard H. Popkin and José R. Maia Neto, eds., *Skepticism: An Anthology* (Amherst: Prometheus Books, 2007): 58.
[9] Ibidem, 59.
[10] *The Cambridge Companion to Ancient Scepticism*, ed. Richard Bett (Cambridge: Cambridge University Press, 2010) emphasises this point.
[11] In his "Notice Concerning the Structure of Lectures in the Winter Semester 1765–1766," Kant writes that 'the special method of instruction in philosophy is *zetetic*, as some ancients called it (from *zetein*), that is to say *investigative*. It only becomes *dogmatic*, that is to say *decisive*, in various parts by well-practiced reason,' see Immanuel Kant, *Akademie-Ausgabe*, vol. 2 (Berlin: Reimer, 1900): 307.

that in the *Meno* Socrates was a zetetic but not a sceptical philosopher.[12] In 2014 the 'Zetesis Research Group' was founded,[13] made up mostly of Italian philosophers devoted to the study of zetetic sceptical philosophy in antiquity and the modern era.

The interpretation of Strauss as a zetetic philosopher is part of this revival, but it is also a special case, for it simultaneously harkens back to the term's classical roots while seeing in it a key to understanding Strauss's ideas. To date, interpreters have sought to define Strauss's scepticism in three different ways.[14] The first view locates his scepticism in his anti-utopianism and in his principled distrust of opinions in favour of an unending search for truth. The second sees his scepticism in his criticism of revealed religion. The third is formulated by Leora Batnizky: 'Strauss's kind of skepticism also is skeptical of itself.'[15] It is important to note that none of these definitions comes off the back of a systematic review of all passages related to zeteticism in Strauss's writings.

III

In sketching out the scepticism attributed to Strauss—and assessing whether it can be called zetetic—I first want to recall several of the basic ideas of Strauss's middle and late periods. It is well known that Strauss argues for antique political philosophy as the authoritative way of doing philosophy. For Strauss, philosophising is a radical, stubborn interrogation of limits, a search for wisdom that is not itself described as wisdom. Scholars—among whom Strauss counted himself—dwell in a cave deeper than the one that Plato famously describes, where they can do no more than rearrange the discussions of great philosophers.[16] True philosophy only begins in the first cave, but reaching it is improbable given the dominant opinions of the day. As a result, religion must provide the orientation that the masses are unable to achieve through philosophy, lacking as they do the mindset for a philosophical form of life. In his 1953 book *Natural Right and History*, Strauss writes:

> No alternative is more fundamental than this: human guidance or divine guidance. The first possibility is characteristic of philosophy [...] the second is presented in the Bible.[17]

---

12 Stewart Umphrey, *Zetetic Skepticism* (Wakefield: Longwood Academic, 1990).
13 See http://zetesisproject.com/tag/zetetic-philosophy.
14 I am drawing here on various ideas, especially those of Steven B. Smith and Michael Zuckert in *The Cambridge Companion to Leo Strauss*, ed. Steven B. Smith (Cambridge: Cambridge University Press, 2009).
15 Batnitzky, *Leo Strauss and Emmanuel Levinas*, 129.
16 For more on this and on other passages I have not singled out individually, see Harald Bluhm, *Die Ordnung der Ordnung: Das politische Philosophieren von Leo Strauss* (Berlin: Akademie Verlag, 2008).
17 Leo Strauss, *Natural Right and History* (1953; reprinted: Chicago: The University of Chicago Press, 1971).

In addition to his return to ancient philosophy, two other areas are useful in approaching Strauss's scepticism: his interpretations of the ancient sceptics—Socrates, Plato, and Xenophon—and his notion of political philosophy. Strauss's scepticism can be characterised as an *existential* scepticism that examines fundamental philosophical questions. In the 1950s, Strauss published several essays tying his sceptical viewpoint to the political. Almost all of those essays have been collected in the influential volume *What Is Political Philosophy? And Other Studies* (1959).[18] There, Strauss describes political philosophy primarily by stating what it is not: it is *not* the history of political philosophy, though it itself is philosophical; it is *not* political thought, for that also includes political opinions; it is *not* political theory, which contains ideas about the political order with the goal of policymaking; it is *not* modern political science, which Strauss associates with positivism and relativism; and it is *not* political theology, which seeks to link politics with divine revelation. Instead, he locates political philosophy in the attempt to safeguard the possibility of philosophy through a tenacious search for truth. This branch of philosophy results from the necessity of taking the conflict between politics and philosophy seriously, and doing this means safeguarding philosophy as the Socratic enterprise of searching for truth and ascertaining the best way of life. Strauss describes ancient political philosophy as classical because it inquires into the natural attitude of the political order unadulterated by previous tradition.

A crucial part of Strauss's understanding of philosophy is its dual mode of presentation: a manifest, exoteric message directed at the public and a hidden, esoteric message directed at true philosophers. This dual mode of presentation is necessary, Strauss maintains, because the masses are unable to absorb the truths of philosophy. The distinction between the masses and the philosophers is one that Plato made after the death of Socrates, which is reflected in the staged drama of the dialogues. By pitching their ideas on two different levels, Plato and other philosophers can dilute ideas that call the existing system into question while allowing the sceptical search for truth to continue. Strauss's rhetoricisation of philosophy places the philosopher in a privileged position, an author who codes his text in different ways for different readers. This not only has consequences for how the philosopher lives, but also highlights his opposition to non-philosophers.[19]

An idea related to this dual mode of communication is Strauss's rarely scrutinised idea of teaching. Shaped by Heidegger's own rhetoricisation of philosophy

---

[18] See Leo Strauss, *What Is Political Philosophy? And Other Studies* (Chicago: Chicago University Press 1959) and Rafael Major, ed., *Leo Strauss' Defense of Philosophic Life: Reading "What Is Political Philosophy?"* (Chicago: The University of Chicago Press, 2013). I would like to thank Thomas Meyer for pointing out to me some additions that Strauss made in the English-language edition of his Hobbes study in 1936 (GS III, 184), including the distinction between classical and modern political philosophy. In letters dated Nov. 27, 1938 (GS III, 558) and Feb. 16, 1939 (GS III, 566), Strauss mentions working on a text about classical political philosophy, which he later published in February 1945.
[19] See Leo Strauss, "Exoteric Teaching," *Interpretation* 1.1 (1986): 54f., written in December 1939.

in his lecture on Aristotle, especially in the summer semester of 1923, Strauss uses the term in a variety of ways to describe a theory's concealed meaning, that part of it that goes unsaid.[20] Teaching, too, is an effort to dilute philosophical ideas that transform systematic constructions into problems of philosophical inquiry. But unlike Heidegger, who reinterprets philosophies and thinks largely in terms of language, Strauss assigns the philosopher an emphatic role as an author who consciously encrypts his writing with multiple meanings. The work of interpretation consists in understanding the philosopher's texts in the way he understood them himself.

In *What Is Political Philosophy*, 'zetetic' appears only in the "Restatement on Xenophon's *Hiero*," Strauss's response to Kojève's critique entitled "Tyranny and Wisdom." Strauss does not use the word in an active sense, but as a casual self-description. He laid the groundwork for this zetetic inquiry in the manuscript of his 1932 lecture "The Intellectual Situation of the Present," in which he writes:

> *Our freedom is the freedom of radical ignorance.* The intellectual situation of the present is characterized by our knowing nothing anymore, by our knowing nothing. Out of this ignorance grows the necessity of questioning, questioning about right and good. And here the following Paradox presents itself: while the present is *compelled to question as any age, it is less capable of questioning than any age.* We *must* question without being *capable* of questioning.[21]

Based on this briefest of sketches, I now want to describe the path to Strauss's scepticism in more detail.

IV

Strauss's novel method of interpretation is closely linked to his scepticism in his understanding of political philosophy. The obvious assumption—that Strauss encountered the idea of the zetetic in his work on Plato and Socrates and developed his scepticism from there—is partly correct, but it is not the entire story. Strauss's understanding of the zetetic is initially informed by the ideas of Xenophon, whose rhetoric, he argues, is simpler than that of Plato and, as such, provides a springboard for un-

---

[20] See Stuart Elden, "Reading *Logos* as Speech: Heidegger, Aristotle and Rhetorical Politics," *Philosophy and Rhetoric* 38.4 (2005): 281–301; also Chacón "Reading Strauss from the Start: On the Heideggerian Origins of 'Political Philosophy'." Chacón shows that the Weimar period put Strauss on the path to Socrates via the 'destruction of tradition,' cf. *ibidem*, 293. He concludes that 'Strauss' bold venture was to reclaim the land that Heidegger discovered but neglected to explore—and to call it Socratic "political philosophy",' cf. *ibidem*, 302. Simon W. Taylor argues that Strauss's turn away from Nietzschean atheism led to his viewing of religion and Zionism from a zetetic vantage point; see idem, "Leo Strauss's Skeptical Engagement with Zionism," *Journal of the History of Ideas* 78 (2017): 95–116. Velkley notes Strauss's nearly life-long engagement with Heidegger's ideas; see idem, *Heidegger, Strauss, and the Premises of Philosophy*.

[21] Leo Strauss, "The Intellectual Situation of the Present (1932)," in *Reorientation*, 237–253.

derstanding more complicated Socratic dialogues.²² Strauss employs his new method of interpretation in his first essay on Xenophon, "The Spirit of Sparta and the Taste of Xenophon."²³ In this now-famous text, he reads Xenophon's comments on the "Constitution of the Lacedaemonians" as a satire, though they are often understood as a panegyric. Some remarks by Laurence Lampert help us to understand the role of Xenophon in Strauss's thinking:

> Over two months pass before Strauss again mentions his work in his letter, but the letter in which he does [February 6, 1939] is the most explosive of them all. He announces his intention to write the essay that appeared nine months later as "The Spirit of Sparta or the Taste of Xenophon": 'I plan to prove in it that his apparent praise of Sparta is in truth a satire on Sparta and on Athenian Laconism.' 'Xenophon is my special *Liebling*,' he says, 'because he had the courage to clothe himself as an idiot and go through the millennia that way—he's the greatest con man I know.' The clothing, the con that so endears Xenophon to Strauss, leads him to conclude that what Xenophon does, his teacher did: 'I believe that he does in his writing exactly what Socrates did in his life.' [...] Strauss here elaborates the most radical aspects [...] of his recovery of esotericism, and he revels in it: 'In any case with [Xenophon] too morality is purely exoteric, and just about every second word has a double meaning.' Socrates and his circle stand beyond good and evil.²⁴

Arguably, by 1939, Strauss had, for the most part, worked out his idea of political philosophy. Even if there is no talk of political philosophy *per se* in his Xenophon essay, Strauss's remark that classical political science is based on foundations laid by Socrates while modern political science follows Machiavelli makes his meaning apparent.²⁵

In "Exoteric Teaching," an essay from the same year, Strauss develops a specific understanding of scepticism that significantly broadens its scope to include morality, religion, political life, and even philosophy. Though Strauss considers philosophy to be an important search for truth, it is not wisdom itself, and cannot and should not provide direct guidance to politicians, scholars, and the masses. As Lampert correctly stresses, philosophers are not moral role models like the prophets. Rather, they are, in Nietzsche's sense, beyond good and evil. Anticipating a possible objection

---

22 See Leo Strauss, *On Tyranny: Including the Strauss-Kojève Correspondence*, ed. Victor Gourevitch and Michael S. Roth (Chicago: The University of Chicago Press, 2000): 26. *On Tyranny* is Strauss's most important text on Xenophon. It was originally published in 1948 and then expanded in 1961 to include the debate with Kojève. The 2000 edition also contains the written correspondence between Strauss and Kojève.
23 Leo Strauss, "The Spirit of Sparta and the Taste of Xenophon," *Social Research* 6.4 (1939): 502–536. See also Heinrich Meier, *Die Denkbewegung von Leo Strauss* (Stuttgart: J. B. Metzler, 1996): 15.
24 Laurence Lampert, "Strauss's Recovery of Esotericism," in *Cambridge Companion to Leo Strauss*, 69.
25 Strauss, *On Tyranny*, 23 f.

here, Strauss states that 'the distinction between exoteric and esoteric speech has then so little to do with 'mysticism' of any sort that it is an outcome of prudence.'[26]

Strauss puts special emphasis on the definition of philosophy as a search for wisdom, and from there draws consequences for the sceptical treatment of politics. He places wisdom in relation to the virtue of moderation, which comes to bear primarily in one's public activity. Here, he uses Machiavelli to argue indirectly against Nietzsche and Heidegger.[27] Like them, Strauss thinks radically, but he does not try to dissolve the tensions between politics and philosophy. For him, political and philosophical life exists in permanent opposition, and it is precisely because the opposition is unavoidable that philosophers must practice moderation. Their scepticism about political opinions and the gods can confuse the body politic and destabilise its order; it is imperative, therefore, that philosophers conceal their radicalism and atheism. For Strauss, radicalism in thought and moderation in politics operate in entirely different spheres.

The point of Strauss's nuanced study is to reconstruct Xenophon's original intentions, not to analyse his arguments. The distinction between form and representations puts Strauss on the path that leads him to discover scepticism, the dialogue form, and the difference between what is said and what is alluded to. Recently, Xenophon scholars have raised a number of objections to Strauss's interpretation of "Constitution of the Lacedaemonians" as satire.[28] Thanks to Strauss's surprising interpretative reversal—returning Xenophon to the status of rousing, accomplished thinker that he enjoyed before the eighteenth century—he manages to remain in the spotlight of current scholarship.[29]

Strauss originally published his second study on Xenophon dealing with the dialogue *Hiero* in 1948. Besides being an extraordinary contribution to the totalitarianism debate and exemplifying his position that big questions demand alternative answers, it is also methodologically interesting, because in it he develops his understanding of political philosophy.[30] Strauss's interpretation of *Hiero* has been

---

[26] See Strauss "Exoteric Teaching," 53. Other candidates for exoteric writing are Maimonides and Lessing, the latter of whom plays a prominent role in "Exoteric Teaching." Strauss writes that Lessing, after 'having had the experience of what philosophy is and what it requires' (57), adopted the distinction between the esoteric and the exoteric in his writing.
[27] Strauss, *On Tyranny*, 184.
[28] See Vivienne J. Gray, ed., *Oxford Readings in Classical Studies: Xenophon* (Oxford: Oxford University Press, 2010) and eadem, *Xenophon's Mirror of Princes* (Oxford: Oxford University Press 2011). In the second book, Gray distances herself from Strauss's readings of Xenophon. However, she too stresses Xenophon's remove from the Sparta of his time.
[29] For a helpful account of Strauss's interpretation of Xenophon, see Richard S. Ruderman, "'Through a Keyhole': Leo Strauss' Rediscovery of Classical Political Philosophy in Xenophon's *Constitution of the Lacedaemonians*," in *Brill's Companion to Leo Strauss' Writings on Classical Political Thought*, ed. Timothy W. Burns (Leiden: Brill, 2015): 213–226 and Eric Buzzetti, "A Guide to the Study of Leo Strauss' On Tyranny," in *ibidem*, 227–257.
[30] See chapter 5 of Bluhm, *Das politische Philosophieren*.

commented on by many. I am only interested in looking more closely at his ideas on scepticism and their two-pronged attack against the mostly positivist, value-judgment-eschewing discipline of political science. In its place, Strauss favours a normative practice of political science that resists historicism, which, besides being relativist, is shaped by a hubristic claim to understanding past authors better than they understood themselves.[31] The starting point for Strauss's interpretation of *Hiero* and the normative philosophy of Xenophon is his understanding of the Socratic dialogues. Like Plato in his dialogues, Xenophon hides his true meaning in *Hiero*. Understanding it involves accessing his original intention. Strauss begins with a brief structural analysis of the two-part dialogue. Simonides, who plays the active role, visits the tyrant Hiero and strikes up a conversation. His intent—Strauss calls Simonides a wise man—is not to give Hiero advice, but to develop an active discussion. Simonides wants to show what is wrong with the tyrannis over which Hiero rules (its pathology) and how to make things right (its therapeutics), but he can only do this if he proceeds indirectly. The idea is to make Hiero at least partially aware of the problems of tyrannical rule by letting him become caught in his own contradictions. In this way, Strauss argues, the tyrant can be turned into the benevolent despot.[32] Whether Simonides achieves this is unclear, but he does manage to show that Hiero's way of life is questionable and could change were he to give more consideration to the *polis*. By moving the dialogue from way of life to the question of virtue, Xenophon puts tyranny and its problem into stronger relief. But in doing so, he also, according to Strauss, employs a radical scepticism, one buried beneath the surface in an esoteric layer that is only revealed by what is not said: the silences, Xenophon's concealments, and Simonides' omissions.

Strauss first mentions the concept of the zetetic in his debate with Kojève—despite his strongly opposed viewpoint, he was one of the few people by whom Strauss felt understood—and only in his "Restatement on Xenophon's *Hiero*" (1950). Kojève, who was influenced by Heidegger in his early life, not only defends Hegel, but, as his own breed of Marxist, even indirectly defends Stalinism.[33] Kojève takes this position because he assumes that the utopia of benevolent despotism described by Xenophon was achieved in the modern era using different means. A Frenchman by choice, Kojéve uses historical arguments to claim that the expanding authoritarian regime, the coming world-state, is a good, the highest form a state can achieve. Furthermore, he believes that tyrants are particularly open to the advice of philosophers, although their recommendations must first be adapted to the circumstances by intellectuals, in whose company he places Simonides. Strauss rejects these extreme views, but he agrees with Kojève on one point: that the understanding of totalitarianism demands a return not to Machiavelli, as many contemporaries believed, but to Xeno-

---

31 Strauss, *On Tyranny*, 24 f.
32 Strauss argues that the compromise of the benevolent despot is strictly opposed to the Athenians, who categorically reject tyrannical rule in any form. Hiero, of course, is no Athenian.
33 Strauss, *On Tyranny*, 188.

phon's *Hiero*. Machiavelli, who intentionally avoids the term tyranny in *Il Principe*, would presumably dismiss a ruler like Hiero. But to Strauss, an ethically rich understanding of tyranny unfettered by a restrictive theory of power is the basic prerequisite for understanding modern tyranny.

The crucial part of the dispute between Strauss and Kojève for our purposes concerns their respective concepts of philosophy. Kojève's historical speculation is fundamentally at odds with what Strauss, in the following passage, calls 'zetetic philosophy':

> What Pascal said with antiphilosophic intent about the impotence of both dogmatism and skepticism, is the only possible justification of philosophy which as such is neither dogmatic nor skeptic, and still less 'decisionist,' but zetetic (or skeptic in the original sense of the term). Philosophy as such is nothing but the awareness of problems, i.e., of the fundamental and comprehensive problems. [...] Yet as long as there is no wisdom but only the quest for wisdom, the evidence of all solutions is necessarily smaller than the evidence of the problems.[34]

To Strauss, Kojève verges on sectarianism because he, like the Hegel of the *Phenomenology of Spirit*, decides for only one solution. Strauss believes his own position is open (though this might confuse readers given his conservative return to virtues, antiquity, and moderation). His "Restatement on Xenophon's *Hiero*" marks a definitive switch from political science to philosophy, to philosophical politics and the political actions of philosophers.[35] By the time of his debate with Kojève, Strauss had come to understand political philosophy as *prima philosophia*, grounded in the irrevocability of the human problem and the unavoidable conflict between philosophy and the *polis*.[36] Strauss continues his interrogation of these basic problems throughout *On Tyranny*, both in his interpretation of Xenophon and in his debate and later correspondence with Kojéve.[37] As I will argue in the next section, Strauss's use of zetetic to explain his own approach is at once a revival of an ancient Greek idea and an act of appropriation to alter its original meaning.

---

34 Ibidem, 196.
35 On the philosophical politics of Strauss, see his *On Tyranny*, 205 f. Here, Strauss emphasises that part of philosophy consists in convincing the state that philosophers are not atheists and that they do not put everything into question.
36 Strauss, *On Tyranny*, 205.
37 A new translation of the "Restatement of Xenophon's *Hiero*" can be found in Emmanuel Patard, "'Restatement' by Leo Strauss," *Interpretations* 36.1 (2008): 3–100. Patard also published the unabridged version of Kojève's contribution; see Emmanuel Patard, *Critical Edition of Alexandre Kojève, "'Tyrannie et sagesse' and 'Tyranny and Widsom',"* in *Philosophy, History, and Tyranny: Reexamining the Debate Between Leo Strauss and Alexandre de Kojève*, eds. Timothy W. Burns and Bryan-Paul Frost (Albany: State University of New York): 287–357.

V

The interpreters of Strauss I mentioned at the beginning of this paper characterise his philosophy as zetetic. I will now discuss this claim using passages from Strauss's writings, especially from statements in letters in which he expresses himself freely.[38] I will confine myself to those passages in which Strauss uses the term 'zetetic' or 'sceptic' to show what he means by this, which are rarely considered collectively.[39] My take on those passages shows that they provide a number of explanations but no systematic justification of zeteticism. Firstly, I want to recall the polemical context: since the late 1920s, Strauss fought against relativism, historicism, and positivism.[40] Notably, these are all movements associated with modern scepticism. As the following passage from 1931 shows, it is no surprise that the young Strauss distanced himself from this kind of scepticism:

> There is no *teaching* of Socrates. Socrates *could* not teach; he could only *question* and through this questioning help others to gain understanding. First, he helped them realize that what they believed they knew, in reality they did not know. Not that he himself knew what others did not know. Instead his wisdom—the famous wisdom of Socrates—meant that he knew that he did not know anything. Even this knowledge of knowing nothing is not a *teaching*. Socrates is also not a *skeptic*. A teaching, at least a philosophical teaching, is an answer to a question. But Socrates did not answer anything. The answer that he appears to give (the knowledge of knowing nothing) is only the most poignant expression of the question. Socratic philosophizing means to question [...]. Why, however, does Socrates *persist* in questioning? [...] How can he persist in questioning *despite* his knowledge? The answer is that he *wants* to persist in questioning [*in der Frage bleiben*], namely because questioning is what matters, because a life without questioning is not a life worthy of man.[41]

I will put aside for a moment the issue of a worthy life to stress again that Strauss expressly does not call Socrates a sceptic; his terminology would not undergo a se-

---

38 As Thomas Meyer observes: 'Strauss as an author of letters is almost completely undiscovered [...] He has been underestimated in this capacity—and, by extension, in his thought. From the beginning, his letters possessed something unconditional: they directly address the subject and its vis-à-vis,' see Thomas Meyer, '"Dass es mir nicht erlaubt ist, für einen Augenblick das Meer von Blut zu vergessen": Hans-Georg Gadamer and Leo Strauss in ihren ersten Briefen nach 1945," in *Nach dem Krieg–Nach dem Exil? Erste Briefe, First Letters: Fallbeispiele aus dem sozialwissenschaftlichen und philosophischen Exil*, eds. Detlef Garz and David Kettler (Munich: edition text + kritik, 2012): 99–118.
39 Restricting my scope in this way seems necessary since it is simply impossible to discuss all of the essays, lectures, and statements by Strauss and the mass of interpretations concerning his view on Socrates and Plato in any one article.
40 In 1929, Strauss heavily criticised Karl Mannheim for dissolving truth into ideology, the hallmark *par excellence* of relativism. He made a similar attack on Max Weber's positivism, though his appraisal of him is different. Strauss makes no distinction between axiological and methodological relativism, all his post-empirical epistemology notwithstanding.
41 Leo Strauss, "Cohen und Maimuni," in idem, *Gesammelte Schriften*, vol. 2 (Stuttgart: Metzler, 1997): 411.

mantic shift until his later period. The passage also shows Heidegger's influence on Strauss.[42] Indeed, it is no exaggeration to say that 'to persist in questioning'—*in der Frage bleiben*—is downright Heideggerian in formulation. What is also interesting about this passage is Strauss's multilayered remark that Socrates has no teaching. The Greek dialogical philosopher does not have a doctrine; he *questions*. Strauss's later distinction between the esoteric and the exoteric for philosophers like Plato who rely on the written word does not apply to such a thinker. Nevertheless, while the early Strauss may have wanted to return to Socrates, his starting point was a modern one. He follows Nietzsche (apart from his criticism of Socrates) and is taken with Löwith, who reads Nietzsche as an author who 'repeats antiquity at the peak of modernity.' In his 1931 review article on Julius Ebbinghaus, Strauss defines the purpose that Socrates and his specific form of scepticism should serve:

> The not-knowing [*Nichtwissen*] that is real in the present day is not at all the natural not-knowing [*Nichtwissen*] with which philosophy must begin; then a long detour and a great effort are first needed in order even to return to the state of natural ignorance [*Unwissenheit*].[43]

The emphasis on 'natural' in 'natural ignorance' should not be overlooked. In the seldom-remarked-on third chapter of his *Natural Right and History*, Strauss alludes to a kind of epistemological explanation of his position: philosophical scepticism develops from 'pre-philosophical experience' with hearsay and appearance. Drawing on Husserl's idea of a natural, pre-philosophical attitude, Strauss defines a normative concept of nature—one opposed to the diversity of gods and mores—that establishes a framework for doing philosophy.

An important aspect of Strauss's concept of philosophy can be found in the 1945 "Farabi's Plato," an essay often assigned special significance in his work. There, he writes:

> It is the way leading to that science rather than that science itself: the investigation rather than the result. Philosophy thus understood is identical with the scientific spirit 'in action,' with σκέψις in the original sense of the term.[44]

The term 'political philosophy' does not appear here—Strauss speaks only of political science—but the phrase 'scepticism in the original sense' is one he will later use when talking about the sceptical character of his philosophy.

---

[42] As often observed, Strauss abandoned the impulses of Hermann Cohen and Franz Rosenzweig that were directed against philosophical systems and epistemic methodology. Like these Jewish thinkers, he focused on ethical questions concerning man in general and open (oral) discussion; see Zank, "Introduction," 35 f.

[43] Leo Strauss, "On the Progress of Metaphysics," in idem, *Early Writings*, 215.

[44] Leo Strauss, "Farabi's Plato," in *Louis Ginzberg Jubilee Volume* (New York: The American Academy for Jewish Research, 1945): 393.

A peculiar feature of Strauss's scepticism is its preoccupation with alternatives. In *Thoughts on Machiavelli* (1958), Strauss writes:

> We did assume that there are fundamental alternatives, alternatives which are permanent or coeval with man. This assumption is frequently denied today.[45]

Similar anthropological claims can be found in *Natural Right and History*: the permanent problems are not only coeval with man; they are always the same, independent of time and context.[46] Strauss frequently claims that all fundamental problems have the character of an alternative. This is more than a preference for a dual code; it recalls Carl Schmitt's notorious distinction between 'friend and foe.' But Strauss does not provide a single argument why, for a sceptic, all problems must assume the form of an alternative. Why should there not be three, four, or five possibilities? Why should unresolvable problems not be trilemmas or pentalemmas? Strauss's fixation on alternatives significantly restricts the scope of his scepticism, though he does concede in his debate with Kojève that multiple philosophical solutions can exist.[47] At any rate, it is a strange turn for someone who expressly rejects problem histories in the neo-Kantian mould and who argues against Hans-Georg Gadamer that the content of problems and their solutions can change.[48] Despite tying the understanding of a problem to the philosophising subject, Strauss remains tethered to the belief in eternal problems as such.

Several passages from Strauss's correspondence with Karl Löwith shed more light on his conception of scepticism. In a letter from July 19, 1951, he responds to an essay by Löwith:[49]

> It is excellently written and compared with the madmen who dominate the world stage, I agree with you 1,000 percent. But compared with the *real σκέψις*, the Socratic-Platonic? You read Plato with Montaignean or Christian eyes. Socrates is no skeptic in a vulgar sense, because he *knows* that he knows nothing. To start, he knows what *knowledge* is—and that's not nothing. Moreover,

---

45 Leo Strauss, *Thought on Machiavelli* (1958; reprinted, Chicago: The University of Chicago Press, 1978): 14.
46 Leo Strauss, *Natural Right and History* (Chicago: The University of Chicago Press, 1971): 32.
47 Cf. Strauss, *On Tyranny*, 196: 'Philosophy as such is nothing but genuine awareness of the problems, i.e. of the fundamental and comprehensive problems. It is impossible to think about these problems without becoming inclined toward a solution, toward one of the very typical solutions. Yet as long as there is no wisdom but only quest for wisdom, the evidence of all solutions is necessarily smaller than the evidence of the problems. Therefore the philosopher ceases to be a philosopher at the moment at which the 'subjective certainty' of a solution becomes stronger than his awareness of the problematic character of that solution. At that moment the sectarian is born.'
48 See Stephan Steiner, *Weimar in Amerika. Leo Strauss' Politische Philosophie* (Tübingen: Mohr Siebeck, 2013): 209.
49 Strauss is most likely referring to the essay "Skepticism and Faith," which appeared in the Jan. 1, 1951 edition of *Social Research*.

he knows that the *problems* are, *the* problems, the *important* problems—that is, what is *important*. In other words, he knows that philosophizing is a unum necessarium.⁵⁰

Strauss goes on to make a distinction between Socratic scepticism and the vulgar scepticism of Pyrrho. In Strauss's eyes, Pyrrho's scepticism boils down to *ataraxia*, a state of philosophical equanimity which is both apolitical and individualistic. Socrates, by contrast, knew that he knew nothing, but he also knew that this was a special form of knowledge. Socratic philosophising is a political act because it seeks, through the interrogation of prevailing opinion, a renewal of the *polis* based on sound principles. The philosophy that Strauss talks about—the *unum necessarium* —is not compatible with stringent scepticism.⁵¹ It would be naïve to assume that Strauss is unaware of the paradox in his position; as an expert in ancient philosophy, he was no doubt familiar with Cicero's maxim that we cannot even be certain that everything is uncertain. Strauss concludes his letter to Löwith by pointing to a particular source of his scepticism:

> To be quite frank, your article helps strengthen the sympathy for Heidegger that recently awoke in me, who remained loyal to himself by making no concessions to belief.⁵²

Sixteen years earlier, Strauss wrote the following to Löwith:

> But these late antique philosophies are far too dogmatic, even the skeptics, for someone like you to remain with them and not go back to their forefather, Socrates, who was *not* dogmatic.⁵³

Around a month later, he wrote to Löwith again:

> Why did I not respond to 'The doctrine of the mean?' Because I know who you mean, namely people like Burckhardt. I would like to believe you that B. was the ideal representative of the moderation of antiquity in the nineteenth century. But the subjects of his philosophizing are

---

50 Strauss, *Gesammelte Schriften*, vol. 3, 675. It should be mentioned in passing that Strauss follows Schleiermacher's interpretation of Socrates. Schleiermacher wrote that Socrates' not-knowing is based on a concept of knowledge that includes knowledge on the path to knowledge, see Daniel Friedrich Schleiermacher, "Ueber den Wert des Socrates als Philosoph [1815]," in Daniel F. Schleiermacher, *Kritische Gesamtausgabe*, vol. I.11 (Berlin: De Gruyter, 2002): 201–228. Andreas Arndt is critical of this view, however; see Andreas Arndt, *Schleiermacher als Philosoph* (Berlin and Boston: De Gruyter, 2013): 285–295. As an aside: Schleiermacher did not see Xenophon as a philosopher.
51 The formula 'the one necessary' ('Das Eine, was not tut') stems from Søren Kierkegard and was made familiar by Heidegger; see Karl Löwith, *Mein Leben in Deutschland vor und nach 1933. Ein Bericht* (Stuttgart: Metzler, 1986): 28. It is interesting and a little ironic that Strauss uses this decisionist formula—which Löwith explains in his "Von Hegel zu Nietzsche," in idem, *Sämtliche Schriften*, vol. 4 (Stuttgart: Metzler, 1988): 195, especially in his letters to Löwith.
52 Strauss, *Gesammelte Schriften*, vol. 3, 675.
53 Letter to Löwith dated June 23, 1935, in Leo Strauss, *Gesammelte Schriften*, vol. 3, 650.

only possible on the basis of modern 'immoderation': no ancient philosopher was ever a historian [...] No, dear Löwith, Burckhardt—that really won't do.[54]

Burckhardt, whom Löwith revered, did not figure similarly for Strauss. He associated Burckhardt, a historian, with relativism and saw no philosophical radicalism in his doctrine of the mean, despite the aristocratic remove from his contemporaries. To Strauss, Burckhardt's moderation was nothing more than a theory of the *juste milieu*. But while Strauss disagreed with Löwith about Burckhardt, they both rejected the decisionism of Heidegger and Schmitt.

VI

Strauss redefines scepticism, or zeteticism, in contradistinction to modern relativism with recourse to Xenophon and Socrates. It is embedded in his political philosophy and in his notion of exoteric and esoteric writing. His rhetoricisation of philosophy, its reduction to zetetic questions, is meant to facilitate and protect political philosophy. Its critical value is primarily polemical; compared with other forms of current political philosophy, it is unable to provide a detailed diagnosis of the present situation beyond a mirroring of theory in antiquity and assuring itself of its impact in the modern era through self-reflection. Instead of being a mere sub-discipline—a 'branch,' as Strauss calls it—political philosophy rises to first philosophy. In this capacity, it is the ceaseless, normative interrogation of fundamental human problems and of the political order. For Strauss, philosophy is the only framework in which this can meaningfully occur.

As I suggested at the beginning, several levels of zetetic questioning can be found in Strauss's writings. He is sceptical of modern philosophy and tradition—including social sciences, political theory, political science, and revealed religion—for being neither radical nor normative enough. The philosopher's scepticism is directed at opinions in general and at the political in particular. Strauss argues again and again for moderation in politics and accuses other radical philosophers such as Nietzsche and Heidegger not only of self-instrumentalisation, but also of not doing enough to prevent misunderstandings by disciples, intellectuals, and the poorly educated. Of course, it is doubtful whether Strauss did enough to prevent such misunderstandings himself, given the later success of some Straussians. His central topos—the warning not to separate wisdom and moderation in *On Tyranny* and in other places—can hardly be ignored, yet he remains vague.

Strauss's implicit set of anthropological assumptions, his concept of political philosophy, and his belief in the insufficiency of reason form the basis of his conservative approach, which was noted by his disciples, political sympathisers, and oppo-

---

[54] Letter to Löwith dated July 17, 1935, in *ibidem*, 565f.

nents alike. Yet one must admit that his zetetic approach, while producing innovative interpretations of canonical political philosophers, yields few substantive guidelines.

Strauss's attempt to ground scepticism anthropologically may be interesting, but he can hardly conceal its limited scope, the lovely line about scepticism being a form of wisdom notwithstanding. Methodically, his philosophising is tied to the distinction between exoteric and esoteric writing, with all its illuminating and surprising insights. According to Strauss's interpretative hermeneutics, the hidden meanings in philosophical texts enable radical questioning while shielding the public from its ramifications. His political philosophy does not aim at specific solutions; rather, it is meant to have humanising side-effects on the city, on the political community, and on gentlemen. Strauss believes that philosophical scepticism, correctly understood, refuses instrumentalisation and, despite its radicalism in theory, is moderate in questions affecting the political order more narrowly.

Nevertheless, the limited scope of his scepticism means that his thinking can be called zetetic only in part. That limited scope grows out of Strauss's commitments to antiquity—to Socratic questioning, to persisting in questioning, and to understanding philosophy as a way of life. At the same time, Strauss wanted to elude criticism of the foundations of modern political philosophy and theory. His insufficiently elaborated existential scepticism can problematise relativism, historicism, and positivism—the spectres, in his mind, responsible for the crisis of modernity—but he cannot shake them systematically. His entire critique of modernism and liberalism stands on feet of clay. Interpreting Strauss's philosophy as sceptical does not do enough to address this or its scant epistemological underpinnings.

Roi Benbassat
Jewish Faith and Scepticism—
The Example of Yeshayahu Leibowitz[1]

Introduction

Religious faith is generally perceived as being in contrast with sceptical approaches, even though some advocates of faith may present doubt as an important feature of religious development. The more you confront and overcome greater doubts, these advocates of faith say, the stronger and firmer your faith. It is quite easy to note, though, that even from this broad-minded religious viewpoint, scepticism is considered an obstacle that should eventually be overcome, and that the ideal of faith still remains the termination of scepticism. Here, however, I would like to discuss a rather different religious approach: one in which scepticism can and should be constantly maintained alongside faith. It is a religious approach that not only accepts scepticism as an essential feature of religious development, but also regards a lack of scepticism as corruptive for a genuinely faithful position. This unusual religious approach is exemplified by the Jewish thinker Yeshayahu Leibowitz (1903–1994).

The term 'scepticism' should first be elucidated here. Usually, it refers to the characteristic of being doubtful in regard to the beliefs and opinions that one confronts. However, the more rigorous meaning of the term, which stems from the ancient Greek sceptical schools of philosophy, is a constant and deliberate aim to detach oneself from one's own judgments, which determine the truth value of views, opinions, and beliefs. The ancient sceptics conceived of *epoché*—the state of mind in which one neither denies nor affirms any belief or knowledge—as leading to the most perfect tranquillity of the mind (*ataraxia*).[2] In the context of our investigation here, scepticism would indeed be considered in the sense of *epoché*, though not as a means of achieving *ataraxia*, but of achieving purified, genuine religious faith. In Leibowitz's religious conception, scepticism is specifically used towards traditional Jewish beliefs, with the aim of achieving the highest form of Jewish faith: אמונה לשמה ('faith for its own sake,' henceforth *lishmah*).

Of course, the term 'faith' must be explicated here too, especially since Leibowitz's understanding of religious faith is certainly not a usual one. In this regard, we must stress Leibowitz's distinction between 'faith' and 'belief.' Whereas 'belief,'

---

[1] This article was first begun at the Maimonides Centre for Advanced Studies, University of Hamburg, and was finally completed within the framework of the Hessian Ministry for Science and Art funded LOEWE research hub "Religious Positioning: Modalities and Constellations in Jewish, Christian and Muslim Contexts" at the Goethe University Frankfurt and the Justus-Liebig-University Giessen.
[2] Sextus Empiricus, *Outlines of Pyrrhonism*, trans. Benson Mates (New York: Oxford University Press, 1996): 3.

in his terms, is a cognitive determination of our minds, 'faith,' he claims, is a *conative* determination:

> [R]eligious faith [...] is rather a value decision that one makes, and, like all value determinations, it does not result from any information one has acquired, but is a commitment to which one binds himself. In other words, faith is not a form of cognition; it is a conative element of consciousness.[3]

'Cognitive determinations' refer to our judgments of whether what we think of as reflecting a state of affairs in reality is true or false. This category generally includes our opinions, beliefs, and knowledge regarding the world that we perceive and its objects. '*Conative* determinations,' by contrast, are determinations of our willpower rather than our intellect. These determinations include our desires and aversions, our tastes, our intentions, and also our values. Faith, according to Leibowitz, belongs to the second category, and as such, in principle, it does not rely on what we know or believe.

According to Leibowitz, religious faith is specifically a value determination, and any value, in his view (including moral values), is the product of one's will rather than one's cognitive capacities. In other words, religious faith, like value determinations in general, does not reflect one's knowledge or beliefs, but what one wishes to realise and fulfil in reality. In a Kantian fashion (which Leibowitz frequently adopted), we may say that faith does not refer to *what is*, but to *what ought to be*.

The philosophical foundation of Leibowitz's concept of faith may be disputable. Our contemporary philosophers of morals, for example, would consider Leibowitz a *non-realist* and a *non-cognitivist*, and challenge him in the ways in which these moral positions are usually challenged. However, it is not our concern here to support or dispute this philosophical viewpoint. We only wish to elucidate Leibowitz's concept of faith in a way that would allow us to understand how scepticism could be integrated into it and even become essential to it. I would only note that the fact that these two realms—our intellect and our willpower—usually interact did not escape Leibowitz's mind. It may be true that our desires are often influenced by our opinions and *vice versa*; nonetheless, this does not exclude the possibility that certain conative determinations are indeed independent of what we know or believe in, just as certain cognitive determinations (for example, mathematical truths) are indeed indifferent to what we want and desire.

Jewish faith specifically, in Leibowitz's conception, is absolutely independent of one's beliefs. It is defined as one's binding decision to live under the restraints im-

---

[3] Yeshayahu Leibowitz, *Judaism, Human Values, and the Jewish State*, ed. Eliezer Goldman, trans. Eliezer Goldman, Yoram Navon, Zvi Jacobson, Gershon Levi, and Raphael Levy (Cambridge, Mass.: Harvard University Press, 1992) [henceforth abbreviated *Judaism*]: 37. I have slightly revised the English translation in the quotation above, which originally employs the misleading term 'evaluative decision.'

posed by the Halakhah (the Jewish system of laws), and this practical decision—analogous to one's determination to abide by moral principles—does not necessarily rely on any belief that one might have. It may only express what a person desires to realise in his or her life as a superior value. This definition of faith, we may observe, enables, in principle, the integration of scepticism in Leibowitz's religious conception.

Despite presenting quite an unusual concept of faith, Leibowitz is not the only thinker who conceives of religious faith in this manner. The Protestant Christian thinker Søren Kierkegaard, for example, had a very similar notion of faith. He too understood faith as a passionate, existential choice rather than a belief or set of beliefs, and like Leibowitz he found proofs, evidence, and demonstrations to be senseless in the realm of religion. I have already elaborately discussed the analogy between these two religious thinkers elsewhere.[4] My interest here, however, is to show how this particular concept of religious faith renders possible the incorporation of scepticism into a religious framework, and especially into the framework of Judaism.

Leibowitz's definition of faith as a pure *conative* determination, independent of all cognitive determinations, lays the ground for the integration of scepticism within the Jewish religion. Belief, from this perspective, becomes a superfluous element of the Jewish religion that may be—or, should better be—suspended. This is certainly a radical and uncommon religious position, and one would want to enquire whether an Orthodox Jewish practitioner may really be sceptical in regard to well-rooted traditional Jewish beliefs while still maintaining his or her faith in Judaism. Could it really be possible, for example, to be sceptical of whether the reception of the Torah on Mount Sinai actually took place, or about the very existence of God, without losing faith in Judaism? This is what we are about to find out by reviewing Leibowitz's approach to some central Jewish beliefs.

1 The Belief in God's Existence

The existence of God is a fundamental matter of belief for religious practices, individuals, and schools of thought, especially within the scope of the monotheistic religions. To others (mainly philosophers), God's existence may be a matter of strict knowledge. In Leibowitz's religious conception, however, the existence of God—specifically the God to which the biblical text refers—is neither a matter of belief nor of knowledge, but of practical decision: the decision to adhere to the halakhic system of duties as absolutely binding, which is essentially what constitutes faith in Judaism.

According to Leibowitz, the belief in or the presumed knowledge of the existence of God has no religious significance whatsoever, since one may very well acknowl-

---

[4] Roi Benbassat, "Yeshayahu Leibowitz – Jewish Existentialism," *Religious Studies* 51.2 (2015): 141–163.

edge the existence of God and yet rebel against Him, or ignore His demands. The biblical story of the revelation on Mount Sinai—and the making of the golden calf right after it—teaches us, according to Leibowitz, this simple lesson: 'even if one cites a notarised approval of God's revelation to the people of Israel on Mount Sinai and of the granting of the Torah from the heavens, one may still refuse to worship the lord.'[5] Therefore, the crucial thing that the Jewish religion demands is not knowing or believing in God, but obeying God's commands in practice.

But isn't obeying God's commands dependent on prior acknowledgment of God's existence? No, claims Leibowitz: religious practice is 'prior to any cognitive and emotional aspect of Jewish religiosity.'[6] In Judaism, one is obliged to undertake the halakhic duties regardless of what one believes, even in regard to the existence of God. This peculiar claim is central in Leibowitz's religious thought. For him, acknowledging the existence of God is the consequence of undertaking the religious practice, not the reason for this undertaking. It is not that 'I believe, and therefore I observe my religious duties,' but rather, 'I observe the halakhic duties and therefore I believe in the God of Israel.' In Leibowitz's words: 'I have been privileged to recognize the giver of the Torah as a result of having accepted the yoke of the Torah and its *Mitzvoth*.'[7]

Hence the importance of distinguishing between 'faith' and 'belief' in Leibowitz's thought. Whereas a 'belief' in God is normally conceived of as a reason for engaging with religious practice, 'faith,' according to Leibowitz, is this very engagement itself —one's commitment to live under the constraints of religious practice. We cannot understand the uniqueness of Judaism, Leibowitz claims, unless we consider the Torah as 'data preceding recognition of the giver of the Torah "to whom there is no analogy whatsoever."'[8]

Note that the concept of 'God' remains here, in itself, quite empty and uncharacterised. God is nothing but 'the giver of the Torah,' whose nature is inscrutable. Following Maimonides' theory of negation of divine attributes ('to whom there is no analogy whatsoever' is a reference to Maimonides), Leibowitz does not claim to know God's nature or works in the world.[9] The only essential assumption of Jewish faith, in Leibowitz's view, is that He is 'the giver of the Torah.' Thus, he claims, 'the

---

[5] Yeshayahu Leibowitz, *Faith, History, and Values* [in Hebrew] (Jerusalem: Academon, 2002) [henceforth abbreviated *Emuna*]: 39. Passages from this text presented in this article are my translations into English.
[6] Leibowitz, *Judaism*, 4.
[7] *Ibidem*, 5.
[8] *Ibidem*.
[9] It is important to note however that Maimonides, contrary to Leibowitz, did consider knowledge— and that of God's existence in particular—as fundamental for Judaism (see *Mishneh Torah, Sefer ha-Madda'*, and *Hilkhot Yesodei ha-Torah*, 1:1, as well as his discussions and demonstrations of the existence of God in the first and second parts of *The Guide for the Perplexed*). This may reflect a general difference between the two thinkers' religious conceptions, which will be touched upon again towards the end of this article.

assumption of the yoke of the Kingdom of Heaven is nothing other than the assumption of the yoke of Torah and its *Mitzvoth*.'[10] I will discuss later, separately, this specific assumption (which does not appear to be sceptical at all), however, we may already note at this point that the assumption of God as 'the giver of the Torah' must not be understood as a cognitive statement (a statement with regard to what *is*), but rather as a normative one, which concerns the absolute validity of the halakhic laws.

Now, specifically regarding the assumption of God's existence, let us be clear about Leibowitz's notion here. He claims that faith does not rely on the cognitive determination (belief or knowledge) of God's existence. This means that a religious practitioner is allowed (in Judaism) to be sceptical with regard to God's existence —that is, neither to affirm nor to deny it—as long as it is a matter of mere cognition. We simply do not know enough about what 'existing' means in reference to God. Nevertheless, the affirmation of God's existence is derived from one's observance of the Halakhah as an absolute duty. The law itself is a given fact, and—although it may have been prescribed by human beings—it determines the exclusive manner of worshipping the divine entity called 'God.' Therefore, one who decides to accept the law as absolutely valid and absolutely binding thereby accepts God as 'the giver of the Torah.' Thus, in Leibowitz's view, it is the Halakhah that posits God as its source and not *vice versa*, just as the Halakhah determines the holy status of the Bible, and not *vice versa*.[11]

In this radical sense, the Halakhah has a constitutive role in Judaism, according to Leibowitz. The law is prior to any belief, knowledge, need, or desire that Jewish practitioners may have. It is even prior to *faith*. As Leibowitz puts it: 'faith is a superstructure rising above the *Mitzvoth*; the *Mitzvoth* do not subserve faith [...] Judaism as a historic entity was not constituted by its sets of beliefs.'[12] Thus, faith in Judaism (unlike Christian faith or any other religious form) cannot be separated from halakhic practice: it consists of nothing but the commitment to this practice. And it is the commitment to this practice that affirms God's existence, rather than it being the affirmation of God's existence that leads to this commitment.

One may observe, then, that although a Jewish practitioner does have to assume the existence of God as 'the giver of the Torah,' this assumption does not belong to the category of beliefs. It is not the type of assumption that could be verified by evidence or by any reasonable procedure of attaining knowledge. The assumption of God's existence is understood here as the product of a pure determination of the will, as a value determination, which, according to Leibowitz, is the nature of faith. By being defined as pertaining to a category distinctive from that of cognition, faith does not contradict scepticism, nor is it undermined by it in the framework of the Jewish religion. From this perspective, as we shall see, a Jewish practitioner

---

10 Leibowitz, *Judaism*, 38.
11 *Ibidem*, 11–12.
12 *Ibidem*, 6.

would be allowed not only to avoid affirming or denying the belief in the existence of God (as a matter of cognition), but also other diverse assumptions with regard to God's nature and deeds, which may be claimed by the Bible. This extraordinary viewpoint has led some of Leibowitz's Orthodox Jewish colleagues to regard him as 'an observant heretic.'[13]

2 The Belief in God's Creation of the World

The belief in God's creation of the world as told by the Bible often seems to separate religious people (in the context of monotheism) from those who consider themselves secular, atheistic, or agnostic. It is commonly thought that one cannot possibly be both religious and an advocate of the theory of evolution, for example, or of the Big Bang theory. This might simply reflect a common misunderstanding of the nature of religiousness, which may not be reduced to a set of beliefs with regard to reality. From ancient to modern times, we have examples of religious figures who disprove this common view, thinkers for whom religion and science do not contradict one another. Leibowitz—himself a scientist and an Orthodox Jew—is not a unique figure in this respect.

Leibowitz was able to reconcile his religious and scientific commitments by separating the realm of cognition from that of values. As we have seen, he proclaimed the absolute independence of these two realms from one another. Scientific claims may affect religious faith only when the latter is conceived as relying on knowledge or belief, but *faith*, conceived as a value determination—a pure determination of the will—is, according to Leibowitz, indifferent to science.[14]

However, the Bible does not seem to correspond easily to such a Leibowitzian notion of faith, as it opens with a cosmological, metaphysical, and theological description of the formation of the world that seems to be very much a matter of cognition, and which was actually a matter of belief for many individuals during centuries and millennia:

> בראשית ברא אלהים את השמים ואת הארץ. והארץ היתה תהו ובהו [...]
> In the beginning God created the heavens and the earth. Now the earth was formless and empty.[15]

The fact that the biblical text opens with statements about the origin and formation of the universe may suggest that this issue is fundamental for the Jewish religion, and the other monotheistic religions to follow. We would therefore want to enquire how Leibowitz deals with this section of the Bible, which appears to undermine

---

13 Michael Shashar, *Leibowitz – Heretic or Believer* [in Hebrew] (Jerusalem: Keter, 2002): 15.
14 See Leibowitz, *Judaism*, 132–141; idem, *Emuna*, 11.
15 Genesis 1:1. English translation from http://www.mechon-mamre.org.

his particular concept of Judaism, according to which cognitive claims about reality are irrelevant. Let us begin by looking at one of Leibowitz's direct statements on this subject:

> The first verse of the Torah does not communicate information concerning what came to pass, since the reader is unable to derive from it any factual data which his mind is capable of grasping. If the reader were to try to impute on it a meaning, he would willy-nilly become involved in the ancient metaphysical problem of the beginning of time, a problem fraught with antinomies and paralogisms. The second word, as well [*bara*], cannot be rendered by any term which might indicate an act, or an event, or a process which the reader is capable of cognizing. What I learn from these verses is [only] the great principle of faith, that the world is not God—the negation of atheism and pantheism.[16]

The weight of the hundreds of years during which human civilisation reviewed and quarrelled over this biblical section is marked in these words from Leibowitz. As a modern thinker, familiar with the achievements of modern science in expanding our knowledge of the physical world as well as with the persistent philosophical difficulties regarding the question of the origin of the world, Leibowitz finds it inapt to defend the biblical text in terms of cosmology. Instead, he employs a sceptical strategy to confront the matter. We simply cannot understand the meaning of the first section of the Bible by using our cognitive capacities, he claims. Therefore, as a matter of cognition, there is nothing to affirm or to deny here.

In order to establish our ignorance regarding the matter, Leibowitz points out the philosophical difficulties that prevent us from understanding what 'in the beginning God created the world' means. These difficulties do not mean that the biblical message is false, but they do render it obscure and incomprehensible.

We cannot understand the first act of 'creation' described in the Bible as analogous to any event in history that we know of. It involves abstract notions such as 'time,' 'first cause,' and 'God,' which in this context are not historical or cosmological, but rather metaphysical. These notions therefore require philosophical elucidation, but the philosophical enquiry into these notions reveals irresolvable problems. Firstly, the Bible does not explain what 'God' is in this context, except for being 'the creator' of the world. Secondly, the act of 'creation' has no clear meaning here either. If we assume that we are told that the world came into existence at a certain point in time—the 'starting point' of time—we then encounter the familiar philosophical difficulties concerning the concept of time. I would hardly be able to review these difficulties properly here, but let me note them very briefly.

We generally conceive of 'time' as being infinite—without a beginning or an end—similar to a line drawn to represent the infinite series of real numbers, for example. Any starting point or ending point that one wishes to mark on this line would naturally be artificial and arbitrary, since the line, in principle, continues before the starting point and beyond the end point. Similarly, positing a starting point for time

---

[16] Leibowitz, *Judaism*, 140.

would always raise the persistent question regarding what is (or was) before this point: a *before* that one wishes to deny by the idea of a 'starting point.'

By the notion of the beginning of time (and this applies to the Big Bang theory just as much), we wish to deny the infinity of time, but at the same time we cannot but assume this infinity (just as we do with regard to the series of real numbers). Any limit imposed on time raises in our minds the notion—from which we cannot escape—of that which is beyond the limit. On the other hand, if we wish to hold on exclusively to our concept of time as infinity, then we are prevented (by the logical form of our thinking) from positing any distinctive points and sections within time, since these divisions produce a multiplicity of infinite sections within time which renders the concept of time paradoxical. For this reason, some philosophers concluded that any infinite whole would be, in principle, indivisible.[17] Nonetheless, in practice, we do have to assume points and sections within time and space if we want to consider everything that we perceive around us (all finite things) as real. This, at a glimpse, is the difficulty that pertains to the notion of 'the beginning of time,' and to the concept of time in general.

With regard to the word ברא used in the biblical text (translated as 'created'), similar difficulties arise. The common way of understanding it would be in the sense of God's 'doing'; an action of some sort. However, the way in which we understand the meaning of 'to do,' 'to create,' 'to act,' 'to build,' 'to design,' etc. is based on our experience of the world of human activity (or, generally, that of finite beings), whereas here it refers to 'God,' and specifically to the creation of the world as a whole. Therefore, it seems that ברא is a *sui generis* type of action, just as 'the creator' would be an essentially different being from any finite being. But since we may hardly know anything about the nature of God (note again Leibowitz's acceptance of Maimonides' negative theology), what then can we possibly know of His act of creation?

Some interpreters of the Bible, in consideration of this philosophical difficulty, suggested that the word ברא specifically denotes a 'formation of something out of nothing': a unique act that only God, as a first cause beyond the world (beyond the succession of worldly causes), could perform. Nonetheless, here too we face difficulties in understanding an action of a transcendent cause. However, it is not necessary to become further involved with these difficulties here, as Leibowitz claims that even if we could supposedly comprehend a transcendent cause's action, it would still be unlikely, and impossible to verify, that our particular notion of it is the true interpretation of the biblical term ברא.[18]

Thus, the effort to make sense of the very first verse of the Bible leads, according to Leibowitz, to an awareness of our ignorance with regard to the biblical message; to an *aporia*, if you like. 'Eventually,' Leibowitz says, 'we do not know the meaning of

---

17 See Spinoza, *Ethics*, I, Propositions 12 and 13.
18 See Leibowitz's discussion of the term ברא in *Seven Years of Discourses on the Weekly Torah Reading* [in Hebrew], oral material, published privately by the Leibowitz family (Israel: 2003) [henceforth abbreviated *Seven Years*): 7–8.

the concept ברא, and we do not recognise an act of creation [בריאה] in any category of human understanding.'[19] For this reason, there is no sense, literally, in believing that 'God created the world.'

Nonetheless, in case someone decides to trust in the Bible and hold on to a belief in a cosmological or metaphysical interpretation of its first verses, this belief, according to Leibowitz, would have no religious significance within Judaism. That is to say, whether one believes in the cosmological meaning of the opening passage of the Bible or prefers scientific theories in this respect, the Jewish religion, in principle, tolerates both viewpoints. This tolerant characteristic with regard to cognitive assumptions is rendered possible by acknowledging that the only essential feature of the Jewish religion is the adherence to its practice, which, as stated, does not rely on any cognition. Thus, faith remains indifferent, and resistant, to any cognitive data.

Again, we have an example of how scepticism may be incorporated into Judaism. However, one may observe that Leibowitz does not seem to be entirely sceptical about the truth value of the first section of the Bible, as he writes at the end of the quotation above: 'What I learn from these verses is…that the world is not God —the negation of atheism and pantheism.' In this respect, it appears that Leibowitz does embrace a 'cognitive' content of the biblical message, though a negative one, namely that God is *different* from the world, or, in other words, God's transcendence. Moreover, this assertion obviously has major importance for Leibowitz, as it forms, in his view, the distinction of Judaism from paganism, pantheism, and atheism.

3 The Assumption of God's Transcendence

The problem posed to Leibowitz's religious conception by the affirmation that 'God is not the world' is that this affirmation appears to be a metaphysical assumption, which belongs to the category of cognition no less than that of cosmological assumptions. If this assumption is crucial for a Jewish religious standpoint, as Leibowitz seems to think, this appears to undermine his religious conception, in which *faith* is supposed to be a purely *conative* determination.

As a metaphysical assumption, the statement that 'God is different from the world' raises no simpler problems than those we observed regarding the cosmological message of the first verse of the Bible. Philosophically, it may be claimed against dualistic worldviews that the distinction between God and the world is self-contradictory. Spinoza had famously demonstrated that an infinite substance—be it God or Nature—does not 'leave room' for a second substance.[20] He thus made clear

---

19 Leibowitz, Seven Years, 8.
20 Spinoza, Ethics, I, Proposition 5. This also applies to the distinction between spirit and matter, which cannot be counted, according to Spinoza, as two substances.

that the distinction between God and Nature leads to grave paralogisms, just as the notion of *bereshit* does. For what reason, then, is Leibowitz sceptical about the assumption of God's creation, but willing to 'learn' the principle of God's transcendence from the first biblical verses?

One might already be able to presume what Leibowitz's reply to this question would be. Certainly, his reply would not consist of resolving the philosophical/metaphysical problems pertaining to the notion of God's transcendence. Rather, it would focus on denying the 'cognitive' nature of this claim. Just as God's existence, God's nature, and God's deeds are not matters of belief or knowledge for Leibowitz, as we have seen, so he would deny that God's transcendence is a cognitive assumption.

'When one realises that the world is not God,' Leibowitz states, 'one thereby recognizes that this world is not the value and the end, but rather the end is beyond the world.'[21] We may observe, therefore, that just as Leibowitz did not relate to the assumption of God's existence as a cognitive one, but rather as a specific practical postulate, so also does he relate to the assumption of God's transcendence within the practical realm, the realm of values, and not in the realm of cognition.

In a rather obscure statement, Leibowitz says that 'God is not a metaphysical entity, but He is beyond metaphysics.'[22] What could 'beyond metaphysics' mean? In light of the quotation above, it is quite clear that God signifies a *value*, and values, as stated above, do not refer to 'what *is*.' Specifically, God denotes an end, which is posited 'outside' the world. That is, God's transcendence must be understood as signifying an absolute value, which does not manifest itself in anything within this world.

In this sense, the affirmation of the faithful person that 'God is different from the world' means that he or she does not consider anything within this world as valuable in and by itself. Anything within the world can only have a relative value, derived from one's relation to God as an absolute value. This is the demand of Judaism as Leibowitz understands it: it demands that one worships God through halakhic practice as an absolute, unconditional value. For the sake of this value, anything in the world might be renounced, for anything else is only relatively, conditionally valuable. Considering anything within the world as valuable in and by itself would be, from the perspective of Jewish faith, idolatry.[23]

The biblical figure of Abraham serves for Leibowitz as the best example of faith in Judaism as a value system. Abraham's behaviour—leaving his family, his homeland, circumcising himself, and later, being willing to sacrifice his beloved son and all the promises related to him—manifests the 'logic' of God's transcendence. For God's transcendence is understood as the postulation of an absolute value, beyond this world. Proclaiming God's transcendence in this sense therefore expresses

---

21 Leibowitz, *Seven Years*, 15.
22 *Ibidem*, 22.
23 Leibowitz, *Judaism*, 24–25.

one's willingness to renounce everything in this world, or to consider anything in this world as lacking true value in and by itself. This is, in Leibowitz's view, 'the stance of Abraham on Mount Moriah, where all human values were annulled and overridden by fear and love of God.'[24]

This understanding of the assumption of God's transcendence also explains Leibowitz's conception of Judaism as an exclusive religion which is essentially in conflict with any other ethical or religious position. Christianity, for example, announces the divinity of a human being, whereas moral humanistic standpoints consider the existence of Man in general as an end in itself. From the Jewish perspective, both these positions are clearly forms of idolatry which annul the principle of God's transcendence. For the same reason, in Leibowitz's view, Judaism also condemns fascism (positing the state as a superior value), as well as nationalism and the sanctification of a land (phenomena that also appear within Judaism, and which Leibowitz denounced). All these are forms of idolatry that Judaism—by proclaiming God's transcendence—denounces.

The rejection of atheism and pantheism by the principle of God's transcendence can also be understood in normative rather than in cosmological and metaphysical terms. Atheistic and pantheistic worldviews may have various moral consequences, be they universal humanism, utilitarianism, or consequentialism. The principle of God's transcendence, as it is understood here, is the negation of all these consequences. All value systems that posit a superior value within the world essentially contradict Judaism, if Judaism is understood as positing an absolute value outside and beyond the world.

Now, a reflection on the way in which the principle of God's transcendence (understood in the realm of values) is manifested by a biblical model like Abraham makes us wonder whether such a religious position could still correspond with a sceptical approach. The decisiveness and pathos that characterise this position do not seem to resemble the nature of sceptical attitudes. However, I would suggest that the sceptical standpoint, as the Greeks conceived of it, was no less decisive and pathos-filled. It takes a great deal of decisiveness to maintain the Socratic position, for example, which stressed human all-encompassing ignorance. And one may recall that Socrates himself did not fail to sacrifice his life for the sake of his awareness of ignorance. Would it be wrong to suggest, then, that Socrates too may have been so decisive in regard to his own philosophical standpoint not because he *believed* it was true, but because he considered it an absolute value?

---

24 *Ibidem*, 14.

4 The Assumption of the Halakhah as a Divine Command

This brings us to consider the question of whether Jewish faith, understood as such a decisive value determination, is necessarily a non-sceptical attitude. For even if one accepts Leibowitz's exclusion of faith from the realm of cognition, we do know that scepticism may apply not only to our beliefs regarding reality, but also to moral certainties and values. This question becomes especially vital as we come to an inspection of Leibowitz's acceptance of the Orthodox Jewish postulation of halakhic practice as the exclusive form of relating to God.

Earlier, during the discussion of Leibowitz's approach to the assumption of God's existence, I already noted this postulate, which determines the *law* as the only positive content of the concept of God. According to Leibowitz, Jewish faith does not attribute anything to God except that He is 'the giver of the Torah.'[25] Therefore, as we have seen, 'the assumption of the yoke of the Kingdom of Heaven is nothing other than the assumption of the yoke of Torah and its *Mitzvoth*.' Now, can this assertion correspond with a sceptical attitude?

It is true, in my view, that if one 'believes' that the law (Torah) was given to the Israelites from God as described by the Bible, then one can hardly be considered sceptical. For if scepticism were an attitude in which one refrains from affirming or denying any opinion or belief as true, then the belief in the divinity of the Torah would be no exception. Leibowitz, however, did not hold that the holiness or divinity of the Torah is based on the belief in the reception of the law by the Israelites from God. His references to the biblical description of the events which took place on Mount Sinai make this clear: 'The event on Mount Sinai was the greatest failure in the history of Judaism,' he says, 'for it did not bring the people of Israel to faith and worship of God.'[26]

It is not whether this event truly occurred or not that is in question here, but rather the connection between revelation and faith. In accordance with his general concept of faith, according to which faith 'does not result from any information one has acquired,' Leibowitz does not think that a testament of a revelation in the past (or even a revelation that one experiences in the present) can establish faith in Judaism. This is precisely the lesson that the Bible teaches us, in his view, by telling the story of the revelation experienced by the Israelites on Mount Sinai, after which the golden calf was made:

> Ḥazal [i.e. the wise old Jewish rabbis] knew that it is possible to know the Lord and rebel against Him. Even if one proves that God created the world during six days, freed Israel from Egypt, opened the Red Sea, and gave them the Torah on Sinai, still one can say 'but I do not undertake to worship the lord.' Psychologically and logically, events do not have the power to establish

---

[25] I also noted above that according to Leibowitz Jewish faith also assumes that 'God is different from the world,' but this is only a negative statement with regard to God's nature.
[26] Leibowitz, *Emuna*, 151.

faith [...] to conclude, any knowledge we have or learn of God's deeds cannot by itself bring a man to act for the sake of heaven.[27]

If these kinds of events cannot bring human beings to faith and worship of the lord, then what can? The answer to this question has already been given to us: only one's *value determination* constitutes faith in Judaism, a determination of the will that is not dependent on any knowledge or belief one might have. This value determination is also the grounds for accepting the Halakhah as a divine command, and as forming the exclusive manner in which one may relate to God, that of worship in practice.

It is true that Leibowitz stressed that the Halakhah is the first and foremost pillar of the Jewish religion, prior even to faith, which is, as stated above, 'a superstructure rising above the *Mitzvoth*.' Nonetheless, in order to accept the Halakhah as an absolute authority, as a divine law, one ought either to believe in a story of its divinity or to have faith in the Leibowitzian sense. In any case, a subjective determination is required so that one adheres to the halakhic system of laws as an absolute authority.

Indeed, the Halakhah proclaims itself as a divine command. The first of the Ten *Mitzvoth* (which are fundamental to the Halakhah) announces the God who commands the Israelites. However, the truth value of this proclamation of the law may be challenged, of course, especially if one wishes to be sceptical. It is plausible, for example, that Moses (like the Egyptians before him and the Greeks after him) presented as divine commands laws that he himself established, for socio-political reasons, as a means of enforcement. However, whether this was indeed the case or not, it is a matter of belief. And as a matter of belief, Judaism, in Leibowitz's view, can in principle tolerate various views on the origin of the law. Leibowitz himself often highlighted the fact that some halakhic rulings were obviously man-made and could often be modified by rabbinic rulings in view of the changing circumstances of the Jewish community. And yet Leibowitz, in consent with Orthodox Judaism, assumes the divinity of the law. The law, at its core, is not aimed to attain any human (personal or social) purpose, but expresses only the demand of God from His people. The sole purpose of fulfilling the law must therefore be the worship of God.

This purpose, however, for Leibowitz, is not determined by belief or knowledge, but by faith as a value determination: it is a product of one's will. A faithful person views the Halakhah as a divine command regardless of the beliefs and opinions he or she might have about the origin of the law. The faithful accept the law's proclamation of its own divinity as a demand to adhere to it as an absolute duty. It is a demand to obey the law unconditionally, despite one's particular beliefs, views, needs, wishes, or requirements—as a 'categorical imperative,' if you will.[28] Accepting

---

27 Ibidem, 145.
28 The analogy of Leibowitz's concept of Judaism to Kant's deontological ethics is quite established in the secondary literature on Leibowitz's thought. See Naomi Kasher, "Leibowitz's conception of Judaism compared to Kant's conception of morality" [in Hebrew], in *Sefer Yeshayahu Leibowitz*, eds. Asa Kasher and Yakov Lewinger (Tel Aviv: Tel Aviv University students union press, 1977): 21–34; Silman

the divinity of the law, in this sense, is simply accepting the law as absolutely binding, in all circumstances and at any cost.

It is important to stress here, though, that the halakhic law cannot pass itself as having such absolute authority over human actions unless the individual person makes a subjective decision to regard it as such. In other words, only by virtue of faith, as a personal value determination, is the law rendered absolutely valid and unconditional.[29] Thus, only faith constitutes the acceptance of the divinity of the law. But faith, as understood in this context, is not belief, nor is it dependent on beliefs.

The truth value of the law's proclamation of its divinity is therefore affirmed here, not as a fact (as a matter of cognition), however, but as a matter of the will. In a way, it might be correct to say that the *law* is rendered divine by one's willingness to accept it as such. But this, in Leibowitz's view, is not a unique feature of Judaism, but generally applies to the realm of moral imperatives and duties. Moral imperatives in general have absolute authority not by the force of any objective determination, but only by one's subjective decision (with this claim, Leibowitz definitively rejects the Kantian concepts of ethics). To act with *decency* and refrain from deception and injustice, for example (an example that Leibowitz gives), is a rule that is not objectively valid: its validity is established only by one's choice to posit decency as a value.[30] Hence, in the realm of values in general, according to Leibowitz, it is not appropriate to speak of 'truth' in the common sense of the term, as if we were in the realm of cognition, but rather of 'truthfulness.' And this is:

> [T]ruth in a completely different sense, truth as a value, the value of truthfulness which is not imposed, which one can ignore, and by which one needs not abide. Such is truth in the relations between man and his fellows, between man and wife, between a man and the task he has undertaken [...]. Here deceit is always possible [...]. The truth of science is not a 'value;' it is datum within science. Values [by contrast] are not anchored in reality. They are what a man aspires to impose upon reality [...]. The value of truthfulness is not a cognitive attribute, but rather a conative one, a matter of intention. A man intends to be truthful [...].[31]

Yochanan, "Kantian motives in Leibowitz's thought" [in Hebrew], in *Sefer Yeshayahu Leibowitz*, 47–55; and Daniel Statman, "Leibowitz's concept of morals" [in Hebrew], in *Olamo Vehaguto shel Yeshayahu Leibowitz*, ed. Avi Sagi (Jerusalem: Keter, 1995): 326–343. Leibowitz himself accepted this analogy to some extent; see idem, "Tguvot" [Hebrew], *Iyyun* 26 (1975): 278–281 and idem, *Emuna*, 31.

29 This reveals that the frequent analogy between Leibowitz's conception of religion and Kant's ethical thought is not entirely correct. There is a structural difference between the two: unlike *reason*, which objectively determines the authority of the moral law in Kantian ethics—determination that can be acknowledged by any reasonable being—Halakhah has no similar capacity and is absolutely dependent on a personal subjective determination in order to gain authority. I have elaborately discussed this issue elsewhere; see Benbassat, "Yeshayahu Leibowitz – Jewish Existentialism."

30 See *Conversations on Faith and Philosophy: Aviezer Ravizki Talks with Yeshayahu Leibowitz* [in Hebrew], broadcasted on the university radio channel *Galei Zahal* (1992) (published and printed privately by www.leibowitz.co.il, 2005): 16.

31 Leibowitz, *Judaism*, 139.

This statement may contribute significantly to our enquiry of whether Leibowitz's assumption of the Halakhah as a divine command can correspond with scepticism. The answer implied here is positive. A man of faith can be sceptical with regard to the assumption of the Halakhah as a divine command, considered as a matter of cognition, but he can still affirm this assumption within the realm of values, in which assumptions do not determine whether something is objectively true, or whether something is 'real,' but rather reflect one's subjective determination to impose his or her values upon reality. In the realm of values, the truth value of our assumptions does not refer to the state of affairs in reality, but to one's will and intention. In this context, then, the assumption of the Halakhah as a divine command only reflects that, for the faithful Jew, the halakhic practice constitutes an absolute, unconditional value—a value that he or she strives to realise in reality.

5 The Belief in Divine Providence

The theme of divine providence generally implies the belief that a godly entity somehow watches over us (as individuals or a collective), cares about our deeds and fate, and can, at will, reward those who please it and punish those who upset it. It may then naturally involve various proposed solutions to the problem of theodicy, which are usually also matters of knowledge or belief. In the specific context of Judaism, this notion may include numerous traditional beliefs, among which are the belief in God as the saviour of the Israelites, the belief in the Israelites (or the Jews) as a chosen people, the belief in miracles, and the belief in the arrival of the messiah. Being sceptical about the notion of divine providence would therefore imply scepticism towards quite a rich spectrum of beliefs.

In Leibowitz's religious thought, however, the question of how one should relate to the notion of providence is of major importance, because it essentially involves the crucial distinction between faith *lishmah* ('for its own sake,' or 'for the sake of God') and not-*lishmah* ('not for its own sake,' faith as a means of achieving human ends). This distinction, for Leibowitz, is one between the genuine notion of Jewish faith, attainable (if at all) only to the very few, and the corrupted notion of faith, which is its common form.[32]

The idea of faith *lishmah* 'was given its most eloquent expression, its most profound and sublime formulation,' Leibowitz states, 'in the doctrine of Maimonides, and especially in his conception of providence.'[33] Maimonides understood general providence simply as 'the course of the world'; that is, as Leibowitz writes:

> Whatever exists in reality, or is necessitated by the causal structure inherent in nature, falls under providence. In this respect the fate of human kind—as one type of natural beings—is

---
32 Ibidem, 67.
33 Ibidem, 55.

> no different from that of any other species, whose existence is secured by the general scheme of causality (final cause!). The individual too, of course, is subject *by nature* to this reality [...]. The consequences of all human deeds are necessitated by the nature of men's actions, the regulation of which is the manifestation of providence.[34]

One may observe that this interpretation of the notion of providence could just as well imply the absolute denial of the belief in providence, in its usual sense. For 'providence' is usually understood as being manifested by deviations from the normal course of nature, by divine interventions in the course of nature or in human history, which may render the impossible possible (miracles, or inexplicable events). Therefore, the Maimonidean notion of providence, understood as the necessary course of nature and of all its events, is the absolute opposite of the ordinary belief in providence. 'The very existence of the world is God's loving kindness,' the powers implanted in all living things are His 'righteousness,' and 'the sequence of events succeeding one another by the necessity inherent in the relations between them' is His 'judgment.'[35]

In this Maimonidean sense of the notion, as Leibowitz explains it, to have faith in God as providence means to cleave to God 'with a strength which is proportionate to the extent of his [or her] knowledge ("according to the knowledge shall be the love"), *and it is this knowledge and this cleaving to God that constitutes "individual providence."*'[36] That is to say, individual providence is never the *lot* of this or that agent (not even of the righteous), but rather is something that 'each individual must achieve [...] by his own endeavor [...] through the perfection of his rational power [...] and through a supreme effort in exercising his capacities for this purpose.'[37]

The point here is that providence is not conceived of as a result of one's effort to develop his rational capacities and the other capacities of the mind related to it, but is established by this very effort itself. This is actually a typically Socratic interpretation of the notion of providence, equivalent to Socrates' statement that the wisest man is also the happiest and most invulnerable of all.[38] The more one knows about the nature of things, according to Socratic-Platonic philosophy, the more one is protected from evil and disaster.

Now, this does not appear to be a sceptical approach, and at this point it is also important to recall again what seems to be an essential difference between Maimonides' concept of Judaism and Leibowitz's own. Maimonides posited דעות ('knowledge,' particularly knowledge of God) as the aim of the Jewish praxis and faith. Lei-

---

34 *Ibidem*, 57.
35 *Ibidem*.
36 *Ibidem*.
37 *Ibidem*, 58.
38 Plato, *Apology of Socrates* (trans. Benjamin Jowett), 41c-d: 'No evil can happen to a good man, either in life or after death. He and his are not neglected by the gods.'

bowitz, by contrast, as we have seen here, completely separated the realm of Judaism and faith from that of cognition. Jewish faith, in his conception, does not rely on knowledge, nor does it lead to more knowledge of the world and of God. Therefore, it seems that Leibowitz's concept of Judaism corresponds much better, in principle, with sceptical attitudes. This difference, however, may be undermined, to some extent, when we go further into the Maimonidean conception of providence, in which knowledge and ignorance become one and the same, just as they do in Socratic philosophy.[39]

Maimonides' interpretation of the book of Job stresses that individual providence is anchored in the human understanding, but this understanding consists not of positive knowledge of the world and its purposes, but of one's own ignorance.[40] In his terrible situation, Job finds relief and comfort not by understanding the lord and His deeds, but by realising that his own severe reproaches of God were based on the illusion of understanding the purposes of things in the world, and particularly the essence of 'good' and 'bad.' It is the awareness of his own ignorance in regard to God and to the purposes of Nature that finally relieves Job's resentment and allows him to establish a new life for himself. And it is this awareness of ignorance that renders Job 'righteous' for God.

Leibowitz connects the lesson taught by the book of Job with that of the story of the *Aqedah* ('The Binding of Isaac') in Genesis: 'Both stories seek to teach the meaning of fear of God.'[41] The fear of God attributed to both Abraham and Job denotes their particular *love* of God[42] which is expressed by cleaving to God in all conditions and circumstances, especially in those in which the purposes of God are incomprehensible. The religious *test* (נסיון) presented to both Abraham and Job is set to verify whether their love of God depends on God's fulfilment of their needs or whether it is unconditional. Both Abraham and Job pass the test, and in both cases it is shown that unconditional love towards God—which is the nature of faith *lishmah*—essentially involves acknowledging one's own ignorance regarding God's purposes, or in other words, the purpose of all that which occurs in Nature:

> Abraham is put to the test when fulfillment of the divine demand requires that he renounce all human values; not only personal values such as those involved in the relationship of a father to his only son, but also promises bearing in his seed for all generations to come. He is expected to forgo the Covenant of the Pieces.

---

[39] The following reading of Maimonides' notion of providence as being Socratic does not deny that Maimonides' thought is embedded in a Neo-Platonic and Aristotelian conceptual framework. Nonetheless, I am claiming here that in his interpretation of the book of Job Maimonides is much closer to Socratic (early Platonic) philosophy, which, in contrast with the speculative scientific endeavours of the later Plato and Aristotle, considers the awareness of one's own ignorance as the highest form of human wisdom and righteousness.
[40] Maimonides, *The Guide for the Perplexed*, III:14 and 23.
[41] Leibowitz, *Judaism*, 49.
[42] Ibidem, 49–50.

> Job is put to the test when God appears to him not as the guardian of his fate who metes out reward and punishment, but *in his sheer divinity* [...] Abraham and Job are tested to determine whether their faith is faith for its own sake, manifested in the worship of God for His sake, and unlike the religious faith of the mass of believers who conceive God as acting for their sake.[43]

Leibowitz highlights the unconditional nature of faith (*lishmah*) as it is expressed in the realm of values, where the contrast between religious values and human needs is exposed. But as he continues to analyse the figures of Job and Abraham as models of faith, he also reveals the cognitive element of faith *lishmah*, which consists precisely of knowledge of one's own ignorance. Like Maimonides (in his interpretation of the book of Job), Leibowitz too stresses the role of human understanding and human judgment in the process of acquiring faith *lishmah*. This role consists precisely of *detaching oneself from one's own judgments and pretentions of knowledge*. According to both Maimonides and Leibowitz, this is the central insight proposed by the book of Job (which is, again, analogous to the Socratic idea). Gradually, Leibowitz observes, during the development of the book of Job, we notice that:

> Job's suffering is no longer the focus of his protest; rather, it is his inability to comprehend the meaning of his suffering, which is but one detail within an incomprehensible world [...] this lack of suffering oppresses and troubles him. But for this suffering there is no remedy. The creator of the world concealed from man its meaning, knowledge of which is the true 'wisdom.'[44]

Job's greatest accusation of God, Leibowitz states, is that God had concealed the meaning of His providence, and this protest is 'ultimately answered by God, an answer that satisfies Job and makes him revoke his accusation.'[45] At first view, God's answer, as described in the last three chapters of the book of Job, seems irrelevant:

> It describes being as it is without judging it. It presents the cosmic and terrestrial world, from the inanimate to the living, from the splendid and wondrous to the awful and monstrous—especially the monstrous phenomena—without hinting at any purpose in this amazing creation, or any secret intention underlying the monstrosity. Such is the Creator's providence, and this is what satisfies Job.[46]

Oddly, this seemingly hollow reply satisfies Job. Something is revealed to Job by these words from God, although there is nothing here but 'a description of natural matters.'[47] Leibowitz adopts Maimonides' notion of the message of the book, an interpretation that he considers to be 'the most profound.'[48] Whatever exists in reality

---

43 *Ibidem.*
44 *Ibidem*, 50–51.
45 *Ibidem*, 51.
46 *Ibidem*, 52.
47 *Ibidem.*
48 *Ibidem.*

reflects God's providence: this, as we have seen, is Maimonides' concept of general providence, which is the case even though we have no understanding of God's intentions and of the purposes of natural events. This is a real revelation for Job, as he now advances from the lower stage of faith—'the way prevalent among the masses, who believe in God and undertake to serve Him because He—in their conception—acts for their benefit'—to the superior stage of faith *lishmah*, of those who undertake to worship God with no expectation, to worship a God 'whose world, precisely as it is, is His providence.'[49] In Socratic terms, we could say, Job advances here from the state of ordinary men 'who pretend to know what they really don't,' to that of the philosopher, the truly wise man, who is aware of his own ignorance.[50]

Conclusion

Through an exploration of Leibowitz's treatment of various beliefs, which are central in the Jewish tradition, I believe I have established the possibility of a strong relation between Judaism and scepticism. This connection is already exposed in Maimonides' concept of Judaism, as we have seen in the last discussion of the notion of providence, and it can be detected even in the book of Job itself. However, in Leibowitz's thought, this connection is significantly reinforced by the stark distinction of the realm of Jewish faith from that of cognition. Leibowitz's definition of faith as a value determination—and his philosophical account of values in general, understood as pure products of the will and intention—renders faith absolutely independent of any belief and knowledge. Consequently, scepticism is no longer considered the opponent of faith, but its natural companion.

I have pointed out Leibowitz's sceptical approach to fundamental matters such as the existence of God, the belief in God's creation of the world, God's transcendence, the perception of the Torah as a divine command, and the notion of divine providence. All these assumptions, although being affirmed within the realm of values (by faith as a determination of the will), are suspended as matters of cognition in Leibowitz's thought. They cannot, and should not, in Leibowitz's view, be accepted as true by human understanding.

They *cannot* be accepted as true, because we simply do not recognise the necessity by which they could be perceived as true (knowledge) and because the attempt to understand them confronts us with paradoxes and paralogisms; and even if we wish to *believe* that these assumptions are true (without knowing this), we mostly do not even understand their meaning—such, as we have seen, is the notion of God's existence, as well as the notion of creation and that of God's transcendence. But also, a religious person *should* not accept them as true by his or her human un-

---

49 *Ibidem.*
50 Plato, *Apology of Socrates*, 23b-d.

derstanding, because by doing so one generally renders religion a service to oneself and thereby annuls it as a genuine religion aimed at worshipping the lord. Such is especially the case with regard to the assumption of the Halakhah as a divine command and to the notion of providence. In general, Leibowitz claims, 'faith that relies on information that explains the world to man, may be called not-*lishmah* ["not for its own sake"].'[51]

For this reason, scepticism towards beliefs—and especially towards prevalent beliefs within Jewish circles—is not only possible, but also crucial for the maintenance of a genuine religious position. This was rendered especially clear in the discussion of the notion of providence. One who believes in providence as being manifested in a particular way in the course of history—be it in miracles or merely in ordinary events that occur in one's own favour—is one whose faith is corrupted. Thus,

> the question of faith addressed to man is: do you have faith in God [...] also when providence is **not** proven to you by the course of history? In other words, do you accept the yoke of the kingdom of heaven—the yoke of Torah and *Mitzvoth*—even if this kingdom is not revealed in certain events in history? The answer to this question differentiates between worship *lishmah* and not-*lishmah*.[52]

Clearly, then, it is not scepticism that jeopardises faith, but rather one's judgments and beliefs. And this applies to a very rich spectrum of beliefs that may be accepted within wide Jewish circles—including beliefs in miracles, in the Israelites as a chosen people, in messianism, in the holiness of Zion, in kabbalistic notions, and more—all of which Leibowitz considered as idolatrous and as corrupting the essential notion of Jewish faith.

Of course, Leibowitz acknowledges that the majority of Jewish practitioners cannot refrain from grounding their faith on such beliefs. He also acknowledges that the Jewish religion generally tolerates this corrupted form of faith by insisting on halakhic practice regardless of its basis. However, as Maimonides emphasised, Judaism and its scriptures speak in a double language: one for the ordinary and one for the extraordinary man. And the highest model of faith—exemplified by Abraham and Job—is that of faith that is not grounded on belief. The sceptical feature of this model of faith, as I have stressed, goes hand in hand with the nature of faith *lishmah*, portrayed as unconditional love. For only the one who acknowledges his own ignorance with regard to God's nature, God's deeds, and generally to the occurrences in this world and their purposes, can relate to God as an absolute, unconditional, and transcendent value, posited beyond this world.

Finally, I have made an analogy between Maimonides' and Leibowitz's understanding of providence and that of Socrates. This must not be understood as if I am claiming that the two Jewish conceptions are analogous to the philosophical po-

---

51 Leibowitz, *Seven Years*, 6.
52 Leibowitz, *Emuna*, 144.

sition of Socrates, which is the source of all sceptical schools. Whereas Socratic philosophy refers to an abstract idea of 'the good'—which is indeed absolute and divine from its perspective, but which actually has no positive or concrete content—Judaism, by contrast, relates to a divinity that has definite, concrete, and positive content: the Torah. Judaism establishes its system of duties as the exclusive manner in which a Jew may relate to God in this world, by subordinating his or her life to it. This aspect is absolutely absent, in my view, from Socratic philosophy.[53]

My claim consisted mainly of showing that Maimonides' and Leibowitz's notion of providence presents a typical Socratic insight, according to which the 'righteous' one—the wise and the faithful alike—is not one who knows or understands the purposes of things in life, who knows what is 'good' and what is 'bad' or what brings favourable results or terrible ones, but is, on the contrary, one who acknowledges his own ignorance with regard to these issues and who therefore refrains from affirming or denying them. This typical sceptical feature, as I have demonstrated, is generally compatible with Leibowitz's concept of Judaism.

---

53 Even when Socrates claims unconditional obedience to the laws of the State in Plato's *Crito*, this claim is contradicted by his no-less-important claim in the *Apology* when he assures the judges of Athens that, in the case of contradiction with his philosophy, he would not obey the law.

Part II: **Lectures**

Josef Stern
What is Jewish Philosophy?
A View from the Middle Ages*

Keynote Lecture at the Grand Opening of the Maimonides Centre for Advanced Studies on 29 October, 2015

My late teacher Professor Sidney Morgenbesser often taught his students the 'laws' of Jewish Philosophy or, more specifically, of Jewish logic, Jewish epistemology, Jewish metaphysics, and so on. For example, the laws of general logic are tautologies like 'If p, then p' or 'If it is the case that if p, then q, then not-q, then not-p.' The first law of Jewish Logic is: 'If p, *why not* q (spoken with a Yiddish accent)?'[1]

The question—What is Jewish Philosophy?—is typically answered by describing Jewish philosoph*ies*, i.e, the books, theories, and doctrines of canonical Jewish philosophers, such as, Saadiah Gaon, Moses ben Maimon (Maimonides), Judah Halevi, Levi ben Gershon (Gersonides). Indeed the distinguished scholar of Jewish philosophy, Julius Guttmann, entitled his classic history, *Philosophies of Judaism*.[2] But Jewish philosophy is more than a sequence of doctrines or books. Like all philosophy, it is an activity, something one 'does.'[3] For some it is an intellectual exercise that solves theoretical puzzles. For others these exercises are practices that constitute a way of life, practices that give central place to the intellect and reasoning but aim at a practical end, the achievement of happiness or a harmonious life in which one's Judaism and intellect are in sync.[4] In either case, philosophy is a pursuit in which one engages, not only a subject matter or the results of the pursuit.

The name of the subject 'Jewish Philosophy' first emerged in Germany in the late seventeenth century and early eighteenth century when we find the first histories of philosophy—and the very idea that philosophy has a history. The earliest histories are in the doxographical tradition, portraying certain historical figures as paradigms of what was then considered to be philosophical wisdom. Slightly later histories were developmental

---

* Many thanks to Michael Fagenblat, Zev Harvey, and David Shatz for very helpful conversations and comments on earlier drafts of this paper.
1 And of Jewish epistemology: 'Your mother always knows best.'
And of Jewish metaphysics: 'To be is to be in *tzures* ("pain, suffering").'
And of Jewish aesthetics: 'Beauty is for the *goyim*.'
2 But only in the English translation which was not authorized by him; the title of the German original uses the singular: *Die Philosophie des Judentums*.
3 See Mark Steiner, "Rabbi Yisrael Salanter as a Jewish Philosopher," *The Torah u-Madda Journal* 9 (2000): 42–57.
4 On philosophy as a way of life, see Pierre Hadot, *What is Ancient Philosophy?* (Cambridge, Mass.: Harvard University Press, 2002) and his collection of essays, idem, *Philosophy as a Way of Life* (Oxford: Blackwell, 1995). On Maimonides' *Guide of the Perplexed* as a guide to a way of life, see Josef Stern, *The Matter and Form of Maimonides' Guide* (Cambridge, Mass.: Harvard University Press, 2013).

OpenAccess. © 2017 Josef Stern, published by De Gruyter. This work is licensed under the Creative Commons Attribution-NonCommercial-NoDerivatives 4.0 License. https://doi.org/10.1515/9783110527971-011

narratives that aimed to show that the past is at most of historical interest and of no contemporary philosophical value. It is in these histories that the category of Hebraic, Mosaic, scriptural, or prophetic and finally 'Jüdische Philosophie' (first coined by Brucker in the 1740's) was introduced, and ironically in some of these books to specifically *exclude* the Jewish tradition (as well as 'barbarian philosophy') from the history of philosophy that traces its origins to Greece. Later in the nineteenth century, historians and philologists of *Wissenschaft des Judentums* appropriated the term 'Jewish Philosophy' in order to claim a field of scholarship of their own in order to legitimate their academic respectability.[5] In short, it is only relatively recent that engagement with ancient, medieval, and early modern philosophers became a historical discipline, creating the history of philosophy. Jewish philosophy is a special case or byproduct of this phenomenon. Unlike the physical world that exists independently of and prior to the scientific discipline 'Physics,' the domain 'Jewish Philosophy' was the creation of the academic discipline, the 'History of Jewish Philosophy,' an artifact *made* by an academic discipline as much as the discipline *studies* it.

What was it, then, that those thinkers and authors were doing—and I will concentrate now on the medieval case since that is what I know best—that we scholars nowadays refer to as 'Medieval Jewish Philosophy'? Well, the simple answer is: Philosophy! However, stating what philosophy is, say, in a definition, or through necessary and sufficient conditions, is no easier than spelling out what *Jewish* philosophy is. Instead I will sketch two examples of different conceptions of philosophy in which two seminal medieval Jewish philosophers were engaged, Saadiah Gaon and Maimonides. But, first, you might reasonably ask: 'If it was simply philosophy they were doing, why label it *Jewish* philosophy?'

What Jewish Philosophy is *Not*

Let me first tell you what Jewish philosophy is *not*. It is not philosophy composed or studied in a Jewish language, say, Hebrew.[6] We do speak of medieval *Arabic* philosophy and medieval *Latin* philosophy, meaning medieval philosophy written in Arabic or in Latin, but we cannot describe the full gamut of medieval Jewish philosophy as medieval

---

[5] I am indebted to Dirk Westerkamp's rich and insightful "The Philonic Distinction: Germanic Enlightenment Historiography of Jewish Thought," History and Theory 47 (2008): 533–559, for the history of the origins of the term 'Jewish philosophy' and of the fields of Jewish philosophy and the history of Jewish philosophy. See also Daniel Frank, "What is Jewish philosophy?," in History of Jewish Philosophy, eds. Daniel H. Frank and Oliver Leaman (London: Routledge, 2004): 1–8. On the emergence of the academic study of the history of philosophy in general, and on varieties of ways of doing the history of philosophy, see Michael Frede, "The History of Philosophy as a Discipline," Journal of Philosophy 85 (1988): 666–672.

[6] Jacob Klatzkin, the author of the famed Oṣar ha-Munaḥim ha-Filosofiyyim (Thesaurus Philosophicus Linguae Hebraicae) (reprinted New York: Feldheim, 1968), makes a claim to this effect.

Hebrew philosophy.⁷ Leaving aside Philo of Alexandra in the first century who wrote in Greek, works written in the Islamic empire (e.g., by Saadiah, Maimonides, Judah Halevi, and many others) were all composed in Arabic or Judeo-Arabic (Arabic in Hebrew characters). Only after 1148 do medieval Jewish philosophers in Christian Europe compose and read works in Hebrew. And, of course, for modern Jewish philosophy after the Enlightenment, the relevant languages include German, French, and English.

Moreover, it is not self-evident that everything philosophical written or read in Hebrew should necessarily count as Jewish philosophy. Many Aristotelian and Arabic philosophical texts were translated into Hebrew, and some only survive in their medieval Hebrew translations. Is this sufficient for them to count as Jewish philosophy? To complicate matters, many medieval Jewish thinkers composed supercommentaries in Hebrew on commentaries originally written in Arabic but then translated into Hebrew (say, Gersonides' supercommentaries on Averroes' Arabic commentaries) on Greek classics by Aristotle. *If* these supercommentaries are part of medieval Jewish philosophy—and why shouldn't they be?—should the Hebrew-translated Arabic commentaries on which they are super-commentaries, or the original Greek texts translated into Hebrew, also cross the boundary? Maybe it would more accurate to say that there is no boundary. In any case, language alone cannot settle the question.

Second, you don't have to be Jewish to do Jewish philosophy and, by the same token, not just any kind of philosophy composed by a Jew, i.e., someone of Jewish descent or confession, need be Jewish philosophy.⁸ Some medieval Jewish philosophical texts were composed after their author's conversion to Islam (e.g., Abu'l-

---

7 Note that some Islamic (Arabic?) philosophy, such as Avicenna's *Danishnamah-yi 'Ala'*, was composed in Persian.

8 See, however, Raphael Jospe, *What is Jewish Philosophy?* (Ramat Aviv: Open University, 1988): 28–29: 'A philosopher's Jewish identity is a necessary condition, but not a sufficient condition, for determining whether his philosophy is, indeed, a Jewish philosophy [...]. Jewish philosophy cannot be developed by a non-Jew. A non-Jew cannot write Jewish philosophy." See also p. 6 where Jospe claims that Aristotle and Al-Farabi, for all their influence on Jewish philosophy, 'have no share in [it] for the simple reason that they were not Jews.' No argument is given, but even if one agrees that a Jewish philosoph*er* (meaning someone who is both a Jew and a philosopher) must be Jewish, it does not follow that Jewish philos*ophy* must be written by a Jew. That would be no different than requiring that feminist philosophy be written only by women. Notwithstanding the counterexamples I mention in the text, of course, the fact—contingent fact of course—is that (almost all?) Jewish philosophy has been written by Jews. But this fact, at least in the past, can be easily explained by historical, sociological reasons (access to languages, training, ethnic divisions). The same was true for at least a thousand years about rabbinics—and for the simple reason that non-Jews (apart from Jewish converts to Christianity) did not have the education or training to do serious rabbinics. Today, however, with the proliferation of academic Jewish studies, we now have extremely well-trained *non-Jewish women*, not to say men, engaged in serious rabbinics. (And if one does not draw an arbitrary line between the academic study of rabbinic texts and non-academic or 'traditional' study of rabbinic texts, then both are part of one tradition that is arguably all part of the continuation of the tradition of 'Oral Torah.') I see no principled reason not to expect that the same will ultimately be true of Jewish philosophy, mutatis mutandis.

Barakat al-Baghdadi) or Christianity (Profiat Duran, Joshua Lorki, Abner of Burgos [=Alfonso of Valladolid] who considered himself a Jewish philosopher even while he was a Christian bishop!). Likewise, whether one regards the medieval sectarian movement, the Karaites, as inside or outside Judaism, philosophy and theology written by Karaites is also generally considered part of the repertoire of medieval Jewish philosophy. And if one looks at modern figures, Henri Bergson, Ernest Nagel, and Saul Kripke are all Jewish (and identify as Jews) and they are all philosophers but their works are not Jewish philosophy. Once again, we cannot define Jewish philosophy using the religion or ethnic identity of the philosopher who composed it.

Is Jewish philosophy something like English, French, or American philosophy—something like a school or style of philosophy? Just as Early Modern empiricist or materialistic philosophy (Hobbes, Locke, Hume) is sometimes labeled 'British empiricism' or just as Early Modern rationalist philosophy (Descartes, Malebranche, Spinoza and Leibniz) is identified with France or the continent,[9] is there one philosophical orientation or movement or style that marks medieval Jewish philosophers or philosophy? Again, No. The standard histories of medieval Jewish philosophy identify Saadiah as a Mu'tazilite dialectical theologian; Abraham ibn Daud, Maimonides, and Gersonides as Aristotelians, or Neo-Platonized Aristotelians; Baḥya ibn Paquda as a theologian and Neo-platonist; Ibn Gabirol and Judah Halevi as Neo-platonists. No one school or orientation characterizes medieval Jewish philosophy or philosophers.

A final suggestion is that Jewish Philosophy is the Philosophy of Judaism or, as we would say nowadays, the 'Philosophical Foundations of Judaism.'[10] This idea is more promising but it immediately raises two thorny questions: 'What is Judaism?' and 'How such a conception of Jewish philosophy differs from Jewish theology,' i.e., the systematic study of the doctrines, practices, and culture of Judaism as a revealed religion, a question that generally makes contemporary scholars of Judaism anxious because of an acquired allergy to theology, perhaps in reaction to its sophisticated development in Christianity with its creedal core. But it has not always been that way, especially if we take theology to be *natural* theology, human reasoning about the nature of God and divinity. Thus one of the most influential texts on medieval Jewish thought was the Neo-platonic *Theology of Aristotle*, the Arabic annotat-

---

[9] Similarly, by 'American philosophy,' we mean either Thoreau and Emerson, so-called American Transcendentalists, or Peirce, James, Dewey, pragmatists. And Continental Philosophy is, if not a school, then a style of 20th-century philosophers living on the European continent. Is 'Jewish philosophy' a euphemism for some school like this? Michael Fagenblat (p.c.) has suggested that we might indeed think of Jewish philosophy as the philosophy (or philosophies) of (the) Jews; the question is whether we are interested simply in knowing what philosophy or philosophies Jews have professed (a sociological question) or whether such a category marks out a philosophically interesting kind.

[10] See Guttmann, *Philosophies of Judaism*, 9–10; Alexander Altmann, "Judaism and World Philosophy," in *History of Philosophy Eastern and Western*, vol. 1, ed. Sarvepalli Radhakrishnan (London: Allen & Unwin, 1952): 76; Leon Roth, "Is there a Jewish Philosophy?," in *Jewish Philosophy and Philosophers*, ed. Raymond Goldwater (London: Hillel Foundation, 1962): 10–11; Eliezer Berkovits, "What is Jewish Philosophy?," *Tradition* 3.2 (1961): 120–122.

ed and expanded edition of central books of Plotinus' *Enneads*. We shall return to philosophical theology, or theological philosophy, in our discussion of Saadiah, but rather than attempt to distinguish the two, let me simply stipulate for now what I mean by this conception of Jewish Philosophy. Understood as the Philosophy of Judaism, it takes Judaism, primarily manifest in its canonical texts, as the *datum* on which it analytically reflects—exploring its presuppositions, making distinctions, articulating its possible claims and concepts, exposing ambiguities and imprecise beliefs, laying out arguments and evaluating their truth and validity—no different from the philosophy, or what we nowadays call the philosophical foundations, of biology, physics, mathematics, or economics. Although Jewish philosophy of this kind may have originated in polemical contexts, its content does not adopt a stance defending or advocating Judaism. And while the philosopher may be *committed* to the claims he is philosophizing about, this commitment need be no more than the kind of authority the philosopher of biology or physics assigns to the biological or physical facts about which he is philosophizing. That is, the philosopher does not challenge the data—of either biology or a religion—when he does not understand them, not because they are metaphysically privileged but because they are the given about which he is philosophizing. As Maimonides says in the name of Themistius, he shapes his theory according to the world rather than makes the world fit his theory (*Guide* I:72). The aim of such a Jewish philosophy is to achieve a critical understanding of the foundational beliefs, assumptions, logical structure, and implications articulated in the data, thus taking the texts and practices of Judaism as given.[11]

Two caveats: First, we must be careful not to adopt an essentialist preconception of Judaism, taking Judaism to be pre-determined, 'an invariable "given," prior to and transcending changing philosophies.'[12] Historically, the Judaism that Jewish philosophy philosophizes about has in part been changed as a result of its philosophical scrutiny. Perhaps the best example is Maimonides' conception of Judaism or, more precisely, his conception of *Talmud Torah*, or the study of Torah. Maimonides' seminal code of rabbinic law, the *Mishneh Torah*, opens with four chapters that provide a streamlined exposition of Aristotelian metaphysics, cosmology, and physics, philosophy which Maimonides identifies with the subject matter of two classical rabbinic terms for esoteric knowledge, 'the Account of the Beginning,' i.e., the rabbinic interpretation of the first chapters of Genesis, and 'the Account of the Chariot,' the rabbinic interpretation of Ezekiel's and Isaiah's prophetic visions of a divine chariot. He then subsumes these two Accounts under another rabbinic heading, *Pardes* (alluding to a famous talmudic story) which he describes as the most noble and sub-

---

[11] An excellent example of a contemporary work on the philosophical foundations of Judaism of the sort I have in mind is Moshe Halbertal and Avishai Margalit, *Idolatry* (Cambridge, Mass.: Harvard University Press, 1998). See also Steiner, "Rabbi Yisrael Salanter;" Moshe Halbertal, *On Sacrifice* (Princeton: Princeton University Press, 2012); and David Shatz, *Jewish Thought in Dialogue: Essays on Thinkers, Theologies and Moral Theories* (Brighton, Mass.: Academic Studies Press, 2009).
[12] Jospe, "What is Jewish Philosophy?"

lime part of Talmud, the classic rabbinic activity of interpreting the Torah. Through these identifications of Aristotelian physics and metaphysics with rabbinic categories, Maimonides radically rewrites our very conception of Torah, its study, and the core of Judaism. He makes the study of Aristotelian physics and metaphysics a subject of Talmud, hence, a religious obligation. Furthermore, philosophy is not just *a* subject of Torah, it is now the *apex*, the *most* noble subject in the study of Torah. Finally, Maimonides makes normative beliefs and knowledge (of Aristotelian physics and metaphysics) rather than pious performance of the practical commandments the most important part of Judaism. Here the Philosophy of Judaism radically recasts our very conception of Judaism.

My second caveat is that the religion of Judaism has never been the exclusive subject matter, or datum, of Jewish Philosophy. No different from ancient and medieval philosophy in general, medieval Jewish philosophy included both the subjects we call metaphysical, epistemological, and moral philosophy nowadays (including topics unrelated to classical Judaism, such as substance, matter and form, causation, the theory of intellects, the nature of motion) *and* natural philosophy: physics, biology, astronomy, cosmology, astrology, mineralogy, meteorology, mathematics, geography, the science of dreams and the physiology of sensation. Medieval Jewish philosophy was inseparable from the sciences regardless of their connection to Judaism.[13] Hence, any restriction of Jewish Philosophy to religious or theological topics will not cut the subject at the right joints.

Judaism before Philosophy

For the remainder of this paper, I want to illustrate through two examples what the thinkers engaged in what we now call 'Medieval Jewish Philosophy' were doing. This approach takes our opening question 'What is (Medieval) Jewish Philosophy?' as an interpretive or explanatory question about an empirical phenomenon: how should we describe and explain the activity of certain canonical thinkers and the works they produced when they were engaged in what is now called 'Medieval Jewish philosophy'? On my view, as I mentioned earlier, they were simply doing philosophy, although these episodes also exemplify two different conceptions of philosophy in its first encounters with Judaism. But what will also emerge from these two examples is a proposal concerning how we might be able after all to reconstruct a sense in which these thinkers were engaged not only in philosophy but also in *Jewish* philosophy, a sense that avoids the criteria we criticized in the previous section.

---

[13] For example, Maimonides wrote a treatise on mathematics, Gersonides was an original creative astronomer, and many more were active in astrology, medicine, and logic. Of course, one might object that this simply shows that Jewish philosophers were *also* scientists. However, this misrepresents the way the medieval figures themselves viewed the sciences as integral to their philosophy, instead projecting backwards a historically anachronistic modern view of their relation.

First, however, in order to appreciate the effect of its encounter with philosophy on Judaism, let me say a word about the religion of the Bible or Israel and of the Rabbis *before* its contact with philosophy and how it treated matters of belief or doctrine or reasoning.

The core of both Biblical and classical rabbinic Judaism is normative *actions* and *practices*, the correct performance of the Mosaic commandments as elaborated by the rabbis in Halakhah. These commandments primarily concern the Temple, sacrifice, agriculture, purity and impurity, and 'holiness' (whose original meaning is connected to separate and to be separated) practices that served to distinguish Israel or the Jews as a people from other nations, among others, dietary laws, dress codes, and the Shabbat. The rabbis expanded the range of practices to cover all aspects of ordinary life, actions that can be performed by any individual, not just priests, in any place, not only in the Temple. But for all their differences, both Israelite biblical religion and rabbinic Judaism are primarily focused on how to *act*.

To be sure, it was also assumed that there are general beliefs shared by all Israelites and Jews, e.g., that there is one God who created the world, who gave Israel the Torah and its homeland, who chose Israel and sends prophets, whom one must love and serve, and so on. However, these beliefs—especially compared to the commanded actions which are thick and dense in rabbinic detail—are thin. They are never systematically organized or justified like a science. Most often, they are mentioned only within narratives or non-legal Aggadah or as terse, epithet-like interpretations of scriptural verses in sermons or exegetical contexts. Unlike the prescribed actions, neither the Bible nor the rabbis attempt to legislate belief or demand explicit, official acceptance of a catechism, confession, or creed—although they do have their red lines, and exclude those who deny various beliefs (concerning God, the Torah and prophecy, or reward and punishment) as heretics and sectarians.[14] On the other hand, the rabbis celebrate sophisticated, abstract theoretical study of Torah, according to relatively well-defined rules of reasoning (or interpretation). This intellectual activity not only becomes a primary mode of religious worship for the rabbis. They are also clearly well aware that the body of law they are creating is the creative product of their own natural reason and reasoning—notwithstanding their repeated attempts to ground their autonomous human creativity on divine foundations. Yet what is almost exclusively studied is normative law, Halakhah, governing behavior, not philosophy, theology, or ethics. Rather than ask 'What is the Good?' the rabbis probe under exactly what circumstances must one perform one or another good act (e.g., saving a life, returning a lost article). Instead of asking 'What is prayer and in what sense does God hear our prayers?,' they ask 'How many blessings should we make in our prayers and can and when should we interrupt our prayers?' The ab-

---

14 On this question of dogmas and obligatory beliefs, see Menachem Kellner, *Must a Jew Believe Anything?* (Oxford: Littman Library of Jewish Civilization, 1999) and David Berger's review in *Tradition* 33.4 (1999): 81–89.

sence of analysis and argument for theological and philosophical doctrines stands in sharp contrast to the detailed, subtle, abstract legal argumentation concerning normative behavior.[15] The heart of biblical and rabbinic Judaism is orthopraxis, right action, rather than orthodoxy, right belief.

We find traces of Hellenistic philosophical influence on the rabbis, e.g., in their conception of the soul, creation, or innate knowledge, and we assume that representatives of Hellenistic philosophical schools (e.g., Stoicism, Platonism, Epicureanism, and even scepticism) were present in Palestine and Asia Minor.[16] However, the little we actually possess are popular versions of philosophical positions, not sophisticated, advanced, nuanced expositions, no sustained or detailed argument for one side or another, or extended debate of a single theme. No doubt there must have also been polemical exchanges with non-Jews and heretics, also known as philosophers, and, like Christians against pagans, or Muslims against Christians, the rabbis would have employed philosophical arguments against their philosopher rivals. But when it came to recording these discussions, the rabbis eschew philosophical terminology and never engage with philosophical dialogue and interrogation. In short, the rabbis seem both uninterested in and simply not curious about philosophy—it is alien to them—not necessarily because they did not know what it was but probably because they did.[17] Indeed, we find suspicion of philosophy, theosophy, and theology. The rabbis prohibit public teaching of certain quasi-philosophical subjects, such as the 'Accounts of the Beginning' and 'of the Chariot' mentioned earlier. In the enigmatic talmudic story of *Pardes*, about four rabbis who entered a garden of theosophical speculation, we sense the dangers of philosophy—one rabbi dies, one goes mad, one becomes a heretic, and only one escapes in peace. We do not know exactly what the rabbis meant by any of these titles (the 'Accounts of the Beginning' and 'Chariot' or *Pardes*), but they do suggest caution toward, even anxiety about, speculation on God, nature, and metaphysics.[18]

---

15 To be sure, many legal, or halakhic, analyses in the Talmud and rabbinic literature rest on definite metaphysical and epistemological, not to say ethical, presuppositions, e.g., about causality, individuation and identity, determinism, time, and more. In recent years there have been a number of fascinating attempts to work out these metaphysical and epistemological presuppositions of the rabbis by analytically trained philosophers. See, for example, papers by Mark Steiner, Eli Hirsch, Dani Rabinowitz, and Aaron Segal. Moshe Halbertal has also argued that ethical reasoning shaped rabbinic 'revolutionary' interpretations of scriptural laws that the rabbis found morally upsetting and unacceptable. Nonetheless, it seems more accurate to say that there is much philosophy to be found in rabbinic literature rather than that the rabbis were philosophers doing philosophy.
16 Stoic motifs: the soul fills the body like God fills the world, that God has created and destroyed worlds, that the soul is estranged in and from this world. Platonic: Knowledge before birth that is re-discovered (Torah, not forms), God created the world by contemplating, or looking at, the Torah or language.
17 I owe this observation to Zev Harvey.
18 Perhaps the best example of the differences between the ideas and thought of pre-philosophical biblical and rabbinic Judaism and philosophy—and no other beliefs conflict as much with philosophical wisdom—is their respective conceptions of God. The Bible repeatedly describes God in anthropomorphic and anthropopathic language: God has a physical form, body, emotions, affect, and person-

The Encounter between Medieval Judaism and Philosophy

Philosophy entered early medieval Judaism through two main avenues, both during the Islamic period (roughly from 750–1300) and both essentially involving Muslim thinkers. The first was through the *kalam* which literally means 'speech' or (like the Greek *logos*) 'word,' 'argument,' or 'reason,' and nowadays is translated as 'Islamic dialectical or rational theology.' (A practioner of *kalam* is a *mutakallim*, pl.: *mutakallimun*.) I will return to this description in a moment.

Kalam, according to our best sources, originated in two ways. First, disagreements over the interpretation of the normative beliefs of Islam led to systematic general accounts of theological doctrine based on reason as well as the Qur'an and oral tradition which were taken to complement rather than contradict each other. Thus Ibn Khaldun (fourteenth century) writes: 'argumentation formed by the intellect (*al-aql*) began to be used in addition to the evidence derived from tradition, and in this way the science of *kalam* originated.'

Second—and here our source is Maimonides (*Guide* I:71.73–75) who left us one of our few systematic descriptions of *kalam* and its origins—early Muslims were forced to develop a rational theology to defend Islam against Syriac Christians, just as even earlier church fathers had been forced to turn to reason to justify and defend Christianity against pagan philosophers.

Thus *kalam* developed out of the impulse to use reason to systematize, conceptualize, and thereby understand the beliefs of Islam and to defend it against rationally based critiques. Among these beliefs, two topics were special foci: (1) the Unity of God which had to be reconciled with the existence of divine attributes and (2) God's unlimited power which had to be reconciled with divine justice and human freedom. But, more generally and more important for us, throughout the ninth and tenth centuries, the 'spirit' of *kalam*, best represented by the dominant Mu'tazila,

---

ality. The philosophers, in contrast, teach that God cannot have a body on pain of being divisible, hence not a unity or one simple God. He cannot have emotions because He cannot be affected in any way. But it is not merely that their two doctrinal stances are contradictory. Even while the Rabbis are aware that God must be transcendent to be Creator, Providential Governor, and the absolutely authoritative giver of the Torah, they also believe that their God wears phylacteries and dons a prayer shawl, that He studies Torah and that He must in order to master it, that He sheds tears when His people suffer even when He also causes that suffering, and that He is exiled when they are. Likewise, He is intertwined with His own law. The rabbis teach that a person blind in one eye need not make a pilgrimage to the Temple because just as the pilgrim must be seen by God with *His* two eyes, so must the pilgrim be able to see God with two eyes—presupposing that God is no less of a pilgrim bound by His own laws! In other words, the rabbis' God is not only a rabbinic Jew, He is one of us, the rabbis, a member of the rabbinic community of Israel, not just a personal god but a person in the fellowship. Like Homer's Greek gods, God is a god, i.e., a rabbinic hero. This is a radically different stance toward the deity in which He serves a certain function for the community. The challenge for the philosophers will be to create a God that satisfies their own desiderata—necessary existence, unity, omnipotence, omniscience, perfection—but also meets these communal and personal demands.

was the view that reason is necessary in order to establish the basic tenets of Islam which otherwise would be based on imperfect grounds of authority and tradition. This conception of the role of reason in religious belief deeply influenced our first Jewish figure, Saadiah.

The second avenue through which Judaism encountered philosophy was via the *falasifa* ('philosophers') and *falsafa* ('philosophy'), the Arabic terms reserved specifically for the movement that saw itself as the heir and continuation of Aristotle whose works were translated into Arabic and in many cases interpreted through Neo-platonic lenses.[19] In this sense of the term, philosophy began in Islam with the translation of the corpus of Greek philosophical and scientific works into Arabic (in the East) in the ninth and tenth centuries. This herculean task was one of the great achievements of Islamic civilization in the Middle Ages: it involved painstaking learning of Greek or Syriac, collection and establishment of manuscripts, and development of an Arabic style and philosophical terminology that combined accuracy with elegance. Works of all kinds were translated, from the natural sciences (mathematics, astronomy, physics, and biology) to metaphysics, logic, and ethics, including the entire Aristotelian corpus and its Hellenistic commentators. So, unlike the situation in the West, almost the whole of Aristotle and Greek science, grammar, and medicine were available to the Muslim philosophers and scientists—and if not for them, may not have survived. The *falasifa* in turn saw themselves continuing, commenting on, and expanding the Aristotelian or Greek heritage. In the case of metaphysics, this elaboration also involved a project to understand and interpret Islam as a philosophical religion in light of Aristotle. And this led to original philosophical works by figures such as Al-Farabi, Avicenna (Ibn Sina), and Averroes (Ibn Rushd)—and, I would add, our second Jewish figure, Maimonides.

In short, both *kalam* and *falsafa* used reason to construct sciences, or systematic bodies of belief and knowledge, either to justify and defend religion or, more generally, to understand nature and metaphysics. In a broad sense of the term, both *falsafa* and *kalam* can be called schools of 'philosophy'—even though, as I mentioned earlier, *kalam* is often translated as '(dialectical) theology.' But the term 'theology' for them did not have the exclusionary sense from 'philosophy' that it has for us—notwithstanding the hostile attitude of the *falasifa* to the *mutakallimun* whom the former depict as opportunistic defenders of their religion who will employ any means at their disposal to defend it, including distorting the empirical facts to fit their doctrines.[20] The main difference between them is that the *falasifa* saw themselves as (justifiably) importing a foreign Hellenistic perspective into Islam, and their allegiance was owed primarily to Aristotle, while *kalam* promoted a much more indige-

---

19 Some of these were in fact Neo-platonic works of Plotinus and Proclus that were falsely attributed to Aristotle.
20 Thus, one of the most important Neo-platonic philosophical texts was the *Theology of Aristotle*. Maimonides' negative presentation of *kalam* was strongly influenced by Al-Farabi, who himself was persecuted by the *kalam*, but he is right to claim that *kalam* has a significant apologetic component.

nous Islamic point of view, based on Arabic language (and grammar) and the Qur'an, *hadith*, and their interpretation as a religion. And *kalam* is 'dialectical' in that its logic or reasoning employs Stoic dilemmas rather than the Aristotelian syllogistic and its writing a dialogical style ('if he says [...], then he should be answered') that reflects dialectical techniques employed in polemical exchanges.

Saadiah Gaon: Jewish *Kalam*

With this background, let's turn to our first major Jewish thinker, Saadiah ben Joseph Gaon (b. 882, Fayyum, Egypt; d. 942, Sura, Iraq [Babylonia]) whom modern scholars often refer to as 'the first medieval Jewish philosopher.'[21] This is a correct description insofar as Saadiah was a philosopher in the broad sense (just mentioned) who used reason to justify and understand his beliefs, including the revealed beliefs of Judaism. But he was not a *falasif*. Not that he was unaware of or entirely unfamiliar with the translated Aristotelian literature; sometimes he adopts Aristotelian and Platonic positions. The crucial point is that he did not see himself as someone continuing, commenting on, or expanding the Aristotelian or Greek heritage. Instead Saadiah's conception of 'philosophy' was that of Mu'tazilite *kalam*.[22] Although part of his motivation was apologetic and polemical, Saadiah's deeper philosophical goal, and his view of the role of reason in religion, was to render revelation as rationally understandable as possible, to use reason to render revealed belief understood and thereby believed or known with certainty. He opens his theological summa, *The Book on Beliefs and Opinions* (932), with a description of his generation as people 'sunk in a sea of doubt and covered by the waters of confusion.' The aim of his treatise is to bring them to certainty, to make doubt vanish, and to turn 'the believer who blindly relies on tradition' into 'one basing his belief on speculation and understanding.'

Beliefs and Opinions is organized along classic *kalam* lines, dealing first with universal questions of theology (creation and a proof of the existence of a divine creator, the unity of God and attributes, prophecy and revelation, command and prohibition and free will) followed by six chapters that address themes and problems more specific to Judaism: reward and punishment, the afterlife, and eschatology. In *kalam* fashion, for each topic he lists competing theories but he does not merely survey actual positions which he had to refute in practice; he considers every *possible* position on a given question, eliminating all but one, which not surprisingly turns out to be the doctrine of Judaism. This is a method of achieving knowledge through a process of argumentation modeled on the purification of metal through the elimination of impurities.

---

[21] 'Gaon' is the title given to the heads of the great Babylonian *yeshivot*, or talmudic academies.
[22] Thus the twelfth-century Neo-platonically inclined Spanish bible commentator and grammarian, Abraham ibn Ezra, referred to Saadiah as 'chief among speakers (*medabbrim*) everywhere,' i.e., chief among *mutakallimun*.

As a system builder, Saadiah sees human reason as a divinely-given instrument to enable humans to achieve both a true understanding of the world and a sound interpretation of Scripture. One must accept the Torah and believe its revealed truths on divine authority, but, as with the Christian philosopher Augustine, through reason one can transform mere acceptance on authority into understanding and thereby knowledge.[23] Thus Saadiah argues, using a design-like argument, that contemplation of the world reveals its created nature, hence, the existence of a creator. Reason, he also argues, can establish that the world was created *ex nihilo*. From the plurality and multiplicity in the world, reason demonstrates that its creator must be one. Following the Mu'tazilites, Saadiah argues that God is benevolent and good—and in the same sense in which these moral evaluative terms apply to humans. And because these divine virtues are good in themselves, humans should also be benevolent, good, and grateful—the core moral traits identified by Saadiah. In each case, Saadiah uses reason, as a tool subordinate to revelation, as far as it can be pressed into service to justify, confirm, and thereby render understandable the revealed Torah. But Saadiah also recognizes limits to reason. In his seminal systematic explanation of the Mosaic commandments, he distinguishes two classes of laws: 'rational' commandments (*sikhliyyot, aqli'at*) that can be given intelligible, utilitarian, or moral reasons and 'heard' or 'obeyed' laws (*shimi'ot, sam'iat*), that vary over and are conventionally adopted by societies and are not rationally necessary or universal but can be given ad hoc reasons given that they are commanded.

Saadiah was also the first to endow Jewish philosophy with a strong hermeneutical dimension. His commentaries on various books of the Hebrew Bible, which he was also the first to translate into Arabic, were the first to constrain the interpretation of Scripture to reason: in verses where Scripture contradicts what reason or science has established—e. g., where God is, contrary to reason, described in corporeal and anthropomorphic terms—reason trumps Scripture which we then re-interpret figuratively —though the particular figurative interpretation we adopt must also conform to our historical knowledge of the language and its metaphors at the time of the Bible.[24]

Saadiah's *Book of Theodicy*, his commentary on the Book of Job, was also the first to treat a scriptural text as a work of philosophy. He identifies Job and his comforters as representatives of different schools of *kalam*. For each speech, Saadiah identifies a main thesis for which he constructs a *kalam* argument out of the highly elliptic verses. A general introduction gives a thematic unity to an apparently rambling set of speeches, transforming the core of Job into a philosophical dialogue, while recasting the supernatural, mythical frame in the spirit of naturalistic reason and science. Satan turns out to be, not an angelic divine rebel, but simply Job's human adversary

---

[23] This understanding of the role of reason is very similar to Augustine's (and others in the Augustinian tradition such as Anselm of Canterbury) for whom reason converts belief, an act of assent to a proposition, into understanding.

[24] Among these commentaries is a seminal Neo-platonic commentary on the enigmatic *Sefer Yeṣirah* ('Book of Creation') (931). Time prevents me from discussing it.

(philologically derived from the Hebrew word *sitnah* for 'enmity'); the 'children of God' (*benei elohim*) are human nobles and judges, the mythical beasts Leviathan and Behemoth nothing more than frightening exotic animals, a hippopotamus and alligator. This naturalistic approach to the Bible is emblematic of Saadiah's general use of reason, including our best scientific knowledge of nature, to understand and justify revealed texts. Moreover, according to Saadiah, the problem addressed by the Book of Job is not the metaphysical justification of evil—on this Saadiah has much to say in his *Beliefs and Opinions*, views that he repeats in the commentary on Job—but rather a phenomenological problem: it shows, through 'the record of Job's trials [...] what is in the hearts of people when they reach the limits of endurance in a trial.' That is, Saadiah reads Job as a phenomenology of suffering, what it feels like to endure the deepest suffering. This is a remarkably original conception both of the task of philosophy and of the kinds of genres of writing employed by philosophy—using a commentary on a biblical narrative whose surface looks nothing like philosophy!

What Medieval Jewish Philosophy Is

We said that Saadiah is often designated as 'the first medieval Jewish philosopher.' Chronologically, he was not first.[25] Nonetheless, there is an important sense in which Saadiah is truly the first figure in what I would call 'Medieval Jewish Philosophy.' And now I want to say more about how we ought to understand that heading. I argued earlier that we should not characterize Jewish philosophy as a *branch* or *domain* of philosophy, distinguishing it by its language, the (ethnic and religious) identities of its authors, its subject matter, or approach or method. What Jewish philosophers do is nothing but philosophy—in one of its senses or forms but none of them specific to Judaism. However, what does make a set or series of individual philoso*phers* into what we might call *a* philoso*phy*, like *Jewish* philosophy, is their shared discourse, who they address and cite, who they support, criticize, or comment on, who influences whom or who is influenced by whom. That is, Jewish philosophy, in Myles Burnyeat's words, 'is a tradition, a succession of thinkers whose thought is conditioned in one way or another by a knowledge of their predecessors in the line,' whose 'conditioning' can include both constructive development of thoughts at earlier stages and critical reactions to them.[26] These relations which are a matter of pos-

---

[25] Apart from Philo of Alexandria in the first century (who had a deep influence on the church fathers but none on medieval Jewish thinkers), the Neo-platonist Isaac Israeli (d. c. 932) and the *mutakallim* al-Muqammas (9th c.) both preceded Saadiah.

[26] Myles Burnyeat, "Introduction," in idem, *The Skeptical Tradition* (Berkeley: University of California Press, 1983): 1. On the idea of influence, see also Avishai Margalit, "Wittgenstein's Knight Move: Hacker on Wittgenstein's Influence on Analytic Philosophy," in *Wittgenstein and Analytic Philosophy: Essays for P.M.S Hacker*, eds. Peter M.S. Hacker, Hans-Johann Glock, and John Hyman (Oxford: Oxford University Press, 2009).

itive and negative 'influence,' have an important *causal* element, which it is possible to identify often only *post facto*. But where a group of individual philosoph*ers* are inter-connected in this way, they inhabit their own sphere of discourse—sharing certain assumptions, speaking a common language, living in one intellectual space. Thus, what marks off medieval Jewish philosophy from the rest of philosophy or from general medieval philosophy is that it is its own tradition. A tradition need not be exclusive, its boundaries can be permeable. The tradition of early medieval Jewish philosophy is embedded in and grows out of the tradition of Islamic philosophy and its Greek sources, while later medieval Jewish philosophy is rooted in a world of Christian, scholastic philosophy. It is not always clear how to distinguish when the Jewish philosophers are talking *to* Muslims or Christians or simply talking *about* them. (Likewise, it may not always be clear when a Christian author, like Aquinas, is simply talking *about* R. Moses and when he is talking *to* him; in the latter case, we may want to claim Aquinas for Jewish philosophy.)

In sum, where we find a continuous dialogue and a succession of exchanges of this sort, we might refer to a distinctive tradition of causally influencing and influenced thinkers as medieval Jewish philosophy—even though what the figures in the tradition are doing is simply philosophy! Without a common methodology and with no linguistic, ethnic, national, or religious conditions for citizenship, what makes the tradition 'Jewish'? No one feature but *causal* relations to many: either Jewish texts or events that triggered philosophical questions, the Jewish identities or languages of its participants that somehow causally affect their philosophizing. So, although being Jewish or written in Hebrew (or in Hebrew characters) or being about Judaism are not individually essential, neither necessary nor sufficient conditions to count as Jewish philosophy, one could allow them as defeasible diagnostic tools, i.e., superficial identifiers of a Jewish philosophical tradition.[27] These causal impacts can also be extremely indirect. Thus a passing comment about meteorology in Maimonides' *Guide of the Perplexed* while explaining the story of creation in Genesis led Samuel ibn Tibbon to translate Aristotle's *Meteorology*; this was the first Hebrew translation of an Aristotelian work—a translation that played a central role in subse-

---

27 Another diagnostic is the use of prooftexts or verses from Scripture or rabbinic literature. Of course, scriptural verses are no proof that the philosophical work belongs to Jewish rather than Christian philosophy, but it is also important to keep in mind the use of the verses. Sometimes the verses are cited as authorities which, in virtue of their identity, are meant to justify a claim. Sometimes the verses are being explicated and explained, say, as a parable. And sometimes, especially when the Jewish philosophical text is a 'translation' or paraphrase of a Greek or Arab text, the scriptural or rabbinic prooftexts are added neither as evidence nor as justification nor as an *explanandum* to be interpreted and explained, but in order to 'Judaize' the original work. (See e.g., Chaim M. Neria, "*It Cannot Be Valued with the Gold of Ophir*" *(Job 28:16): Rabbi Joseph B. Shem-Ṭob's Commentary on Aristotle's* Nicomachean Ethics. *Sources and Analysis* [Chicago: PhD typescript, 2015]: 180 and 182.) Likewise, the use of rabbinic terms for Aristotelian notions—see Neria, "*It Cannot Be Valued with the Gold of Ophir*," 201 ff., 205: on *'ones raḥman petirah*, and 217: the use of Hebrew names in examples are attempts at 'Judaization.'

quent discussions of Genesis, providence, and prophecy, hence, arguably, an important text in medieval Jewish philosophy—even though it is a scientific work by Aristotle, not by a Jew, not originally in Hebrew, and not directly about Judaism.[28]

Some will see my proposal as a deflationary 'definition' of 'Medieval Jewish Philosophy.' Others will object that really I am denying that there is such a thing as 'Medieval Jewish Philosophy.' However, that conclusion underestimates the importance of particular discourses or traditions in the history of philosophy in general.

From the perspective of founding a tradition, Saadiah was the first medieval Jewish philosopher—because he initiated a discourse and conversation to which others added and responded, in which he was addressed by later parties, beginning with Baḥya ibn Paquda and Maimonides. As we turn to the second encounter, I will try to develop this theme in more depth.

Maimonides: Judaism and *Falsafa*

The second encounter between medieval rabbinic Judaism and philosophy began when Jewish thinkers met *falsafa*, Arabic Aristotelian philosophy. Unlike their exposure to *kalam*, which led to their appropriation of human reason and reasoning to justify, conceptually systematize, and understand revealed truths, the encounter with *falsafa* was more like a collision between two competing authorities, Moses and Aristotle, and two canonical texts, the Torah, and its rabbinic legal (halakhic) and non-legal (aggadic) interpretation (the so-called Oral Torah), on the one side, and the Aristotelian corpus including its Hellenistic and Arab commentators, on the other. This encounter was a confrontation between two different conceptions of human perfection: piety achieved through the performance of the commandments versus intellectual perfection achieved through science and knowledge; between a transcendent God who is the necessarily existent cause of the motion and being of the eternal cosmos and a voluntaristic personal God (often described anthropomorphically and anthropopathically) who created the world *ex nihilo* and who intervenes in history and changes nature miraculously; and between two ways of life, each with its own education or training leading to its own brand of happiness: a rabbinic education based on laws governing the Mosaic commandments and the Aristotelian curriculum that goes from logic through the natural sciences to metaphysics. The challenge in this encounter was not merely whether and how to use reason to understand and thereby render certain beliefs held on the authority of revelation. This was a confrontation between two rival authorities and two entirely different, and often opposed, intellectual cultures and conceptions of truth. Our best witness

---

[28] For this fascinating story, see Aviezer Ravitzky, "Aristotle's Meteorology and the Maimonidean Modes of Interpreting the Account of Creation," *Jerusalem Studies in Jewish Thought* 9 (1990), The Shlomo Pines Jubilee Volume, Part 2: 225–50; reprinted in idem, *Maimonidean Essays* [in Hebrew] (Jerusalem: Schocken Publishing House, 2006): 139–156; English translation in *Aleph* 8 (2008): 361–400.

to this encounter is Moses Maimonides (b. 1138, Cordoba, Spain; d. Fustat, Egypt 1204), arguably the greatest rabbinic thinker of the Middle Ages, both in matters of law and philosophy, and there is no better description of the intense tension of the encounter than his description in his *Guide of the Perplexed* of perplexity as a mental tug-of-war between the 'external sense' of the Torah and the demands of the intellect, namely, philosophy.[29]

We first see the impact of this second encounter in Maimonides' monumental halakhic compositions that integrate philosophy with classical rabbinic law; indeed Maimonides reconceives Judaism as a philosophical religion. Recall that classical rabbinic Judaism focused almost exclusively on how to *act* according to the Torah, with relatively little to say about what one should *believe*. Maimonides radically shifts this focus. He lays down thirteen foundational principles—about God, prophecy and the Torah, reward and punishment, the messiah and resurrection—that everyone in the community of Israel *must* believe *regardless of how they act*, beliefs that are both necessary and sufficient to belong to the community of Israel or, in classic rabbinic terms, to 'have a share in the world to come.' As we mentioned earlier, his Code opens with an exposition of Aristotelian metaphysics, cosmology, and natural science, whose study he makes a religious obligation and even the summit of the rabbinic curriculum.[30] And throughout his Code, Maimonides complements detailed legal discussions with philosophical rationales and conceptualization. This blending of philosophy and Halakhah, or law, created a new Judaism, a philosophical religion the core of whose worship of God is not through praxis but by correct belief and the acquisition of scientific and philosophical knowledge.

---

29 Maimonides' given Arabic name was Musa ibn Maymun, but he is best known by his Hebrew name *R*abbi *M*oshe *b*en *M*aimon, or the acronym Ra*MBaM*. Maimonides was a product of the great Judeo-Arabic culture of Andalusia, although he and his family were forced to flee when the Almohades invaded in 1148, and he lived most of his mature life in Fustat, Egypt, where he served as the rabbinic and political head of the Jewish community and as a physician in the court of the Fatimid and then Ayyubid sultans, most notably Saladin's son and his vizier. Apart from living this extremely active life, Maimonides was prolific to a degree that it is difficult for us even to imagine. He wrote three main works in his lifetime, any one of which would have been sufficient to earn him a place in the world to come of Jewish literature:

1. *Commentary on Mishnah* (1158–1168), the first running commentary on the canonical rabbinic anthology of legal opinions;

2. *Mishneh Torah* (1168c-1178), the first and to this day the only comprehensive code of rabbinic law, covering obligatory beliefs, rituals, festivals and the Shabbat, marriage, torts, property, purity and impurity, sacrifices and the Temple, and laws governing the polis and messianic monarchy;

3. *Guide of the Perplexed* (1185–1190), the seminal work of Jewish philosophy.

30 This by way of identifying the contents of the enigmatic rabbinic 'Account of the Beginning' and 'Account of the Chariot' with Aristotelian physics and metaphysics, respectively, and including them both under the enigmatic rabbinic title *Pardes* which in turn is taken to be the apex of the activity of study of the Oral Torah that Maimonides calls 'Talmud.' See *Mishneh Torah*, "Laws concerning the Foundations of the Law," chapters 1–4 and especially 4, x-xiii, and "Laws concerning Study of the Torah," chapter 1, xi–xii.

Maimonides' philosophical masterpiece, the *Guide of the Perplexed*, set the agenda for all subsequent Jewish philosophy up to the present day. If we think of Jewish philosophy as a causally-intraconnected discourse, or conversation, what I called a 'tradition' within philosophy, then Maimonideanism is a sub-tradition within the medieval Jewish philosophical tradition. The *Guide* generated a tradition of commentaries and treatises that stretches over at least three centuries either elaborating and applying Maimonides' program, interpreting his enigmatic, puzzle-like work, supporting his views by reference to Muslim or Greek authorities, or criticizing him.[31] In a letter to his Hebrew translator, Samuel ibn Tibbon, Maimonides directed him to his Arabic and Hellenistic sources—which in turn produced translations over the following centuries from Arabic into Hebrew that made the Aristotelian corpus and its commentaries accessible to Jews outside the Arabic-speaking world, and in turn produced a significant philosophical literature in Hebrew, including authors like Gersonides (Levi ben Gershon), Ḥasdai Crescas, and Joseph Albo, whose interests go beyond theology to logic, physics, astronomy, and the sciences, written either in the genre of commentaries or supercommentaries or in distinct treatises or encyclopedias. This full range of shared discourse and conversation, triggered by Maimonides' *Guide*, comprises much of what we call 'Medieval Jewish Philosophy.'

One of the central topics in this tradition, or conversation, is the very relation between philosophy, aka Aristotle, and the Torah, which, according to many, also shaped the way in which the *Guide* is composed. Maimonides tells us that he conceals his own beliefs from the popular reader by dividing and scattering topics to create an appearance of *dis*organization and by employing deliberate contradictions. Instead he hints at his own true beliefs for philosophers using 'chapter headings' and parables. Maimonides' thirteenth and fourteenth-century disciples and commentators[32] and, in the past century, Leo Strauss picked up on this unique literary form of Maimonides' treatise, producing the influential view that the *Guide*—and, by analogy, its predecessors in the tradition of writing to which it belongs, from the Torah itself through rabbinic writing as well as Plato—is written on multiple levels of meaning: with a revealed, exoteric meaning for the consumption of the community at large and a concealed, esoteric meaning addressed to a philosophical elite. The precise relation between these different levels is, however, a matter of endless controversy.

In the spirit of many medieval thinkers who, facing contradictions between competing authorities, tend to gloss their differences and harmonize the two rather than conclude that one is right and the other wrong—one view is that the *Guide* aims to

---

[31] Cf. Shlomo Pines' comment in the "Introduction" to his translation that Maimonides does not mention any previous Jewish philosophers since he had no recourse to a 'Jewish philosophical tradition;' see Moses Maimonides, *The Guide of the Perplexed*, trans. Shlomo Pines (Chicago and London: The University of Chicago Press, 1963): xxxiii. Even if this is true, which is arguable, by initiating a tradition, Maimonides ipso facto belonged to it.

[32] These include Samuel ibn Tibbon, Shem-Tov Falaquera, Moses of Narbonne, Isaac Abravanel, Profyat Duran (Efodi), and Joseph ibn Kaspi.

harmonize, or synthesize, revelation and reason, the Torah with Aristotelian philosophy.[33] Thus Maimonides accepts both exoteric and esoteric meanings, and gives arguments in the latter that rationally support the revealed views of the former. A second group claims that the secret of the *Guide*, hidden by its literary form, is that reason and revelation, or Aristotle and the Torah, are insurmountably incompatible and that Maimonides' own true beliefs are on the side of reason or philosophy as opposed to the Torah. Thus, Maimonides really believes in eternity rather than creation and in the God of the philosophers, not of Scripture. The Torah is at best a kind of popular philosophy by means of which the philosopher can found and control a community, and Maimonides (like the author of the Torah) wrote the *Guide* in his secretive way to control the dissemination of philosophical truth and prevent it from reaching the wrong ears.

Yet, a third class of medieval readers thinks that the secret of the *Guide* is that Aristotle is *identical* with the Torah according to its concealed, esoteric meaning. That is, the true but hidden meaning *of the Torah* is philosophical truth. The Torah describes God exoterically as a body, in anthropomorphic and corporeal terms, only in order to accommodate the general reader or multitude. But the true meaning of those descriptions is that God is a perfect immaterial, transcendent, necessarily existing intellect. This last approach led to a long tradition of Maimonidean philosophical scriptural exegesis, deepening the hermeneutic dimension introduced by Saadiah, but now decoding or translating scriptural terms and claims into Aristotelian categories and doctrines by establishing semantical equivalences between words or concepts: e.g. 'woman' is matter, 'image' is Aristotelian form. The point is to show that the true meaning of the Torah is nothing but Aristotle; hence, the one can be translated into the other. Its rich development of this genre of philosophical scriptural commentary, exegesis as a way of doing philosophy, is one of the great contributions of medieval Jewish philosophy to the history of philosophy.[34]

Underlying all these approaches is the assumption that the Torah, or Mosaic revelation, and Aristotle, or Aristotelian reason, are distinct insofar as they are the sorts of things that can be (or cannot be) harmonized, made mutually consistent, or identified. But there is a fourth way to read the *Guide* that aims to work out how Maimonides might have read the Torah as a unique work with its own unique philosophy. On this reading, the Torah and rabbinic literature are philosophical works, but not works of Aristotelian philosophy. Instead they emerged from what Maimonides sincerely believed was a rich indigenous ancient Israelite philosophical world containing competing schools, schools roughly parallel to all those he knew from his contemporary Arabic philosophical literature—including Plato, Aristotle, the Stoics, Epicureans,

---

[33] See, for example, Al-Farabi's *Harmonzation of the Opinions of Plato and Aristotle*.
[34] For examples, see the commentaries of Kimḥi, Kaspi, Gersonides, Naḥmanides, Abravanel—and, in a sister genre, the sermons of Nissim of Gerona and Isaac Arama.

sceptics, and various Islamic schools of *kalam*.[35] The philosophical arguments found in the *Guide* for and against Aristotle and the *kalam* are not borrowed to philosophically understand or legitimate the Law, nor are they a key to decipher Scripture. Rather they provide a *context* for original philosophical positions that Maimonides finds expressed, especially in parable form, in the Torah, the text he takes to be *the* exemplary philosophical work of all time. To be sure, the Torah and rabbinic literature do not 'look like' a typical philosophical text, and much of the challenge of reading scriptural literature (and the *Guide*) is seeing through its outer form to its inner philosophical wisdom. But rather than think of Torah *and* philosophy, Maimonides thinks of the two as one: *Torah/philosophy*. If there are tensions, they are not between two separate domains but within one body. And if the Torah is itself a distinctive philosophy, that in turn implies that Moses, the prophets, and the rabbis were themselves philosophers, the native philosophical sages of ancient Israel and Judaism. On this view, medieval Jewish philosophers were simply continuing, in part by re-discovering and reconstructing, the philosophical tradition of their ancestors.

What is the distinctive philosophy of ancient Israel that Maimonides finds in the Torah that he, in turn, elaborates in the *Guide?* The first three approaches we surveyed took Maimonides to be primarily concerned with a *meta*-philosophical problem: the problem of the relation between philosophy and Torah. On this last approach, the *Guide* is primarily addressed to a classical *philosophical* problem: In what does human perfection and true happiness consist? Is it material or intellectual or something else? Are perfection and happiness realizable by humans or unachievable ideals? And how does one negotiate the competing, conflicting demands of being a complex, composite, hylomorphic human being—composed of both intellect and body, form and matter?

The distinctive philosophy of ancient Israel—which Maimonides presents in the *Guide*—takes the *ideal* human perfection to be intellectual—the acquisition of all possible knowledge and constant, exclusive engagement in intellectual activity—but it also takes that ideal to be humanly *un*realizable because of limitations on the intellect imposed by the human's body and bodily faculties, like the imagination. It is neither possible for a human to achieve all knowledge and, in particular, knowledge of cosmology, metaphysics, and God and it is not possible for an embodied human to engage exclusively and constantly in intellectual apprehension and contemplation as if she were disembodied. Thus Maimonides takes a sceptical stance at least with respect to human scientific knowledge of metaphysics and God. Neither the author of

---

35 This view should be distinguished from another position, found in authors as diverse as Judah Halevi and Falaquera, that the Jews discovered philosophy from whom it was then stolen by the Greeks or others. According to Maimonides, philosophy would seem to be a natural development of the use and perfection of the human intellect that would arise in any culture independently of any other. Philosophy was not stolen from the Jews but lost, as a result of its originally oral character, the various restrictions on its dissemination within the community, and the difficulties of continuous transmission because of persecutions and exile.

the Torah, rabbis, nor Maimonides have the kind of understanding of metaphysics that could be expressed in the explicit, axiomatic form of a science; instead they employ semantically multi-leveled texts like parables that give us momentary glimpses or insights of the truth that reflect their own incomplete, partial understanding of metaphysics. Thus, on this view, the function of the parable is not to control the *dissemination* of truths fully grasped by the prophet, sage, or philosopher, but to *express* their merely *partial* knowledge and *incomplete* understanding. Finally, Maimonides shifts our focus away from fully demonstrated and intellectually known *doctrines* whose grasp is the stuff of the happy, perfected intellectual life to a way of life cultivated through exercises and practices—including scientific inquiry and other intellectual activities—that minimize our bodily impulses and train us to engage ourselves with as much concentration as is humanly possible in intellectual activity.[36]

In conclusion, we have now surveyed two ways in which philosophy and Judaism, or the Jews, first came into contact in the Middle Ages—through the use of reason to understand and justify beliefs and in a confrontation between two authoritative bodies of knowledge. In both cases, the individuals in question were simply doing philosophy—giving and evaluating arguments, exposing presuppositions, drawing distinctions—on classic philosophical problems. What united them under one umbrella, *Jewish* philosophy, was nothing more than a variety of causal relations among themselves of influence, positive and negative, somehow connected to Judaism or the experience of the Jews, by which they came to constitute a tradition. Being causal, this notion of a tradition is in part sociological but it proved extremely productive philosophically, not just for Judaism but also by yielding philosophical insight into classical problems of (or that ought to be of) interest to all philosophers: the ultimate cause of being, the nature of human happiness, the character and scope of human knowledge. This is why medieval Jewish philosophy is both philosophy, Jewish, and a rich and distinctive contribution to the traditions of philosophy.

---

[36] For further discussion of this last conception of Maimonides' philosophical stance, see Josef Stern, *The Matter and Form of Maimonides' Guide* (Cambridge, Mass.: Harvard University Press, 2013).

WORKSHOP: Jewish-Christian Polemics in the Middle Ages and in the Early Modern Period

15 June, 2016

Daniel J. Lasker

Polemics, Religion and Scepticism in Judah Halevi's *Book of Kuzari*[1]

The present talk allows me to revisit some themes of the research I have been carrying out for the last four decades. Over the years, my interest in medieval Jewish philosophy has centered on a number of themes, one of which has been interreligious polemics, most specifically Jewish anti-Christian polemics, with a special attention to those debates in the Islamic realm; and another theme has been the philosophy of Rabbi Judah Halevi, especially his view of the opponents of Rabbinic Judaism, whether they be philosophers, members of other religions or Karaites. Two articles which I particularly enjoyed writing were "Proselyte Judaism, Christianity and Islam in the Thought of Judah Halevi," which appeared in 1990;[2] and "The Jewish Critique of Christianity Under Islam in the Middle Ages," which appeared in 1991.[3] Since it is now been a quarter century since these articles appeared, it is appropriate to consider them once again.

Since Judah Halevi wrote the *Kuzari* in an Islamic country, and since it includes polemics against Christianity, let me begin with that topic, namely the nature of the Jewish debate with Christianity in those countries with Muslim governments.[4] When I began studying Jewish-Christian polemics, at the behest of my late, lamented Doktorvater, Prof. Alexander Altmann, I assumed like most Jews that these works were a reaction to Christian attempts to convert Jews to Christianity, resulting in the Jewish critique of Christianity. Now, it is true that my dissertation, which became my first book, included Jewish philosophical arguments from Islamic countries written in Ju-

---

[1] Research for this paper was sponsored by the Israel Science Foundation (grant 531/12) as part of a larger project dedicated to writing an academic commentary on Judah Halevi's *Kuzari*. I would like to thank Prof. Giuseppe Veltri, director of the Maimonides Center, Prof. Carsten Wilke, who made the first arrangements for the workshop at which this talk was presented, and Dr. Racheli Haliva who organized the workshop. Only partial annotation is provided in this written version of the lecture.
[2] *Jewish Quarterly Review* 81.1–2 (1990): 75–91.
[3] *Proceedings of the American Academy for Jewish Research* 57 (1991): 121–153.
[4] The demographic issues during the first few Islamic centuries are not as simple as we usually think and some Judaeo-Arabic anti-Christian polemics might have been written in areas which had a Christian majority but a Muslim government.

daeo-Arabic;[5] and the article I mentioned from 1991 was dedicated specifically to Judaeo-Arabic texts; and an article published in 1993 outlined the Andalusian Jewish origin of anti-Christian arguments used in Provence in the twelfth century;[6] and the book I edited with Sarah Stroumsa in 1996 presented all the texts associated with the highly influential *Book of Nestor the Priest* and demonstrated that it was written in the ninth century in the Islamic Middle East and not in sixth-century Byzantium as once believed;[7] and despite all this, I never addressed specifically the question: if Jewish anti-Christian polemics are a reaction to a Christian mission, why are there so many such polemical works in Islamic countries?

As I continued my research, I realized that there were other anomalies in the history of Jewish-Christian polemics, for instance, that in Ashkenaz (I refer to northern and eastern Europe as a collective), where there was much Christian pressure on Jews and active persecutions, forced baptisms, blood libels and expulsions, there were almost no Jewish polemical compositions, let alone the use of rationalist arguments.[8] I also started doubting whether Ashkenazi biblical commentaries were as chock full of anti-Christian polemic as claimed by some important students of the genre.[9] And I asked myself as well: why in seventeenth- and eighteenth-century Italy, not a Garden of Eden for Jews but not a place with an oppressive anti-Jewish mission, there were dozens of Jewish anti-Christian works;[10] but in Eastern Europe, home of many more Jews and many unsympathetic Christians, there were almost no such treatises. It

---

[5] *Jewish Philosophical Polemics Against Christianity in the Middle Ages* (New York: Ktav Publishing House, 1977; 2nd ed., Oxford and Portland, Or.: Littman Library, 2007).
[6] "Judeo-Christian Polemics and Their Origins in Muslim Countries" [in Hebrew], *Pe'amim* 57 (1993): 4–16; for a shortened English version, see "The Jewish-Christian Debate in Transition: From the Lands of Ishmael to the Lands of Edom," in *Judaism and Islam: Boundaries, Interaction, and Communication*, eds. Benjamin H. Hary, John L. Hayes, and Fred Astren (Leiden: Brill, 2000): 53–65.
[7] Daniel J. Lasker and Sarah Stroumsa, *The Polemic of Nestor the Priest*, 2 vols. (Jerusalem: Ben-Zvi Institute, 1996).
[8] "Jewish Philosophical Polemics in Ashkenaz," in *Contra Iudaeos: Ancient and Medieval Polemics Between Christians and Jews*, eds. Ora Limor and Guy G. Stroumsa (Tübingen: Mohr-Siebeck, 1996): 195–213; "Joseph ben Nathan's *Sefer Yosef Ha-Mekanné* and the Medieval Jewish Critique of Christianity," in *Jews and Christians in Thirteenth-Century France*, eds. Elisheva Baumgarten and Judah D. Galinsky (New York: Palgrave Macmillan, 2015): 113–122.
[9] "Rashi and Maimonides on Christianity," in *Between Rashi and Maimonides: Themes in Medieval Jewish Thought, Literature and Exegesis*, eds. Ephraim Kanarfogel and Moshe Sokolow (New York: Michael Scharf Publication Trust of the Yeshiva University Press, 2010): 3–21.
[10] Károly Dániel Dobos and Gerhard Langer have identified at least 56 anti-Christian treatises in Hebrew from that period, which does not include treatises written in other languages; this information is contained in a research proposal which the authors were kind enough to share with me. See, as well, Daniel J. Lasker, "Anti-Christian Polemics in Eighteenth-Century Italy" [in Hebrew], in *Proceedings of the Eleventh World Congress of Jewish Studies*, Division B, vol. 1 (Jerusalem, 1994): 185–192.

slowly dawned on me that the old narrative of Jewish criticism of Christianity as a reaction to Christian pressure was under need of revision.[11]

In searching for a new narrative concerning Jewish anti-Christian writings, I have come to the conclusion that the Jewish critique of Christianity is not necessarily tied intrinsically to a so-called Christian threat, even though sometimes they are connected.[12] When there was increased pressure on Jews to convert, there usually was a Jewish reaction.[13] But that does not mean that when there is no such pressure, there are no Jewish anti-Christian polemics. They still exist in the absence of any presumed need, without a specific stimulus.

Yet, not all Jewish thinkers engaged in polemic. Which Jews did write anti-Christian polemics in the Middle Ages? The answer is that Jewish anti-Christian argumentation was mainly a function of Jewish rationalist theology. Almost every Jewish author of a philosophical treatise was involved in one way or another with interreligious polemic, sometimes against Islam but usually against Christianity. If we start at the beginning of medieval Jewish philosophy, we see that Daoud al-Muqammas's ninth-century pioneering *Twenty Treatises* is replete with anti-Christian polemic, and, in addition, he wrote two specifically anti-Christian treatises.[14] Saadiah Gaon takes on Christianity in his *Beliefs and Opinions*, as well as in his commentaries on the Torah and other writings.[15] The Karaite followers of *kalam*, such as Yaqub al-Qirqisani, Yefet ben Eli, and Yusuf al-Basir, all include anti-Christian argumentation in their legal code, biblical commentaries, and theological works respectively. In Andalusia, Judah Halevi's predecessors, including Baḥya ibn Paquda, Abraham bar Ḥiyya, and Judah ben Barzilai of Barcelona, all have anti-Christian passages in their works.[16] After Judah Halevi, we can look to Maimonides, Ḥasdai Crescas, Isaac Abravanel, and many other Jewish rationalists as sources for anti-Christian polemic. In contrast, in Ashkenaz, where Jewish rationalism was suspect if not worse, Jewish authors rarely engaged in specific anti-Christian polemics, and those who did

---

11 See Daniel J. Lasker, "The Jewish Critique of Christianity – In Search of a New Narrative," *Studies in Christian-Jewish Relations* 6 (2011): Lasker 1–9.
12 I was reminded of this conclusion on a recent trip to Panama. I had a guide who said that although there is crime in Panama, it is really not necessary since anyone who wants a job can find one. The guide assumed that when the economy is not doing well, then crime is understandable, but in a good economy crime is unnecessary. I do not know if the guide's facts or analysis were accurate, but it is clear that crime exists even when there is no economic threat to the criminal. It is part of the human condition and does not need a specific stimulus to occur. Such is the case with polemics as well.
13 See Daniel J. Lasker, "Jewish Anti-Christian Polemics in Light of Mass Conversion to Christianity," forthcoming.
14 Stroumsa, Sarah, *Dâwûd ibn Marwân al-Muqammiṣ's Twenty Chapters ('Ishrûn Maqâla)* (Leiden: Brill, 1989).
15 Daniel J. Lasker, "Saadya Gaon on Christianity and Islam," in *The Jews of Medieval Islam: Community, Society, and Identity*, ed. Daniel Frank (Leiden: Brill, 1995): 165–177.
16 See note 6.

were not in the forefront of Ashkenazic Jewish intellectual activities. We do not even know the name of a number of these polemicists. The leading Ashkenazic rabbinic authorities, such as the tosafists, who were not inclined to philosophical investigation, never wrote anti-Christian treatises. When there was an eruption of anti-Christian polemics in late fourteenth-century Prague, it was executed by a small coterie of philosophically adept authors, which may be the reason they engaged in polemics.[17] Jewish anti-Christian polemic, therefore, is first and foremost a rationalist enterprise, even when specifically rationalist argumentation is not in use, not necessarily a defense mechanism against a real or perceived threat.

And Judah Halevi was a Jewish rationalist.[18] I know that he is often considered the anti-philosophical Jewish philosopher, and such a judgment can be reinforced by a number of statements in *Kuzari*, such as:

> But we have been promised that we are to be attached to the divine order through prophecy and whatever approximates it and that this divine order will be attached to us through acts of providence, marvels, and miracles[19] [...]. [God said]: 'The world will conduct its affairs according to the natural course of events, except for you, because simultaneously with the indwelling of the Divine Presence among you, you will see the fertility of your land and the regulation of your rainfall, the times of which will not exceed what is needed. You will conquer your enemies without preparation, by which you will understand that your affairs do not proceed according to a natural norm, but one that is willed [...]. And then you will also know that your affairs are governed by an order that is higher than the natural order.' All this has come to pass, and so the promises of this Law guaranteed.[20]

It would seem that Halevi's denial of a central aspect of philosophy, namely that the laws of nature have a necessary and immutable status, and his positing of a special divine order which attaches itself solely to Israel, are hallmarks of anti-rationalism.

Nevertheless, I would argue, and indeed have argued, that Halevi is not an anti-rationalist but rather a critic of Aristotelian a priori rationalism in favor of a sort of

---

17 See my "Jewish Philosophical Polemics in Ashkenaz" (n. 8).
18 When calling Halevi a rationalist, I do not mean that he believed in innate ideas or non-empirical truths (similar to the early modern Continental Rationalists), but that he used reasoned argumentation to support his doctrines (even if one might think that his argumentation is unreasonable). Thus, he was part of the Jewish philosophical tradition and not an anti-rationalist in the style of some of the opponents of Jewish philosophy in the Maimonidean controversies of the thirteenth and fourteenth centuries.
19 'Divine order' is Barry Kogan's translation of the key term, *amr ilahi*; Michael Schwarz renders it *ha-davar ha-elohi*.
20 Judah Halevi, *Kitāb al-radd wa-'l-dalīl fī 'l-dīn al-dhalīl (Al-kitāb al-khazarī)*, eds. David H. Baneth and Ḥaggai Ben-Shammai (Jerusalem: Magnes, 1977): 36 (1:109) (below: *Kuzari*). The English is from the forthcoming translation by Barry S. Kogan; I would like to thank Prof. Kogan for making this translation available to me. I have also made use of the new Hebrew translation of the *Kuzari*: R. Judah Halevi, *The Book of Kuzari. The Book of Rejoinder and Proof of the Despised Religion*, trans. Michael Schwarz (Beer-Sheva: Ben-Gurion University of the Negev, 2017). I would like to thank the late Prof. Schwarz for making his translation available to me before its publication.

empiricism.[21] His goal in the *Kuzari* is to present a defense of Jewish theology and to refute those who challenge it. Thus, it is only natural that one of the major targets in the book would be Christianity, even though he lived mostly in Jewish communities in Islamic lands which were not the target of Christian missionary activity. And so, even though Judah Halevi did not write a specifically anti-Christian polemical treatise, he can be added to a list of medieval Jewish anti-Christian polemicists.

All this leads me to consider how exactly Halevi's arguments against Christianity fit into the tradition of anti-Christian polemics in Islamic countries and what is specific to the author of the *Kuzari*. In my articles outlining the Andalusian influence on Jewish anti-Christian polemics in Christian Europe, I identified six features of the Jewish criticism of Christianity as found in works written by Iberian Jews who were either Andalusian or influenced by Andalusian culture. These features are: 1) Christian interpretations of the Hebrew Bible are distorted; 2) a correct understanding of divine attributes precludes the doctrines of Trinity and incarnation; 3) Jesus was not the messiah; 4) Jesus was not as bad as Paul, the true founder of Christianity; 5) Christianity contradicts reason; and 6) even though Christianity is a poor imitation of Judaism, it does have a role to play in the divine scheme for salvation. Not all Iberian authors made all six points, but these form the general outline of their critique of Christianity.[22]

If we look specifically at Judah Halevi's *Kuzari*, we see that he does not provide exegetical arguments against Christianity based on verses from the Hebrew Bible. He does interpret verses concerning the suffering servant of the Lord (Isaiah 52–53) as referring to Israel (2:44), and makes a number of other references to this verse as proof that Jewish temporal degradation is a sign of the truth of Judaism (4:22–23). Missing from the *Kuzari*, however, are most of the classical texts of the Jewish-Christian debate, such as Genesis 1:26 ('Let us make man'); Genesis 18 (the three men who visit Abraham); Genesis 49:10 (scepter of Judah); Isaiah 7:14 (the *almah* who will give birth); Jeremiah 31 (new covenant); Psalm 110 (Melchizedek); and many more.

Halevi also does not make a connection between the correct interpretation of divine attributes and the Christian doctrine of the Trinity. As Harry A. Wolfson demonstrated, the medieval philosophical discussions of attributes have their original source in Christian-Muslim debates over the Trinity. Among Jewish philosophers writing in Arabic, including Daoud al-Muqammas, Saadiah Gaon, Yaqub al-Qirqisani, and Maimonides, the connection between attributes and Trinity is expressed clearly.[23] For Halevi, the technical discussion of attributes at the beginning of Book 2 of the *Kuzari*, and the longer discourse on divine names at the beginning of Book 4, both ignore any Christian aspect of the topic.

---

21 Daniel J. Lasker, "Judah Halevi as a Philosopher – Some Preliminary Comments," in *Judeo-Arabic Culture in al-Andalus. Proceedings of the 13th Conference of the Society for Judaeo-Arabic Studies Cordoba 2007*, ed. Amir Ashur (Cordoba: CNERU – CSIC; Oriens Academics, 2013): 99–109.
22 See note 6 above.
23 See Lasker, *Jewish Philosophical Polemics*, 51–63.

The third point, Jesus was not the messiah, is implicit in the refutation of Christianity, but there are none of the specific arguments based either on the unredeemed nature of the world, such as Saadiah's arguments against the view that messianic promises were fulfilled in the past, or denigrations of Jesus, as found in *Toledot Yeshu* or the *Account of the Disputation of the Priest*, the Judaeo-Arabic original of *Nestor the Priest*. No mention is made as well of Paul and his founding of Christianity, as explicit in al-Muqammas's work as cited by al-Qirqisani, and implicitly in Maimonides's *Epistle to Yemen*. The Christian interlocutor with the King of the Khazars does say (in *Kuzari* 1:4) that Christianity follows the laws of Peter (perhaps under the influence of certain versions of *Toledot Yeshu*). He contrasts these laws with the statement of Jesus in Matthew 5:17, in Halevi's rendering: 'I have not come to remove even a single one of the Moses' commandments. Rather, I have come to support them and to enlarge them.' This verse is perhaps the one most cited by Jewish critics of Christianity and it is the only New Testament verse cited in the Talmud (*Shabbat* 116b); Halevi also cites Matthew 5:39–40 concerning turning the other cheek and giving up one's cloak (1:113).

Halevi is closer to previous anti-Christian polemics concerning the fifth point, namely, Christianity is illogical, and this accusation is made at the beginning of his book. As is well known, the literary framework of the *Kuzari* is based on the story of the King of the Khazars who searches for a new religion to replace his Khazarian one, because he dreams repeatedly that an angel-like figure tells him his intentions are desirable but his act is not. He first calls upon a philosopher, whose Aristotelian views represent twelfth-century Andalusia and not eighth century Khazaria. This encounter is unsatisfying since Aristotelianism is incompatible with the dreams which stimulated the King's search for the correct way of divine worship. After dismissing the philosopher, the King then calls upon a Christian who is the first representative of a revealed religion. The Christian begins his exposition of Christianity in *Kuzari* 1:4 with the assertion of a belief in the creator God who revealed Himself to the Jews, revelation which was pervasive among the Jews and cannot be denied because of its public nature and widespread exposure. Turning to specifically Christian doctrines, the King's interlocutor states that at the time of the last of these things and closely following upon them, divinity became incarnate and turned into a fetus in the womb of a distinguished virgin. She gave birth to a person who was human in his external appearance, but divine internally; in his outer appearance, a prophet who was sent, but in his inner character, a God who sends. This is the messiah, Son of God. There is a triune divine unity of Father, Son and Holy Spirit, a God whose divine order dwelt with Israel until they rebelled against Him and crucified the messiah. The followers of the messiah are now those who please God and are properly called Israel. All peoples are called upon to become Christians, whose laws, as I mentioned, follow those of Simon the apostle, namely Peter, since Jesus himself had stated that he had not come to abolish the law but to support it and to enlarge it.

This description of Christianity reflects not only a Jewish understanding of that religion, but also a literary device which is part of the strategy intended to force the King eventually to turn to a Jewish Sage. The Christian's opening statement about creation, mirrored by the same initial comments by the Muslim, allows Halevi to portray both religions as political and conventional but not divine ones. The assertion that the divine order dwelt among the Israelites introduces this key term into the book and establishes Jewish temporal priority to Christianity. In addition, the unique Christian doctrines of Trinity, incarnation and virgin birth are presented to the pagan King who is likely to reject them. Ultimately, the pervasiveness of the references to Judaism by the Christian sage, and in turn by the Muslim sage in 1:5–9, is what leads the King to find out more about Judaism.

As noted, the King immediately objects to Christianity as illogical by saying: 'there is no place here for logic (the Arabic is *qiyās*, a central term in the book); indeed, logic rejects most of these things.' The King does say that if he had been brought up a Christian, he would have felt a need to manipulate his logic to justify these beliefs, a task not dissimilar to that of the Jewish Sage who explains Jewish doctrines and practices which at first glance might appear illogical. It is also of interest that the King does not indicate which of the Christian doctrines logic rejects, nor does he explain why. We can assume, however, on the basis of previous Jewish critiques of Christianity in Andalusia as well as from the East, that he was referring specifically to Trinity and incarnation. He may also have had in mind virgin birth, even though Halevi's predecessors did not discuss the illogical aspects of that doctrine.[24]

In contrast to their views that Christianity is illogical, Jews under Islam did not generally consider the latter religion to be false because it is contradicted by reason. Instead, they argued that Muhammad's status as a prophet is not amenable to historical verification, and the so-called inimitability of the Quran is a fabricated claim, also not subject to substantiation.[25] Thus, the King's major objection to the Muslim's

---

[24] For arguments against Trinity and incarnation in Islamic countries, see my *Jewish Philosophical Polemics*, e.g., 51–63; 93–96; 109; 126. In his response to my talk, Prof. Lawrence Kaplan suggested that the King may well have considered other Christian doctrines which were held in common Judaism, such as creation of the world, the choice of Israel and prophetic revelation, to be against logic as well. It is true that the philosopher had rejected creation of the world, and it is obvious that the King is sceptical of the possibility of divine-human communication (e.g., *Kuzari* 1:8, in response to the Muslim sage). Since, eventually, the King is convinced by the Jewish Sage that such communication really occurred, it is important for Halevi's argumentation that the specifically Christian doctrines be judged illogical, since religion could not maintain a patently illogical belief (1:67; 89).

[25] See, e.g., David E. Sklare, "Responses to Islamic Polemics by Jewish Mutakallimun in the Tenth Century," in *The Majlis: Interreligious Encounters in Medieval Islam*, eds. Hava Lazarus-Yafeh, Mark R. Cohen, Sasson Somekh, and Sidney H. Griffith (Wiesbaden: Harrassowitz, 1999): 137–161.

speech was his inability to read the Quran in the original in order to verify its unique status.²⁶

Before turning to the last point, the contribution of Christianity (and Islam) to the coming of the messiah, I would like to review a few more references to Christianity in the *Kuzari*, most of which consider Christianity and Islam as almost one unit. Adherents of both religions are called incomplete proselytes (4:11), since they adopt some of the beliefs of Judaism but continue to maintain pagan practices, such as their adoration of 'the wood and the stone' of Deuteronomy 28:36, namely the cross of Christianity and the black stone of the Kaaba of Islam. Followers of both religions once saw *lack of worldly success* as proof of their truth, although now they point to *worldly success* as such a proof (1:113 and 4:22). Both religions are fighting wars and promising their followers a reward in the afterlife (1:2), and both have a high regard for the Land of Israel (2:23); both try unsuccessfully to imitate Judaism (3:9). Ironically, it is a perceived closeness to Judaism which distances these two religions from their source, compared to philosophy which has no pretensions of superseding Judaism (4:12–13). Halevi also argues in 1:83 that the Law of Moses did not annul the commandments given to Adam and Noam, perhaps an allusion to the Christian and Muslim views that that God can replace previous laws with a new revelation. In a passage in 4:29, Halevi mentions only the Christians in the context of an argument concerning the Jewish calendar and its incompatibility with astronomical calculations.²⁷

Returning to Jewish responses to Christianity in Iberia, the last point was the perception that Christianity is part of the redemptive process (along with Islam). In actuality, that was not part of the Judaeo-Arabic polemical tradition but rather Judah Halevi's own innovation, which was later adopted by Maimonides. Using an imagery which I argue has its origins in Romans 11 (with perhaps a nod to I Corinthians 15:36), the Jewish Sage compares Judaism to a tree growing out of a seed which appears to decompose into the earth, water and manure which surround it. In reality, however, the seed transforms the earth and water into itself as it grows into a mature tree which casts off husks, leaves and other such things, leaving the pure kernel suitable to receive the divine order. This will be the case with the Christians and Muslims who had originally rejected the tree, but actually serve as 'a preparation and prelude

---

26 Here, again, Prof. Kaplan suggested that the King considered the Muslim's belief in creation and revelation to be impossible, but the language of logical syllogism (*qiyās*) is not used. Without the objection that a reader who did not control Arabic would not be able to judge whether or not the Quran is inimitable, there would be no way to refute Islam once the possibility of prophecy were granted.
27 Ehud Krinis has argued that Halevi's polemic against Christianity and Islam should be understood not only in the context of the traditional rivalry among the three religions but also specifically in terms of Halevi's innovative view of Jewish chosenness based on Shi'ite concepts and themes. Thus, the true dispute is over 'legitimate succession' from Adam and his select descendants, in which Halevi presents the Christian and Muslim views that they are the legitimate successors. In contrast, the Jewish sage convinces the King of Jewish legitimacy and chosenness; see Ehud Krinis, *God's Chosen People: Judah Halevi's* Kuzari *and the Shī'ī Imām Doctrine* (Turnhout: Brepols, 2014): 241–283.

to the awaited messiah, who is the fruit of this process [...]. The Christians and the Muslims will come to be [the messiah's] fruit when they recognize him, and the tree will also become one. At that time, they will recognize the excellence of the root that they used to disdain.'

As I noted, Maimonides says similar things about these two religions at the end of the *Mishneh Torah*, and some Jewish thinkers to this very day have adopted the position that the other religions are part of salvation history, in an attempt to fashion a positive Jewish evaluation of Christianity and Islam. What remains unclear, however, was Judah Halevi's motivation for such a positive evaluation of these two religions, in light of the many negative comments he makes about them in the rest of the *Kuzari*. I believe the answer has to do with Halevi's view of theodicy and providence. Throughout the *Kuzari*, the point is made that temporal success is not a criterion for determining the truth of a religion. This assertion was part and parcel of Halevi's defense of his despised religion, as the alternate title of the book has it. Christianity and Islam, with all their wars between them, had a great measure of temporal success; Judaism did not. How, then, can Jews claim to be God's chosen, essentially different from their more successful competitors and subject to a non-naturalistic providence? And if temporal success is so unnecessary for a truth claim, why did Halevi choose the story of the conversion of the Khazars as the framework for his book; was not their success after conversion, as described at the beginning of Book 2, an indication of the truth of Judaism? Undoubtedly, Judah Halevi had to find some reason why Christianity and Islam prospered.

The answer to Halevi's quandary is his assertion that Christianity and Islam are imitators of Judaism. They adopted Jewish beliefs, but not fully, since they misunderstood the place of Jesus and Muhammad. They adopted Jewish practices, but also not fully, since they distorted some rituals, such as the correct day of the Shabbat, while not fully jettisoning their old rituals, the idolatrous use of wood and stone. Nevertheless, they were successful enough imitators in order to prosper and grow strong; after all, they offered the same benefits of being a Jew but at a much lower price. Eventually, however, they and all mankind will take upon themselves the full burden of Judaism although, as proselytes, they will never be fully equal to native-born Jews.

I would say that Halevi hints at another positive aspect of Christianity and Islam. Throughout the book, references are made to belief systems which are human inventions based on the diligent exertion (*idjtihād*) of unapproved cognitive methodologies like logical analogy, arbitrary judgment, intellectual speculation, supposition, conjecture, or ingenuity (Halevi uses quite a number of terms, such as *qiyās*, *tafarruḍ*, *taʿaqqul*, and *taḥakkum*). These parallel human endeavors include philosophy, Karaism, astrology, the use of amulets, dualism, sun-worship, child sacrifices, alchemy, and golden calf worship. Christianity and Islam are not included in Halevi's lists of mistaken intellectual systems. If anything, he hints to a certain divine help which was instrumental in the spread of Christianity and Islam (1:80–81), a divine help which endows them with a role to play in salvation. Presumably in the messianic age, all of Rabbinic Judaism's competitors will disappear: Karaites, philosophers, sun-worshippers, dualists, spiritualists, astrologers, purveyors of amulets, materialists and the like. Christianity and Islam will disappear as well but perhaps their former adherents will look back fondly on them as semi-inspired, incomplete forms of Judaism necessary to bring them to the truth, just as they were stepping stones on the King's journey to the one true religion. This will not be the case of the other competitors, whose doctrines were fully human in origin.

If my analysis of Judah Halevi's critique of Christianity is correct, then it is obvious that he was not a typical anti-Christian polemicist who used the standard arguments developed by Jews ever since the ninth century. He took on Christianity and Islam as the most successful of non-Jewish religions, just as he took on philosophy as the most successful of the non-religions, and Karaism as the most successful of non-rabbinic Judaisms. A Christian mission did not bring him to refute Christianity; rather, his rationalistic defense of Judaism required a reasoned rejection of that religion. This interpretation reinforces the point I made at the beginning of the talk: Jewish critiques of Christianity are not necessarily tied to a Christian threat. They can be, but they do not have to be. Even Jews not threatened by Christianity can find a good reason to polemicize against that religion.

I would like to add a comment about scepticism, the main raison d'être of this Centre. Without giving a second lecture about Judah Halevi, let me say that with all the self-assurance of the Jewish Sage's defense of Judaism in the *Kuzari*, with the claim that empirical facts substantiate the Bible's narrative, there remain many aspects of Jewish belief and practice which are beyond intellectual explanation. In 1:88, the King states that in light of the veracity of the theophany on Sinai, the Jews can be forgiven for believing that God is corporeal. The Sage denies divine corporeality and explains revelation in terms of a created glory which is not God Himself. Although the King says that that explanation is convincing, the Sage declares that that is only one possible explanation and he is not committed to it; there has to be some explanation of the corporeal aspects of revelation which do not imply a corporeal God, but one cannot know what they are with full confidence. When the King asks for the reasons for sacrifices, the Sage gives a detailed interpretation of the relation between the ritual and the functions of the human body and other aspects of the cosmos, again without a commitment to the details of his explanation. And at the beginning of Book 5, when the King asks for an account of Aristotelian philosophy and *Kalam* theology, he does so by admitting that he has not reached the level of acceptance of the tradition without question. The Sage responds that such reliance on tradition is the ultimate goal, but very few people can reach it. Thus, it is necessary to investigate other systems and refute them in the pursuit of truth. It would seem, then, that Judah Halevi understood that his defense of Judaism is not necessarily meant as a definitive statement of truth since absolute truth may be beyond human comprehension. I think that a full examination of the *Kuzari* will allow us a greater appreciation of Judah Halevi's scepticism, but that will have to wait for some other opportunity.

Lawrence Kaplan

Response to Daniel J. Lasker's "Polemics, Religion, and Scepticism in Judah Halevi's *Book of Kuzari*"

As did Professor Lasker, I, too, would like to start out by thanking both Prof. Giuseppe Veltri, founder and director of the Maimonides Center, and my former doctoral student, current colleague, and co-director of the center, Dr. Racheli Haliva, who planned this workshop.

Above all, I am deeply honored to have been chosen to be the respondent to Professor Daniel Lasker's paper, "Polemics, Religion, and Scepticism in Judah Halevi's *Book of Kuzari*." But this honor brings with it a daunting task. Lasker modestly notes. Over the years my interest in medieval Jewish philosophy has centered on a number of themes, one of which has been interreligious polemics, most specifically Jewish anti-Christian polemics, with a special attention to those debates in the Islamic realm; and another theme has been the philosophy of Rabbi Judah Halevi, especially his view of the opponents of Rabbinic Judaism, whether they be philosophers, members of other religions, or Karaites.' In truth, Lasker is widely acknowledged as being as one of the world's leading scholars in both these areas (and other areas as well). To have to respond, then, to a paper of Lasker that deals with *both* these areas of his expertise is no small challenge.

Lasker begins his paper with a thoroughly documented and entirely convincing critique of 'the old narrative of Jewish criticism of Christianity as a reaction to Christian pressure.' In its stead, he skillfully, learnedly, and, again, entirely convincingly argues in favor of a 'new narrative' that 'Jewish anti-Christian argumentation was mainly a function of Jewish rationalist theology. Almost every Jewish author of a philosophical treatise was involved in one way or another with interreligious polemic, sometimes against Islam but usually against Christianity.'

Coming to the subject at hand, Judah Halevi's *Kuzari*, Lasker argues that Halevi's polemic against Christianity in the *Kuzari* fits, with certain variations, into this model, inasmuch as Halevi himself was a rationalist. To be sure, Lasker immediately notes that Halevi 'is often considered the anti-philosophical Jewish philosopher,' and even brings evidence that might be used to support that view. But he rejects this view, and, referring to his excellent and illuminating article, "Judah Halevi as a Philosopher–Some Preliminary Comments,"[1] he argues that 'Halevi is not an anti-rationalist, but rather a critic of Aristotelian a priori rationalism in favor of a sort of empiricism. His goal in the *Kuzari* is to present a defense of Jewish theology and to refute those who challenge it.'

---

[1] Daniel J. Lasker, "Judah Halevi as a Philosopher – Some Preliminary Comments," in *Judeo-Arabic Culture in al-Andalus. Proceedings of the 13th Conference of the Society for Judaeo-Arabic Studies, Cordoba 2007*, ed. Amir Ashur (Cordoba: CNERU – CSIC; Oriens Academics, 2013): 99–109.

Here I must pose a question. I agree entirely with this characterization of both Halevi and his goal in the *Kuzari*, but, I do not see how this makes Halevi into a rationalist. What it makes him, as Lasker correctly notes, is an empiricist. To be sure, Halevi, as an empiricist, was not an anti-rationalist, but neither was he a rationalist. He was, to repeat, an empiricist.

To elaborate: As Lasker notes, the key claim of Jewish rationalists against Christianity is that it 'contradicts reason,' or, as I would put it to be more precise, that it, unlike Judaism, 'contradicts reason.' A bit later, Lasker reformulates this claim to read that 'Christianity is illogical,' or, again, as I would put it, that, unlike Judaism, which is logical, 'Christianity is illogical.' Since Lasker believes that Halevi was a rationalist, he sees him as leveling this accusation against Christianity at the beginning of his book. But is this the case?

The Christian scholar's speech in *Kuzari* 1:4,[2] is, we may say, divided into two parts: a shorter 'Jewish' part, in which he sets forth the belief in the providential, creator God who revealed Himself to the Jews, followed by a longer 'Christian' part, in which he sets forth such specifically Christian doctrines as Jesus as the Messiah and son of God, as God incarnate, and as the Father, Son, and Holy Spirit. The King objects to this presentation as illogical by saying: 'there is no place here for logic (*qiyās*); indeed, logic rejects most of these things' (1:5). Note my formulation, 'The King objects to this presentation as illogical,' as contrasted to Lasker's formulation, 'The King immediately objects to Christianity as illogical.' Lasker insightfully observes that 'It is also of interest that the King does not indicate which of the Christian doctrines logic rejects, nor does he explain why;' but he does not pursue this insight, and immediately continues 'We can assume, however, on the basis of previous Jewish critiques of Christianity in Andalusia as well as from the East, that he was referring specifically to Trinity and incarnation.' But why, indeed, doesn't the King spell out to which Christian doctrines he is objecting?

Moreover, since the Christian scholar's speech includes as already noted, both a Jewish part and a Christian part, why should we assume that the King objects only to the speech's specifically Christian doctrines? After all, the Christian, in the speech's Jewish part, refers to such teachings as God's 'providential concern for creation, and contact with human beings [through expressions of] anger, satisfaction, mercy, speech, self-disclosure, and revelation to His prophets and pious friends' (1:4). All these doctrines, which, as the Christian states, are contained in the 'Torah and in the traditions of the children of Israel,' were already dismissed by the philosopher in his lengthy opening speech to the King (1:1) on the basis of arguments that the king himself admitted were persuasive, even if not demonstrative (1:2). So why not

---

[2] For a critical edition of the Judeo-Arabic original, see Judah Halevi, *Kitāb al-radd wa-'l-dalīl fī 'l-dīn al-dhalīl (Al-kitāb al-khazarī)*, eds. David H. Baneth and Ḥaggai Ben-Shammai (Jerusalem: Magnes, 1977). The English is from the forthcoming translation by Barry S. Kogan. I would like to thank Prof. Kogan for making this translation available to me. All references in the body of my essay are to the Book and Section of the *Kuzari*.

assume that the King also had in mind these Jewish teachings as being illogical, as being rejected by *qiyās?*

But to return to the main question: Why doesn't the King in his response to the Christian scholar's speech specify to which doctrines set forth in that speech he is objecting?

Perhaps an examination of the exchange between the King and the Muslim scholar, immediately following upon the former's exchange with the Christian scholar, will help us answer our question. Asked by the King about 'his knowledge and actions' (1:5), the Muslim scholar responds:

> We affirm the unity and eternity of God, the complete innovation of the world, and [our common] descent from Adam and Noah. We deny the corporeality [of God] completely, and if something [implying corporeality] appears in speech, we interpret it and say that it is a metaphor and an approximation [of the truth]. At the same time, we affirm that our book [the Quran] is the word of God. It is in itself a miracle that we must accept because of its very nature, since no one can produce anything like it or even anything like one of its verses. Our prophet is the seal of the prophets, who abrogates every previous Law and summons all nations to accept Islam. The reward for one who obeys is the return of his soul to his body in a garden and [a state of] bliss, which does not lack for eating, drinking, sexual intercourse, and anything else he desires. The punishment for one who rebels is for him to be consigned to a fire from which the torment never ends. (1:5)

Let us note that the Muslim scholar in his presentation, unlike the Christian scholar, speaks about God in a philosophical manner, referring to His 'unity and eternity.' More important, as if he were directly responding to the Christian scholar,[3] he de-anthropomorphizes all the anthropomorphic expressions used by the latter in his presentation, explicitly stating 'We deny the corporeality [of God] completely, and if something [implying corporeality] appears in speech, we interpret it and say that it is a metaphor and an approximation [of the truth].'

This philosophical, non-anthropomorphic description of God on the part of the Muslim scholar and his immediately following assertion that the Quran is the word of God, as evidenced by its miraculous inimitable nature, lend support to Lasker's historical claim that 'In contrast to their views about Christianity as illogical, Jews under Islam did not generally consider that religion to be false because it is contradicted by reason. Instead, they argued that Muhammed's status as a prophet is not amenable to historical verification, and that the so-called inimitability of the Quran is a fabricated claim, not subject to substantiation.'

These general historical observations are certainly valid, though one would imagine that many Jewish rationalists—though certainly not all Jews—would also find the Muslim scholar's highly corporeal description of the afterlife objectionable.

---

3 Of course, in truth, the King only 'called upon a certain scholar of Islam, and asked him about his knowledge and his actions' (1:5) *after* he had dismissed the speech of the Christian scholar as unsatisfactory, and had resolved to 'investigate further.'

But let us set that point to the side. What I find problematic in Lasker's discussion is that he uses these generally unimpeachable historical observations to draw a conclusion about the nature of the King's objections to Islam in his response to the Muslim scholar's speech. Thus, Lasker concludes, 'Thus'—that is, in accord with the immediately above mentioned historical observations—'the King's major objection to the Muslim was his [the King's] inability to read the Quran in the original in order to verify its status.' But is this the case? How does the King respond to the Muslim scholar's speech, and what objections to it does he in fact raise?

> Then the Khazar said to him: Someone who wishes to be rightly guided in connection with God's command and also to have it confirmed that God speaks to flesh and blood, when he thinks that that is quite unlikely, ought to have it established in his mind by well-known facts that cannot be rejected. And [even then], it would hardly be verified for him that God has really spoken with a human being. Now if your book is a miracle, but the book is in Arabic, then a non-Arab like myself will not be able to recognize its miraculous and extraordinary character. Even if it is recited to me, I won't be able to distinguish between it and anything else expressed in Arabic. (1:6)

In this response of the Khazar King, we, in my view, arrive at the heart of Halevi's view. As the King's response indicates, his major objection to the Muslim scholar was not 'his [the King's] inability to read the Quran in the original in order to verify its status,' but rather the Muslim scholar's claim that God speaks to and comes into contact with man. The point the King makes about his inability to read the Quran in the original in order to verify its status, is that on account of his inability he is unable to judge whether the Muslim claim that the inimitability of the Quran shows that it is the word of God is sufficiently grounded to *overcome* his key objection to the Muslim scholar, which, to repeat, is the latter's claim that God speaks to and comes into contact with man. That is, the King's default position is that God does not speak to and come into contact with man. If someone claims otherwise, as does the Muslim scholar, it follows that the burden of proof is upon him—that is, it is incumbent upon him to bring proofs that are of sufficient weight to overcome the default position. And, in the King's view, the Muslim scholar's claim about the inimitability of the Quran does not possess that sufficient weight, or, at least, he is unable to judge whether it does so or not.[4]

That this, indeed, constitutes the King's major objection is reinforced by the subsequent exchange between him and the Muslim scholar:

> Therefore, the scholar said to him: Miracles have been performed by him, but they have not been offered as proof for accepting his Law. (1:7)
>
> The Khazar said: Yes, of course. But people are not inclined to affirm that the deity enters into contact with human beings, unless it is by means of a miracle through which the essences [of things] are transformed. Then we know that only He who created things from nothing has the

---

4 The King seems to be suggesting between the lines that the Muslim doctrine of the inimitability of the Quran is so subjective in nature, that even were he proficient in Arabic—as, of course, Halevi himself was—he would be unable to accord it sufficient weight to overcome the default position.

power to do that. Moreover, this should take place in the presence of multitudes which see it with their own eyes, and not come to them by means of a report and a chain of authorities transmitting it. It should be studied and tested time and again, so that it would not occur to anyone to think that imagining or magic were involved there. And [even then] people would hardly accept this grand thing, I mean, that the Creator of this world and the next, of the angels, the heavens, and the luminaries enters into contact with this dirty piece of filth—I mean man—speaks to him, and also fulfills his longing as well as his arbitrary whims. (1:8)

What we have in 1:8, I would suggest, is a variation of the objection set forth in 1:6. In 1:6 the King's objection is directed against the claim that 'God's command' can provide 'right guidance' for man, 'that God speaks to flesh and blood,' and 'that God has really spoken with a human being.' The background of this objection appears to be the philosopher's speech in 1:1 denying that God can address men and reveal a Law to them, inasmuch as He, precisely on account of His divine perfection, is 'beyond desires and aims,' as well as 'beyond the knowledge of particulars,' as a consequence of which God is 'not aware of [individuals] let alone of [their] intentions and [their] actions.' In 1:8, the King's objection is directed against the claim 'that the deity enters into contact with human beings,' and more elaborately, 'that the Creator of this world and the next, of the angels, the heavens, and the luminaries enters into contact with this dirty piece of filth—I mean man,' and the specific objection to the claim that God speaks to man is just a subsidiary point. As Ehud Krinis, developing an observation of Shlomo Pines,[5] notes,[6] the King here is expressing a 'late Hellenistic pagan worldview'[7] that God is so spiritual, sublime, and pure that He cannot come into contact with corporeal, filthy, flesh and blood man.[8]

But, I believe, this key objection of the King to the Muslim scholar, namely the implausibility of the latter's claim that God speaks to and comes into contact with man, whether that implausibility flows from philosophical or late Hellenistic pagan principles, is also his key objection to both Judaism and Christianity as revealed religions. And here, I would suggest, we may have an answer to our question as to why the King did not spell out his objections to the Christian scholar's teachings. No doubt the King—and in this respect he faithfully reflects Halevi's views—felt that many of the specific doctrines of the Christian scholar, such as Trinity and incarnation, are, indeed, illogical. But, in light of the King's fundamental objection to the claim that God speaks to and comes into contact with man, espoused by all three

---

[5] Shlomo Pines, "Shī'ī te Terms and Conceptions in Judah Halevi's *Kuzari*," *Jerusalem Studies in Arabic and Islam* 2 (1980): 65–166 and 196–210.
[6] Ehud Krinis, *God's Chosen People: Judah Halevi's Kuzari and Shī'ī Imām Doctrine* (Turnhout: Brepols, 2014): 171–177.
[7] *Ibidem*, 171.
[8] *Ibidem*, 174; Krinis does not distinguish between the King's objection in 1:6 and his objection in 1:8. Instead, he reads 1:6 in light of 1:8, and sees them both as stemming from the King's adherence to the 'late Hellenistic pagan worldview.' This, in my view, is to ignore the differences between the two paragraphs, and to make the King repeat himself unnecessarily.

Abrahamic religions, they are beside the point—and had Halevi had the King discuss them, it would have just muddied the waters. Unlike, however, the many problematic theological claims set forth in the Christian scholar's speech, the *only* problematic theological claim set forth in the Muslim scholar's speech is that God speaks to and comes into contact with man. Halevi, therefore, had the King wait until the latter's speech in order to object to this claim, so that, thereby, this core issue would be, as it properly ought to be, at the center of discussion.

Here we return to the issue of Halevi's 'rationalism.' For what I believe emerges from my discussion is that Halevi in the *Kuzari* confronts us with two conflicting claims: the claim that God neither speaks to nor comes into contact with man, whether based on the arguments of the philosopher that God's perfection entails that He has no knowledge of human beings and their actions, much less is concerned about them and pleased or displeased by them, or on the principles of late Hellenistic paganism that God's spirituality and sublimity preclude His coming into contact with corporeal man; and the common assertions of all three Abrahamic religions affirming the contrary. The King's point—and Halevi's point—is that the claim that God neither speaks to nor comes into contact with man, whether based on philosophical or late pagan principles, is intrinsically more reasonable than the common claim of the three Abrahamic religions affirming the contrary. In this respect one cannot call Halevi a rationalist.

What the King—and Halevi—maintain on the other side, however, is that since the claim that God neither speaks to nor comes into contact with man, while intrinsically reasonable and plausible, has not been established through demonstration, one can *defeat* this claim and vindicate the common Jewish-Christian-Muslim claim, even if it is intrinsically less reasonable and plausible than the contrary claim of the philosophers and the late pagans, by bringing empirical evidence indicating that God in fact did speak to and come into contact with men. In this respect, as Lasker correctly notes, Halevi is an empiricist.

Coming to the competing claims of all three religions to be the true revealed religion, positively, the *Haver*, the Jewish sage—who here is a faithful spokesman of Halevi—maintains that only the history of the Jewish people provides empirical evidence in the form of God's performing ongoing and public miracles before the eyes of multitudes sufficient to both establish the veracity of Judaism as a revealed religion and to defeat the philosophical/late pagan claim.[9] Negatively, what emerges from the King's discussions with both the Christian and the Muslim scholars is that neither has brought empirical evidence in the form of God's performing ongoing and public miracles before the eyes of multitudes sufficient to establish its veracity as a revealed religion and to defeat the philosophical/late pagan claim. The empirical evidence the Christian scholar offers in support of the specific Christian part of his speech is the historical suffering of those Jews who rejected Jesus as the Messiah

---

9 This, of course, is the point of the *Haver*'s famous parable about the king of India; see *Kuzari* 1:17–25.

and the historical temporal success of those Gentiles who accepted him as the Messiah. The King does not respond to this point, but the *Haver* addresses it at length later in the *Kuzari*.[10] Lasker analyzes this issue with his customary learning and insight, and thus I need not discuss it.[11] The empirical evidence the Muslim scholar offers in support of the Quran being the word of God is its inimitability, and we saw why the King did not accept this argument.[12] The bottom line—the empirical bottom line—remains that only Judaism is supported by empirical evidence sufficient to establish its veracity as a revealed religion and to defeat the philosophical/late pagan claim God does not speak to and come into contact with men.

Regarding Lasker's incisive and authoritative discussion regarding the nature of Christianity and Islam as semi-inspired imitations of Judaism and the role these religions will play in the coming of the Messiah, I have nothing to add.[13]

I certainly agree with Lasker that Halevi's 'defense of Judaism required a reasoned rejection of Christianity.' But I do not agree with him, for reasons which I have tried to explain, that that defense was a 'rationalistic defense.'

To conclude: In an article in which he took issue with certain theses of Gershom Scholem, Yehudah Liebes commented that it was only owing to Scholem's towering scholarly accomplishments that he, Liebes, was able to take issue with him. And, Liebes concluded, this is the way that scholarship progresses.[14] In a similar vein, let me state that if I have expressed certain reservations regarding some of Lasker's theses, I have been able to do so only thanks to his many learned, brilliant, and enduring contributions to both the fields of Jewish anti-Christian polemics and the philosophy of Rabbi Judah Halevi. And, let me close with the hope that here too this is the way that scholarship progresses.

---

10 See *Kuzari* 1:113; 2:29–44; and 4:22–23.
11 See, as well, Krinis, *God's Chosen People*, 243–282 (Chapter 12: The Question of Legitimate Succession in the *Kuzari*).
12 As Lasker commented in the discussion following his presentation and my response, *once* the King accepted the claim of the *Haver* that the history of the Jewish people provides empirical evidence in the form of God's performing ongoing and public miracles before the eyes of multitudes that God in fact did speak to and come into contact with men, at *that* point his major and only objection to the claim that the Quran is the word of God would, indeed, be 'his inability to read the Quran in the original in order to verify its status'. This is no doubt the case, but since Halevi does not bring the Muslim scholar back on stage for an encore, any suggestion as to how a further, 'post-*Haver*,' exchange between them might have proceeded must remain speculative and beside the point. One can judge the *Kuzari*'s world view and defense of Judaism only on the basis of what it says, not on what it does not but might have said. See above, Note 4.
13 See Daniel Lasker, "Proselyte Judaism Christianity and Islam in the Thought of Judah Halevi," *Jewish Quarterly Review* 81.1–2 (1990): 75–91.
14 I cannot remember in which of the many articles of Liebes I have read I came across this comment, and am citing from memory.

Racheli Haliva
Abner's Double Standard Approach towards the Jewish Rabbis

From Judah Halevi's *Kuzari* who argues against Christianity while living under Muslim rule, now we turn to Abner of Burgos, a Jewish convert to Christianity who lived in Christian northern Spain between the second half of the thirteenth century and the first half of the fourteenth century.

In this article I focus on Abner's approach towards the Rabbis as it appears in his *Teshuvot la-Meḥaref* ('Response to the Blasphemer'), a long letter he addresses to Isaac Polqar, his former student, who defends the philosophical interpretation of the Jewish faith. On the one hand, in several places in his letter, Abner harshly criticizes the Jewish sages for creating the Oral Law in order to establish two different ethical systems, one for Jews and one for non-Jews; and for stubbornly rejecting Christianity as the true religion. On the other hand, however, it seems as if Abner puts a great effort in convincing his readers, most likely a Jewish audience whom he tried to convince to convert to Christianity, that the Jewish sages were, in fact, Christian believers who had to conceal their true belief for political reasons. In *Teshuvot la-Meḥaref*, Abner consistently uses Jewish sources in order to prove that the doctrines of the Christian faith are true from the Jewish sources themselves. He aims to show that although the Jews of his own time reject Christianity altogether, the talmudic sages, upon whom they rely, tacitly accepted Christianity's fundamental beliefs.

First, I will cite a passage from the *Teshuvot la-Meḥaref* where Abner slanders the Jewish sages' ethical behaviour, accusing them of teaching their adherents to behave immorally. Then, I shall focus on two Midrashim, which Abner interprets in such a way as to justify his claim that the Jewish sages embraced Christian doctrines but had to conceal this fact from the Jewish community. At the end of this article, I will offer several possible explanations regarding Abner's motivation to ascribe two opposing views to the Jewish sages.

At the beginning of *Teshuvot la-Meḥaref*, Abner accuses the Jewish sages of behaving unethically, as a result of which others behave unethically towards them.[1] He writes:

> In the *Teacher of Righteousness* (Moreh Ṣedeq), I have already described those ten evil commandments which were juxtaposed to the Ten Commandments. They are found in their Babylonian Talmud and include theft and swearing falsely in a deceitful manner. On account of them, it would be fitting for it to be designated darkness and gloom [...]. This is the Babylonian Talmud. It is said after that, 'That is the curse which goes out over the whole land. For everyone who has stolen, as is forbidden on one side [of the scroll], has gone unpunished; and everyone who has sworn [falsely], as is forbidden on the other side of it, has gone unpunished.' That is their *eifah* and 'measurement,' through which they receive and give. As they say, 'the degree to which a man measures, they measure him.' Just as they made that Oral Law in order to injure others,

---

1 *Teshuvot la-Meḥaref*, 33b; 34b.

it, in turn, was the reason for their being injured by others. On account of this, it [the Oral Law] was extended and spread among them, which is the opposite of (the verse) *For out of Zion shall go forth the Law* (Isaiah 2:3). This is the meaning of (the verse), what is this approaching? (There the angel) says, 'This is the *eifah* which is approaching.' He then gives a reason for why he called the scroll an *eifah* and the 'measurement.' He says, 'This is their eye in all the land.' It is the 'eye,' the 'vision' of reasoning they present to the world concerning their commentary on the Torah. According to this, they 'were seen' and judged 'in all the land,' that is, for themselves and by others. This is what happened to them: Just as they declared from the logic of the Talmud that it is permitted to steal and to swear falsely for such and such a reason, they were robbed and false testimony was given about them for those very reasons.[2]

Abner claims here two things: First, the Talmud, or more precisely, the rabbis of the Talmud changed the ten 'good' commandments of the Written Law to ten 'evil' commandments of the Oral Law. In the *Moreh Ṣedeq* ('Teacher of Righteousness') he spells out what these ten 'evil' commandments are: (1) to steal, (2) to rob, (3) to give false testimony, (4) to pervert justice, (5) to be proud, (6) to swear falsely, (7) to kill, (8) to be unchaste, (9) to loan at interest, and (10) to serve and worship idols.

His second claim is that since the talmudic rabbis replaced the original 'good' Ten Commandments with these ten 'evil' commandments, those who act in accordance with these 'evil' commandments, will find themselves mistreated in the same way by others. In other words, if they allow stealing from and killing gentiles, then they, in turn, will be subjected to the gentiles stealing from and killing them. This is the *middah ke'neged middah*, the degree to which one judges, he will be judged himself.

Contrary to this negative view of the rabbis, ascribing to them an unethical double standard, Abner also presents a positive view of them. According to him, the talmudic sages were esoterically Christians. Naturally, Abner claims, the sages could not openly teach their disciples to believe in the three persons of God or in the incarnation, for, were they to do so, they would be charged with heresy. But, this indeed was their true opinion, which they concealed and only obliquely alluded to.[3] By claiming this, Abner implies that the sages used the Maimonidean method of concealing true knowledge from the multitude because of the latter's inability to understand it. However, while for Maimonides the knowledge that the sages concealed from the multitude was *philosophical* knowledge, for Abner the knowledge they concealed were the *fundamental doctrines of Christianity*.

---

[2] *Teshuvot la-Meḥaref*, 33b.
[3] One might wonder why the sages could not have explained to their disciples that these three persons do not contradict God's unity. Perhaps we can suggest that acknowledging the three persons was so closely identified with Christianity that the rabbis, even if they possessed the 'true' knowledge of the Trinity, could not disclose this knowledge to their disciples. Since they would have been accused of heresy, they could only allude to God's three persons.

Abner uses several examples to substantiate his argument. Here I shall focus on two Midrashim, which, according to Abner, clearly show that it was this Christian position that the Jewish sages genuinely espoused.

The first Midrash that Abner cites is from *Genesis Rabbah*; his reading of this Midrash focuses on the grammatical analysis of the plural name *Elohim* and the singular verb *bara'* that follows it. Abner's main purpose in this Midrash is to demonstrate that, in the sages' view, *Elohim* alludes to the Trinity. The Midrash states:

> The sectarians asked Rabbi Simlai: 'How many deities created the world?' 'I and you must inquire of the first day,' replied he, as it is written, *For ask now of the first days* (Deuteronomy 4:32) Not 'since the days gods created man' is written here, but 'God created (*bara'*).' Then they asked him a second time: 'Why is it written *in the beginning Elohim* [plural] created?' '*In the beginning baru* Elohim is not written here,' answers he, 'but *bara'* Elohim.' Rabbi Simlai said: 'Wherever you find a point [apparently] supporting the sectarians, you find the refutation at its side.'[4]

The second Midrash Abner cites is from *Exodus Rabbah*, which elaborates on the first Midrash. The Midrash states:

> Some sectarians once asked R. Simlai:[5] 'Are there not many deities in the world?' He replied, 'What makes you think so?' 'Because,' they said, 'it is written, *Did ever a people hear the voice of God* (*Elohim* in the plural form)? (Deuteronomy 4:33)' To which he replied, 'It does not say *medabberim* but *medabber*.' Whereupon his disciples said to him: 'O teacher, you have thrust those off with a broken reed, but what answer will you give to us?' R. Levi then offered this explanation. It says, '*Did ever a people hear the voice of God?* What does this mean? Had it said, "The voice of God in His power," the world would not have been able to survive, but it says instead, *The voice of the Lord is with power* (Psalm 29:4)—that is, according to the power of each individual [each one] according to the power of the young, the old, and the very small ones.'[6]

---

4 *Genesis Rabbah* 8:9.
5 Rabbi Levi is referring to the Midrash in *Genesis Rabbah* 8:9, which states: 'The sectarians (*minim*) asked Rabbi Simlai: "How many deities created the world?" "I and you must inquire of the first day," replied he, as it is written, *For ask now of the first days* (Deuteronomy 4:32) Not "since the days gods created (*bar'u*) man" is written here, but God created (*bara'*). Then they asked him a second time: "Why is it written *in the beginning Elohim* [plural] created?" "*In the beginning* baru Elohim is not written here," answers he, "but bara' Elohim *the heaven and the earth*." Rabbi Simlai said: "Wherever you find a point [apparently] supporting the sectarians, you find the refutation at its side." They asked him again: "What is meant by *And God said: Let us make a man*?" "Read what follows," replied he: "not, And god created [*va-yevr'u*] man, is written here, but *And God created – va-yivra*' (Genesis 1:27)." When they went out his disciples said to him: "Them you have dismissed with a mere makeshift, but how will you answer us?"' Cf. Jonathan Hecht, *The Polemical Exchange between Isaac Pollegar and Abner of Burgos/Alfonso of Valladolid according to Parma MS 2440* (PhD thesis, New York University, 1993): 489–491.
6 *Exodus Rabbah*, 29:1; cf. Shalom Żadik, *Trinity and Determinism in the Thought of Abner of Burgos* (PhD thesis, University of Ben Gurion, 2011): 47–51.

The name *Elohim* in the plural form appears to suggest, so the sectarians claim, that there are many gods, which raises troubling theological questions. Rabbi Simlai's grammatical explanation, according to which the use of the form *medabber* in the singular form indicates that *Elohim* should be understood as referring to one God, is criticized by his disciples as being unsatisfactory.[7] Abner emphasizes that Rabbi Simlai's students did not accept his simple reply as representing his true view. This is crucial, for it suggests that his genuine opinion differed from the answer he offered to the sectarians: Rabbi Simlai, then, must have believed that the true meaning of the biblical verse needed to be hidden from outsiders.

Abner suggests that for both Rabbi Simlai and Rabbi Levi, the plural form of *Elohim* indeed carries with it a plural meaning, but this plural meaning refers not to God's 'honor and exaltation,' but to 'relationships and actions.'

Abner first refers to the end of the Midrash in *Exodus Rabbah* and goes on to give his analysis:

> Then Rabbi Levi came and explained it. He said: 'If "the voice of the Lord (YHVH) in His power" had been written, the world could not have stood. Rather: *The voice of God* (*Elohim*) (is written in Deuteronomy 4:33). Each and every one according to his power, the young man according to his power and the old man according to his power.' His answer was that the plural form of the name, *Elohim*, of the one God was not for honor and exaltation—just as it was not for the plurality of His substance, according to the opinion of us who believe in unity—for then the students would have required a different answer (for them) from the questioner, [the question being] why this plurality is mentioned in the name 'God.' Neither Rabbi Levi nor Rabbi Simlai answered that it was for honor and exaltation, rather it was because of the *relationships and* the *actions* (between the names). Our rabbi, Moses Maimonides, wrote in chapters 51 and 52 of the first part of the *Guide of the Perplexed* that it is possible to attach (a notion of) multiplicity of attributes to the Creator, since a change in relationships does not necessitate a change in His essence [...]. Rather, Rabbi Levi interpreted the 'voices' as a metaphor to all the changing actions coming from the Holy One, blessed be He. So, since there is no multiplicity in His essence, the verse uses the singular form, 'speaking out of a fire,' and not 'speaking' in the plural form. Thus, 'God created,' 'and God created,' (are written) and not 'Gods created,' nor 'and Gods created,' and others be-

---

7 In *Teshuvot la-Meḥaref*, 17a-b, Abner also examines the Midrash in *Genesis Rabbah* and states, 'It is explained in *Genesis Rabbah*, and also in *Exodus Rabbah*, that the name "God" was not written in the plural form for embellishment and exaltation as the commentators who argue with us thought. It is not as they understand from Rabbi Simlai, when he argued with the sectarians who believed in the plurality of deities, when he said, "In every place that the sectarians profane, the answer to them is at their side: When the Gods began to create [...] is not written here, rather: (When God began to) create. And the Gods created man [...] is not written, rather: And (God) created. The voice of Gods are speaking is not said, rather (the voice of God) is speaking. Thus it is in every case like this." They (the students) wished to say that this response is not convincing. That is to say because of the mention of unity, plurality cannot be understood in it in any way. For the students say to Rabbi Simlai: "You have put (the sectarians) off with straw. What do you say to us?" (The students) called that particular response concerning His uniqueness, "straw," and a weak response. It is not a convincing answer. This is because there still remains doubt so they ask him, saying, "if the deity is one, why is the name 'God' (Elohim), which indicates plurality because it is in the plural form, used. After all, we have found the name, 'God' (Eloha), in the singular?"'

sides these. Rather, because the power of the Holy One, blessed be He, is actually infinite, and the world—because it is created—is not actually infinite, it must be that the power of the Holy One, blessed be He—which is actually infinite must in actuality perform an infinite number of actions—one after the other—which are the details of existence. Thus, the world will be one, qua totality and purposive, appropriately coming from the One; and it [the world] will be [filled with] multiplicity by virtue of the many parts which deserve to exist because He is a power without end.[8]

Abner employs here Maimonides' view of God's attributes, which stresses that God's unity is not diminished by ascribing these attributes, for they do not cause any change in Him. Rabbi Levi explains that the verse does not states 'the voice of the Lord [YHVH],' but rather 'the voice of God [*Elohim*] is with power' in order to affirm God's unity and at the same time to allow for His multiple actions and relationships, which do not diminish His unity and perfection. The 'voices,' according to Rabbi Levi, are the sum of all the actions that occur in the world.[9] However, according to Abner, the only way we can explain the multiplicity of actions in the world is to accept the three aspects of *Elohim*. If we look carefully on Abner's analysis of the two Midrashim, we arrive at Abner's conclusion that the talmudic sages possessed the knowledge that *Elohim* in its plural form alludes to the three aspects in God. However, they had to conceal it from the people for social and political reasons, namely, that the people were not ready to accept these truths and consequently could believe that God is not only one, but also three.

Now, the main question remains: why would Abner introduce two contradictory opinions regarding the talmudic sages, namely, on the one hand claiming that they were esoterically Christians, and on the other, accusing them of creating a set of laws which educate their adherents to act in as an unethical manner?

Teshuvot la-Meharef should be seen, in my view, as an apologetic treatise whose main goal is to attack Jewish principles, while showing the superiority of Christianity. In this light I would like to suggest three possible answers to this question:

1. From an apologetical/ political point of view—One of Abner's main goals, writing his *Teshuvot la-Meharef* is to convince as many Jews as possible to convert to Christianity. That means that he mainly addresses his writings to a Jewish audience, which would explain his extensive use of rabbinic texts. His audience—Jews, who are familiar with rabbinic literature, biblical verses, and biblical commentaries, are more likely to understand the weak points of the Jewish Law pointed out by Abner.

2. From a theological point of view—Abner adopts the Christian method of interpreting the Bible, namely, on the one hand, it has been replaced by the New Testament. On the other, it alludes to Jesus. Here too, only true philosophical teaching of the Rabbis should be taken seriously, while the political/social laws must be disre-

---

8 *Teshuvot la-Meharef*, 17b.
9 See Hecht, *The Polemical Exchange between Isaac Pollegar and Abner of Burgos/Alfonso of Valladolid*, 489.

garded. What is important is the inner meaning—the *tokh*, the internal meaning of their teaching, and the exoteric, the external meanings are useless and misleading. In other words, the Christian method is to disregard the exoteric message of the bible —for example the practical commandments—and to accept the internal/esoteric truth of the Old Testament, namely, the verses which allude to Jesus. Here too, the Oral Law conveys two different types of teaching; an exoteric one—the Jewish Law; and an esoteric one—accepting the Christian doctrines.

3. The last option, which in my view is unlikely to be true, would be to suggest that Abner truly believed that the talmudic sages were esoterically Christians and that the only reason they did not disclose their Christian belief to the Jewish community was their [the sages'] fear that the Jewish community would aggressively reject the sages' new Christian view. The main reason I doubt this explanation is the correct one is because presenting the talmudic sages as esoterically Christians would serve Abner's purpose perfectly; by presenting to the Jewish community the option that the talmudic rabbis accepted the Christian doctrines, would bring the desired result—more Jews would convert to Christianity. Why, then, does Abner spend so much time and effort attacking the rabbis? It is difficult, then, to accept that the rabbis were esoterically Christians. Abner understood that this argument does not hold water from the point of view of the Jewish community.

This paper does not aim to provide a decisive conclusion to the question: what was Abner's motivation in presenting two contradictory opinions about the Jewish sages. I merely wish to point out to the way Abner employs the Maimonidean method—conveying two different messages to different audiences—and to suggest few options of reading his treatise *Teshuvot la-Meḥaref*.

Michael Engel
Response to Racheli Haliva's "Abner's Double Standard Approach towards the Jewish Rabbis"

At the heart of Haliva's thought-provoking reading of Abner, one finds two conflicting approaches towards Judaism and Jewish sources. Haliva finds these approaches at the heart of Abner's reply to Isaac Polqar, and the crux of her argument is an attempt to contextualize and harmonize the two seemingly conflicting attitudes. My reply is concerned less with Haliva's attempts at reconciliation and regards more fundamentally the aforementioned tension she locates in Abner's reply. On the one hand, Abner is explicitly critical towards Jews and Jewish sources. On the other, Abner is sympathetic towards the early sages of Judaism, whom he perceives as esoteric Christians. As I will argue, in viewing these sages as Christians, Abner, himself a converted Christian, is interpreting the Jewish sources too broadly. The Midrashim cited by Abner, which concern a certain plurality within God's essence, do not necessarily indicate a Trinitarian position. In fact, a certain tension between God's unity on the one hand and some aspects of Divine plurality on the other was also acknowledged by a host of Jewish thinkers, first and foremost by Maimonides. This last point, in fact, was acknowledged by Abner himself.

Haliva begins by illustrating Abner's critical stance towards Judaism. She presents a powerful accusation made by Abner against the Jewish sages, formulated in particularly harsh language. Abner refers to the 'ten evil commandments' that are 'juxtaposed to the ten commandments.' The Oral Law, he argues, was made 'to injure others,' and he concludes with the following assertion: 'This is what happened to them: just as they declared that from the logic of the Talmud it is permitted to steal and to bear false witness for such and such a reason, they were robbed and false testimony was given about them for those very reasons.'[1] These are undoubtedly harsh criticisms, directed at the moral code (and core) of the Jews as manifestly expressed in the ultimate source of Jewish law, the Babylonian Talmud.

Yet in addition to this highly critical stance and derogatory depiction of the Jewish moral position, Haliva cites another view expressed by Abner concerning the teaching of the Jewish sages, a view less explicit, yet far more favorable. According to this view, the sages of the Talmud were in fact secretly Christians. Haliva correctly notes that both Rabbi Simlai and Rabbi Levi, in the Midrashim cited by Abner, appear to conceal a secret concerning God's plurality and the plural form *Elohim*. Furthermore, in these Midrashim, she observes that 'Abner interprets [this] in such a way as to justify his claim that the Jewish sages embraced Christian doctrines but had to conceal this fact from the Jewish community.' Yet it should be noted that in the passages cited by Abner, there is no reference to Christianity, but to a certain tension concerning Divine unity, which is not to be equated with an allusion to the

---

1 *Teshuvot la-Meḥaref*, 33b.

Christian Trinity. In other words, a Trinitarian Christian model is not the only model which can resolve the tension between God's unity and certain aspects of plurality associated with God. We find one such example in Maimonides. As Abner himself acknowledges, Maimonides offered a model for reconciling unity and plurality with regard to the Divine in his *Guide*:

> Every attribute that is found in the books of the deity, may He be exalted, is therefore an attribute of His action and not an attribute of His essence [...]. There accordingly is not, as these people believe, an essence composed of diverse notions. [...]
>
> Thus it has become clear to you that these attributes too are not to be considered in reference to His essence, but in reference to the things that are created. (*Guide*, I:53; Pines' translation)

Maimonides does not see a concession to Trinitarian ideas in this, and in one of the preceding chapters he says explicitly:

> If, however, someone believes that He is one, but possesses a certain number of essential attributes, he says in his words that He is one, but believes Him in his thought to be many. This resembles what the Christians say: namely, that He is one but also three, and that the three are one. (*Guide* I:50; Pines' translation)

What is relevant here is the general structure of Maimonides' reasoning. Maimonides does not reject the idea of God's attributes altogether, but only the idea of essential plurality. In other words, he interprets—and thus implicitly accepts—certain authoritative passages which seem to jeopardize God's unity, but without succumbing to a Trinitarian model or any similar model which relies on essential differentiation in God.

In sum, this reply seeks to highlight that the tension in Abner's response, which Haliva attempts to resolve, is to a large extent an artificial one. The presence of an esoteric Christian position, embraced by the Jewish scholars and hinted at Abner, is highly contentious, and is not based on solid textual grounds—at least not in the Midrashim cited above. This is not to undermine the value of Abner's general direction nor Haliva's interpretation. The reply does, however, point to the strong ideological undercurrent in Abner's response to Polqar, of the kind that one may indeed expect in a medieval treatise which bears, to a very large extent, a polemical nature.

Paolo L. Bernardini

Fighting For the Truth? Some Remarks on the Real Meaning of the Early Modern Jewish-Christian Controversies and the Briel-Pinamonti Polemics (1694–1702)

This paper aims to shed some light on the 'real meaning'—or rather the nature—of the Jewish-Christian polemics in the early modern age. While I have most recently been working on Jacob ben Amram's *Porta Veritatis* (1634–40), providing an edition of one of its codices, I will refer in this paper to another polemic, the Briel-Pinamonti controversy, which took place between the end of the seventeenth and the beginning of the eighteenth century. Father Giuseppe Pinamonti (1622–1703), a rather prolific author and 'ghost writer' for the much more famous Paolo Segneri, wrote a great number of theological works. *La sinagoga disingannata* (Bologna and Rome, 1694) met with a certain success (the second edition was produced in 1754 and it was reprinted in 1911), but also with a fierce attack from the Mantuan Rabbi Leone ben Eliezer Briel (1643–1722), who wrote a confutation of Pinamonti's work in 1702. Never published, Briel's work, *La sinagoga disingannata dagli inganni di P. Pinamonti*, circulated widely in manuscript and is probably the most important of his works. Before addressing Judah Briel's replies to Giuseppe Pinamonti, however, I will briefly reflect on the nature of theological controversies in general. This preliminary reflection will allow me to approach Briel's work and the entire controversy, attempting to offer some new ideas in order to approach both it and the general spiritual environment in which the controversy took place.[1]

---

[1] This case has been studied in depth by Piergabriele Mancuso, who provided the first (and only) edition of the work by Judah Briel, or Leone Brielli, in response to *La sinagoga disingannata* by Father Pinamonti. The work is preserved in six codices, henceforth quoted as S. or its complete and critical edition, see Piergabriele G. Mancuso, "Evangelizzazione gesuitica e tattiche di difesa a Mantova tra Sei e Settecento sotto il Rabbinato di Yehudah Leone Brielli," *Materia Giudaica* 19.1–2 (2014): 331–445. I am most grateful to Dr Mancuso for having shown me his critical edition in advance, well before its publication. I first encountered Judah (Leone) Briel (Brielli) in the early 1990s when working on the Jewish community of Mantua. There are a number of similarities between the *Porta Veritatis* and Briel's work, although it is likely that Brielli never read Jacob bem Amram's text. As for the *Porta Veritatis*, while my edition of the text is close to completion, I would like to refer in the meantime to my essay published in this volume and to my other more historical and less theoretical paper devoted to the *Porta*: "Mysteries at the Gate of Truth. A Reappraisal of the *Porta Veritatis* (1634–1640)," *Nuova Rivista Storica* 101.1 (2017): 65–82. Before Mancuso approached the theme, the only publication about the Pinamonti-Briel controversy—still extremely valid from the theoretical point of view—was William Horbury, "Judah Briel and Seventeenth-Century Jewish Anti-Christian Polemics in Italy," in idem, *Jews and Christians in Contact and Controversy* (Edinburgh: T&T Clark, 1998): 276–96. As Horbury pointed out, the main reference for this work, which is often used, is Cardoso's *Excelencias*, which the author sent to Briel, who replied with a poem in Hebrew. Briel uses Cardoso extensively when dealing with miracles (a crucial passage in the structure of the text) and in many other passages. Briel writes—contrary to Pinamonti—in a very uncertain Italian, devoid of any style and occasionally

If there is a spiritual domain where 'truth' must be absolute, it is religion. Truth derives from a single source, the word of God, which, by definition and *per se*, cannot and may not be questioned. From a certain point of view, we find the same dogmatic truth in classical Aristotelian philosophy, where the principle of contradiction, A=A, is as dogmatic as the theological truth of the word of God. It cannot be denied, 'cannot be outraged;' it is an absolute, dogmatic truth whose stability is both at the *theoretical* and at the *moral* level. Interpreters are asked to identify the 'real meaning' of the word of God when it is subject to obscurity and contradiction. They cannot alter the meaning when it is clear, as it often is. Even when, in the Renaissance, the truth was often conceived as a product (daughter) of time—*veritas filia temporis*—it lost its immediacy, but not its content; the same truth that was hidden becomes evident over time.[2]

It has not changed, it is only 'revealed.' 'Revelation' is a key word, and not only in the domain of theology. There is a lay form of revelation 'by arguments' and a correct usage of it, even within a purely speculative and non-theological context. In the Middle Ages, the Jewish-Christian controversies were deeply philosophical, for their authors used logical along with theological arguments. From renewed research on the 'history of emotions,' it is clear that there was a strong 'emotional adherence' to the arguments by both contenders. Emotions also play an important role in the early modern controversies, where, occasionally, references to the current philosophical debates emerge, although there are strong similarities, in the construction of the arguments as well as of the controversial treatises themselves, with their antecedents from the Middle Ages.[3] The line of continuity is stronger than the breaks, and quite often contemporary authors are not even mentioned in the controversies, or are only marginally cited, as if their relevance to the arguments could be easily dismissed or is quite remote.

The Jewish authors often reacted to Christian provocations, although occasionally they stood up to defend their own faith without any particular reason or *casus belli*. The dimension of public controversy was also progressively lost. If a public controversy, as a contest for the truth, had quite a lot to do with a theatrical conception of life, where dialectic fights with arguments and the final victory is often left in the

---

very poor. Sometimes, it is difficult to understand what he really meant, even for a native Italian speaker. In the translations of some passages, I have tried to render its obscure Italian in English, so the translation is far from being completely adherent to the letter of the text, although I have tried to preserve the meaning of the sentences.

2 I am working on a manuscript provisionally entitled "The Daughter of Earth and Time. Truth in the Renaissance," which will be completed, *si Deus vult*, by the end of 2017.

3 It is worth noting that the new discipline of the history of emotions is growing all over the world. Most recently, the Society for the History of Emotions was created in Australia. I deem that emotions play a substantial role in the controversies we are discussing, and theoretical tools coming from the history of emotions as a new discipline can provide important ideas for new approaches to this old theme. I wish to thank my colleague and friend Professor Giovanni Tarantino, University of Melbourne, ARC Centre for the History of Emotions, for this information.

hands of the public, a merely 'bookish' controversy was, in a way, blind and most often completely devoid of an audience. The reason for this is that in many cases Jewish books against Christianity remained in manuscript, and even as manuscripts, they had a very limited circulation. Occasionally, they did not circulate at all. With no stage, or even a public, a Jewish anti-Christian work remained a 'dead letter,' although possibly it had a real benefit as a sort of 'stream of consciousness' for the author who wrote it. It was a personal and intellectual as well as, once again, an 'emotional benefit.'[4] So, both Pinamonti's and Briel's works are aimed at Christians and Jews alike; they are not simple apologetic works, but aim to convince all their readers of the truth of their statements. Briel denounces the surge of 'atheism' as a threat to both religions.

In many ways, the genre of the anti-Christian treatise or pamphlet was a mere exercise of logic and erudition, with an extremely limited circulation. If written by a rabbi, he demonstrated to his community that he was indeed able 'to defend Judaism' and to oppose counter-arguments, possibly solid and grounded in the Holy Scripture, against those who attacked Judaism and the Jews. This was probably enough within the Jewish community and was what the Jews required from him. It was not necessary, therefore, to publish the work. Furthermore, it could be extremely difficult to find a publisher prepared to accept the risk.

The speculative dimension of those works is normally inferior to their practical aim. They could be written in cold blood, as exercises of a speculative and erudite mind, or, more often, because there was an immediate threat to the community (more than a generic intellectual threat to the tenets and the very essence of Judaism). Contrary to the controversial literature of the Catholics and Protestants, of extreme importance from Luther's time up until the end of the seventeenth century, there were no major events or upheavals at stake. However, every apologetic work was normally meant as a weapon of defence against immediate threats, particularly when the force of a Catholic preacher's arguments was able to convert, or bring close to conversion, a large number of Jews. Acute heirs to a long medieval tradition, the Jesuits, this new, vibrant, brilliant, and incisive cohort of soldiers of Christ, were a major threat for the Jews. During the difficult period of the last half—and particularly the last quarter—of the seventeenth century, the Jesuits actively pursued a conversionist policy in Italy and all over the world. Clearly, the Jews were their main target, at least where they were present.

In those polemics, when Jewish authors defended their faith, the immediate needs—to prevent mass conversions, even occasionally expulsion, and so on—were

---

[4] This is also true for the Christian authors, who, by writing these anti-Jewish polemics, were looking for a rational as well as an emotional confirmation of their own faith. The degree of 'passion' in Pinamonti's writing caught the attention of James Joyce, as is well known. On Joyce as a reader of Pinamonti, see Vincent J. Cheng, "James Joyce and the (Modernist) Hellmouth," in *Hell and Its Afterlife: Historical and Contemporary Perspectives*, eds. Margaret Toscano and Isabel Moreira (Farnham: Ashgate, 2010): 165–174.

stronger than the merely theoretical needs, to provide readers with absolute genuine and incontestable arguments based on the purest doctrine and speculation. The issue was not to demonstrate the *veritatem religionis Christianae* or the *veritatem religionis Judaicae*, but to demonstrate that some legends, held to be 'true,' were not such. All the theoretical content of merely speculative disputes—such as those which involved philosophers such as Leibniz, Malebranche, Spinoza etc.—were either lost or not present at all in the Jewish apologetic works. The matters at stake were much more concrete and contingent. Some arguments were merely historical and deprived of any theoretical side. Some arguments were more logical, but never went so far as to deny the entire 'truth' of the opposite religion and to reduce the adversary to *nihil*. Masters of rhetoric, the Jesuits had to be opposed by authors who had the same skills in rhetoric and eloquence. The adherence to one or to the other, opposite thesis was often—or rather could often be—more 'emotional' than 'rational,' instinctive rather than theoretical. The Catholics aimed to convert the Jews. The contrary was not true. In a way, this hampered the ability of Jewish authors, often confined to the Ghetto and unable to obtain all the works they needed to write sound apologetic texts, to provide solid counter-arguments. But in general, counter-arguments were solid and 'passionate'—once again, we enter the realm of the history of emotions—enough to give substance to lengthy and profound works. Unfortunately, in most cases those works remained unpublished and unnoticed even by those whom they aimed to attack and debunk. The game was not a fair one.

Rabbi vs. Jesuit, however, was a battle of titans. The new religious company and the heirs of the oldest revealed religion—the 'tragic couple' with much shared history and occasionally a common destiny of 'expulsion' in the eighteenth century—shared a passion for offering and constructing their arguments, reviving the passion that had been alive and well in the Middle Ages, during the public controversies. In polemical works, and in most of the Christian-Jewish polemics in general, the space reserved for 'passion' is almost equal to that reserved for 'reason.' A false argument, prone to be debunked by the adversary, is usually based on the intention to lie, on bad faith, and on the writer's sheer hatred of the Jews and their religion. For Briel, the misinterpretation of the biblical and talmudic texts is derived from the fact that the Christian interpreters are often driven by the most anti-rational force, the power of hatred; 'la forza dell'odio' in Italian. This goes well beyond any logical and dialectical reasoning.[5]

Let us analyse some of the passages where the word 'odio' ('hatred,' 'hate'), is present in the lengthy apologetic work by Briel:

> It is a matter of pain for a wise man, when the opposite sect tries to completely alter his own reasonings, turning them into the most blasphemous and erroneous things, when, in reality,

---

[5] See James W. Bernauer and Robert A. Maryks, eds., *The Tragic Couple: Encounters between Jews and Jesuits* (Leiden and Boston: Brill, 2014), particularly Gianfranco Miletto's essay in this collection, "Jesuit Influence on Italian Jewish Culture in the 16th and 17th Centuries," see *ibidem*, 103–123.

it is clear that those arguments and the relevant way of reasoning are entirely metaphorical and allegorical. They had much more fortune with the Heathens and the Christians, by the way, all peoples who borrowed from the Jews whatever beauty and goodness is in their own doctrines. There are so many allegories and metaphors in the classical authors, Aesop and Ovid, and they all praise those works, although they are all metaphorical and often filled with impious and blasphemous phrases, but they do not want to accept that there are also metaphors and allegories in Hebrew works, and they take everything according to the literal sense, which is not the appropriate one. So did Aristotle, a bad pupil, with his Master Plato in his work on Ideas. Oh, how mighty is the power of Hatred that shades the light of reason and forces us to see poorly those things that are enlightened by the purest divine Truth.[6]

Here, Briel defends the metaphorical and allegorical interpretation of the Jewish texts, which is as legitimate for them as it was and is legitimate for the classical texts, for example, Ovid and Aesop. Only the 'power of hate' forces the Christian interpreters to see only the literal meaning and base their attacks of Judaism on it. Furthermore, it also legitimates a degree of 'error' in the writings of a talmudic author. There are also quite a few errors in Christian authors. Hatred, an irrational element, prevents the correct reading of the text. The force of hatred not only prevents a correct understanding of the metaphors and allegories in the sacred text, but also forces misreading where the correct sense is literal, such as in the case of Leviticus, with references to the obligation of marriage of the brother's widow:

> It is laughable to state that the Talmud suggests marriage to your own sister or daughter, as if the doctors of the law wanted to destroy the same Law they were meant to preserve; it is all but slander, *invented by Hatred*, as if it was legitimate for a man to marry the daughter of his own sister. It is all based on false translations, for the translator did not know Hebrew, even very simple Hebrew, for the real meaning of that passage is clear even to children.[7]

---

6 S., 357: 'Ma è Infelicità troppo grande d'un savio che La setta nimica vog[li]a tirare in sentimenti ridicoli, Ingiuriosi, et Impossibili i suoi raggionamenti, quando effettivam[en]te è Infallibile esser quelli mettafforici, et allegorici, in somma hebbero piu fortuna appresso i Cristianj, i Gentili, che gl'Hebrei, da quali presero q[uan]to di buono, e bello, hano nelle loro Dottrine, Li passano da loro gl'Appologi d'Esopo, le metamorfosi d'Ovidio con amiratione di quei grand'huominj, che fecero cosi virtuose compositionj, per le moralità e Dottrine, che rachiudono, se bene nell'apparente , hano coperte non solo Improprie, ma sacrilighe e pure non vogliono tollerare i discorsi mettaforicj che gl'Ebrei hano con sensi piu reconditi e fondati nelle sacre carte , e vogliono malamente, e litteralmente intenderle per malevolenze, e derisione, come si dice haver fatto il Cattivo discepolo Aristotele con Platone suo maestro nel trattato dell'Idee, *Oh forza dell'odio*, [my italics] ch'offusca il lume dell'Intelletto in modo tale che non vede gl'oggetti ben che Illuminati dalla fulgentissima Luce della Verità [...].'

7 S., 364: 'E ridicolo poi il dire ch'il Talmud stabilisce esser opera di merito il pigliarsi per moglie la sua propria sorella, o la figliola, ne so, come posse credersi ne anco che i veri professori della Legge di D:o volessero appertamente distruggere la med[esi]ma Legge, che conservino, e qui devo altamente esclamare, e chiamare tutti i Dotti, acio possino argomentare giustam[en]te dalla parte al tutto esser mere calunie *Inventate dall'odio* [my italics], quelle che si dicono dall'autore, contro la Dotrina del Talmud, hor sentite, dicesi collà ch'è opera meritoria il prendere per moglie la figlia di sua sorella, puotendosj, secondo la legge di D:o nel livitico maritare il Zio con la nipote, e chi trasportò questo

Finally, the Christian authors, imbued with hatred towards the Jews, attribute to them the same hatred they personally feel by a typical psychological reversal of the arguments:

> As for what the Author [Pinamonti] says about the hatred felt by the Jews towards the Christians and Christ, he offers the cases of children allegedly killed by Jews, and he says that those killings actually happened, for the Jews were condemned for them. As a matter of fact, every religion says evil things about the other religions and hates them, but the cases he brings forth are but inventions, and the depositions against the Jews were all false, dictated by hatred. It is not the fault of the judges, for they judged according to the depositions, *iuxta allegata et probata*, and they did not possess divine inspiration so as to be able to know hell on earth and enter therefore in the righteous Truth.[8]

If we go looking for merely rational arguments and reasoning, the references to logic, as well as those to reason, are few. The example of an irrational argument *par excellence* is the incarnation of God in Christ, an argument shared by the whole Jewish apologetic tradition:

> The author [Pinamonti] admits that he cannot understand through reason how God could become a man. The Jew does not believe that, and he is not obliged to this belief by reason or by authority. On the contrary, he deems that the humanisation of God is impossible; it is a contradiction for what is indivisible to be divided, and this is just one of the arguments that prove its impossibility.[9]

At the very end of the long confutation, Briel makes another interesting appeal to 'reason':

> When a Jew appears in front of the Divine Tribunal, he will be able to defend his own faith, for he will say to God that he followed the law that God himself has given in a solemn way, so that there was never in history a more abundant people, all contemplating the same God, as it is said

---

Testo ha detto con Vizio, ò con Ignoranza Crassissima sua figliola, e sua sorella, anzi ben considerando si scorge haver cosi fatto vitiosamente poi che quanto che fosse Ignorante, ò Imperito della Santa Lingua, non poteva dare tall' interpretat[io]ne alle parole del Testo chiaro anco a Fanciulli, e principianti nella notitia dell'Heb[rai]co.'

8 S., 413 (and see also Mancuso's introduction, 338): 'Quanto al resto che và dicendo l'autore in questo unumero dell'Odio che portano gli Hebrei al Cristo e Cristiani, adducendo alcuni casi d'Innocenti uccisi da hebrei, provandoli dalle pene ripportate da trasgressori; si dice ch'ogni religgione per il piu odia, e dice male delle religgioni contrarie, ed i casi addotti furono inventioni de malevoli contrarij, che volsero sfogare la loro Rabbia contro gl'Ebrei, onde deposero falsamente, ed'impegnati sostenessero le depositioni, non però se ne Incolpavano i Giudici, per che giudicavano iuxta allegata et probata, e non havevano spirito Divino di poter conoscere L'Inferno degl'huomini, e penetrare nella Giusta Verità [...].'

9 S., 440: 'Gia che confessa l'autore, non poter con la ragione penetrare, come dio, potesse farsi huomo, L'hebreo, non lo vuol credere; non trovandosi obbligato a tal Credenza, ne dalla raggione, ne dalle autorità, anzi stima impossibile L'humanarsi una sol delle persone Divine, essendo contraditorio l'esser Indivisibile, e diviso, appresso ad'altri motivi che ne fanno conoscere L'Insussistenza [...].'

in Deuteronomy 4, that law will never be repealed, a law that God declared to be the most perfect, and as in the Psalms (18; 19 for us), perfectly adhering to reason; the Jew will say to God that in spite of all the persecutions, difficulties, and miseries, he always lived in that faith and never wanted to listen to things that are against reason and against the authority of the Prophets.[10]

In order to prove his arguments, therefore, Briel attributes a good deal of 'irrationality' to the adversary. Hatred plays a fundamental role in Pinamonti's argument, but so too does the goal to convince in order to convert, not to convince for the sake of a pure truth. The combination of 'reason' and 'revelation'—in an age in which free thinkers were questioning the same ratio of revelation, considered as a myth—seals Briel's argument in a strong and unbeatable mechanism. He is rather diffident towards a merely philosophical argumentation. This is made clear by the references to philosophy in the text, which are normally negative:

> He [Pinamonti] says that the Law of Moses does not teach that much on the perfections of God; it merely teaches that God is One, who cares about everything, gives rewards and punishments, and is holy and perfect, completely; I do not know what more a philosopher might add to this with his own sophisms. On the contrary, a philosopher can meet with heresies, an occurrence not present for the believer, who stays with God and does not engage himself with human speculations.[11]

As has been noted by Mancuso, Brielli's rigid defence of Jewish orthodoxy counted among its targets not only Pinamonti, but also all the Jews who, devoted to mysticism, Kabbalah, and messianic views, were potential 'Trojan horses' within those same Jewish communities. Here, the key concept of this polemical skirmish, the 'inganno'—'deceit,' but also 'deception,' 'trick,' or, as Professor Horbury suggests, 'enchantment'—plays another major role. 'Inganno' can be everywhere, not only in the literal interpretation of some talmudic passages, not only in texts and arguments, but also in souls and hearts. And here the controversy appears to be well rooted in the Baroque sensibility, where 'inganno' and 'simulation' as well 'dissimulation' played a major role.

---

10 S., 440: 'L'Hebreo quando comparirà avanti al Tribunal divino, renderà buona ragione della sua fede, dicendo, sig: Iddio io hò seguitato la legge, data da voi con Sollenità tale, che non hà pari, dove mai si trovò popolo si numeroso, tutto sollevato alla visione d'Iddio, come nel Deutoronomio cap: 4, legge che non fu mai abrogata, legge dichiarata da voi perfettissima, come in davide Salmo 18 (a noi 19) legge unniforme alla raggione, e non ostante le persecuzioni, turbolenze, captività, e [f. 151b] miserie, hò vissuto sempre costante in questa Fede, et non hò volluto credere cose repugnanti, et alla ragione, et all'autorità de vostri Profeti [...].'

11 S., 356: 'Dice ancora che la Legge di Moisè poco insegna delle perfettioni di D:o et basta ch'insegna, che ci è un sol Id: autore della tutta providente , premiante e castigante, santiss[i]mo, e perfett[issi]mo, ne sò che possa Intendere di piu un filosofo colle sue sottigliezze, anzi con questa puo urtare nello scoglio di qualh'eresia cosa che non succeede a chi stà con la parola di D:o, e non aplica ad humane speculat[io]ni.'

If we analyse the use of the word 'verità,' truth, we see it on many occasions with different meanings, ranging from the moral to the theological, from the theoretical to the practical. As I have said, my paper is merely an attempt to invite scholars to reflect on the 'hidden meaning(s)' of a controversy, or, in general, of Jewish-Christian polemics.

Also, the structure of the polemics is not systematic. As a matter of fact, Briel does not confute a large number of points in Pinamonti's work. Why? Does he agree with Pinamonti's point, or does he simply not deem that those criticisms and attacks are worth a reply? This is difficult to establish. Perhaps there were points of contact in the two 'enemies' about some 'errors' in Judaism, not so much in orthodoxy, but certainly in post-talmudic reading and interpretations.

The means of proving the 'truth' are twofold and only very occasionally based on reason. In most cases, authorities play a leading role in the construction of the truth, not only religious authorities and the Old Testament, in Hebrew, but often lay political authorities: Charles V, denying the blood libel accusation, certainly not a 'thing of the past,' or felt as such, at the end of the seventeenth century.

Jonathan Garb
Doubt and Certainty in Early Modern Kabbalah

Maimonides Lecture on 3 May, 2017

I would like to open with a homage to a great German writer, Herman Hesse, whose books are pervaded with mysticism. In his magnum opus, *The Glass Bead Game (Magister Ludi)*, we find the following dialogue between the young student Joseph Knecht, the future master of the glass bead game, and his mentor, the old music master:

> 'Oh, if it were only possible to find understanding' Joseph exclaimed. 'If only there were a dogma to believe in. Everything is contradictory [...] there are no certainties anywhere. Everything can be interpreted one way and then again interpreted in the opposite sense [...] isn't there any truth?' [...] The Master, after a short silence replies thus: 'There is truth, my boy. But the doctrine you desire, absolute, perfect dogma [...] does not exist. Nor should you long for a perfect doctrine, my friend. Rather, you should long for the perfection of yourself. The deity is within *you*, not in ideas and books.'[1]

Joseph's outcry is shared by textual scholars, bewildered by the endless contradictions of possible interpretations. As we shall see today, the Master's response, as is fitting for a book that prominently mentions German Pietism, follows the path of the Ḥasidim, who internalised theosophy, thus enabling them to embrace doubt. Or, as Hesse describes Knecht's more mature understanding:

> For even as he was familiarizing himself with the ever more recondite mysteries [...] his doubts had by no means been silenced. He had already learned by experience that faith and doubt belong together, that they govern each other like inhaling and exhaling.[2]

The studies of Giuseppe Veltri, and more generally recent discussions here at the Maimonides Centre, have alerted us to the pivotal role of scepticism in the formation of modern Jewish discourse. Veltri and others (such as Richard Popkin, Yossi Chajes, and Allison Coudert) have pointed out the role of conversos such as Uriel da Costa, who experienced the relativity of religious identity and contributed to the proliferation of sceptical approaches. One should also mention here the intriguing connections which were already being made between Kabbalah and atheism in the seventeenth century, as discussed by Yossi Schwartz. To these should be joined Yaakov Dweck's forthcoming discussion of the role of scepticism in resistance to the spread

---

[1] Herman Hesse, *The Glass Bead Game (Magister Ludi)*, trans. Richard and Clara Winston (Harmondsworth, UK: Penguin, 1973): 79–80.
[2] *Ibidem*, 127.

of the Sabbatean movement. However, as we shall see, I wish to consider the presence of this theme in even earlier stages of modernisation.

The different ratios of doubt and certainty clearly distinguish pre-modern Kabbalah from that of the last few centuries. As Elliot R. Wolfson has shown, the use of the term *vadday* ('for sure' in colloquial English) marks zoharic rhetoric and exegesis. In tandem, one should note the recurrence of the phrase *bli safeq* ('without doubt') in influential texts such as the pseudo-Rabad commentary on *Sefer Yeṣirah*, actually penned by R. Joseph ben Shalom Ashkenazi, who may well have taken part in the formation of the *Sefer ha-Zohar*. This is not to say that this locution is absent in major texts in modern Kabbalah, *Sefer ha-Tanya* by R. Shneur Zalman of Liadi being one striking instance. Nonetheless, it is doubt, rather than its absence, that one encounters in some of the better-known modern literatures.

Three examples should suffice. One, discussed quite recently as part of a wider study by Shaul Magid, is found in the nineteenth-century *Liqquṭei Moharan* by R. Nahman of Bratzlav: in an oft-discussed passage in *Torah* 64, he differentiates between the questions and quandaries—*mevukhot*—arising from the primordial rupture of the breaking of the vessels, which can be resolved, and those stemming from the seeming absence of divinity created by the *ṣimṣum*, or contraction, and the resultant 'empty space.' The correct response to the latter *qushiot*, or difficulties, is silent faith, rather than any discursive effort. It is true that this passage does not employ the term 'doubt,' yet *sfeqot*, or doubts, appear, alongside confusion, in a parallel discussion (which is not the parallel that Magid cites from the same section) of the seeming absence of God in the second part of *Liqquṭei Moharan* (*Torah* 12). Nahman's references to *eppiqorsut*, translatable here as 'heresy,' clearly disclose the historical background of this teaching, and many of his other teachings, in contending with the Haskalah, or Jewish Enlightenment.

Our second example is that of the radical ḥasidic teacher R. Mordekhai Joseph Leiner of Izbica. As I have written briefly elsewhere,[3] in Leiner's psychological typology of religious characters (which predates Jung by several decades), he grants both prominence and legitimation to the religious personality characterised by constant doubt. I have selected a discussion that I did not cite in my book: this homily is blatantly national (and should be read in light of Elliot Wolfson's foundational studies of the attitude towards Gentiles in Kabbalah). Although, as a rule, one who encounters doubts and successfully clarifies them 'for the good' is greater than one who avoids doubt, this is only true of the 'seed of Jacob,' for God only 'clarifies Israel for the good' so that even converts are forbidden to experience doubt.[4] In other words, the national divide is established partly as a bulwark against the increasing encroachment of doubt. More generally, it should be stressed that Leiner's positive

---

[3] Jonathan Garb, *The Chosen Will Become Herds: Studies in Twentieth Century Kabbalah* (New Haven: Yale University Press, 2009): 84.
[4] Mordekhai Joseph Leiner, *Mei ha-Shiloaḥ* [Hebrew], vol. 1 (Bnei Brak: Mishor, 1995): 33–34.

assessment of doubt echoes similar statements in other schools branching off from the Seer of Lublin, R. Jacob Isaac Horowitz.

A final late modern instance is located in *Orot ha-Qodesh*, a compilation of mystical reflections by the twentieth-century author R. Abraham Isaac Ha-Kohen Kook. In texts assembled in the first volume, Kook writes of the relativity of certainty, of the ascending and increasing degree of certainty in each world and each individual. Typically for such a unitary thinker, Kook (reworking a text from *Tiqqunei Zohar*) stresses the unification of the *nahar ulay* ('river of maybe') with the river flowing from Eden, from the *Yesod*, or foundation of certainty; in kabbalistic terms, the phallic aspect of the higher feminine, *Binah*. For him, the source, higher up in the layers of *Binah*, is that of both certainty and doubt. In other words, Kook aspires, in an almost Zen-like fashion, to transcend the differentiation between doubt and certainty. At this source, doubts are transformed into joyful positivity, which reveals their true interiority. Yet in his dialectical poetics, when a certain level aspires to a level of certainty that is inappropriate for it, this necessitates a fall, a rupture, and an explosion (in other words, the breaking of the vessels that begins below *Binah*) until it can re-ascend to the source in a resurrection-like process.[5] While R. Nahman contended with the beginnings of secularisation, Kook repeatedly explicitly engaged with its full-fledged form.

Yet I would like to move away from these more obvious cases and interrogate the first stirrings of doubt in early modern Kabbalah. In this phase, doubt is less a psychological experience or cognitive event, as it is for the ḥasidic writers and R. Kook, and rather pertains to ontology. I believe that the point of transition can be found around the time of Kant's sharp differentiation between the ontological and epistemological realms, namely in the eighteenth century. Clear formulations of the embedded doubt in the very pattern of divine revelation can be found in the circle of R. Moses Hayyim Luzzatto, one of a set of fellowships whose writings became foundational for subsequent schools of modern Kabbalah. He also belonged to the same family as the seventeenth-century author R. Simone Luzzatto, whose sceptical stance was addressed in one of Veltri's above-mentioned studies.

In his most important kabbalistic treatise, *Adir ba-Marom*, Luzzatto discusses the highly exalted divine aspect known in the *Idrot* section of the *Zohar* (and its canonical sixteenth-century Lurianic interpretation) as *reisha de lo ityada* (acronym: *radla*), the 'unknown head.' For Luzzatto, who reads such mythical, anthropomorphic terms as metaphors for historiosophical dialectic, *radla* signifies the nexus between the temporal *hanhagah*, or divine guidance of the world, and eternity. Thus, when we learn of the doubts in *radla* in Lurianic Kabbalah, this does not mean that it is possible that these aspects have no being. Rather, *ha-kol yesh* ('all is'). However, they currently shine 'by way of doubt,' while in the eschaton they will 'shine by way of

---

[5] Abraham Isaac Kook, *Orot ha-Qodesh* [Hebrew], vol. 1 (Jerusalem: Mossad Ha-Rav Kook, 1963): 205–207.

certainty.' Elaborating on this terse, axiomatic statement, Luzzatto writes that in the present the vision of the divine lights 'always comes in a doubtful manner' due to their constant movement and complex re-combination. In this constant flux (echoing Judah Muscato's image of steam, as discussed by Veltri), certainty is unavailable, and this is why they transcend human apprehension. In sum, epistemological doubt is a product of the present deep structure of the divine realm, with the promise of its transformation into certainty being part of the Messianic horizon.[6] In other words, Moses Hayyim Luzzatto goes beyond his relative Simone in relocating doubt from human knowledge to the divine realm. Our text echoes an earlier (1730) epistle by Luzzatto, demonstrating 'a small part of the way of the *Idra*' (addressed to R. Isaiah Basaan, one of his early teachers), where he confides that *radla* is seen differently from moment to moment, and thus 'gives birth to doubt.'[7] However, this is nonetheless a source of pleasure, as this is how the *radla* shine, given that they are unknown lights. In this earlier version of the commentary, composed around 1731–2, it appears that this is the nature of the light rather than being a problem.

Luzzatto's approach is fleshed out in an influential text, the so-called *Qelaḥ Pithei Ḥokhmah* ('138 Gates of Wisdom'), based on his writings but probably edited and expanded in ḥasidic circles towards the end of the century. Before reading this text, one should note the introduction to the text of *138 Gates* as found in one version (*Ma'amar ha-Wikkuaḥ*) of the larger work in which it is embedded, a debate between a kabbalist and a 'researcher,' or philosopher. Here, the author asks why we should know the list of doubts related to *radla* (as we shall see anon), and goes on to say that 'there must be a great root in this matter, which was mentioned for a very great secret.'[8] Now let us turn to our main text (influenced by formulations by the sixteenth-century kabbalist R. Meir Ibn Gabbay):

> The head that is not known is one light, where all the connections stand [...] however, it is a light which is not perceived or grasped at all. And whoever looks at it will have several unresolved doubts, for it does not appear that all the connections are found in it, but rather that it is a kind of light that cannot be grasped. And indeed, one cannot see its content, for sometimes it seems that there is one connection in it and sometimes it seems that there is another or even an opposite connection.
>
> So we find that even though we know that all the connections are found in it, the light itself stands in a manner that cannot be grasped and seems to be in another manner. And its power is that we do not know the guidance [of *radla*], because if we follow any given matter that is below in [the world of] emanation to locate its source in this head, we cannot find our hands and feet because we cannot discuss it at all. Rather, sometimes it appears thus, some-

---

6 Moses Hayyim Luzzatto, *Adir ba-Marom ha-Shalem* [Hebrew] (Jerusalem: Yosef Spinner, 1995): 188–189.
7 *Igrot Ramhal u-Bnei Doro* [Hebrew], ed. Mordechai Chriqui (Jerusalem: Makhon Ramhal, 2001): 67.
8 *Sha'arei Ramhal* [Hebrew], ed. H. Friedlander (Bnei Brak: Sifrayati, 1986): 71.

times otherwise, in a manner that we cannot grasp, and thus it is called the head that is not known.⁹

In the core text, which may be have been penned by Luzzatto, *radla* is a site of radical doubt, which manifests in a confusing and contradictory manner. Already here, we find a move away from temporality and messianism towards a version of the epistemological problematic, coupled with the limitations of language: 'is not perceived and grasped at all,' 'whoever looks at,' 'one cannot see,' or 'we cannot discuss it.' This trend is strengthened in the commentary, which is almost certainly later and Eastern European, perhaps ḥasidic:

> It seems difficult that we should not say that it has doubts, because, on the contrary, we said that it has all the connections, but the matter is that we are speaking about perception, that one who perceives its light cannot stand its light.¹⁰

This ḥasidic weakening of the radical ontological implications of *radla* can be found in a recently published testimony (*Early Years* by Boruch Oberlander and Elkanah Shmotkin) by the last Lubavitcher Rebbe, R. Menahem Mendel Schneerson, in the name of his father, the renowned kabbalist R. Levi Isaac Schneerson. According to the son, his father rejected the possibility of doubt in the divine structure and read the Lurianic formulations that we shall soon encounter as referring merely to the limits of human understanding.

It is now high time to turn to the Lurianic sources, which, as in many other matters, are formative and authoritative for most of modern kabbalistic writing. As noted above, as in many cases Luria's teachings take the form of creative exegesis of the mythical-anthropomorphic layer of the *Zohar*, the *Idrot*, or gatherings. One should recall here the important discussions by Susan Schreiner and Stefano Tutino, addressing at length the tension between certainty and doubt in mysticism and religious thought in general that was already present in the earlier parts of the sixteenth century.

The twelfth gate (concerning *'atiq*, the aspect of the 'ancient of days') of *Derekh 'Eṣ Ḥayyim*, the most widespread formulation of Luria's teachings, as transmitted by his main student R. Hayyim Vital and edited in Europe by R. Meir Poppers in the middle of the seventeenth century, discusses the connections (alluded to in the text that we just saw) that emend the primal trauma of the breaking of the vessels. At the end of the first chapter of the gate, the aspect of *radla* is discussed, and the term 'unknown' is interpreted as follows: its existence is known, but not its content. In listing the numerous doubts and *tmihot* ('wonders') that follow from this general question, the text (chapter four) gives mnemonic 'signs' for each one of them. The gate concludes (chapter five) thus: 'Here we have explained all the doubts that I

---

9 *Qelaḥ Pitḥei Ḥokhma* [Hebrew], ed. Joseph Spinner (Jerusalem: Ha-Mesora, 1987): 248.
10 *Ibidem*, 249.

heard from my teacher [Luria], and there are also innumerable and endless doubts, and I have not merited [hearing] them. And also, just like these doubts in ʿatiq, there are similar doubts in the rest of the order of emanation.'[11] In other words, doubt is both pervasive and infinite. Perhaps it is also built in, for Vital writes 'doubts in ʿatiq,' not 'about ʿatiq.' The entire gate is edited from Oṣrot Ḥayyim by Poppers' teacher, R. Jacob ben Hayyim Zemah, who was of converso origin. If one turns to Zemah's own conclusive rendition, in his Mevo Sheʿarim (Gate 3, part 1, chapter 1), we read as follows:

> And ʿatiq is known [in the Zohar] as the supreme head, which does not know and it is not known what is in this head [...] and it says 'does not know,' that is to say that this head, which is ʿatiq itself, cannot know and apprehend the ein sof ('infinite'), which is in this head. And relative to us it is said, 'and it is not known what is in this head.' And it is difficult, for it is obvious, if he himself does not know, all the more so that it is not known to us, but this means that we already know the reality of this head, what it is, that it is ʿAtiq, but what is inside this head is not known.[12]

Zemah's locution seems to be the source for Luzzatto's formulation, as we have seen, according to which doubt here has two layers. The deep level is that of the lack of divine autognosis. The lower level is relative to human comprehension and parallels the discussion in Oṣrot Ḥayyim. In a sense, Zemah, who assumes a lack of self-knowledge in the divine, is more radical than Luzzatto, who only goes so far as to embed doubt in the structure of divine revelation. In view of these sources, it is interesting that R. Joseph Ergas, an Italian kabbalist from the same milieu as Luzzatto, described Lurianic Kabbalah as putting an end to all doubts.

One should recall that Zemah's writings (Oṣrot Ḥayyim and Mevo Sheʿarim) were interpreted by R. Moses Zacuto, who corresponded with him, and his student R. Benjamin Kohen. In addition, Kohen's own student R. Moses Hayyim Luzzatto also wrote glosses on Oṣrot Ḥayyim. If this lineage is upheld, we can trace a central vein of the modern kabbalistic discourse on doubt to a writer of converso origin. However, once the Shaʿar ha-Haqdamot ('Gate of Introductions') in the original manuscript of ʿEṣ Ḥayyim is published later this year, joining the greater part of the manuscript's eight gates which have already been published, then we will be able to determine whether this text also appears in Vital's own writing and thus to uphold or refute this hypothesis.

I would like to cite one more textual source, in which radla is associated with silence as an epistemological stance in a Maimonidean manner. R. Kook's teacher and/or study partner R. Shlomo Elyashiv writes as follows on radla in his Leshem Shvo ve-Aḥlama: Haqdamot u-Sheʿarim, published in 1909 (not long after the period in which the two kabbalists studied together):

---

11 (Derekh) ʿEṣ Ḥayyim [Hebrew], ed. Meir Poppers (Jerusalem: Yerid ha-Sefarim, 2013): pt. 1, 60 A.
12 Jacob Zemah, Mevo Sheʿarim [Hebrew] (Jerusalem: Shaʿarei Yitzhak, 2016): 138.

But [of] *radla* there is no grasp (*tfisa*) [...] for it is totally removed [alluding here, based on an earlier discussion, to *'atiq*] and negated from apprehension, for it has no place and revelation [...] and to him silence is praise [based on Psalm 65:2].[13]

This, of course, is the famous proof-text for Maimonidean negative theology, and, as I have shown elsewhere, the *Zohar* gives this verse a negative slant, as belonging to the fallen state of exile, although the verse refers to Zion! Indeed, the *Guide for the Perplexed* is a central source, particularly for this book, but also elsewhere in Elyashiv's writing.

These texts call for further comparative, theoretical, and interdisciplinary examination (see, e.g., *Rig Veda* X, 129: 'Only he knows—or perhaps he does not know').[14] One tool which can be of value is psychoanalysis. Michael Feldman has written about patients who attempt to fill the analyst with doubt in the process of psychoanalysis. One goal here is to remove the discrepancy between analysand and analyst by acknowledging that they share a disturbing state of mind. From this point of view, statements about God's self-doubt could be an attempt to mitigate the discrepancy between an omniscient deity and an increasingly doubtful religious subject.

A concluding historical comment: the gradual prominence of doubt as a theme of modern kabbalistic discourse parallels similar developments in the field of Halakhah, especially around the eighteenth century. Here one should note especially *Quntres ha-Sfeqot* ('Treatise on Doubt') by R. Judah Kahana Heller (1750–1819), brother of the more famous Aryeh Leib ha-Kohen Heller (1745–1812), who devoted a large part of his early work *Shev Shma'tata* to the question of doubt and doubt of doubt (*sfeq sfeiqa*) and had familial connections with Prague. Actually, the treatise on doubt responds to an earlier discussion by R. Shabbetai Kohen in his *Taqfo Kohen*. Kohen also authored 'the rules of *sfeq sfeiqa*' within his *Siftei Kohen* supercommentary on the *Code of Law* (*Shulkhan 'Arukh*). These set the stage for the extremely prominent place given to the question of doubt in an early twentieth-century classic of Talmudic analytics, *Sha'arei Yosher* by R. Shimon Shkop, head of the Telz Yeshivah where Elyashiv studied. These mostly unstudied discussions should be placed alongside recent explorations of the origins of reasonable doubt (as in the writing of James Q. Whitman).

I would like to conclude with two comments pertaining to the history of Kabbalah scholarship and the role of German Jewry in this history. One is the need for closer attention to kabbalistic rhetoric, as recently exemplified in Roee Goldschmidt's work. The other relates to the reception of Gershom Scholem's *Major Trends in Jewish Mysticism*. Seemingly, the 1941 publication of this series of lectures marks the transition of the centre of Kabbalah scholarship, besides Jerusalem, from Germany to America. However, Scholem was disappointed by the published reviews and asked a colleague who shared his German background to respond to his book. This review

---
13 Shlomo Elyashiv, *Leshem Shvo ve-Ahlama: Haqdamot u-She'arim* [Hebrew] (Petrakov, 1909).
14 *The Rig Veda: An Anthology*, trans. Wendy Doniger O'Flaherty (London: Penguin, 1981): 26.

was published in an abbreviated form in *The Jewish Frontier*, and in full in Scholem's correspondence with Hannah Arendt (now also translated into Hebrew). Arendt claims in her review that Scholem has clarified, for the first time, the role of the Jews in the formation of modern man. *Inter alia*, she notes the connection between the modern *cogito* and the mystical subject, as well as the affinity between the scientific experimental approach and mystical experience. Following on from Arendt's observations, one should stress the contribution of Kabbalah to the interplay of doubt and certainty that characterises the evolution of modern subjectivity.

Wilhelm Schmidt-Biggemann
Lingua Adamica and Philology: The Rise and Destruction of a Concept[1]

Maimonides Lecture on 6 June, 2017

1 Introduction: The Origin of Language and the Shift of Credibility

The *lingua Adamica* seems, at first glance, to be a strange and merely academic subject.[2] However, one has to consider that the idea of the divine origin of language was **the** common theory in the Western tradition from the first century CE until the first half of the eighteenth century. So, for 1700 years, the theory of the *lingua Adamica* was a remarkably stable view of the notion of language and of its origin and potential. Yet from 1740/50 onwards, the question of how languages had emerged was discussed anew. Discussions of the genealogy of language led into a set of complicated arguments. In particular, the question of whether logic—which is evidently dependent on language and syntax—has a temporal index provoked unsolvable paradoxes. It is obvious that the question of whether there was a time when logic was not valid does not make any sense. Sensualist accounts of the origin of languages may perhaps have been capable of explaining the origin and etymology of single words, but they were unable to deliver a plausible account of how syntax and logic emerged. That is why, just at the apex of the discussions about the natural origin of language, the Berlin pastor Johann Peter Süßmilch (whose work on demographic statistics anticipated that of Malthus) wrote a booklet in 1766 entitled *Essay on a Proof That the First Language Had Its Origin Not from Mankind, But from the Creator*.[3] His argument was precisely this: that there is no plausible argument that can explain how logic could develop naturally. And indeed, the discussion on the origin of languages ended without a result: in 1832, the 'Société Linguistique' in Paris declared in its statutes that it would not permit any discussion of the origin of language.

---

[1] The first part of this lecture has already been published; see Wilhelm Schmidt-Biggemann, "*Lingua Adamica* and Speculative Philology: Philo to Reuchlin," in *For the Sake of Learning: Essays in Honor of Anthony Grafton*, eds. Ann Blair and Anja-Silvia Goeing (Leiden: Brill, 2016): 572–580. The English translation of this lecture was aided by Millay Hyatt and Andrew Johnston.
[2] Allison P. Coudert, ed., *The Language of Adam – Die Sprache Adams* (Wiesbaden: Harrassowitz, 1999). Philologically and philosophically, this book (including my own paper in it) does not really achieve its goal.
[3] Johann Peter Süßmilch, *Versuch eines Beweises, daß die erste Sprache ihren Ursprung nicht vom Menschen, sondern allein vom Schöpfer erhalten habe* (Berlin: Buchladen der Realschule, 1766; reprinted Köln: Themen, 1998).

OpenAccess. © 2017 Wilhelm Schmidt-Biggemann, published by De Gruyter. This work is licensed under the Creative Commons Attribution-NonCommercial-NoDerivatives 4.0 License.
https://doi.org/10.1515/9783110527971-018

Any discussion of the subject of the *lingua Adamica* inevitably leads to a second, even more intriguing question: how is it possible that philosophical and theological truths may lose their believability? In what way are they true? Is it plausible to say that Kant's transcendental philosophy, Hegel's objective idealism, or Wittgenstein's theory of *Sprachspiele* ('language games') is true? Or is it more convenient to say that they are plausible? But what can that mean? Plausibility does not mean anything more than meeting with approval. Is approval sufficient for the claim of philosophical truth, which arguments had in the past? The question that is most intriguing within the subject of the *lingua Adamica* can thus be phrased: how did the idea of the divine origin of language achieve and lose its credibility? Here I present the first part of this history of truth claims: the rise of concessions to the truth in philosophers from Philo to Reuchlin.

2 The Rise of Credibility: from Philo to Reuchlin

2.1 Philo's Cosmic and Earthly Adam

Few books have been provided with so many commentaries as the Book of Genesis; I think it is by far the most discussed book in the world. The reason for this astonishing fact is possibly that Genesis contains an account of the becoming of the world, of the creation of men, of the beginning of human wisdom, and of the origin of evil. All this is told in a brief, concise story, without any philosophical pretensions. Yet no other story has provoked so many philosophical interpretations. One of them is the subject of this paper, viz. the idea of the *lingua Adamica*: can such a discussion can be classified as philosophical at all, or is it merely a vain speculation?

The Book of Genesis has two accounts of man's creation. The first is:

> 'Let us make man in our image, after our likeness; and let them have dominion over the fish of the sea, and over the birds of the air, and over the cattle, and over all earth, and over every creeping thing that creeps upon the earth.' So God created man in his own image, in the image of God he created him; male and female he created them. (Genesis 1:26 f.)

The second account contains Adam's creation from dust and Eve's creation from Adam's rib:

> Then the Lord God formed a man of dust from the ground, and breathed into his nostrils the breath of life; and man became a living being. (Genesis 2:7) [...]

> So the Lord caused a deep sleep to fall upon the man, and while he slept took one of his ribs and closed up its place with flesh; and the rib which the Lord God had taken from the man he formed into a woman and brought her to the man. The man said, 'This at last is bone of my bones and

flesh of my flesh; she shall be called Woman, because she was taken out of Man.'⁴ (Genesis 2:21–23)

In between stands the passage concerning the *lingua Adamica* in Genesis 2:18–20:

> And the Lord God said, it is not good that the man should be alone; I will make him a help meet for him.
> And out of the ground the Lord God formed every beast of the field, and every fowl of the air; and brought them unto Adam to see what he would call them: and whatsoever Adam called every living creature, that was the name thereof.
> And Adam gave names to the cattle, and to the fowl of the air, and to every beast of the field; but for Adam there was not found a help to meet for him.

Philo of Alexandria conceived the first (and, moreover, a very long lasting) interpretation of these passages. In his commentary on the Book of Genesis, he interprets Adam in a twofold way. The Adam created in God's image is identified with the Platonic cosmic man, the androgynous macro-cosmos who is the archetype of the word; the spiritual Adam, 'he that was after the image was an idea or type or seal, an object of thought, incorporeal, neither male nor female, by nature incorruptible.'⁵ In opposition to this pure, spiritual, supra-individual, androgynous Adam, the individual Adam is composed of soul and body. His body was created, though Philo does not say from where. The Adam who was made from dust and whose wife was formed from his rib is composed of bodily and spiritual parts, and this bodily Adam is the one who fell into sin. His soul, however, partakes of the eternal Father and Ruler of all:

> For that which He breathed in was nothing else than a Divine breath that migrated hither from that blissful and happy existence for the benefit of our race, to that end that, even if it is mortal in respects of its visible part, it may be in respect of the part which is invisible be rendered immortal.⁶

The earthly Adam was created by the hand of God. Because of this immediate creation, he is 'a born ruler and master'⁷ of all beings, and, before his fall, he named all things, thanks to divine grace. In the process of naming, Adam had insight into the inner essence of things. His names denote the signatures of the things and indicate the archetypes of creation before they were called into extra-mental existence. Their power can be evoked again by their Adamic names:

---

4 'Man' in Hebrew: *ish*; 'woman' in Hebrew: *isha*; Vulgate: *vir, virago*.
5 Philo, *De creatione mundi. On the creation*, in Philo, *Works*, trans. Francis H. Colson and George H. Whitaker, vol. 1 (London: Loeb Classical Library, 1929): 134.
6 *Ibidem*, 135.
7 *Ibidem*, 83.

> For the native reasoning power of the soul being still unalloyed, and no infirmity or disease or evil affection having intruded itself, he received the impressions made by bodies and objects in their sheer reality, and the titles he gave were fully apposite, for right well did he divine the character of the creatures he was describing, with the result that their natures were apprehended as soon as their names were uttered.[8]

2.2 Dénis Pétau on Philo and Chrysostomus

Before the nineteenth century, Philo was not accepted as part of the Jewish tradition. Instead, from the time of St. Jerome onwards, he was counted as one of the Church Fathers, because he taught a logos theology that was close to the Gospel of St. John and to the spirituality of St. Paul. He was part of the Christian tradition, before the Hamburg philologist Johann Albert Fabricius destroyed the pious myth,[9] and so it is obvious why the Jesuit Dénis Pétau (1583–1652), one of the great important theologians, philologists, chronologists, and intellectual historians of the seventeenth century, summarised Philo's theory in his *Dogmata Theologica* (1644). However, his interpretation gave Philo a new slant: it was not so much the participation in the divine wisdom that he attributed to Adam, but rather the more rational interpretation that Adam had command over the animals.

> Philo Judaeus says in his *De mundi opificio:* God let Adam give perfect names to all the animals. These names encompassed wisdom and the dignity to rule. Adam was wise because he learned by himself and was not taught by anyone, only accompanied by an act of divine grace, and that was the reason why he was king. It is the task of leaders and princes to give proper names to all their subjects.[10]

Pétau also quotes the Church Father John Chrysostom, who shares Philo's (and Pétau's) interpretation of the *lingua Adamica* as wisdom and command over the animals. He combines Genesis 1:26 ('let man and woman have dominion over the fish of the sea, and over the birds of the air, and over the cattle, and over all earth, and over every creeping thing that creeps upon the earth') with the account of the divine origin of Adam's language, and therefore emphasises that man was the ruler over all species of animal. For him, Adam was like an owner and master of slaves who changes the names of his servants after he buys them. Chrysostom em-

---

8 *Ibidem*, 150.
9 Johann Albert Fabricius, *De Platonismo Philonis Judaei* (1693), repr. in idem, *Opusculorum Historico-Critico-Literariorum Sylloge* (Hamburg: Felginer, 1738): 147–160.
10 Dionysius Petavius (Dénis Pétau), *Dogmata Theologica* (Paris: Vives, 1866): T. IV. Theologicorum dogmatum De opificio sex dierum, Lib. II, Cap. VIII, 265b: 'Philo Judaeus in libro *de mundi opificio*, Optime, inquit, et impositionem nominum primo homini tribuit. Id enim opus est sapientiae, ac regiae dignitatis. Porro ille sapiens erat, qui a seipso didicerat, nec ab alio perdoctus fuerat, divina quadam id gratia consecutus; sed etiam praeterea rex erat. Est autem duci, ac principi consentaneum, unicuique subjectorum sibi proprium nomen assignare.'

phasises the force of the *lingua Adamica* to command, whereas the idea of participation in the divine logos evidently does not play an important role for him. Of course, as a consequence of the fall, Adam's dominating power over the animals was lost for all mankind.[11]

In any case, the quotations in Pétau clearly prove that Philo was still counted as an authority of Christian Dogmatic until the seventeenth century.

2.3 Reuchlin: *De Arte Cabalistica*

a Logos Theology
In the early modern era, it was Reuchlin who renewed the Church Fathers' theories and made the idea of the *lingua Adamica* a key concept of the Christian Kabbalah. Reuchlin shared Giovanni Pico's conviction that no art 'makes us more certain of the divinity of Christ than magic and the Kabbalah.' The divinity of Christ includes the doctrine of the Holy Trinity, the incarnation of the logos in Jesus Christ, and his resurrection.[12] To prove this theory, Reuchlin used the topos of the wonderworking word, *verbum mirificum*: an intertwinement of logos theology, magic of the word, and Christological prophecy. He merged all this in the *Ars Cabalistica*, and this Christian Kabbalah had the aim of reconstructing the paradisiacal *lingua Adamica* lost with the fall.

The real wonderworking word was the divine word, which created the world from nothing. The wonderworking word encompassed two elements: the first was the essence of all things, which were preconceived in the divine mind (the divine Sophia); the second was the force to make these ideas of the divine Sophia extra-mentally real (*fiat, vehementia essendi*). The *lingua Adamica* revealed insight into the divine Sophia, i.e. into the essential concepts of things, and Adam's command over them was the shadow of God's power to call things from mental into extra-mental material existence. God's primordial intellect and the might of His word were united in the divine logos in which Adam participated when he was granted the right to name God's creatures.

This is how—according to Philo of Alexandria—the prologue to the Gospel of St. John could and should be read. Obviously, the prologue begins as an allusion to the

---

[11] Chrysostomos, *Homilia XIV in Gen. Pétau, Dogmata Theologica* (Paris: Vives, 1866): T. IV., col. 265: 'Hoc impus admirabilis cujusdam in Adamo sapientiae specimen praedicat Joannes Chrysostomus, sed et alteram causam adjicit, dominatus in animantia caetera, ‚cujus argumentaum in illa nominum imposition praebuit. Nam et hominibus usitatum illud est, hoc uti signo dominationis, ut cum servos emerint, eorum nomina commutent.'
[12] Johannes Reuchlin, *Gutachten über das jüdische Schrifttum*, ed. and trans. Antonie Leinz-v. Dessauer, Pforzheimer Reuchlinschriften 2 (Konstanz: Thorbecke, 1965): 75: 'There is no art that makes us more certain of the divinity of Christ than magic and the Kabbalah.' The quote is from Pico's *Apologia*, see Giovanni Pico, *Opera omnia* (Basel, 1557–1573; ND Hildesheim: Olms, 1969): 166.

first words of the Hebrew Book of Genesis: *bereshit bara elohim* ('In the beginning God created'). The beginning of St. John's Gospel is analogous: ἐν ἀρχῇ ἦν ὁ λόγος. The complete verse reads as follows: 'In the beginning was the Word, and the Word was with God, and God was the Word. The same was in the beginning with God.' For Christians, this text could only, in the first instance, be read as a hint towards the Holy Trinity: Christ is God's Word, by which God becomes aware and cognizant of himself, and this reciprocity was considered as Father, Son, and Holy Spirit. Therefore, the 'Word' was intertwined with the inner-Trinitarian concept of the Deity. Secondly, the Word's power became obvious in the creation of the world through the Word: 'All things were made by Him (i.e. the Word); and without Him was not anything made that was made.' On the one hand, this verse shows the process of creation through the word, and this creating word was communicated to Adam when God revealed the names of the animals to him (Genesis 2:19 ff.). On the other hand, it is obvious that this logos is also the inner-Trinitarian one and therefore the logos of the Father. The prologue to St. John's Gospel has a third interpretation of the logos: ὁ λόγος ἔνσαρκός: 'And the Word was made flesh, and dwelled among us, and we beheld his glory, the glory as of the only begotten of the Father, full of grace and truth.' (John 1:14) St. Paul, in his letter to the Philippians, corroborated this interpretation and concentrated the whole process of logos theology in the name of Jesus: 'Wherefore God also hath highly exalted him, and given him a name which is above every name. That at the name of Jesus every knee should bow, of things in heaven, and things in earth, and things under the earth. And that every tongue should confess, that Jesus Christ is the Lord, to the glory of God the Father.' (Philippians 2:9–11)

So, it was obvious for Christian theologians how the 'Word' was intertwined with the Divine Trinitarian essence, with the process of the conceiving and becoming real of the creation, with Jesus as the Christ, and Adam participated in this process when God revealed the divine language to him.

b Kabbalah as *symbolica receptio*: JHSWH

Reuchlin takes the consequences of the theology of logos even further; he alludes to St. Paul's typology of Christ and Adam[13] and quotes Genesis 3:22, where God says: 'Ecce, Adam sicut unus ex nobis.' This verse corroborates a typological correspondence between Christ and Adam. For Reuchlin, Adam therefore has both a cosmic and a Christological meaning, and he quotes the appropriate passage from *Onqelos*, the Aramaic (Chaldaic) paraphrase of the Book of Genesis: 'Behold, Adam was my only begotten Son, the only one and in eternity from me.'[14] In other words, prelapsarian

---

13 1 Corinthians 15:22: 'For as in Adam all die, even also in Christ shall all be made alive.'
14 Johann Reuchlin, *On the Art of Kabbalah/De Arte Cabalistica*, trans. Martin and Sarah Goodman (Lincoln and London: University of Nebraska Press, 1993): 70: 'Ecce, Adam fuit unigenitus meus sive unicus meus in aeternitate ex me ipso.'

Adam, too, participated in this inner divine logos of God. Human paradisiacal knowledge culminated in the *lingua Adamica*, with which Adam, the 'protoplast,' named the animals (Genesis 2:18–20). 'And it was incidentally this singular and astute insight with which the protoplast himself, who already was master of the world, gave a name to each and every thing that presented itself to him.'[15]

This human insight into the will and knowledge of God was lost with Adam's fall. With the fall, the analogy between the Christological cosmic and the earthly Adam takes on a new meaning. Christ, the cosmic Adam, *sicut unus ex nobis*, who was preferred to the angels, now has to be newly revealed as the coming redeemer to the fallen human souls by the angels:

> After this unhappy fall of the race of man, God taught his angels about redemption, 'the coming salvation, and through whom it would come.' Of course, he only taught them as much as the angels, with their status, could comprehend. He showed them the presence of the one who would redeem the human race, for man's salvation was completely predestined. And so he said: 'Behold, here is that Adam who not only existed in essence after you and the world came into existence, but who also was one of us in eternity before all creation and before time began.'[16]

Restoring the knowledge of the redeemer is part of the divine project of the salvation of mankind after the fall. This knowledge has its magical focus in the saviour's name, which is the core of the *lingua Adamica*; it is the divine name in which all wisdom and might was united, and the aim of all the attempts of the Christian Kabbalah. It is participation in the logos, who is part of the life of the Holy Trinity, who created the word, and who became flesh.[17]

It is for this reason that the messianic Christological aspect is the dominant theme of Reuchlin's Kabbalah, and he has a key narrative for his access to the core of the *lingua Adamica*, the name of Christ. In the terms of his Kabbalah, this means that the Kabbalah of the name of God is based on the *shin* in the tetragrammaton, which thereby becomes a pentagrammaton.

---

[15] Reuchlin, *On the Art of Kabbalah/De Arte Cabalistica*, 66: 'Caeterum et hoc ingenii erat videlicet singularis et acerrimi cuique rei protoplastus ipse iam orbis dominus spontaneo positu nomen adderet.'

[16] Reuchlin, *On the Art of Kabbalah/De Arte Cabalistica*, 70: 'Post miserabilem itaque generis humani casum docuit angelos suos deus de restitutione aliquando futura salutis, per quem nam ventura esset, et quidem docuit non quantum ipse docere, sed quantum capere angelica conditio poterat, in praesentia demonstrans quis esse humanum genus redempturus, tunc enim praedestinata plane fuerat salus hominum, quapropter Ecce inquit hic est ille Adam qui non tantum post orbis et uestri ortum essentialiter est, sed etiam ante omnem creationem in aethernitate fuit unus ex nobis antequam tempus fieret.'

[17] This intertwinement of logos speculation, Trinitarian theology, theology of creation, and Christology obviously cannot be accepted by Jews. Rabbinic theology—if a theo'**logy**' exists—can only accept creation through the word; the rest of logos speculation is suspicious.

Reuchlin begins the story of these kabbalistic revelations with the promise of the Messiah, imparted to the fallen Adam by the angel Raziel. This is the key story of his messianic Kabbalah:[18]

> And so the angel Raziel was sent to fallen Adam, who was filled with grief, in order to comfort him. The angel said: Do not succumb to excessive pain and grief, because under your guidance the human race was plunged into the worst perdition. Original sin will be atoned for like this: from your descendants will be born a just and peaceable man, a man of peace, a hero whose name exists **in mercy** and in the four letters **i.h.u.h.** He will extend his hand for the true faith and a sacrifice agreeable to God and take from the wood of life, and the fruit of that wood will be the salvation of all who hope.[19]

This is the messianic hope, fulfilled for the Christians in the wood of the cross, but still to come for the Jews.

The following passage is proof of Reuchlin's philology as well of his speculative kabbalistic abilities. It is a little complicated; however, it makes clear that Kabbalah, too, is philology, and that it is also the summit of speculation. It is speculative philology.

Genesis 4:26 reports that Adam's clan began calling on God's name שם (*shem*) beginning with the birth of Adam's grandson Enosh. 'God' is written as a tetragrammaton (יהוה) here. The key words are *shem* and the tetragrammaton: שם יהוה. Reuchlin now highlights the special meaning of the *shin* in the word *shem*, which is spelt with the Hebrew letters *shin* and *mem*. He combines *notaricon* and *gematria*, the kabbalistic methods of interpretation. (*Notaricon* means that the letters of a word are read as the first letters of other words. *Gematria* is the interpretation of letters as numbers.[20]) According to the *notaricon* method, the Hebrew letters ש (*shin*) and מ

---

18 The surviving part of the *Book of Razi'el* consists of mystical, cosmological, and magical texts. It has nothing in common with Reuchlin's account. It includes writings from *Merkavah* and *Heikhalot* literature and from the *Sefer ha-Razim* as well as a version of the *Sefer ha-Malbush*. The title and the legend of the *Book of Razi'el* presumably derive from the introduction to the *Sefer ha-Razim*. According to this legend, the angel Razi'el revealed the secrets (of all ages) to Adam shortly after he was driven out of paradise. In addition to these early writings, the collection also includes literature by the thirteenth-century Ḥaside Ashkenaz, primarily from the *Sode Razayya* by El'azar ben Yehuda of Worms, as well as kabbalistic texts on the Sefirot and interpretations of the name of God. The book was first published in Amsterdam in 1701 and, since owning it was widely believed to keep fire and other dangers away from the home, it was reprinted many times.

19 Reuchlin, *On the Art of Kabbalah/De Arte Cabalistica*, 72: 'Missus est igitur angelus Raziel ad Adam collapsum et moerore plenum, ut consolaret eum, cui sic dixit. Ne supra modum conficias gemitu et molestia quod te duce genus humanum in summa corruit perditionem. Quoniam originale peccatum hoc expiabitur. Nam ex tua propagatione nascetur homo iustus et pacificus, uir heros, cui nomen continebit in miserationibus, etiam quas quatuor litteras **i.h.u.h.** et ille per rectam fidem et placidam oblationem mittet manum suam, et sumet de ligno uitae, et ejus ligni fructus erit omnium sperantium salus.'

20 The word 'notarikon' derives from the Latin and means 'shorthand;' it is also used as a kabbalistic exegetical method.

(*mem*) of the word שם (*shem*, 'name') stand for the spelled-out letter שין (*shin*) and מתוך (*mitokh*, 'in the middle'). Thus, following the *notaricon* method, Genesis 4:26, שם יהוה can be read: '*Shin* is in the middle of the tetragrammaton.' So much for the *notaricon* explanation of the word שם. According to *gematria*, the letter ש *shin* has a numerical value of 300. This is also the numerical value of ברחמים (*be-raḥa-mim*, 'in mercy').[21] The prophecy the angel Raziel revealed to Adam was: 'A hero whose name exists **in mercy** and in the four letters **i.h.u.h.**' So, when the *shin* ש is introduced into the tetragrammaton, you have the solution to the riddle. With the *shin* in the middle of the tetragrammaton, which means 'in mercy,' the tetragrammaton can be pronounced as Jehoshua; Jesus. So the *shin* makes the tetragrammaton pronounceable, which means that the *shin*, the symbol of Jesus Christ, when positioned in the middle of the divine name יהשוה, reveals the divine mercy and grace, because through the *shin* God's name is pronounceable. The *sensus anagogicus* thus is: Jesus is the way to the otherwise unpronounceable God.

Divine might and wisdom are focused in the name of God, thus the newly invented pentagrammaton יהשוה is the kernel and centre of the magic of the *lingua Adamica*; this is the name before which 'every knee should bow, of things in heaven, and things in earth, and things under the earth.' (Philippians 2:9–11) Reuchlin was convinced here that he had found the key to universal wisdom and magic. So if one tries to find a combination of *lingua Adamica* and philology—viz. speculative philology—one has it here with Reuchlin, and on a remarkable level.

What truths does Reuchlin tell? What kind of philological proofs does he present? He transferred Philo's concept of *lingua Adamica* into Christian Kabbalah. Reuchlin does not copy Philo's interpretation at all. He has his own much more comprehensive approach to explain the *lingua Adamica*. His theology of language elevates speculative philology into the only truth that matters, the name of God himself, of which everything else is a derivative, such as the naming of the animals which Adam then does. Reuchlin is a believer in the truth of the Bible as well as in the truth of the divine ideas directly communicated to human minds. His theological speculations and his philological skills laid the ground for the credibility of kabbalistic exegesis in the early modern era. With this exegesis, he set the standards of anagogical interpretations, which founded the fruitful development of Christian Kabbalah for 200 years. It took until the eighteenth century for critical philology to murder her speculative sister. But that is another story.

---

21 In detail: ב (= 2), ר (= 200), ח (= 8), מ (= 40), י (= 10), מ (= 40).

3 The Destruction of the *Lingua Adamica*. The Process of Discrediting Theories

Discrediting something is in many cases a silent, but very effective process; it works like calumny.[22] Such a decrease in credibility and credit can also be observed in theories and in varieties of speculation. However, it is difficult to understand this process. It constitutes something like a miracle in the histories of philosophy, philology, and the humanities that certain theories lose their credibility, although it cannot be said that their arguments become explicitly wrong; however, they look increasingly aged, no longer seem up to date, become dull and finally are considered absurd. This was also the case with the *lingua Adamica*, and the process of its discrediting is rather long. I shall try to sketch some of the stages of this process of disillusionment.

For the Jewish tradition, Philo was no authority, and for good reason. His theology of logos was too close to Christian Trinitarian theology and Christology, and this was of course unacceptable for the Jewish rabbis. Even though the Jewish theology of creation highlighted the word through which the world was made, Jewish theologians (if one can speak of 'logians' at all) did not follow the Greek speculations on logos. The platonic interpretation of the *lingua Adamica* which Philo, a Greek Jew, offered them, was too close to Trinitarian and Christological trains of thought. Consequently, the idea of the *lingua Adamica* became a Christian rather than a Jewish doctrine. So it is hardly astonishing that competing interpretations of the passage Genesis 2:18–23 which proved the idea of the *lingua Adamica* first came from Jewish exegetical traditions.

Just to recall: the passage which Philo first interpreted as an account of the *lingua Adamica* began with God's deliberation in Genesis 2:18–20: 'And the Lord God said, it is not good that the man should be alone; I will make him a help meet for him.' The following verse is the passage which triggered the interpretation of the *lingua Adamica*:

> And out of the ground the Lord God formed every beast of the field and every fowl of the air; and brought them unto Adam to see what he would call them: and whatsoever Adam called every living creature that was the name thereof. And Adam gave names to the cattle and to the fowl of the air and to every beast of the field; but for Adam there was not found a help to meet for him.

So much for the account of Adam's naming of the animals. The biblical text continues:

> So the Lord caused a deep sleep to fall upon the man, and while he slept took one of his ribs and closed up its place with flesh; and the rib which the Lord God had taken from the man he formed into a woman and brought her to the man. The man said, 'This at last is bone of my bones and

---

[22] Cf. the aria 'La calunnia è un venticello' in Gioachino Rossini's opera *Il barbiere di Siviglia*.

flesh of my flesh; she shall be called Woman, because she was taken out of Man.' (Genesis 2:21–23).

3.1 Naḥmanides (1195–1270) and Isaac Abravanel (1437–1508): No Help for Adam Which He Would Be Able to Call 'a Living Soul' Like His Own Name

It was Naḥmanides (aka Ramban) who took into consideration that Adam's naming of the animals had nothing to do either with the divine creating word or with the philosophical speculations of human insight into the divine logos embracing the essence of things. In his commentary on Genesis 2:19, Naḥmanides writes:

> It is possible that the phrase be explained in connection with the matter of 'the help' that God gave to Adam, and the meaning is the *ha'adam nefesh ḥayyah* ('the man is a living soul'), as is said, *And man became a living soul* [Genesis 7], and it is as I have explained it there: 'And He brought before him all species so that every one of them unto which Adam would give a name and say it is a living soul like himself, that would remain its name and be a help to him. So Adam gave names to all, but as for himself he found no help which he would be able to call 'a living soul' like his own name.[23]

The interpretation is obvious: *nefesh* ('soul') and *shem* ('name') are connected, and the name is the expression of the soul. Therefore, the meaning of the biblical passage is that Adam did not find a living being that had a soul like his own. Since Adam had no help and companion who had the same kind of soul as him, Eve was to be made from Adam's substance. Consequently, the story of Eve continues with her creation from Adam's rib. The whole account receives its meaning without any mention of the *lingua Adamica* with all its Platonic implications. This is not a lengthy and elaborated interpretation like Philo's or Reuchlin's, but it concisely makes sense of the whole difficult account of Eve's creation.

Precisely this exegesis could be found about three hundred years later in Isaac Abravanel's (1437–1508) *Commentary on the Book of Genesis* (c. 1505)—that is, just to recall, exactly the time when Reuchlin conceived his ideas of the *lingua Adamica* and the wonderworking word. Abravanel writes:

> Comme il est dit ensuite: 'Et l'homme ne trouva point d'aide qui lui corresponde'. Il n'a pas trouvé parmi les animaux, en face et devant lui, une femelle capable de lui être une aide qui le serve alors que tel était le but de ce rassemblement. En effet, D. n'a pas volu lui donner une femme avant qu'il en ressente la nécessité, qu'il la recherché, et qu'il ne trouve pas de femelle qui lui convienne parmi toutes les espèces animals. C'est alos qu'Il la lui a faite, de sa chair et de sa substance.[24]

---

[23] Naḥmanides, *Commentary on the Torah: Genesis*, trans. Charles B. Chavel (New York: Shilo Publishing House, 1971): 77.
[24] Isaac Abravanel, *Commentaire du récit de la creation (Genèse 1:1 a 6:8)*, trans. Yéhouda Schiffers (Paris: Verdier 1999): 350f.

So here, at least for more prosaic philological and hermeneutical minds with no interest in logos theology, it became obvious that the *lingua Adamica* was mainly a Christian speculation or—in Jewish eyes—rather a phantasm.

3.2 Marin Mersenne

Marin Mersenne, a French Franciscan monk, astronomer, philologist, and mathematician and one of the best and busiest networkers in the seventeenth century, a friend of Gassendi and Descartes and an avid anti-kabbalist, wrote a huge commentary on the Book of Genesis with the title *Quaestiones celeberrimae in Genesim*, which was printed in 1623. The book has a chapter entitled "De scientia Adami, & intellectus ornamentis."[25] Mersenne comments on Genesis 20:2, which in Latin reads: 'Appellavit Adam nominibus suis cuncta animantia, & universa volatilia coeli, & omnes bestias terrae. Adae verò non enveniabatur adiutor similis eius.'[26]

a Quotation of Naḥmanides

It is important that Mersenne cites the last verse of this famous biblical passage, since it is here that the germ of the destruction of the concept of the *lingua Adamica* lies hidden. Mersenne does not openly draw the hermeneutical conclusions of the last sentence. However, he quotes Naḥmanides as the best commentary on this passage: Adam did not find any animal to whom he could have given a name corresponding to his own as *ish* ('man') until he saw a woman, whom he called *isha* ('woman'), because she was obviously suited to him.[27] He evidently knew the sceptical and dry elimination of the *lingua Adamica* by the Jewish exegete, but that did not prevent him from giving an explicit explanation of how Adamic wisdom could be imagined and explained in terms of the Aristotelian theory of knowledge.

b Philosophical Considerations about the Adamic Language
1 The Limits of Adam's Knowledge: Hebrew Grammar Sufficient for the Explanation of the Holy Scriptures

Firstly, he deals with the philosophical question of whether the names of the things are imposed on those things or whether they derive *ab ipsa natura*. Evidently, he believes that Adam was given insight into the essence of the things by God. It is remarkable that the sceptical Mersenne concludes: 'It is not dangerous if we concede to

---

[25] Marin Mersenne, *Quaestiones celeberrimae in Genesim* (Paris: Cramoisy, 1623): col. 1201–1221.
[26] Ibidem, col. 1201.
[27] Ibidem, col. 1201: 'Ramban ait nullum animal reperissse Adamum, cui nomen ex proprio suo nomine איש [ish] deductum imponere posset, donec foeminam videret, cui אשה [isha] nomen inderet, quia solum sibi convenire perspexit.'

Adam the knowledge of all things corporeal and elementary, as well as the knowledge of the stars and the sciences.'[28] His proof is biblical; he quotes Ecclesiasticus (Jesus Sirach) 17:3.4.6:

> He gave him the number of his days and gave him power over all things, that are upon the earth. He put fear of him upon all flesh, and he had dominion over beasts and fowls. [...] He created in them (scil. Adam and Eve) the science of the spirit, he filled their heart with wisdom, and showed them both good and evil.[29]

It seems that one has to conclude from this that the first parents *omni decore, virtute atque scientia ornatos fuisse.*

Mersenne offers some critical objections; it is, however, not completely clear whether he does so in order to destroy or to corroborate the biblical passage. On the one hand, he argues that Adam only had sufficient knowledge to explain the Holy Scriptures and the veneration of the godhead. It was not a knowledge of all particulars, but a form of wisdom which derived from *optimum ingenium & maximam aetatem.*[30] Here Mersenne again draws on evidence from Jesus Sirach 17:11: 'And their eyes saw the majesty of his glory, and their ears heard his glorious voice, and he gave them a heart to understand.' These were practical abilities which mostly concerned *voluptas animi*—the 'joy of the soul.' This knowledge did not deal with theoretical subjects such as mathematics and the liberal arts. On the other hand, he seems convinced that Adam was able to answer questions about astronomy and grammar, particularly the latter as he gave names to the animals. God gave him the Hebrew language which he handed down perfectly to Eve and their descendants. Moreover, when the discussion turns to these encyclopaedic questions, Mersenne seems to lose his sceptical attitude completely. He is sure that Adam mastered the problems of metaphysics, angelic knowledge, and all the secret sciences of the wise men from the Orient before the fall: 'Indorum Gymnosophistae, Sacerdotes Aegyptorum, Prophetarum Cabalistae, Chaldaei Babyloniorum [...] Adamus omnibus Philosophis hic enumeratis doctior.' Additionally, he had a perfect knowledge of natural magic.

It is hard to decide whether Mersenne is being ironic with this list from a secret Adamic encyclopaedia. It is precisely the list of magic sciences he rejects in his acrid polemics against Robert Fludd which feature in this very same volume on the Book of Genesis.

---

[28] *Ibidem*, col. 1211: 'nullum esse periculum si rerum omnium corporearum, atque elementorum, quam syderum cognitionem, atque scientiarum Adamo tribuamus.'
[29] *Ibidem*: 'Numerum dierum et tempus dedit illi (viz. Adam). Et dedit illi potestatem eorum quae sunt super terram. Et deinde: & disciplina scientiae replevit illos (viz. Adam and Eve). Creavit illos scientiam spiritus, sensu implevit cor illorum, & mala & bona ostendit illis.'
[30] *Ibidem*.

2 Philosophical Theory of Knowledge: *Species Infusa* (How is it possible to know what a species is without having sense perception of an individual of this species? God presented the individual animal to Adam in the moment when he infused him with the knowledge of the species.)

Be that as it may with the encyclopaedia of magic and secret sciences, Mersenne's substantial considerations concerning the concept of the *lingua Adamica* are philosophical. His question is: what kind of knowledge could Adam have had? How can infused empirical knowledge be possible?[31]

Mersenne's first rather sceptical question is: is it possible to know particular things without having achieved a habitus that administrates the species deriving from sensual experience with the extra-mental things? Knowledge of extra-mental things is always knowledge of species, and therefore abstract. It is abstracted from the extra-mental things, represented spiritually by an abstract phantasma which is given a name. A phantasma, viz. a species or scheme, can be given a name, and with the combination of scheme and name one can communicate knowledge and identify an individual extra-mental thing. This is the Aristotelian theory of science: giving a species a name is creating a concept of an individual, extra-mental being.

The second question is how an intra-mental species can correspond to an extra-mental object without previous experience and without a mental habitus of episteme. It is not at all clear how it is possible that infused knowledge of species, prior to any experience, can meet the external individual object. In order to produce empirical knowledge, one must always compare external individual things and mental species. But this was precisely not the case for the names Adam gave the animals.

Mersenne solves this difficulty as follows: he suggests that God conceded his peculiar knowledge of things, namely the *lingua Adamica*, to Adam in this way: at the very moment when God infused the cognition of all things into Adam's mind, he showed the animals to him physically. Therefore, the divinely infused species perfectly corresponded to the things presented to him.[32] Through this construction, the correspondence between the *species infusa* and empirical knowledge was granted.

Adam therefore knew the essential divine language, since the knowledge of the *species infusa* which God conceded to Adam entailed more than the empirical knowledge of species achieved by the habitus of abstraction.[33] He was given the *verbum mentis mediante specie intelligibili* ('the mental word through the medium of the intelligible species'). The essential word which corresponded to the divine logos of the

---

[31] *Ibidem*, col. 1215: 'Itaque primò videndum est, an quis aliquo habitu scientiae infuso peraeque uti valeat, ac si illum proprio labore comparasset; 2 quomodo novit Adamus scientias praedictos ibi divinitus concessas fuisse.'

[32] *Ibidem*, col. 1216 f.: 'Existimo autem Deum tantam rerum omnium cognitionem Adamo concedisse, ut statim atque occulos aperiret, viderit hanc & illam plantam, astra & quaecumque subjecerit occulis, perfecte correspondere illi cognitioni, quam habeat à Deo.'

[33] This question is discussed in Articulus VI: Quomodo potuit Adamus de rebus, quas agnoscebat, edissere, cùm loqui nusquam didicisse?

creation entailed the knowledge of the *proprietates rerum* and their substance. This language was the original divine Hebrew, lost with the fall. But before this misfortune, Adam taught the original Hebrew, his *lingua Adamica*, to Eve in paradise.

3.3 Samuel Bochart (1599–1667): *Hierozoicon*

Samuel Bochart was one of the outstanding Calvinistic philologists of the seventeenth century; his *Hierozoicon*, an encyclopaedia of all known animals compared with those mentioned in the Bible, was **the** reference dictionary of seventeenth- and eighteenth-century biblical exegesis.[34] Bochart, a model Calvinist, was a dry philological positivist. He asks three questions concerning the *lingua Adamica*: 1. What is a species of animal? According to the biblical account, were animals also presented to Adam that derived from mixtures of species, like mules or amphibious creatures? And what about the species of animals in the waters,[35] which do not feature in the biblical account? 2. The second question is even more positivistic: how could one reconstruct the situation when God presented the train of animals to Adam? To Bochart, it is a wonder that the crowd of animals proceeded peacefully in a line before Adam, just as all animals lived peacefully together in Noah's ark. 3. A further question is how so many animals could come to a place where Adam could impose names on them. Was this possible through the might of angels or *arcano Dei impulsu*?[36] Bochart leaves these questions open and flees into exegetical obedience: it is sufficient that we know that God, who has absolute mastery over the creatures, has means by which he can arbitrarily realise whatever he decided needed to be done.[37] *Qui movent quaestiones tam superfluas* should recall that nobody knows why storks and cranes fly to Egypt in the autumn and return to Europe in spring.

Facing all these problems of biblical realism, Bochart only allows one interpretation of the *lingua Adamica*: 'Itaque in servitutis notam Adam illis omnibus nomina imposuit, nempe ut domni servis solent.'[38] Before the fall, the animals were obedient to Adam and Eve; after the fall, most of the animals became wild and disobedient, although there were traces of the original obedience in dogs and horses.

As a philologist, Bochart is interested in the history of the Hebrew names Adam gave to the animals. He also argues that Adam transmitted the animals' names to later generations, which gives him the opportunity to list a vast number of animal names that can etymologically be traced back to their Hebrew origin.

---

[34] Samuel Bochart, *Hierozoicon sive bipartitum opus de Animalibus S. Scripturae*, ed. quarta (Leiden and Utrecht: Guillielmus van de Water, 1712): vol. 1, lib. 1, Cap. IX.
[35] The question of fish was already a subject of discussion in St. Augustine's *De Genesi ad literam*.
[36] Bochart, *Hierozoicon*, vol. 1, col. 56.
[37] *Ibidem*: 'Sufficit enim ut sciamus, Deo, qui absolutam habet in creaturas dominium, non deesse rationes, quibus eas pro arbitrio suo impellat quaecunque decrevit et destinavit.'
[38] *Ibidem*, col. 57.

3.4 Hermann von der Hardt and Johann Albert Fabricius

Johann Albert Fabricius was the chief lexicographer of Latin and Greek philology of the late seventeenth and the early eighteenth centuries. His *Bibliotheca Graeca*, *Bibliotheca Latina* and *Bibliotheca Mediae et Infimae Latinitatis* were the key reference works/dictionaries/encyclopaedias of classical philology through the eighteenth and nineteenth centuries, until the *Realenzyklopädie für klassische Philologie und Altertum*, the so-called *Pauly-Wissowa*, replaced them. Fabricus' philology also included theological philology. Therefore, he collected dates and texts concerning the pseudepigraphy of the New and Old Testaments.[39] Important for the subject of the *lingua Adamica* is his *Codex pseudepigraphicus Veteris Testamenti*;[40] here, under the lemma 'Adam,' he discusses: 1. 'Adamus Litterarum Inventor'; 2. 'Adami Commentarius de Nominibus Animantium'; and 3. 'Adamus edoctis ab angelis.'

Fabricius, like Bochart, was a dry character. In most cases, he only cites others' opinions; however, concerning the first section, the invention of the script and peculiarly the revelation of the Hebrew letters and their punctuation, he is ironic and shows clear judgement.[41] He quotes the Calvinistic polyhistor Johann Heinrich Alsted and the Imperial librarian Peter Lambeck, who were convinced that Adam handed over the complete knowledge of the Hebrew language including its punctuation. As a philologist who knew the state of the art, he was of course convinced that the punctuation of the Hebrew letters was a rabbinic invention. Therefore, he ridicules all attempts to elaborate this thesis and denotes it as 'nugae' ('cloudy'). Although he insists that he wants to save money and time since otherwise he would have to report too many ridiculous opinions, he nevertheless quotes a lot of literature concerning this subject.[42]

The second section comes to the heart of the problem, viz. Adam's naming of the animals; this is the famous locus Genesis 2:19. In fact, Fabricius quotes works by some very well-known authors who argued in favour of the *lingua Adamica*: Petavius'

---

[39] The best monograph on Fabricius is Erik Petersen, *Johann Albert Fabricius: En humanistz in Europa* (in Danish) (Copenhagen: Museum Tusculanum Forlag, 1998).
[40] Johann Albert Fabricius, *Codex pseudepigraphicus Veteris Testamenti* (Hamburg and Leipzig: Liebenzeit, 1713): 1.
[41] *Ibidem*: 'Litteras Hebraicas una cum punctis vocalibus ab Adamo repertas & Setho traditas non dubitant Henricus Alstedius in Chronologia p.253. & Petrus Lambecius quem vide sis in Prodoromo Hist. literariae p.5. Alii diversa longe & mirifica plane Alphabeta tribuunt Adamo, quae vel ab ipso excogitate, vel ab Angelo Raziel ille tradita nugantur, quae hic descxribi aere curassem, nisi in ridiculis commentis ac per tot alios jam explosis voluissem opera et sumptui parcere.'
[42] Cf. *ibidem*; he mentions Thomas Bangius, *Tou makaritou coelo Orientis*, 100–101; Giulio Bartolocci, *Bibliotheca Rabbinica*, vol. 1, 80; Scipio Sgambati, *Archiva V.T.*, 28 ff.; Paul Christian Hilscher, *Bibliotheca Adami* (Dresden, 1703, 1711 4°); Gottfried Volkerot, *De societatibus literariis antediluvianis*, 14; Angelus Roccha, *Commentarius de Bibliotheca Vaticana*, 79, 82, 88, 295; Theseus Ambrosius in *Appendice introductionis ad Varias linguas*, and many others.

Theologia dogmatica,⁴³ Johann Heinrich Heidegger's *Historia patriarcharum*,⁴⁴ and Samuel Bochart's *Hierozoicon*.⁴⁵ But his most important source is the Helmstedt polyhistor Hermann von der Hardt, who doubted the whole theory concerning the *lingua Adamica*. In a letter to Paul Martin Nolte, printed in Helmstedt in 1705, von der Hardt states that he shares Isaac Abravanel's opinion⁴⁶ that Moses did not intend to say anything about Adam giving names to the animals, but that he merely wanted to express that Adam did not find a being among the animals that was suitable to become his wife. The story in Genesis 2:19 was also told, as Abravanel explains, as an allegorical example for the Jews that they should guard against the infamy of the heathens who, like beasts, often violate their contracts.⁴⁷ In his letter to Paul Martin Nolte, von der Hardt states:

> Adam carefully examined all living beings, says Moses, of whatever name, for he should judge himself in God's mandate whether there was one among them who could become his desired partner, who could nourish him and establish a family with him.⁴⁸

---

43 Denis Pétau, *Dogmata Theologica*, ed. Nova (Paris: Vives, 1866): T. IV. Theologicorum dogmatum De opificio sex dierum, Lib. II, Cap. VIII, 265b.
44 Johann Heinrich Heidegger, *Historia sacra Patriarcharum. Exercitationes selectae*, ed. Secunda (Amsterdam: Abraham à Someren, 1688): 148 (the passage deals with the **essential names** Adam gave the animals): 'Quippe quae jamjam impositum nomen fuerat, idem multò ante in ipsa natura inclusum fuisse, adeóque suam illam in appellato quoque appellationem antegressum esse declarant, quam deinde vir ille divino afflatus vi quadam superiore imposuit. Quod etiam secundum naturam imposita sint nomina, arguit appellato coniugis אישה [*isha*] *vira*, quae ejus originem plane pandit. Et animalium nomina Hebraica, quae in Sacris occurrunt, naturam ipsam animalium aperiunt.'
45 Bochart, *Hierozoicon*, vol. I, lib. 1, Cap. IX.
46 Abravanel, *Commentaire du rècit de la creation*, 350 f.: 'Comme il est dit ensuite: "Et l'homme ne trouva point d'aide qui lui corresponde." Il n'a pas trouvé parmi les animaux, en face et devant lui, une femelle capable de lui être une aide qui le serve alors que tel était le but de ce rassemblement. En effet, D. n'a pas volului donner une femme avant qu'il en ressente la nécessité, qu'il la recherché, et qu'il ne trouve pas de femelle qui lui convienne parmi toutes les espèces animals. C'est alos qu'Il la lui a faite, de sa chair et de sa substance.'
47 Fabricius, *Codex pseudepigraphicus Veteris Testamenti*, 3: 'Nuper tamen Vir acutissimus Hermannus ab Hardt universum hoc vocavit in dubium, Epistola ad Paulum Martinum Noltenium Helmstadii 1705.8 edita, & cum Arbabanele sentit Moysen nihil eo loco dicere de animantibus ab Adamo nomine donatis, sed tantum voluisse docere quod Adamus considerata quorumcunque animantium natura, nullum offenderit aptum ad vitae & coniugii consuetudinem, ut adeo Adami exemplo Judaei monerentur cavere sibi ab Ethnicorum turpidine, qui brutis bestiis quandoque foede sunt abusi.'
48 Hermann von der Hardt, *Ad Clarissimum virum Paulum Martinum Noltenium ... in Mosis Gen. II, 18.19.20*, in *Bochartum Epistola* (Helmstedt, 1705): 25: 'scopus erat, Adamo divinitus destinatam fuisse sociam;' 29: 'Omnia, inquit Moses, viva animantia, quocunque veniant nomine, attente consideravit et expendit sedulo, pro divino nutu & instinctu ipsemet ingénue judicaturus, an aliquod illorum esset, quod ad auxilium desideratum societatemque ineundam, alendam, remque familiarem conservandam facere posset.' But he did not find any, and this was reason why God made Eve from Adam's rib, 'flesh from my flesh and bone from my bone,' as his companion and helper: *isha*.

However, he did not find any, and this was the reason why God made Eve from Adam's rib 'flesh from my flesh and bone from my bone' as his companion and helper: the *isha* for the *ish*, the fe-male as the partner of the male. Fabricius confesses that he finds this opinion the only plausible interpretation of the biblical passage.[49] With this statement from a leading philologist in the first decade of the eighteenth century, it finally became obvious that the idea of the *lingua Adamica* had lost its credibility.

3.5 Zedler's *Universallexikon*/Pierre Bayle/Hermann Samuel Reimarus: "Adam"

A couple of years later, this opinion shared by the philological elite had become common. In the article entitled "Adam," which was printed in Johann Heinrich Zedler's *Universallexikon* in 1732, all the elements of the spiritual tradition are still mentioned; however, they are all rejected. Only the post-paradisiacal biblical story of Adam remained accepted as historical truth. Zedler—or whoever the author of the article was—writes:

> Adam, the first man, whom God has created after His image. [...] His age amounted to 930 years, and he begot Cain, Abel, Seth, and additional sons and daughters whom we do not know by name. One honestly cannot relate anything else about him on the basis of scripture. All other stories about him are based on conjectures which are at best likely or evidently fabulous and absurd, e.g. one knows so much about Adam's peculiar physical beauty and his magnificent knowledge. Some say that the angel Raziel was his teacher. They attribute to Adam different books, one on the names of the animals, an apocalypse, Psalm 92 and other psalms, the kabbalistic book Raziel, the book Yeşirah, likewise one on alchemy, and others. Among the Jews, there are many who pretend that Adam was a being of a gigantic size, also that he was created circumcised. And it is also a product of absurd fantasy if some, and especially the well-known Lady Bourignon, believed that Adam was bisexual and that, before the fall, he could procreate the human race without woman.[50]

---

[49] Fabricius, *Codex pseudepigraphicus Veteris Testamenti*, 3: 'Fateor non destitui ingenio quae à Viro praestantissimo disputantur & communi sententiae objiciuntur, sed ab tota antiquitate cui ratio & verba Moysis aperte vidnetur favere, ideo neutiquam recesserim.'

[50] *Zedlers Universallexikon*, vol. 1 (Leipzig, 1732): s.v. Adam: 'Adam, der erste Mensch, welchen Gott nach seinem Ebenbilde erschaffen. [...] Er hat sein Alter auf 930 Jahre gebracht, und ausser Cain, Abel und Seth, noch andere ungenannte Söhne und Töchter gezeuget. Ein mehreres lässet sich von ihm mit Wahrheits-Grunde und nach der heiligen Schrifft nicht melden. Denn was man sonsten von ihm erzehlet, beruhet entweder auf lauter Muthmassungen, die auf eine Wahrscheinlichkeit gegründet sind, oder ist offenbarlich fabelhaft und ungereimt. Also weiß man viel von seiner sonderbaren Leibes-Schönheit und grosser Wissenschaft zu sagen, wobey einige den Engel Raziel vor seinen Lehrmeister ausgeben, ihm auch ein und andere Schrifften, als ein Buch von denen Namen der Thiere, eine Apokalypsin, den 92. und andere Psalmen, das cabbalistische Buch Raziel, das Buch Jezira, imgleichen eines von der Alchemie, und noch andere mehr andichten. Unter denen Jüden werden viele gefunden, welche vorgeben, er sei von ungeheurer Riesen-Grösse gewesen, auch beschnitten erschaffen worden. So sind auch ungereimte Phantaseyen, wann einige, und sonderlich die bekannte Bourignon, gemeinet, daß in Adam beyderley Geschlecht vereinigt gewesen, und daß er bis auf seinen Fall das menschliche Geschlecht allein, und ohne Weib hätte fortpflanzen können.'

Although the article in Zedler's book widely depends on Pierre Bayle's *Dictionnaire Historique et Critique*, it is also much more sceptical than it. Whereas Bayle still accepts Adam's vast knowledge as legitimate biblical exegesis according to the analogy of faith,[51] the article in Zedler doubts this. It looks as though it had been written by Hermann Samuel Reimarus, Fabricius's unbelieving son-in-law. The credibility of Adam's universal knowledge is completely abandoned here. The doctrine of the divine origin of the human language and its implication that the divine logos opens an insight into the essence of the things created is drawn into serious doubt. The terrain is paved for new naturalistic theories of the origin of languages which, from the 1750s on, grew like mushrooms from the earth.

In the 1730s, the same decade in which "Adam" appeared in *Zedlers Universallexikon*, Hermann Samuel Reimarus wrote his *Schutzschrift für die vernünftigen Verehrer Gottes* ('Apology for God's Reasonable Venerators'), an acrid criticism of the Old and New Testaments which remained unpublished until 1972. Lessing knew the manuscript and published parts of it in the 1770s.

Reimarus was a brilliant Hebraist, virtuoso student of Johann Albert Fabricius and Johann Christoph Wolff, the author of the famous *Bibliotheca Hebraea*. During his working life, he was a professor of Oriental languages at the Hamburg Gymnasium Johanneum. In the 1730s, he conceived his clandestine *magnum opus*, the aforementioned *Schutzschrift für die vernünftigen Verehrer Gottes*, and here the historicity of the whole paradisiacal story, and with it the historical Adam, were taken apart.

Reimarus still seems to believe that Adam was a historical figure; however, the only Adam he accepts is the one after the fall and the expulsion from paradise.[52] For him, the whole paradisiacal story is dubious. His doubts especially concern the question of original sin and its relationship to Adam and Eve's knowledge and wisdom. His crucial question is: if Adam was created in God's image and was so wise by God's instruction, and if he taught the divine language and wisdom to Eve, how could one imagine that this wisdom did not include the distinction between good and evil? Why did Eve trust the serpent rather than God's wise command? And how was it possible that the wise Adam was seduced by Eve in the ridiculous manner of eating an apple? And a little later, the scripture says that 'the eyes of the first parents were opened' with this act of the disobedient eating of an apple—

---

[51] Pierre Bayle, *Dictionnaire*, s.v. Adam: Bayle first tells the biblical facts about Adam; this is then taken over by the Zedler article. Bayle continues: 'Voilà tout ce que nous savons de certain sur son Chapitre. Une infinité d'autres choses, que l'on a dites de lui, sont, ou très fausses, ou très incertaines: il est vrai qu'on peut juger de quelques-unes, qu'elles ne sont point contraires à l'analogie de la foi, ni à la probabilité. Je mets en ce dernier rang ce que l'on dit de sa vaste science.' This positive judgement is not taken up by the Zedler article.
[52] Hermann Samuel Reimarus, *Apologie oder Schutzschrift für die vernünftigen Verehrer Gottes*, ed. Gerhard Alexander, vol. 1 (Frankfurt: Insel 1972): 193–195.

what was this new kind of wisdom? Reimarus comments sarcastically: 'Nobody is so foolish that he thinks he can become a doctor by consuming fruits.'[53]

Here, the paradisiacal Adam, and with him the *lingua Adamica*, was dissolved into vapour. Adam became a mythic figure, and the question of the origin of languages was henceforth discussed naturalistically, without any reference to divine intervention. From the 1750s on, naturalistic theories of the origin of languages sprang up like mushrooms. But that is another story.

---

[53] *Ibidem*, 758: 'Dann aber sieht Eva den Baum an, daß gut davon zu wäre, weil er klug mache. [...] Sollte die Klugheit im Apfel stecken, und als eine Quintessenz durch die Verdauung des Magens herausgezogen werden, damit sie so ins Geblüt treten, und in die Seele übergehen könnte? Welche Vorstellung! So albern denkt jetzt niemand, daß er sich im Obst zum Doktor fressen könnte.'

Part III: **Reports**

Activities and Events

Opening of the 2nd Academic Year on 8 November, 2016

Giuseppe Veltri: The Limits of Scepticism and Tolerance

Sceptical thinking has often been regarded as being dangerous to social and political stability; or, as the Enlightenment philosopher Christian Wolff stated: 'The sceptic is dangerous for religion because the sceptic does not consider anything without doubting it.' Almost every heresy has sprung from an answer to a question about the validity of norms, customs, and dogmatic patrimony. While past scholarship was interested in emphasising the role of sceptical groups or individuals and their impact on society, as well as their alleged danger to the social order, recently researchers have increasingly directed their attention towards sceptical challenges to hegemonic power structures and to (state) religion (which was a topic already discussed in the eighteenth century by Moses Mendelssohn). Here, Stuart Sim is worth mentioning for his emphasis on 'why we need more scepticism and doubt in the twenty-first century.' Sim envisages the problem of the entanglement between politics, dominant culture, and (political) belief and the need for a sceptical attitude as a privileged form of attacking authoritarianism in daily life. Although scepticism is commonly considered a negative attitude, it becomes a positive and necessary resistance to excessive power and to the suppression of dissent. Hence, a possible impact of scepticism on modern society could be the generation of tolerance.

In this lecture, Veltri discussed three fundamental and debatable points. The first question is whether a sceptical attitude can be considered a danger or a profit to society. The second is the origins and nature of tolerance, namely, what are the paradigms which enable a tolerant approach to controversial aspects of social and political life. The third and more complicated question is the relationship between tolerance and scepticism, or what limits are implied by a sceptical and/or tolerant vision of society.

Regular Events

Dialectical Evenings

The Dialectical Evening is an informal meeting every four weeks (in fortnightly rotation with the Reading Evening) for discussions and readings, which is designed to promote dialectical culture and sceptical thought within the research unit. Members of the Maimonides Centre and occasional guests convene to challenge, doubt, and explore theses in various subject areas.

[DE09] 29 August, 2016
Asher Salah: **Scepticism and Dogmatism in the Religious Debate in 19th Century Jewish Italy**

In the early days of Jewish Studies, the so-called Science of Judaism ('Wissenschaft des Judentums'), along with its scholarly pursuits, implemented an extensive process of revision of the religious foundations of Judaism. Reform and *Wissenschaft* are believed to have concomitantly arisen in the first decades of the nineteenth century in the German cultural area, later to spread their influence east and west to other parts of Europe and to the United States. Recent scholarship has challenged the germanocentric interpretation of the origins of these movements. As far as Italy is concerned it is still generally assumed that 'the question of reform was never seriously considered' (Cecil Roth), albeit the flourishing of the Science of Judaism there.

But was it really so? Not in the eyes of Moritz Steinschneider, an observer well-acquainted with Jewish life in Italy. In his review of a sermon by Rabbi Marco Mortara, Steinschneider could not refrain from expressing his surprise at the strength of the Italian reform movement: 'dass in Italien die hier bekämpfte extreme Partei so bedeutend sei, haetten wir kaum geglaubt.' Indeed, Italy had numerous Jewish reformers, from Aron Fernandez of Leghorn to the school teacher Moisè Soave of Venice and the Rabbi Daniel Pergola of Turin. They promoted radical reform programs in their writings concerning liturgy, education and Halakhah. Some even implemented significant reforms in their own communities.

Where they isolated figures or did they give voice to significant trends inside an otherwise conservative Italian Judaism? Which models of reform did they refer to and how did they interact with the orthodox camp? And first and foremost, did reformers recur to sceptical tools to attack the dogmatic foundations of Judaism?

[DE10] 20 September, 2016
Almut-Barbara Renger: **Confronting Sceptical Authorities**

Sextus Empiricus, the main authority of Pyrrhonian scepticism, showed that we cannot develop a universally valid art of living because we are unable to determine the supreme good without reference to interests that are always shaped by our belonging to a community. However, Sextus' scepticism does hold out the promise of arriving at a beneficial state of mind, by pointing towards an attitude that can be maintained only performatively. If one abandons the search for the good by itself, tranquillity can be attained without putting forth a general argument against the possibility thereof, thus freeing oneself from the burden of dogma.

At this dialectical evening, Renger explored the potentials and limitations of comparison by juxtaposing this attitude with other stances and ways of life that have been labelled sceptical, such as the teachings of Nāgārjuna, the first historically significant authority in the context of Mahāyāna Buddhism, which contain a comparable promise. The 'Middle Way' (*Mādhyamaka*) of this Indian philosopher puts forth the view that one can calm or still one's thinking by refraining from taking up any position, holding instead to an inconceivable middle among all extremes.

What happens when famous authorities that are seen as sceptics, like Sextus and Nāgārjuna, along with their modern 'descendants' (in the sense of a Wittgensteinian family resemblance), are brought into dialogue with one another in a sceptical fashion?

[DE11] 28 November, 2016
Stephan Schmid: **History of Philosophy and Scepticism about Philosophy: Three (Alleged) Routes from History to Scepticism**

Some are sceptical about the possibility of ahistorical or timeless philosophical knowledge on the grounds that philosophy itself has a history (and is perhaps more closely related to its history than many other academic disciplines). Three arguments for this kind of scepticism concerning philosophical knowledge were discussed during the Evening. Schmid concluded that all these arguments are quite problematic. Thus, there are good reasons to be sceptical about historical scepticism about philosophy.

[DE12] 12 December, 2016
Roi Benbassat: **Thesis—Religious Faith and Scepticism do Not Contradict One Another**

Scepticism is normally considered to be an attitude opposed to religious faith, even though some advocates of faith present doubt as an important feature of religious development. The more you confront and overcome greater doubts, these advocates of faith say, the stronger and firmer your faith will be. However, it is evident that even from this 'tolerant' religious viewpoint, scepticism is viewed as something that should eventually be overcome, and that the ideal of faith is still the termination of scepticism. However, Benbassat discussed a different religious approach here: one in which scepticism can and should be constantly maintained alongside faith. This is a religious approach that not only regards scepticism towards religious beliefs as essential for maintaining one's faith, but also considers any form of faith that does not incorporate a sceptical element to be mostly corrupted. This unusual religious approach is exhibited by the Jewish thinker Yeshayahu Leibowitz (1903–1994), whose fusion of faith and scepticism will be called into question in our discussion.

[DE13] 23 January, 2017
Charles E. Snyder: **Anti-Political Animals**

Anti-Political Animals: On more the one occasion, Aristotle defended the view that the human being is by nature a political animal (*Nicomachean Ethics*, I 1097b, *Politics*, I 1253a). Such a view does not entail for Aristotle that the human is the only political animal, since he also believes that certain non-human animals–bees, wasps, cranes–are political (*History of Animals*, 487b33, 488a9 – 10). And yet critics and loyalists of Aristotle continue to ascribe to him the view that what distinguishes the human from other animals is this natural propensity for politics. Both camps obscure the real issue and let Aristotle off easy, it seems to me. Snyder opposed Aristotle's old commonplace about the human from a different direction. In this opposing view, the human is according to nature the anti-political animal; if not the most sociopathic animal; and it is this anti-political element that distinguishes the human from other animals. This view is one that Aristotle should have developed given his own metaphysical commitments. His reticence is unfortunate and revealing. To register this reticence, Snyder refrained from any presupposition of a modern perspective or theory in opposing Aristotle and from appeals to the recent U.S. congressional and presidential elections, the ongoing threat of nuclear war, and the accelerating destruction of human-fueled climate change as evidence for the rising tide of anti-political power were kept to a minimum. Instead, Snyder opposed Aristotle according to the very same metaphysical presuppositions he used to support *inter alia* his view of the human being. If this opposing view is correct, this need not mean that Aristotle's commonplace was entirely false, or that the annihilation of life on earth is inevitable. Nor does it entail that we should abandon Aristotle's metaphysics or immunise political thought from metaphysics, generally. It could mean however that his metaphysical and political commitments combine to conceal the shadowy truth of the anti-political human, a view that he was apparently unfit to theorise.

[DE14] 14 March, 2017
Teresa Caligiure: **The Sceptical Approach in Petrarch's *Secretum***

The purpose is to discuss the suspension of judgment proposed by Petrarch in his work entitled *Secretum* regarding the lack of a definitive choice regarding his search for Truth; in the literary *fictio*, a dialectic meeting takes place just in her presence between the teacher Augustine and his disciple Francesco, which is one of the greatest manifestations of a sceptical thought strategy that refuses to embrace a univocal moral position in the dialogic genre. The author's ethical scepticism reflects man's inability to pursue and apply the teachings of Christianity, despite wanting to, which is why the writer moves away from the rigid morality of stoicism. In the dialogue, based on the Augustinian motif of rediscovering oneself, the moral project, suggested by the beloved *praeceptor*, is without any doubts definitely postponed by Francesco at the end of the work and substituted for a literary *otium* dedicated to the celebration of Laura and to classical scholarship. The sceptical approach in Petrarch's *Secretum* is also intended as a continuous question from the disciple Francesco, who doubts the dimension proposed by his teacher Augustine and continuously contests the principle of authority.

[DE15] 18 July, 2017
Thomas Meyer and Bill Rebiger: **The Use of Sceptical Strategies to Undermine Authority**

Although they do not appear in ancient scepticism, topics such as knowledge, certainty, and doubt are essential in early modern scepticism. In particular, questioning the certainty of traditional sources of knowledge and doubting the established authorities became more and more common in early modern times, even in discourses outside the traditional philosophical schools. In this non-philosophical context, the posing of questions of certainty and the casting of doubt on authorities were realised by means of sceptical strategies in a broader sense, as Rebiger defined during this dialectical evening. In short, sceptical strategies are a set of literary or rhetorical means intended to induce doubts, questions, and intellectual uneasiness. Eventually, when successful, the use of these sceptical strategies will result in undermining the reliability or trustworthiness of (any) authority as a source of knowledge.

From a modern, i.e. post-1945, point of view, for many Jewish philosophers and intellectuals the (old) difference between 'the ancients and the moderns' (known since the eighteenth century as the 'Querelle des Anciens et des Modernes') became a starting point for revaluating the sceptical tradition from Pascal to Kierkegaard on the one side and Jewish sceptical traditions since Maimonides on the other. For example, Hannah Arendt, Karl Löwith, and Leo Strauss addressed and answered the problems of '1) relativisation, 2) historicisation, 3) indictment of heresy, 4) delegitimation, 5) ridiculisation, and, finally, 6) objectification' (Rebiger) in different ways: their 'solution' was the ancient way of understanding 'political things' (Aristotle's Πολιτικά). Their observations could work as a basis to systematise the understanding of 'Jewish scepticism.'

[DE16] 22 August, 2017
Giuseppe Veltri and Dirk Westerkamp: ***Quaestio sceptica disputata de philosophia judaeorum*: Is there a Jewish Philosophy?**

Leon Roth's (in)famous question 'is there a Jewish philosophy?' has been the subject of an ongoing and controversial debate. What may seem a mere argument of nomenclature among philosophers and historians of philosophy in fact raises important questions concerning the particularistic ('-ish') or universalistic ('philosophy') status of systems of philosophical thought that are intertwined with religious 'truth claims.'

At the Dialectical Evening, both the basic arguments in favour of the 'existence' (not in the quantificational sense) of a Jewish philosophy and their counter-arguments were presented and controversially discussed. The form of the dispute was reminiscent of a mediaeval scholastic *questio* in order to provide a lively and fruitful discussion.

Reading Evening

The Reading Evening is an informal meeting every four weeks (in fortnightly rotation with the Dialectical Evening). Fellows and researchers read and discuss primary texts that are specifically relevant to their respective projects. Each meeting, one fellow or research team member selects and presents a text of particular importance for her research. In reading together, the group benefits from the expertise of the individual researcher.

[RE09] 9 August, 2016
Marietta Horster, Christiane Thompson and James Thompson: **Ludwig Wittgenstein —On Certainty**

Wittgenstein certainly belongs to the most challenging and puzzling philosophers of the twentieth century. Even though he has been regarded as an important figure for positivism and analytic philosophy, it has been incredibly difficult to situate his philosophical work. The *Tractatus logico-philosophical*, published in 1921, is nearly the only work published during Wittgenstein's life time and its reception has been rather one-sided. One important theme of Wittgenstein's work is the critique of philosophy as the bewilderment of language. Wittgenstein's works strongly portray a therapeutic notion of philosophy. The text collection, *On Certainty*, goes back to notes written by Wittgenstein shortly before his death in 1951. The notes have been published posthumously in a collection by Anscombe and Wright in 1969. According to the editors, Wittgenstein's notes deserved to be published separately under the heading of 'certainty.' A central theme of these notes is that propositions—once uttered—can be conceived as 'certain' without being scrutinized in their validity claim (see, e.g., the statement 'This is my hand'). Here, Wittgenstein engages with George Edward Moore, who had published contributions about 'common sense' and the 'proof of the outside world' (cf. Moore 1969). Wittgenstein criticizes Moore for treating certainty as a form of knowledge. The experience of certainty cannot, according to Wittgenstein, be taken as a foundation of knowledge. The goal of this reading evening is to discuss the possibilities and limits of scepticism following Wittgenstein's reflections on certainty. How are belief/certainty/conviction and knowledge related? How does Wittgenstein treat scepticism and doubt? Under which circumstances is the sceptical attitude warranted? These questions were tackled with a selection of text passages from *On Certainty*.

[RE10] 6 September, 2016
Cedric Cohen-Skalli: **Isaac Abravanel's Preface to his Commentary on Former Prophets (1483–1484): Scepticism and New Rhetorical and Philological Attitudes Toward the Biblical Text in the Renaissance**

In his ground-breaking 1937 article "Don Isaac Abravanel and His Relationship to Historical and Political Questions," Baer bluntly states: 'Abravanel was the first Jew to combine Renaissance ideas with the Torah of Israel. He was the first to study tradition in the light of the new historical and humanistic method.' Baer's affirmation, although exaggerated, relied greatly on the reading and interpretation of Abravanel's preface to his *Commentary on the Former Prophets* (on Joshua, Judges, Samuel, and Kings) written in Castile in the years 1483–4, and especially of its discussion of the question: who wrote the books of the Former Prophets. In the discussion, Abravanel develops a new historical sensitivity toward the texts' history and composition. Moreover, he describes the making of the books of the Former Prophets as a multilayered process entailing firstly the sources written by the historical redactors and later the work of compilation and edition made by the editors. This view opened new pathways for later biblical criticism, but also for a new scepticism about the transmission of the divine message within the biblical text itself. Far from Baer's celebration of Isaac Abravanel as the Jewish 'father' of biblical criticism, Cohen-Skalli proposed a new reading and interpretation of this important preface, also taking other parts of it, such as Isaac Abravanel's autobiographical narrative and his discussions on the rhetorical and historical finality of the books of the Former Prophets and on prophecy into account. The reading tried to present the link that unites biographical narrative, historical narrative, biblical narrative, and prophecy in Abravanel's preface.

[RE11] 15 November, 2016
Oren Hanner: **Sceptical Arguments against a Mind-Independent World in Vasubandhu's *Twenty Verses***

The *Twenty Verses* (Sanskrit: *Viṃśikā-kārikā*) is one of the central works of the Buddhist 'Consciousness Only' (*Vijñapti-mātra*) School. It is ascribed to the Indian Buddhist philosopher Vasubandhu and is dated to the end of the fourth century or the beginning of the fifth century CE. This work is dedicated to defending the school's idealist claim, according to which our experiences do not originate from external objects outside the mind (or at least, we cannot be certain that this is the case), while questioning and refuting realist assumptions concerning an objective external reality. Consisting of a polemical dialogue between the author and a hypothetical opponent, the text raises various objections to the idealist stance and then addresses them, relying to a large extent on various Buddhist doctrines and principles.

Modern scholarship has offered different readings of the *Twenty Verses*, with some interpreters suggesting that it articulates a form of ontological idealism, others claiming that it maintains a form of epistemological idealism, and still others seeing it as making principally phenomenological claims. During the reading evening, a recent interpretation by Birgit Kellner and John Taber (2014) was followed, who argue for an idealist interpretation of the *Twenty Verses* and suggest that Vasubandhu's strategy of argumentation in the work is based on an extended *argumentum ad ignorantiam*, where the absence of external objects is derived from the absence of evidence for their existence.

[RE12] 28 February, 2017
Harald Bluhm and Bill Rebiger: **The Function of Experience in Montaigne's Scepticism**

The focus of the reading evening was a specific aspect of Montaigne's scepticism. This was not the well-known, long, and sophisticated *Apology for Raymond Sebond* (II.12), but the essay *On experience* (III.13), the concluding part of *Les Essais*.

Montaigne's existence-philosophical approach forms the basis of his scepticism, his criticism of de-contextualized thinking and ethnocentrism. Some interesting topics in this framework are different elements of scepticism regarding reason and experience, such as the function of experience in critiquing endless conceptual distinctions, in critiquing incorrect ideas of certainty (e.g. interpretations of law, texts, and norms), and in critiquing 'incorrect' ascriptions of relevance.

A starting point for the second text of this Reading Evening, written by Marie de Gournay, was Montaigne's revised view of friendship after his experience of intellectual friendship with her. With this text, a shift of the perspective took place to the experience of a contemporary female author who wanted to become a member of the male-dominated 'république des lettres.' This perspective will open up a new field of insights into scepticism.

[RE13] 21 March, 2017
Josef Stern: **Maimonidean Scepticism**

Two short selections from the *Guide of the Perplexed* were read in order to give a taste of Maimonides' brand of scepticism. Unfortunately, the way Maimonides wrote the *Guide* makes it impossible to understand one passage in isolation; 'you must connect its chapters one with another' (Introduction, Pines 15). So, in addition to the two selections, related chapters were given as background.

The first selection and background chapters (Selection: III: 9: Pines 436–437; Background: III: 24: Pines, 500, paragraph in brackets, II: 33: pp. 363–366, II: 24: pp. 326–7, material within brackets, Introduction, pp. 11–12, material in brackets) is one of Maimonides' clearest sceptical statements about the impossibility of knowledge of immaterial beings by hylomorphic substances (like us) as part of a parabolic interpretation of the scriptural descriptions of the divine 'revelation' at Mt. Sinai. The second selection and background chapters (Selection: I: 32: Pines, pp. 68–70; Background: *Mishneh Torah*, 'Laws of the Foundation of the Torah,' iv, §§10–13, pp. 152–153) describes the kind of perfection that can be achieved by a human who recognizes the limitations of his intellect with respect to knowledge of metaphysics. Again, this is in the context of a parabolic interpretation of a text (here: the rabbinic text about *Pardes*).

[RE14] 25 April, 2017
Emidio Spinelli: **Ancient Scepticism and Its Philosophical Self-Justification (Sextus Empiricus, *Outlines of Pyrrhonism*, I 1–30)**

Against the background of a new complete commentary on Sextus Empiricus's *Outlines of Pyrrhonism*, this lecture aims to offer a first analysis dedicated to a general introduction to Sextus's work and his Pyrrhonian philosophy. Accordingly, after some preliminary considerations of the (non-'linear') history of ancient scepticism in its Pyrrhonian form, it will present a global picture of the self-justification of this 'movement' (which Sextus particularly sets forth in the first book of his *Outlines of Pyrrhonism*, §§ 1–30). After examining the structure of the main reference points at the roots of ancient Pyrrhonism, there was space to offer some reflections on the role of a specifically sceptical use of rationality as well as for underlining (and hopefully clarifying) some general difficulties usually linked to the ethical proposal of ancient Pyrrhonism.

[RE15] 13 June, 2017
Guido Bartolucci: **Political Scepticism and Grotius' Theory of Natural Law**

The Protestant Reform contributed to the formation of a rift in European ethical and religious unity, which for centuries had formed the basis of collective security. This historical transformation was a factor in determining a conflict between different ideas of what was true, holy, and right.

Montaigne and Charron were witnesses to and the greatest interpreters of this period and they used sceptical philosophy to provide interpretive keys to this transformation. One target of their analysis was the traditional idea of natural law, which they criticised using the tools of scepticism. In 1625, Hugo Grotius published his work *The Rights of War and Peace*. In this book, the Dutch jurist reacted against Montaigne's and Charron's ideas of natural law by proposing a new theory that on the one hand was linked to sceptical critique and on the other attempted to go beyond it. The purpose of this Evening was to read the passages in which Grotius discussed this issue and to frame them within the broader transformation of the political thought of this period.

Occasional Events

Lecture Series 2016/2017: Scepticism and Anti-Scepticism in Medieval Jewish Philosophy and Thought

Convenor: **Racheli Haliva**

The tension between reason and revelation has for centuries occupied Jewish philosophers who were committed, on the one hand, to defending Judaism, and, on the other hand, to remaining loyal to philosophical principles.

Maimonides is considered the most prominent Jewish religious philosopher, whose aim was to reconcile philosophy, in particular Aristotelian philosophy, with the fundamental principles of Judaism. But many other Jewish thinkers, before and after him, also struggled with this task, raising the question whether it is possible to attain this reconciliation.

The connection between philosophy and religion was often not an obvious one. As a consequence, it could serve in some cases as grounds for supporting Maimonides' project, while in others it could lead to rejection.

The lecture series 'Scepticism and Anti-Scepticism in Medieval Jewish Thought' focuses on sceptical questions, methods, strategies, and approaches raised by Jewish thinkers in the Middle Ages. In the series of lectures, the variety of attitudes presented by these thinkers, and the latest readings of contemporary scholars concerning those attitudes were examined.

29 November, 2016
Charles Manekin, University of Maryland, College Park/USA
On the Role of Certain and Near-Certain Knowledge in Maimonides' Religious Philosophy

In his famous parable of the palace in the *Guide of the Perplexed*, Maimonides claims that one who has achieved demonstration to the extent possible of everything demonstrable, and who has come close to certainty in those matters in which one can only come close to it—draws near to 'the ruler,' i.e. God (*Guide*, 3.51). Yet why should the psychological state of certainty be relevant for approaching God? Wouldn't it be more appropriate to emphasize the attainment of knowledge? And why would anything less than demonstrated truths affect this process? These questions were considered in light of the importance Maimonides' accords towards the possession of well-established truths in the rational soul. This importance was discussed with special reference to his views on the education of the multitude, the indubitability of the prophetic message, and the necessity of putting deviant philosophers to death. Manekin argued that the possession of well-established or well-grounded truths in the rational soul lies at the heart of his project, and that the achievement of rational certainty and near-certainty are among the means for achieving this goal.

13 December, 2016
Warren Zev Harvey, The Hebrew University of Jerusalem/Israel
Ḥasdai Crescas' Sceptical Critique of Maimonides

In his *Guide of the Perplexed*, Maimonides (1138–1204) sought to anchor the Jewish religion in the principles of Aristotelian science and philosophy. Rabbi Ḥasdai Crescas (c. 1340–1410 or 1411), in his *Light of the Lord*, presented a radical critique of Aristotelian physics and metaphysics, and on the basis of this critique he rejected Maimonides' approach. According to Crescas, human reason can prove the existence of a first cause, but cannot prove God's unity or goodness, that is, it cannot prove the God of the Bible. Religion, he argues, is based on prophecy not philosophy.

20 December, 2016
Yehuda Halper, Bar-Ilan University, Ramat-Gan/Israel
The Sex Life of a Metaphysical Sceptic: Platonic Themes in Gersonides' ***Commentary on Song of Songs***

Gersonides' *Commentary on the Song of Songs* transforms the celebration of the erotic courtship between Solomon and a young woman into a tale of longing between the material intellect and the acquired intellect. On the whole, the presentation of the *Commentary* is Aristotelian: longing is connected to actualising potential, and the active intellect is acquired through the orderly study of the sciences—beginning with logic, then continuing on to mathematics, physics, astronomy, and metaphysics. Yet, at the same time, many main themes of the *Commentary* are Platonic. Like Diotima's description of *eros* in Plato's *Symposium*, the object of desire is never reached in the *Commentary*. Indeed, this kind of *eros* comes from Song of Songs itself, where the erotic courtship is never consummated in the work. In Gersonides' reading, metaphysics is not grasped by the intellect in the way that mathematics and physics are, since it is not grounded in sensory perception, but in common opinions. Moreover,

Gersonides' tale of the material intellect's journey to scientific knowledge is similar in a number of ways to the account of Plato's search for scientific knowledge—and ultimately Plato's lack of solid metaphysical knowledge—in Al-Farabi's *Philosophy of Plato*. Gersonides probably did not read Arabic, but could have read Falaquera's paraphrase of Al-Farabi's work in *Reshit Ḥokhmah*, or else Falaquera's own account of a similar journey to philosophy in *Sefer ha-Mevaqqesh*. According to Al-Farabi and thus Falaquera, Plato's intellectual journey ends with the formation of a city that uses the myth of creation presented in the *Timaeus* as the basis of opinions on which a metaphysics can be built. For Gersonides the Bible, when properly understood, can provide a similar basis of common opinions for grounding metaphysics. Nevertheless, Gersonides himself preferred to study mathematics, physics, and astronomy—sciences he viewed as properly grounded in sensory observation.

10 January, 2017
Howard Kreisel, Ben-Gurion University of the Negev, Beer-Sheva/Israel
Between Philosophic Optimism and Fideistic Scepticism: An Overview of Medieval Jewish Philosophy

In this talk Kreisel showed that the philosophic tradition that penetrated Jewish thought was essentially an optimistic one grounded primarily in the Arabic translations of the writings of Plato, Aristotle and the Neoplatonic philosophy of Plotinus. The Jewish thinkers, following in the footsteps of the Islamic ones, essentially believed that the intellect was capable of apprehending the most fundamental truths regarding God and the structure of the world, whether these truths are attained by way of logical syllogism in the tradition of Aristotle or by way of the illumination of the intellect in the tradition of Plotinus. This optimism can already be detected among the Islamic theologians (*Kalām*) and it also influenced R. Saadiah Gaon (tenth century). Philosophic optimism also characterises the Islamic philosophers, beginning with Al-Kindi (ninth century), and in the Jewish world, beginning with Isaac Israeli, Saadiah's older contemporary. Subsequently, the Jewish philosophic tradition in Andalusia, particularly the philosophy of Solomon Ibn Gabirol, gives expression to this optimism. In later periods, philosophic optimism characterises the Jewish philosophers of Provence (thirteenth and early fourteenth centuries), whose most important exponent was Gersonides, as well as most of the Jewish philosophers of Spain up to the expulsion.

The most blatant example of philosophic scepticism in medieval Jewish philosophy can be found in the thought of Judah Halevi (twelfth century), who on this issue may have been inspired by Al-Ghazzali. Yet in his case, as in the case of Al-Ghazzali, the use of scepticism came in order to defend religious doctrines and the truths of revelation (what some scholars have termed 'fideistic scepticism'). In later periods, the use of scepticism was often tied to the defence of religion, and did not come to question all forms of knowledge, most notably knowledge attained through revelation.

The Evening was concluded with the problem of how to interpret Maimonides on this issue. Maimonides' approach to the ability of philosophy to discover fundamental truths, while at times stressing its severe limitations in the area of metaphysics and even natural philosophy, has led to widely divergent interpretations of his thought. Kreisel argued that Maimonides was a qualified optimist in his philosophic approach, and that some of his more radical sceptical statements regarding the limitations of philosophic knowledge may have served a religious purpose.

17 January, 2017
David Lemler, Université de Strasbourg/France
Halakhic Dogmatism, Aggadic Scepticism: a Duality of Medieval Philosophical Exegesis

As regards the legal aspects of the Jewish tradition, Maimonides might be described as a dogmatic. In his *Mishneh Torah*, he proposes a final and exhaustive codification of the law, without mentioning the diverging views expressed in his talmudic sources. He also proposes a dogmatic list of compulsory beliefs. When one turns to the non-legal aspects of the biblical and rabbinical tradition, Maimonides appears far lesser assertive. He proposes philosophical allegorical interpretations of prophetic parables, but often stresses the fact that other interpretations are possible and sometimes offers several interpretations of one and the same passage. Maimonides' abandoned project of writing a treatise dedicated to deciphering rabbinical *aggadot* was taken over by post-Maimonidean philosophers especially in Provence. In their philosophical exegeses of *aggadot*, authors such as Moses Ibn Tibbon or Levi ben Abraham of Villefranche show the same doubts as regards the possibility of offering a 'true' and final interpretation. What is at stake in this dual epistemic attitude of these philosopher-exegetes? Lemler argued that it reflects an essential aspect of their philosophical practice understood as a Foucaldian 'spirituality.'

24 January, 2017
Lawrence J. Kaplan, McGill University, Montreal/Canada
Does Maimonides' Theory of Parables in the *Guide of the Perplexed* Support a Sceptical Reading of the Work?

On the face of it there would seem to be little or no connection between Maimonides' theory of parables in the *Guide of the Perplexed* and a sceptical reading of the work. But is this the case?

Maimonides characterises parables as possessing either an external meaning (Arabic *ẓāhir*) or an internal meaning (Arabic *bāṭin*). In the introduction to the

Guide however, Maimonides seems to contradict himself regarding the value of a parable's external meaning. On the one hand, he states that the parable's *ẓāhir*, per se, is worth nothing—except that the *ẓāhir* serves the paradoxical dual function of first concealing the *bāṭin*, but then pointing to the *bāṭin*, once, that is, one has succeeded in, as it were, 'decoding' the *ẓāhir*. On the other hand, he states that the parable's *ẓāhir* does possess intrinsic value, since it 'contains wisdom that is useful in many respects, among which is the welfare of human societies.'

How are we to resolve this contradiction? Might a sceptical reading of the *Guide* provide us with a solution to this problem? Or should we seek to resolve this contradiction in light of the more traditional view of the *Guide* as a bibliocentric work, concerned primarily with the meta-philosophical problem of showing how those parts of the Bible that appear to lack wisdom, do, in fact, if read and understood properly, contain it, if in different ways. The talk was devoted to an exploration of these alternative approaches.

7 February, 2017
Ariel Malachi, Bar-Ilan University, Ramat-Gan/Israel
Scepticism at the Service of Revelation: Logic and epistemology in Judah Halevi's ***Kuzari***

Many scholars have acknowledged the importance of Judah Halevi's criticism of philosophy. Some of them even indicated Halevi's use of philosophical tools to establish his criticism, in a way that might be regarded as a sceptical approach to philosophy. Nevertheless, the general impression from scholarly studies is that the criticism of philosophy is merely a secondary assisting goal for the main goal of the Kuzari, namely proposing revelation as an alternative to philosophy, and accepting revelation in a very unsceptical manner. Maybe that is the reason those scholars did not tend to analyse Halevi's criticism of philosophy systematically. In the talk, Malachi tried to identify the principles of Halevi's criticism of philosophy. In this regard, he argued: (a) that the criticism of philosophy represents a sceptical approach based on logical and epistemological principles of Aristotelian logic; (b) that this sceptical approach is used not only to criticise philosophy, but also to establish revelation. Consequently, he suggested that for Halevi, the same sceptic approach can propose revelation not only as a philosophically legitimate option, but also more persuasive and therefore preferable.

14 February, 2017
Racheli Haliva, University of Hamburg
Anti-Scepticism within the Jewish Averroist School

Numerous attempts were made in the Middle Ages by philosophers and theologians to explain the origin of the world. Positioning themselves with regard to this crucial issue was particularly important for medieval thinkers of all religions, since it indicated their relation to one of the fundamental principles of their faith. The present lecture presents the anti-sceptical approach, offered by Yitzhak Albalag and Yitzhak Polqar—two Jewish Averroists of the fourteenth century who lived in northern Spain, to one of the most fundamental questions every religious philosopher has to address: is the world created by God ex nihilo, that is from absolute non-existence, as suggested by religious tradition, or, is the world eternal, as argued by Aristotle?

Albalag and Polqar adopted the philosophy of Ibn Rushd and considered him to be the best commentator of Aristotle. Their interpretation of Judaism, in light of Averroes' Aristotelianism, was based on the assumption that Judaism and true philosophy must always coincide. These two thinkers, then, explain the origin of the world, from a philosophical point of view which clearly rejects the traditional belief.

8–11 May, 2017
Conference: Scepticism from Antiquity to Modern Times

The First International Conference on Scepticism at the University of Hamburg, organised by the Maimonides Centre for Advanced Studies in close co-operation with the Department of Philosophy at La Sapienza University of Rome, addresses the main elements, strategies, and definitions of scepticism with a focus on ancient, medieval, and early modern philosophy. A group of established professors and young scholars working on PhDs and post-docs lectured on the main questions of sceptical philosophy, such as the criteria for defining and distinguishing ancient scepticism from modern scepticism and the debates on the existence and meaning of a Jewish (anti-) scepticism.

Lectures

Antiquity

> Emidio Spinelli, Sapienza Università di Roma/Italien
> 'Dialectic and Sophisms: the Sceptical Dissolution of Dogmatic Logic'

Katja Vogt, Columbia University New York/USA (via web conferencing)
'Ancient Scepticism and its Interlocutors'

Charles Snyder, University of Hamburg/Germany
'Academic Scepticism and the Teachability of Practical Ethics'

Stéphane Marchand, ENS de Lyon/France
'Sextus Empiricus' Use of δύναμις'

Diego Machuca, CONICET Buenos Aires/Argentina
'Agrippan Pyrrhonism, Questionable Assumptions, and the Epistemic Challenge of Disagreement'

Jan Opsomer, Katholieke Universiteit Leuven/Belgium
'Plotinus and Scepticism'

Charlos Lévy, Université Paris-Sorbonne/France
'Scepticism and Monotheism: A Specific Relation?'

Gisela Striker, Harvard University/USA
'Ancient vs. Early Modern Scepticism: Was There a Cartesian Revolution?'

Middle Ages

Josef Stern, University of Chicago/USA
'What is Maimonidean Scepticism?'

Zev Harvey, Hebrew University of Jerusalem/Israel
'The Problem of Many Gods in Al-Ghazali, Averroes, Maimonides, and Crescas'

Henrik Lagerlund, University of Western Ontario/Canada
'The Sources of Medieval Scepticism and the Origin of Divine Deception'

Heidrun Eichner, University Tübingen/Germany
'Reason and Revelation: Fighting Scepticism in the Context of Islamic Theological Manuals'

(Early) Modern Times I

Sébastien Charles, Université du Quebec à Trois-Rivières/Canada
'Scepticism in Modern Times'

Stephan Schmid, University of Hamburg/Germany
'Varieties of Early Modern Scepticism'

Yitzhak Melamed, Johns Hopkins University/USA
'The Road not Taken: Why was Spinoza not a Sceptic?'

Gideon Freudenthal, Tel Aviv University/Israel
'Salomon Maimon: Scepticism of the First and Second Order'

Keynote Speech

Giuseppe Veltri, University of Hamburg/Germany
'Enquiring into (Jewish) Scepticism'

Roundtables of Early Career Researchers

Benjamin Wilck, Humboldt-University Berlin/Germany
'Sextus Empiricus' Criticism of the Foundations of Ancient Mathematics'

Máté Veres, University of Hamburg/Germany
'Lapsarian Scepticism in Cicero's *De Natura Deorum*'

Ariel Malachi, Bar-Ilan University Ramat-Gan/Israel
'When Scepticism Turns Against the Sceptic: The Use of Scepticism by Medieval Religious Thinkers—The Case of Al-Ghazali, Halevi and Maimonides'

José María Sánchez de León Serrano, Hebrew University of Jerusalem/Israel
'The Role of Sceptical Doubt in Spinoza's Naturalism'

Ville Paukkonen, University of Helsinki/Finland; Boğaziçi University Istanbul/Turkey
'Scepticism Concerning Self-Knowledge in Early Modern Philosophy: the Case of George Berkeley'

Nancy Abigail Nuñez, Universidad Nacional Autónoma de México/Mexico
'Narrowing Process and the Context-Sensitivity of Knowledge Attribution Sentences'

Maimonides Lectures on Scepticism

The Maimonides lectures were established to invite international researchers to give a talk within the field of scepticism. The lectures are recorded and published on the webpage of the Centre in order to make them available to a larger audience.

8 February, 2017
Moshe Idel, Hebrew University of Jerusalem/Israel
From Mysticism to Scepticism

The lecture dealt first with an early passage by Maimonides, found in his *Commentary on the Mishnah, Sanhedrin*, dealing with the post-mortem union of the human intellect with the angelic world, which reflects the impact of the rational mysticism of Avicenna. This passage was accurately translated from Arabic into Hebrew by Naḥmanides, which puts into relief aspects that correspond with his understanding of Kabbalah.

Then, following the lead of Leo Strauss and Shlomo Pines, there was a brief discussion of the sceptical aspects of the late Maimonides, in the *Guide for the Perplexed*, concerning his attitude to the Hebrew language and the limits of human speculation, and, finally, a discussion of a passage from the *Guide* dealing with the manner in which the secrets of the Torah should be extracted from the biblical text, and compare it to Abraham Abulafia's ecstatic Kabbalah.

1 March, 2017
Nuccio Ordine, L'Università della Calabria/Italy
The Search for Truth in Giordano Bruno's Work

For Giordano Bruno, we do not possess the truth, but we search for it. His philosophy begins with Copernican heliocentrism and approaches an endless view of the universe: in an infinite universe, in fact, there can be no absolute centre; the centre of the universe is the one who observes the universe. Bruno therefore criticises two rigid and opposing but complementary positions: dogmatism (which posits that there is one truth), and some radical currents of scepticism (which deny the existence of truth). Bruno praises a point of view that encompasses doubt, uncertainty, and relativity, interwoven with typical arguments of scepticism, but places them in a perspective in which the search for truth is essential to give meaning to life.

3 May, 2017
Jonathan Garb, Hebrew University of Jerusalem/Israel
Doubt and Certainty in Early Modern Kabbalah

This lecture contrasted the rhetoric of certainty in medieval Kabbalah with the increased recurrence of doubt in modern Kabbalah, tracing the development of the ontological discourse on doubt and stressing the radical possibility that doubt is not limited to human perception of the divine, but could also limit divine self-knowledge. Then the lecture turned to psychological discussions of doubt and certainty of the Hasidim and R. Kook. Finally, Garb considered the broader historical context of this development: the rise of scepticism in the seventeenth century, Jewish enlightenment in the nineteenth century, and full-fledged secularisation in R. Kook's time.

16 May, 2017
Jani Hakkarainen, University of Tampere/Finland
Hume on Possible Duration without Possible Temporal Parts—A Sceptical Solution

In *A Treatise of Human Nature* Book 1, Part 2, Section 5, Paragraph 29 (1739), David Hume (1711–76) seems to put forward the view that an atemporal, steadfast, and unchanging object has the capacity to endure. This is deeply puzzling, for Hume believes that any enduring object divides into temporal parts. However, this is not possible for an atemporal object, that is, for temporal nothingness, so temporal nothingness cannot endure.

Hakkarainen argued that Hume should be read as claiming that in such cases it merely appears to us that temporal nothingness has the capacity to endure, and that it is causally possible that *reality* is different from *appearance*: really, there is a duration and composition of temporal parts. Therefore, the lecture draws on a distinction which Hume himself employs at the end of *Treatise* 1.2.5: the traditional sceptical distinction, familiar from the work of the ancient sceptic Sextus Empiricus, between appearance and reality in the sense of perceptions being distinguished from their real causes.

6 June, 2017
Wilhelm Schmidt-Biggemann, Free University Berlin/Germany
***Lingua Adamica* and Philological Scepticism—Rise and Fall in Kabbalistic Key-Concepts**

God spoke and the world became real; and the pre-lapsarian Adam was given insight into the essence and the power of the divine language. It was one of the aims of both Jewish and Christian Kabbalah to regain this paradisiacal knowledge, which was lost with the fall of the first human beings. The idea of the *lingua Adamica* stems from

Philo; it was later shared by the Christian Church Fathers as well as Jewish rabbis, and it was fully developed by the Christian Kabbalists Pico and Reuchlin. The concept was harshly criticised in the High Middle Ages by Naḥmanides (Ramban), and in the course of the sixteenth and seventeenth centuries, biblical criticism following these traces made it obvious that Philo's allegorical exegesis of Genesis 2:19 f. could not provide the philological basis for those far-reaching pious speculative and mystical consequences. However, the idea remained vivid, in spite of acid criticism in the age of Enlightenment, and it finally survived in Benjamin's theory of language.

20 June, 2017
Omri Boehm, The New School for Social Research, New York/USA
Maimonides, Spinoza and Kant on Enlightenment and Prophecy

It is common to understand Kant's notion of enlightenment as having the courage to 'think for oneself.' While not contesting this definition, the assumption that 'selbst denken' in Kant consists in refusing the guidance of another over our own thinking was rejected. Paradoxical though it may seem, following another's guidance—in the strong sense of following without understanding—emerges in Kant as a necessary condition for thinking for oneself. In this light, the relationship between enlightenment (thinking for oneself) and religion (prophecy/revelation) must be reconsidered. Far from depending on the rejection of the prophets' authority—as it is in Spinoza's concept of enlightenment—Kantian enlightenment is impossible without it.

11 July, 2017
Carlos Fraenkel, McGill University, Montreal/Canada
Metaphysical Scepticism and Sufi Alternative: Al-Ghazali, Maimonides, and Abraham ben Maimonides

In the talk, Fraenkel offered a solution to the puzzle of why Abraham ben Maimonides staunchly defends his father's intellectual legacy against critics in the West and the East and presents himself as his intellectual heir while at the same time strikingly departing from this legacy: whereas Maimonides interprets Judaism as a philosophical religion, Abraham proposes a Sufi interpretation. Al-Ghazali's account of the relationship between *falsafa* and Sufism was used as a model to explain the relationship between father and son. Both al-Ghazali and Maimonides are metaphysical sceptics—i.e., they hold that reason cannot conclusively settle metaphysical questions. However, in contrast to al-Ghazali and Abraham, Maimonides does not try to overcome scepticism through the Sufi path to God. Therefore, Abraham's departure from Maimonides turns out to be (at least in part) an attempt to solve a specific epistemological problem.

Sceptical Ateliers

A Sceptical Atelier is required whenever we are faced with a multifaceted phenomenon which can only be understood in an interdisciplinary way by combining various disciplinary perspectives into a unified understanding which can account for how and why these facets are united in the phenomenon in question. The Sceptical Atelier is designed as a discussion forum, in which specialists in their fields contribute to the understanding of a certain topic or phenomenon. Thus, the participants will not have prepared a particular talk or paper, but will rather have studied the object of common inquiry in advance so as to share their notes and thoughts about it in the joint discussion.

6–9 February, 2017
Sceptical Atelier: Salomon Maimon's *Lebensgeschichte*: Reading a New English Translation
Convenors: Yitzhak Melamed (Johns Hopkins University/USA) and Stephan Schmid (University of Hamburg/Germany)

> Participants:
> Leora Batnitzky (Princeton University/USA)
> Florian Ehrensperger (University of British Columbia/Canada)
> Warren Zev Harvey (Hebrew University of Jerusalem/Israel)
> Moshe Idel (Hebrew University of Jerusalem/Israel)
> Ada Rapoport-Albert (University College London/UK)
> Paul Reitter (Ohio State University/USA)
> Oded Schechter (HSE Moscow/Russia)
> Abraham Socher (Oberlin College/USA)
> Shaul Stampfer (Hebrew University of Jerusalem/Israel)

Salomon Maimon's *Lebensgeschichte* has fascinated readers ever since its first publication in 1792/3. In light of Maimon's exceptionally vivid description of his life as a Talmudic prodigy from—as he puts it—'the woods of Lithuania,' a preadolescent husband, an aspiring kabbalist-magician, an earnest young philosopher, a bedraggled beggar, an urbane Berlin pleasure-seeker, a Hamburg gymnasiast, and, eventually, the philosopher of whom Kant would speak in highest terms, the widely shared fascination with and admiration of his *Lebensgeschichte* should not come as a surprise.

At the same time, fascination with Maimon's vivid prose led later editors of this text to omit the philosophical passages found in his original version, which they found anathematic or even obstructive to the narrative of Maimon's thrilling life story, or to banish them to appendices. In fact, there is no modern edition of Maimon's *Lebensgeschichte* (whether in German, Hebrew, or English) which preserves the original order of the text. Given that it was via his *Lebensgeschichte* that Maimon publicly introduced himself (under his newly adopted pseudonym 'Maimon') into the philosophical scene of the German Enlightenment, the omission of Maimon's philosophical 'digressions' constitutes a fatal distortion of the original text: it prevents modern readers from seeing the extent to which Maimon conceived of himself as picking up the Jewish rationalist tradition founded by his medieval namesake Moshe ben Maimon (or Maimonides) so as to transpose it into transcendental philosophical terms inspired by Kant.

The Sceptical Atelier on Maimon's *Lebensgeschichte* consisted of an intense close-reading workshop in which a new English translation of this text was discussed. This translation was prepared by Paul Reitter and edited by Yitzhak Y. Melamed and Abraham P. Socher. It is acually the first modern edition of Maimon's *Lebensgeschichte* to preserve its original order. The collaborative study of this text promises to foster a deeper and better understanding not only of Maimon's intellectual biography, but also of his philosophical thinking in general. The Atelier is a preread event devoted to a chapter by chapter discussion of the book (devoting roughly one hour to each chapter).

22 – 24 May, 2017
Sceptical Atelier: Simone Luzzatto's *Socrates*: Reading the Forthcoming First English Translation
Convenors: Michela Torbidoni and Giuseppe Veltri

> Participants:
> Guido Bartolucci (University of Calabria/Italy)
> Paolo Bernardini (University of Insubria/Italy)
> Antonella del Prete (Tuscia University of Viterbo/Italy)
> Cristiana Facchini (University of Bologna/Italy)
> Fabrizio Lelli (Salento University of Lecce/Italy)
> Anna Lissa (University Paris 8/France)
> Luciana Pepi (University of Palermo/Italy)
> Emidio Spinelli (La Sapienza University of Rome/Italy)
> Josef Stern (University of Chicago/USA)
> Syros Vasileios (University of Jyväskylä/Finland

The Sceptical Atelier is a pre-read event devoted to the discussion of the forthcoming bilingual (Italian/English) edition of Simone Luzzatto's *Socrate overo dell'humano sapere* (1651) prepared by Giuseppe Veltri and Michela Torbidoni. It is an important but overlooked work, which provides a critical perspective on the place of Jewish scepticism within the seventeenth century.

Simone Luzzatto (ca. 1583–1663) was the chief rabbi of the Jewish community of Venice as well as a highly talented classicist and a passionate reader of medieval Italian literature.

Stephan Schmid and Yitzhak Melamed
Report on the Sceptical Atelier on Maimon's *Lebensgeschichte* (6–9 February, 2017)

Salomon Maimon's *Lebensgeschichte*

Salomon Maimon's *Lebensgeschichte* is an exceptional book which has fascinated readers ever since its first publication in 1792/3. In light of Maimon's vivid description of his life as a talmudic prodigy from—as he puts it—'the woods of Lithuania,' a pre-adolescent husband, an aspiring kabbalist magician, an earnest young philosopher, a bedraggled beggar, an urbane Berlin pleasure-seeker, a Hamburg gymnasiast, and, eventually, the philosopher of whom Kant would speak in highest terms, the widely shared fascination with and admiration of this book should not come as a surprise.

Apart from this, Maimon's *Lebensgeschichte* is a unique historical source of Jewish life and culture in eighteenth-century Eastern Europe and an important document about both the emergence of the (New) Hasidism founded by Israel Ben Eliezer (also known as Baal Shem Tov or Besht) and the social status of Jews in Western Europe, comprising such different groups as the enlightened Jewish circle around Moses Mendelssohn in Berlin and Jewish salesmen in Amsterdam. It also testifies to the huge impact of Jewish Enlightenment on late eighteenth-century German philosophy in general.

Moreover, the *Lebensgeschichte* is particularly key for understanding Maimon's philosophy, as it meticulously describes the development and formation of his thought: his early talmudic studies, his teenage digressions into kabbalist magic, his fascination with Maimonides, and his encounter with Enlightenment philosophy in Berlin and its empiricist and rationalist forerunners such as Locke, Hume, Spinoza, and Leibniz, which eventually led him to synthesise their views in a 'Coalitionsystem' that he self-consciously opposed to Kant's transcendental philosophy.

In fact, the *Lebensgeschichte* was Maimon's first published book. Despite being often unknown (or at least unmentioned), this is a highly significant fact, as it reveals an altogether new facet of this book. The *Lebensgeschichte* is far more than a mere collection of autobiographical memories. It is his official introduction to the German Enlightenment under his newly adopted pseudonym of 'Maimon'—derived from his philosophical hero Maimonides—and also, at the same time, the constitution of his public philosophical persona. It is an integral part of Maimon's public presentation as a Jewish philosopher.[1]

---

[1] For a rigorous defence of Salomon Maimon as 'the only modern Jewish philosopher worthy of the name,' see Yitzhak Y. Melamed, "Salomon Maimon et l'échec de la philosophie juive modern," *Revue germanique international* 9 (2009): 175–187.

That Maimon's purpose in the publication of his *Lebensgeschichte* was partially also to introduce himself to the philosophical community of his days as a Jewish thinker adopting the legacy of Maimonides helps to explain the otherwise startling fact that he opens the second part of his book with ten chapters (comprising 135 pages in the original German edition published in 1793) of a summary and vast excerpts of Maimonides' *Guide for the Perplexed*.[2] Maimon prefaces his digression into Maimonides' philosophy by confessing that his intellectual development was highly influenced by Maimonides' writings and his wish to 'familiarise the reader, at least to some extent, with the *spirit* of these writings' in order 'to enable the reader to assess the influence this great man's writings had on me.'[3]

Now, Maimon was well aware of the fact that not all of his readers would be interested in his digression about Maimonides' philosophy, writing that '[r]eaders looking for mere incidents or a novelistic story can skim these pages, which will not, however, be unimportant for intelligent readers.'[4] What is striking, however, is that none of the editors of modern editions of Maimon's *Lebensgeschichte* (whether in German, Hebrew, or English) seem to belong to these 'intelligent readers' addressed by Maimon, since they all omit the first ten chapters of the second part of his *Lebensgeschichte* or banish them to appendices. In light of the significance of these chapters, this 'emendation' of the original text seems to be fatal: it prevents modern readers from seeing the extent to which Maimon conceived of himself as picking up the Jewish rationalist tradition founded by his medieval namesake Moshe ben Maimon (or Maimonides) so as to transpose it into transcendental philosophical terms inspired by Kant.

For this reason, a new edition of Maimon's *Lebensgeschichte* which preserves the original order of the text is urgently required. Precisely such an edition has been prepared by Abraham Socher and Yitzhak Y. Melamed, which is presented in a widely accessible English translation by Paul Reitter. It was to the discussion of this text that we devoted the Maimonides Centre's first Sceptical Atelier.

The New Format of the Sceptical Atelier

But what is a Sceptical Atelier and why do we need this new format? Unlike familiar event formats such as conferences or workshops, in which participants speak about

---

[2] As Warren Zev Harvey reported during the Sceptical Atelier on Maimon's *Lebensgeschichte*, some scholars have explained Maimon's vast digression by the (alleged) fact that Maimon was paid by the page and was trying to augment his salary by filling some of them—135 in total!—with excerpts from Maimonides' *Guide*. This explanation could neither be confirmed nor refuted by the participants of the Sceptical Atelier.

[3] Salomon Maimon, *Lebensgeschichte von ihm selbst geschrieben und herausgegeben von K. P. Moritz*, Zweiter und letzter Theil (Berlin: Friedrich Vieweg dem älteren, 1793): 4; MS 230.

[4] *Ibidem*.

their research and findings by giving talks or papers, the Sceptical Atelier is designed as a discussion forum, in which specialists in their fields contribute to the understanding of a certain topic or phenomenon. Thus, participants in a Sceptical Atelier will not have prepared a particular talk or paper, but will rather have studied the object of common inquiry in advance—in our case, the new edition and translation of Maimon's *Lebensgeschichte* prepared by A. Socher, Y. Melamed, and P. Reitter—so as to share their notes and thoughts about it in the joint discussion.

A Sceptical Atelier is, by nature and design, 'sceptical' in the original sense of the term: it is an open and unbiased investigation of a certain topic in which arguments from different perspectives are weighed and compared.[5] Being concerned with Salomon Maimon, our Sceptical Atelier was also sceptical with respect to its particular subject: given that we have only a finite capacity for understanding, Maimon held that we are never able to acquire infallible (and thus true) knowledge about empirical matters and are thus doomed to empirical scepticism.[6]

So much for the new format of the Sceptical Atelier. What is the advantage of this format, and why is it needed? The format of the Sceptical Atelier is particularly apt when it comes to understanding a multifaceted phenomenon or object of study whose full appreciation requires a combination of a whole gamut of disciplinary perspectives. It is a format that makes interdisciplinary research extremely fruitful and rewarding: by being devoted to a single yet multifaceted subject of study, the format of the Sceptical Atelier guarantees a focused and unified discussion. It ensures that the contributions from different disciplinary perspectives are indeed concerned with the same subject and will therefore lead to a comprehensive understanding of one topic, as opposed to a collection of various views about different things (as unfortunately happens all too often in interdisciplinary discussions). By developing the single disciplinary perspectives in real time, as it were, and in the presence of experts from other disciplines, the format of the Sceptical Atelier ensures that the different perspectives do in fact complement and inform one another. In this way, a Sceptical Atelier is not only likely to provide us with a better grasp of one multifaceted subject of study, but rather with a *unified* understanding of this subject: an understanding that does not only yield knowledge *that* the subject in question exhibits various fac-

---

[5] The Greek word 'skepsis' means 'search' or 'investigation.' In line with this, Sextus Empiricus wrote: 'Those who are called Dogmatists in the proper sense of the word think that they have discovered the truth [...]. [...] Academics have asserted that things cannot be apprehended. And the Sceptics are still investigating.' See idem, *Outlines of Scepticism*, ed. and transl. by Julia Annas and Jonathan Barnes (Cambridge: Cambridge University Press 1994): 3 (I.i.3).

[6] As Maimon explains in his *Lebensgeschichte*, ch. 16 (original edition: 254; MS 381), his empirical scepticism is part of his philosophical '*coalition system*,' which 'takes up the problem that Kant's *Critique* tries to solve—namely, the, *quid juris?*—but [...] leaves room for *Humean skepticism* in all its force.' For more on Maimon's empirical scepticism, see the "Concluding Note" of his *Essay on Transcendental Philosophy*, eds. and trans. Nick Midgley et alii (London: Continuum, 2019): 220–227, and as a commentary the essays collected in Gideon Freudenthal, ed., *Salomon Maimon: Rational Dogmatist, Empirical Skeptic; Critical Assessments* (Dordrecht: Kluwer, 2003).

ets, but an understanding that also reveals *how* and *why* these multiple facets are *unified* in the subject in question. To make a long story short, then, a Sceptical Atelier is required whenever we are faced with a multifaceted phenomenon which can only be understood in an interdisciplinary way by combining various disciplinary perspectives into a unified understanding which can account for how and why these facets are united in the phenomenon in question.

As has become plain in the section above, Maimon's *Lebensgeschichte* is precisely this kind of multifaceted phenomenon. Touching upon such diverse topics as the history of Eastern European Jews in the eighteenth century, the various traditions and manifestations of Jewish life, faith, and scholarship, the emergence of Hassidism, and the German philosophy of the Enlightenment, an adequate treatment of the *Lebensgeschichte* calls for an interdisciplinary approach in which the single disciplinary perspectives are integrated into a unified understanding of this exceptional book.

Participants and Programme

The Sceptical Atelier on Maimon's *Lebensgeschichte* was organised by Stephan Schmid and Yitzhak Y. Melamed. Schmid is professor of the history of philosophy at the University of Hamburg and one of the co-directors of the Maimonides Centre for Advanced Studies—Jewish Scepticism, who is particularly interested in the philosophy of Spinoza and the way it was developed and transformed by Salomon Maimon. Melamed is Charlotte Bloomberg Professor of Philosophy at the Johns Hopkins University in Baltimore, USA. He is a world-leading scholar of Spinoza and Maimon with a particular interest in how they shaped or even initiated the development of German Idealism. Particular relevant to the Sceptical Atelier is the fact that Melamed is one of the editors of the new annotated English translation of Maimon's *Lebensgeschichte*.

Fortunately, we managed to attract not only Abraham P. Socher, professor of Jewish studies and religion at Oberlin College (Ohio, USA) and the other editor of the new edition of the *Lebensgeschichte*, but also an excellent group of scholars specialising in Jewish thought, the history of Hassidism, East European Jewry, and the philosophy of Salomon Maimon. Aside from this, we were also able to arrange a Skype conference with Paul Reitter, professor at the Department of Germanic Languages and Literatures at The Ohio State University (Columbus, USA), who translated the document discussed in our Sceptical Atelier.

The participants invited to this Sceptical Atelier were:

Leora Batnitzky, Ronald O. Perelman Professor of Jewish Studies and professor of religion at Princeton University, USA. She is a specialist on (the emergence of) modern Jewish thought and the development of the idea of Judaism as a religion in the sense in which German Protestants coined this term.

Florian Ehrensperger, who works at the School of Library, Archival and Information Studies at the University of British Columbia in Vancouver, Canada. He has published on "The Problem of Individuality and Subjectivity in the Philosophy of Salomon Maimon" and has edited a German critical edition of Maimon's *Essay on Transcendental Philosophy* (*Versuch über die Transzendentalphilosophie*).

Warren Zev Harvey, professor emeritus of Jewish thought at the Hebrew University of Jerusalem (Israel). He is an expert on medieval Jewish philosophy with a particular focus on Maimonides and Ḥasdai Crescas, and he is also famous for his work on Spinoza and Mendelssohn.

Moshe Idel, Emeritus Max Cooper Professor of Jewish Thought at the Hebrew University of Jerusalem (Israel) and a world-famous specialist in Jewish mysticism and Kabbalah studies.

Ada Rapoport-Albert, professor emerita of Jewish history at the Department of Hebrew and Jewish Studies at University College London (England). She has done ground-breaking work on the emergence and dissemination of Hasidism in eighteenth-century Poland and on gender issues in the history of Judaism.

Oded Schechter, professor at the School of Philosophy of the National Research University, Higher School of Economics in Moscow (Russia). He is an expert on rabbinic hermeneutics and the philosophy of Spinoza and Salomon Maimon.

Shaul Stampfer, professor of Soviet and East European Jewry at the Hebrew University, who specialises in Lithuanian yeshivas as well as Jewish demography, migration, and education.

Apart from these, many members and (prospective) fellows of the MCAS, as well as graduate and doctoral students—some even travelling from other German cities—attended our discussions. Among them were Giuseppe Veltri, Racheli Haliva, Patrick Benjamin Koch, Josef Stern, Máté Veres, and Dirk Westerkamp.

The Sceptical Atelier on Maimon's *Lebensgeschichte* lasted for three and a half days. During these days, we discussed the whole book page by page. Furthermore, our discussions were complemented by a satellite talk on "Maimonides: From Mysticism to Scepticism" held by Moshe Idel on Wednesday evening. Idel argued that Abraham Abulafia's ecstatic Kabbalah was (at least in part) inspired by his reading of Maimonides' recommendations on how to extract secrets from the Torah in his *Guide for the Perplexed*.

The combination of distinguished specialists in various disciplines, each of whom could illuminate certain aspects of the *Lebensgeschichte*, and a generous time schedule led to a unique atmosphere for an exceptionally fruitful discussion. This discussion not only resulted in intellectual satisfaction for our participants, but also in major improvements to the discussed manuscript.

Results

The Atelier proved to be an unparalleled event in the study of Maimon's philosophy and thought and made an immense contribution to the development and success of the new edition of his *Lebensgeschichte*. The rare opportunity to bring together the very best world scholars in various sub-fields of Jewish studies and to have them give a close study of this key text enabled the editors to solve numerous scholarly problems, test their conjectures, and overall to develop an extraordinarily rich overview of Salomon Maimon, the person and his philosophy.

For Socher and Melamed, the Atelier proved to be a once-in-a-lifetime opportunity, and they hope and strive to share the fruits of the event in the forthcoming book. The input we received from other participants was equally enthusiastic, to the extent that many suggested using this kind of intellectual forum for the study of other works and thinkers as well. In fact, we already held a second Sceptical Atelier on Simone Luzzatto's *Socrate* in May 2017, and we have planned another for 2018.

The new edition and translation of Maimon's *Lebensgeschichte*, discussed at the Sceptical Atelier, is expected to be published in spring 2018 with Princeton University Press.

Michela Torbidoni
Report on the Sceptical Atelier on Simone Luzzatto's *Socrates*: Reading the Forthcoming First English Translation (22–24 May, 2017)

The second Sceptical Atelier took place from 22 to 24 May 2017 at the Maimonides Centre for Advanced Studies in Hamburg. It successfully accomplished the aim of gathering a group of ten experts together with the editors of the volume (Giuseppe Veltri and Michela Torbidoni) to discuss the philosophical and historical questions raised by Simone Luzzatto's *Socrates or on Human Knowledge* (1651) and the adequacy of the English translation.

In order to make the most of the available time, a number of key topics were defined, such as authority, imagination, and memory, the soul and the intellect, and the enigmatic final part of the book, with a corresponding number of pages being selected from the *Socrates*. The guest scholars were provided with these selections along with the entire book in the original language and a list of recommended literature one month before the beginning of the Atelier. They were then asked to focus more specifically on one of the key topics according to their areas of expertise and to be able to lead a debate on different crucial issues within those contexts. The different contributions followed a predetermined programme scheduled according to the key topics, which was intended not only to give exhaustive room to each of the Atelier's guest scholars, but also to advance progressively into the heart of *Socrates*' main topics.

The topic of authority in the frame of Luzzatto's work and thinking was explored in an intense debate promoted by the significant inputs given by the invited scholars Vasileios Syros, Cristiana Facchini, and Anna Lissa.

Vasileios Syros, professor at the Academy of Finland whose work deals with the political thought of Simone Luzzatto, pointed out the importance of the reason of state in early modern Jewish thought and especially the influence of the Jesuit Giovanni Botero on Luzzatto's political thinking. He also highlighted some common ideas shared by many French libertines, such as Gabriel Naudé, and Luzzatto's philosophical work. He also stressed the attempt of Luzzatto's political and philosophical reflection to conciliate neo-Stoicism and scepticism in order to shape new arguments in favour of tolerance, cosmopolitanism, and the coexistence of different groups in the same city.

Cristiana Facchini, professor at the University of Bologna, emphasised the role played by the Inquisition and censorship and the actual circulation of the books in seventeenth-century Venice. She also invited us to overcome the usual categories of 'traditionalist' and 'anti-traditionalist' for defining Luzzatto's work and to focus more on the complex Baroque atmosphere of his time. The facts that many of Luzzatto's biblical quotations were also widely used in public sermons and that the trial, which is a significant pattern in the framework of *Socrates*, was also a recurrent metaphor in the literature of the time suggest that we should read Luzzatto's evidence as an element of urban history and of a policy in favour of tolerance within communities.

Anna Lissa, maître de conférences at the University of Paris 8, focused on the image of the trial as a linking pattern between Luzzatto's two Italian books: *Discourse on the State of the Jews* (1638) and *Socrates or on Human Knowledge* (1651). The first is an apologetic treatise and the second a fictional trial in which Socrates is to be sentenced because he promoted and spread a suspension of judgement, namely the suspension of judgement concerning what is fair and unfair in a society. She stressed the fact that the authority against which Luzzatto was arguing is political and that he acknowledged a state of political and cultural decay that must be solved not through violence, but rather through the tools offered by wisdom.

The topic of imagination and memory was investigated by the ideas presented by the guest scholars Paolo Bernardini, Antonella Del Prete, and Luciana Pepi.

Paolo Bernardini, professor at the University of Insubria, pointed out that Luzzatto approaches the issue of the imagination differently from Descartes. According to Luzzatto, imagination is like a 'referendary,' namely like those officials charged with the duty of examining and reporting on petitions or requests. Thus, he invited us to interpret Luzzatto's concept of imagination within the framework of Aristotelian philosophy, especially *On the Soul*, of which Gianfrancesco Pico della Mirandola was the mediator. The many quotations from Lucretius' *On the Nature of Things*, a book that was on the list of prohibited books, as well as from Dante's *Comedy* reveal the nature of an eclectic thinker influenced by Epicurean tendencies as well as the teaching of the well-known Aristotelian Cesare Cremonini at the University of Padua.

Antonella Del Prete, professor at the Tuscia University of Viterbo, also stressed the Aristotelian origin of Luzzatto's psychology. She pointed out that most of the information transmitted by the Aristotelian medieval tradition cannot be found in *On the Soul* itself, but rather in the works of Averroes and Thomas Aquinas, and that these same commentaries on Aristotle's works were drastically reduced and simplified during the early modern period. By offering an interesting overview of the development of the concept of the imagination throughout the epochs, she underlined that there are no traces of Renaissance tradition, which had highlighted the internal and external effects of imagination, in Luzzatto's *Socrates*. Luzzatto, on the contrary, seems to have focused more on the epistemological value and on the physiological and bodily nature of imagination: this aspect revealed his work to be mostly influenced by medical studies and thus its entirely materialistic approach to that issue.

Luciana Pepi, researcher at the University of Palermo, explored the meaning of the enigmatic absence of Maimonides in Luzzatto's *Socrates*. She furthermore underlined that the passages on imagination and memory seem not to have been updated with the philosophical tendencies of his time, and that this was responding to a common attitude among the Jews of reviving more ancient texts, probably also with the aim of holding back any trend that could then turn out to have dangerous effects on the Jewish community's survival.

The third session of the Atelier was devoted to the role of the soul and intellect in Luzzatto's speculation and was debated by Fabrizio Lelli and Emidio Spinelli.

Fabrizio Lelli, professor at Salento University of Lecce, focused on the significant elements which reveal the possible readership of Luzzatto's book: like the case of Judah Leon Abravanel's *Dialogues of Love*, the use of the vernacular and the lack of sources from the Jewish tradition are evidence of the Christian readership for which the book was intended. The recurring quotations from Dante's *Comedy* strengthen the awareness of the double identity: to be Jewish and Italian also means to be intimately familiar with the Italian culture and to adopt it for themselves. He emphasised that the circulation of works composed by Jewish and Christian authors on the topic of the soul in this period in Venice was intense and that they all displayed a rhetoric very similar to that of Luzzatto's *Socrates*. Some examples are offered by the critical response of Sara Copio Sullam's *Manifesto* to the discourse on the immortality of the soul addressed to her in 1621 by Baldassarre Bonifacio, by Daniel Arón Afia's treatise on ancient philosophers' opinions on the soul published in 1568, or by Troilo Lancetti's compendium of Platonic and Neo-Platonic theories also focused on the soul published in 1643.

Emidio Spinelli, professor at Sapienza University of Rome, highlighted the Pyrrhonian methodology adopted by Luzzatto's arguments and thus the possible sceptical sources of his work. *Socrates*' doxographical style agrees with the Pyrrhonian strategy of achieving a *diaphonia*, which automatically leads to the suspension of judgement. Thanks also to the reference to Sextus Empiricus, mentioned in the *Discourse* (1638), one might suppose that Luzzatto owned the Renaissance edition of Sextus' works or that he adopted Pyrrhonian arguments by reading Montaigne's *Essays*. Yet the passages on the soul or the intellect show that Luzzatto's philosophy cannot be entirely defined as Pyrrhonian: he weakened a specific idea of the intellect by using sceptical strategies, but he still seems to accept that it is enlightened by divine revelation. This aspect also seems to clarify Luzzatto's evident inclination towards Platonic positions demonstrated by the abundant indirect quotations as well as by the clear appreciation of Platonic theses. Spinelli underlined Luzzatto's positive view of the Platonic logos together with a preference for an Averroistic *nous poietikos*, which appears to be the only one able to promise any kind of knowledge.

From the session on the soul and the intellect, the Atelier moved on to the final topic, namely that of the closing pages of Luzzatto's *Socrates*. Guido Bartolucci and Josef Stern expounded their interpretations of the philosophical and religious dimensions of the final part.

Guido Bartolucci, researcher at the University of Calabria, explored the nature of Luzzatto's political position by opposing the discourses held by Ippias and Timon, the two final interlocutors of Socrates. Ippias' refusal to trust in the perfection of human nature and the Socratic inclination of Timon's view reveal much more than a mere confirmation of Luzzatto's sceptical approach. In these two discourses, crucial issues are summarised: an idea of nature's perfection coherent with the practice of the probable that seems to strengthen the hypothesis of a Stoic tendency in Luzzatto's philosophy, and also the pivotal role played by religion. Luzzatto seems to exempt the religion of the city as well as the religion of the wise man, the so called 'true religion,' from the sceptical inquiry. Bartolucci underlined the existence of a dichotomy in Luzzatto's thought: on the one hand, the human sphere being threatened by the fallacies of human intellect, the actual realm of the probable, and on the other hand, the religious sphere enlightened by divine revelation being relieved by sceptical doubt. This also reflects the relationship between philosophers and rabbis as presented by Luzzatto in his previous work, the *Discourse*. The obedience due to religious authority was indeed a crucial concept in the framework of the religious and political crisis during the early modern period as well as for sceptical thinkers such as Montaigne himself. For this reason, he stressed that Luzzatto must be considered a refined voice of the so-called political scepticism of the time, which has nothing to do with the idea of sovereignty endorsed by Jean Boden and with the issue of the reason of state.

Josef Stern, professor emeritus of the University of Chicago, suggested not interpreting Socrates' inclination towards Timon's view as Socrates'/Luzzatto's full agreement with his motion. Rather, he underlined the existence of a separation between the theoretical and the practical in Luzzatto's work that must be applied to the final *epochè* itself and thus limit it to the realm of theory, while the probable is a term for the domain of action without an epistemic commitment once the attempt to achieve the truth has been excluded. The way Luzzatto talks about nature and the fact that the probable is instilled in us by nature seem to be problematic and to contradict his sceptical premise. This opens up the possibility of suspecting that there is a kind of reverence for the first cause, and thus for a dogmatic position, in Luzzatto's thinking. Despite the coherency between the suspension of judgement promoted by Socrates and the suspension of decision finally supported by the judges, as well as the appropriate use Luzzatto made of Pyrrhonian sources, nevertheless, as soon as he starts adopting expressions of praise for nature as 'the best cause,' the hermeneutic of his scepticism becomes problematic and even contradictory.

This short overview of the issues raised and the enthusiastic participation of the Atelier's guest scholars clarifies the importance of promoting events such as this, in which the rich intellectual exchange achieves not only the goal of increasing and extending the knowledge of an author and his work, but also of enhancing the certainty of the significance of a scholarly project, and so in this case the philosophical and historical value of a translation of Luzzatto's *Socrates*. The English edition will indeed provide the readership with the opportunity to access this work that, thanks to the experience of the Atelier, has already the potential to set out different options for further reflection on the cultural dynamism and admirable modernity of Venetian Jewish culture in the ghetto. Thanks to the guidelines of our new edition, we hope to help the reader in comprehending this immensely complicated work and in grasping some aspects of the composite cultural framework behind it.

Silke Schaeper
Report on the Library of Jewish Scepticism

Electronic Resources

This year, we have been purchasing more electronic books with campus licence, which will benefit all members of the University of Hamburg. E-books can be accessed on and off campus. A few E-books were bought with an institutional license, for use at the Centre.

In the course of the last months, the librarian has negotiated the purchase of several important electronic resources. These will become available in the upcoming academic year.
- *Arabic-Hebrew Dictionary of Modern Arabic* (Hebrew University of Jerusalem, 2006 ff.), one-year subscription to this electronic dictionary, with updates. Access via IP-range of the Centre.
- *Religion in Geschichte und Gegenwart = Religion Past and Present* (Brill, 2015 ff.), German and English versions of this important reference work with annual updates. Campus-licence, bought in cooperation with the Faculty of Humanities.
- *Encyclopaedia of Jews in the Islamic World Online* (Brill, 2010 ff.). Campus-licence, bought in cooperation with the Faculty of Humanities.

Subject Information Service in Jewish Studies

Since November 2016, the 'Fachinformationsdienst Jüdische Studien' (FID Jewish Studies), funded by the German Research Foundation, provides national access to aggregated periodical content in Jewish Studies (JSTOR) and to databases with original content in Hebrew. The FID Jewish Studies is managed by Dr. Rachel Heuberger and her team at the University Library Johann Christian Senckenberg, Frankfurt am Main.

At present, the following databases can be accessed via the FID web platform:
Index to Hebrew Periodicals
JSTOR Complete Jewish Studies Collection (incl. Hebrew Journals)
Otsar ha-Hokhmah
Rav-Milim Dictionary Online
We have discontinued our institutional subscription to *Otsar ha-Hokhmah*, because this resource is now available via the FID Jewish Studies.

German Institutions of Higher Learning in Jewish Studies are licensed to grant FID access to their members (http://juedische-studien.fid-lizenzen.de/nutzerkreis). Independent researchers can apply individually to the FID.

FID subscriptions at our Centre in the academic year 2016/2017:

Staff   12
Fellows   4

Periodicals

In the field of research into Jewish mysticism, we continue to purchase the journal *Kabbalah*, as well as all monographs published in the series 'Sources and Studies in the Literature of Jewish Mysticism.' These are both issued by Cherub Press.

In the coming academic year, we are planning to subscribe to the following periodicals:
Jüdische Allgemeine, German weekly
Haaretz Online Edition, in Hebrew, with institutional license, including remote access.

Student Assistants

Student assistants continue to contribute to the daily running of the library. We thank our assistant, Femke Isermann, who gave up her position in June 2017 in order to prepare for her theological exam. She provided invaluable independent background support to the librarian and the administration team, and her calm sense of humour will be greatly missed. Julius Mann has worked in tandem with Ms Isermann and will take over some library duties until October 2017.

Faculty Library Committee

Library managers and academics from every department in the Faculty of Humanities of the University of Hamburg have formed a library committee, which meets regularly in order to make budget and library policy decisions. Between these formal meetings, the library managers hold regular Jours Fixes in order to discuss budgets and other administrative and bibliographic matters. Special library collections at the University of Hamburg are represented by the manager of the larger library they are attached to. The Maimonides Centre collection is represented at the departmental Jours Fixes by the manager of the Central Library for Philosophy, History and Classics.

From October 2015 until May 2017, the librarian attended Faculty Library Committee meetings on behalf of the Institute for Jewish Philosophy and Religion, in lieu of Professor Giuseppe Veltri. The Institute has now formally become part of the Department of Philosophy, which has an academic representative on the committee.

German Association of Jewish Studies

The association was founded in 1976 in Cologne. The annual meetings organized by its members are a valuable forum for the informal exchange of professional information for professionals working in public and private collections, libraries and institutions in Germany, Switzerland, and Austria in the field of Jewish Studies and Jewish Culture.

At the fortieth annual meeting of the association in Berlin, the librarian gave a presentation about the library of the Centre (September 8, 2016). The association in Würzburg takes place in September 2017.

Book Donations

The library wishes to thank Michael Studemund-Halévy (Eduard-Duckesz Fellow, IGdJ, Hamburg) and Susanne Küther (IGdJ, Hamburg) for their generous book donations. Further book gifts were kindly made by Giuseppe Veltri (University of Hamburg), Karin Hörner (Africa-Asia Institute, University of Hamburg), Josef Stern (University of Chicago), Libera Pisano (University of Hamburg), Jan Wiebers (University of Hamburg), Meir Buzaglo (Hebrew University of Jerusalem), Evelien Chayes (CNRS, Paris), Rico Gutschmidt (Technical University, Dresden), Mr Repsold (Hamburg), and Asher Salah (Bezalel Academy of Art and Design, Jerusalem).

Statistics

Institute for Jewish Philosophy and Religion
July 2016 to June 2017

Bibliographic units (editions)	281
Of which: Donations (editions)	209
Of which: E-Books	1
Periodicals (larger runs)	1
Physical volumes	351

Maimonides Centre for Advanced Studies
July 2016 to June 2017

Bibliographic units (editions)	236
Of which: Donations (editions)	21
Of which: E-Books	18
Periodicals (larger runs)	2
Physical volumes	245

Newsletter

The librarian publishes an occasional newsletter entitled *Library News* containing information about important acquisitions (databases, reference works) and guidance about the library system of the University of Hamburg (retrieval, interlibrary loan, document delivery). The newsletter is distributed by email to Fellows, Research Associates, members of staff, colleagues, and affiliates of the Institute and the Centre.

www.ingramcontent.com/pod-product-compliance
Lightning Source LLC
Chambersburg PA
CBHW060418300426
44111CB00018B/2894